HUNTING

HUNTING

**MARSHALL
CAVENDISH
EDITIONS**

HUNTING has been originated, designed, and produced by AB Nordbok, Gothenburg, Sweden.

Editor-in-Chief: Turlough Johnston.
Editor: Kerstin M. Stålbrand.
Assistant Editor: Jeremy Franks.
Graphical Designer: Roland Thorbjörnsson.
Picture Research Editor: Inge Larsson.
Lithographics: Nils Hermansson, Anette Johansson, Lars Jödahl.

Most of the freehand artwork has been drawn by Ulf Söderqvist. The other drawings have been made by Syed Mumtaz Ahmad, Tommy Berglund, Lars Jödahl, Hans Linder, Lennart Molin, Yusuke Nagano, Regina Richter, Holger Rosenblad, and Roland Thorbjörnsson. The freehand artwork and the watercolors are based on concepts by Roland Thorbjörnsson. The watercolors have been painted by Syed Mumtaz Ahmad (pages 77, 172–173, 200–201, 212–213, 236–237, 240–241, and 244–245), Tommy Berglund (pages 276–277), Erland Holmström (pages 220–221 and 232–233), Ewa Stranne (pages 216–217), Roland Thorbjörnsson (151, 158, 159, 161, 166, 170–171, 177, 204–205, 208–209, 268–269, 272–273).

The photographs have been provided by the following:
Ardea: /page 51, upper; 107, upper left; /*Kenneth W. Fink* p. 53, right; /*M.E.J. Gore* p. 54, left; /*Claude Nardin* p. 54, right.
Erwin Bauer: p. 28, lower; 28–29; 32, upper; 36, upper and lower; 37, upper; 43; 61; 73; 76, center; 83; 87, upper; 90, lower; 94, upper; 97, lower; 110, lower right and left; 114, right; 253; 265.
Tommy Berglund: p. 104, lower.
Bildhuset: /*Per Klaesson & Bengt Olof Olsson* p. 12; 20–21; 20; 21, lower left and center; 28, center; 32, lower; 33; 58; 63, upper; 71; 72, lower; 77; 110, upper; 115; 208–209; 257; 284–285; 288.
Black Star: /*David Beal* p. 13; /*Charles G. Summers jr.* p. 45, lower.
Gordon Carlisle: p. 59, upper; 224–225.
Explorer: p. 249.
Fauna Foto: /*Eddie Granlund* p. 24–25; /*Stefan Rosengren* p. 69.
Robert Harding: p. 87; 103, lower; /*Carol Jopp* p. 98, upper; /*Sassoon* p. 97, upper; 103, upper; /*Faulkner Taylor* p. 82.
Jacana: p. 100; /*Alain Antony* p. 95; 98, lower left; /*Arthus Bertrand* p. 87, lower; 118–119; /*J.P. Champroux* p. 100, inset; /*Manfred Danegger* p. 64, upper; /*Ducrot* p. 65, lower; /*Ermie* p. 44; /*Gens* p. 45, upper; /*R. König* p. 53, left; 76, lower; /*Claude Nardin* p. 80, inset; /*Pissavini* p. 36–37; 41; /*A. Rainon* p. 110–111; /*J. Robert* p. 48, lower; 56; 90, upper; 114, left; /*Jeffrey C. Stoll* p. 42; /*Varin* p. 46; 47, upper; 56–57; 65, upper; 72, upper; 102; 104, upper; 107, top right and lower; 118, upper; /*Zani Vendal* p. 118, lower.
F. Lind: p. 16–17.
Lea MacNally: p. 196–197.
Naturfotograferna (N): /*Ulf Bergström* p. 60, lower; /*Ingmar Holmåsen* p. 28, upper; 48–49; 55; 59, center; 62, upper; 62–63; 64, lower; 68, upper; 80, upper and lower; /*Viking Olsson* p. 289.
Pressens Bild: /*Shostal* p. 47, lower; /*C.G. Ward* p. 91.
Nick Sisley: p. 60; 252.
Text & Bilder: /*P. Fera* p. 94, lower; /*H. Reinhard* p. 40; /*Shostal* p. 50, lower; 51, lower.
Roland Thorbjörnsson: p. 9; 21, lower right.
Åke Wintzell: p. 256; 260–261; 264.

Published by Marshall Cavendish Editions, a division of Marshall Cavendish Books Limited, 58 Old Compton Street, London W1V 5PA

First printing 1980

ISBN 0 85685 833 1

Printed in Great Britain

NORDBOK would like to thank the following for their advice and kindness in providing illustration reference material: Stellan Andersson; Anders Bjärvall for the illustrations on page 286; Professor Erik Fabricius, for the illustrations on page 70; Bengt Ole Röken, for the illustration on page 211; Per Klaesson and Bengt Olof Olsson for pages 287–289, 292, 293, and 298–299; Savage Arms Company.

Supervising Editor

ROBERT ELMAN (RE) has participated in the project from its conception, and all along, he has worked closely with the Nordbok editorial and art departments in guiding the authors, editing their material, and collecting the illustration material. He has written over a dozen books on hunting, has hunted widely, and, as editor, has specialized in books on hunting and the outdoors. He has written the chapter "Arms for Hunting in Africa and Asia" in Part IV and several other pieces in Parts II and V.

Authors

The authorship of the various contributions to Parts II and V is indicated by the relevant author's initials at the end of each piece.

ERWIN BAUER has written the chapter "The Mountain Horse" in Part VI. An accomplished wildlife photographer, he has written many books on hunting.

JIM CARMICHEL is an arms expert and has written the chapters "Rifles for American Hunting" and "Handguns" in Part IV. He is the Shooting and Hunting Editor of *Outdoor Life*.

LEE CULLIMORE has contributed all the material on hunting methods in South America, where he has wide hunting experience. He is presently editor of *Outdoors* magazine.

DAVID MICHAEL DUFFEY is a well-known dog-trainer. He has written the chapter "Training Hunting Dogs" in Part VI. He is the Hunting-dog Editor of *Outdoor Life* and has written several dog books.

J. A. MAXTONE GRAHAM (JMG) is a freelance writer specializing in the outdoors. He has contributed the chapter "The English Shotgun" in Part IV as well as several pieces in Parts II, IV, and V.

GEORGE GRUENEFELD (GG) is an outdoor writer, hunter, and wildlife photographer. He has contributed to the game descriptions in Part II.

BRIAN HERNE (BH) was born in Kenya and is the youngest hunter ever to get a professional hunter's license. He hunted professionally until the closure of hunting in 1977. He has written all the African material in the book.

NICHOLAS KARAS (NK) is an outdoor columnist and has hunted game in many parts of the world. The author of two books on hunting and shooting, he has contributed to Part II.

JEROME KNAP (JK) has provided most of "Hunter's Lexicon" in Part IX and has written many pieces in Parts II and V. The author of over ten books on hunting, he is Canadian Editor of *Field & Stream* and Gundog Editor of *Petersen's Hunting*.

RICHARD LAROCCO is Associate Editor of *Outdoor Life* and has a life-long interest in conservation and game management. He has written all of Part VII, "Conservation."

ALBERTO LLERAS (AL) has contributed to the game descriptions in Part II. He is a world-class international skeet shooter.

WILF E. PYLE is a game biologist, game manager, hunting writer, and wildlife photographer, as well as an expert on firearms and handloading. He has written the chapter "Maintenance, Sighting-in, and Ammunition" in Part IV.

JOHN F. REIGER, who has written Part III, "The History of Hunting," is Associate Professor of History at the University of Miami. The author of several books, he is an avid hunter.

GEORGE REIGER, editor, author, and hunter, has written Part I, "Nature." Conservation Editor of *Field & Stream*, he is former national correspondent of the *Audubon* magazine.

JAMES RIKHOFF (JR) is president of the National Sporting Fraternity and is a well-known hunting author, editor, and columnist. He has supplied the South American game descriptions in Part II.

NICK SISLEY (NS) has written many of the pieces in Parts II, IV, and V as well as the chapter "The Hunting Dog" in Part VI. He is a syndicated hunting journalist and a wildlife photographer.

TOM TURPIN (TT) is a licensed hunting instructor in Germany. He has written the chapter "European Arms" in part IV as well as pieces for Parts II and V.

GORDON YOUNG (GY) was born in China and has spent most of his life in Southeast Asia, working as a naturalist and professional hunter. He has contributed the Asian material.

WILSON STEPHENS, author, hunter, and former editor of *The Field*, has written Part VIII, "The British Isles," and has contributed several pieces to "Hunter's Lexicon" in Part IX.

Contents

I Nature

Chapter 1

Man, the Unique Predator

George Reiger

The world of the hunter is the world itself. Everywhere man evolved and migrated, he did so as a hunter.

On the grasslands of Africa and the Americas, only five or six generations ago, men with tools of stone as sharp-edged as a surgeon's scalpel moved with and among vast herds of ungulates, taking from them the bison, wildebeest, and antelope they needed for food, clothing, shelter, and new tools.

On the Arctic ice and in the deserts, where workable stone and wood were in short supply, hunters devised and decorated sophisticated weapons made from the bones and sinews of the seal and walrus, ibex and gazelle that they hunted for food.

In Eurasia, the horse—once hunted for food—was domesticated in the hunt for other animals. In Africa, another hunted species, the camel, was tamed to enable desert foragers to move swiftly from one waterhole, where game was scarce, to another, where more might be found.

In North America, red men hunted camels until there were no more; in South America, red men domesticated the llama and alpaca, but in the process they became herders, not hunters. Elsewhere, men learned to keep pigs, sheep, and goats—although goats particularly would make major and often adverse impacts on local environments when concentrated in numbers beyond the carrying capacity of the land, even as settling down would have significant and often adverse consequences on man's living conditions, sense of community, etc. Man even taught one of his oldest hunting allies, the dog, to be a "shepherd."

Historians have made much of the apparent fact that the wheel was invented in Asia, implying that this part of the world must, therefore, be regarded as the cradle of what we call *civilization*. Since wheelmakers were tillers of the soil, many historians have also concluded that settled agricultural societies were a prerequisite of urban civilization, while nomadic hunters were somehow inferior—incapable of intellectual and creative progress toward civilization.

Yet hunters in other lands were not less thoughtful or creative than wheelmaking Asiatics. They merely had no use for wheels on the tundra, in the mountains, among foothills drained by rivers, in dense forests, or on rock-studded plains and coasts. Some actually carved and attached wheels to their children's toys, but as hunters, they found the sled and the travois, the canoe and the river raft better adapted to their needs and local conditions than wheeled carts would have been.

It is significant that the wheel was invented in conjunction with agriculture, which implies permanent or at least semi-permanent settlement. Of what earthly use would a wheeled vehicle have been to predominantly hunting or herding peoples—Masai or Zulu, Mandan or Sioux—when they could achieve a civilization comparable or superior to that of settled farmers without sacrificing their freedom to roam?

Sixty years ago, H.G. Wells observed that "a certain freedom and a certain equality passed out of human life when men ceased to wander. Men paid in liberty and they paid in toil, for safety, shelter, and regular meals . . . There was a process of enslavement as civilization grew."

And, as civilization grew, it developed a hierarchy of complex and sometimes imaginary needs which required major alterations to the natural world. Forests were cut, rivers dammed, swamps drained, valleys filled, and mountains leveled, sometimes merely to serve the whims of kings and priests or, in modern times, politicians and engineers.

Where hunting peoples had once lived in harmony with the land, they now lived in competition with those who had settled down. And the environment of the hunter was disrupted by his civilized brethren in ways every bit as discordant as changes wrought by geological upheavals and periodic ice sheets.

Agriculture evolved in the tropics and subtropics and generally moved north. In North America, the process of concentrating people into towns and cities began in Guatemala and Mexico. The populations of these countries were supervised by a hierarchy of leaders whose job it was to maintain control as well as to inspire the people to do work that often seemed unnecessary or was sheer drudgery. Since two or three crops of corn, beans, and squash could be produced every year in these warm latitudes, there was no leisure in the Aztec calendar for the common man. Kings and priests used superstition and terror to keep him at his perennial labor.

In the lower Mississippi Valley, a corn economy enabled complex societies to evolve, but winter provided a respite during which hunters could once again follow their immemorial ways, supplementing the society's larder as well as providing skins and sinews for clothing, bones for tools, and fat and tallow for lighting. The religious beliefs of these Mississippi Indians were elaborate and linked with farming, but when times were hard—or exceptionally good—they could be invoked in the making of wars, in which hunting skills were used to take food and treasure from other tribes.

Farther north, as deciduous forests gave way to those of pine and spruce, it became increasingly difficult, and then impossible, to grow crops. Thus, religious ceremonies did not concern the renewal of life in the spring and the harvest of corn in the fall, but celebrated the hunt in all seasons. Priests (shamans) were more like physicians, and belief derived from a community of feeling with animals and wildlife, not from the authority of kings.

It is significant that, in agricultural societies that have evolved a concept of an afterlife, the orthodox view is that life after death is many times better than life itself. However, for some hunting peoples, "heaven" has never meant anything more or less than a continuation of the good, full life on earth.

For the Ojibwa and the Cree, the Creator, who has given a special meaning to each plant and animal, each rock and stream, and who has made existence so beautiful, has prepared an eternal "hunting ground" for all those who respected the red gods.

Natural man—man as he has evolved and as he remains—is a predatory species, despite the gloss of civilization. A recreational hunter learns this, either consciously or instinctively, and as such, man may be thought to

The early North American Indians gave the moose its name and learned to imitate its mating calls in order to lure it within range of their weapons. Later, when Europeans settled the country, they learned from the Indians how to lure the animal which, perhaps more than any other, embodies the remoteness and the majesty of the seemingly endless northern woods.

be most in harmony with, and most comfortable in, his natural environment.

But man is also unique among predators. He is the only predator capable of exercising consciously benign foresight in his interactions with his prey. Various ecological and biological controls maintain the proper balance between other predators and their prey, but no such restraints limit him: his only restraints are self-imposed. Intelligence, self-interest, and appreciation of wild beauty (an emotion that may also be unique to our species) motivate the hunter to preserve the habitat and its other denizens for future generations.

In still other ways, man is different from other predators. Physically, he is inferior not only to them but to his prey. He cannot run or swim or climb as fast; he cannot pursue winged prey through the air; he has far less stamina than most prey, less strength than some; his hearing is relatively poor; his eyesight is ill adapted for dim light; his scenting ability is almost nil; and his capacity to withstand cold, heat, hunger, and thirst is unimpressive. Yet he is the most efficient of all predators.

His brain and technology are such that he can, if he chooses, devastate

all prey. But he also has a conscience—probably linked closely with his aesthetic appreciation—and thus he can evolve as a benign predator. Likewise, his brain and technology enable him to survive visits to the wilds and thoroughly enjoy the experience, while his foresight and conscience urge him to preserve them as a crucial habitat for all creatures, including himself. Yet it is his civilization—urbanized, industrialized— that diminishes the game and threatens to engulf the remaining habitat, which is the habitat of man himself.

Hunting for pleasure, the oldest sport on earth, is also the most natural: a direct and atavistic interaction with nature. When in tune with its surroundings, it does not destroy them. Man has long hunted in this way and always will, if other activities do not annihilate flora and fauna alike. But today, hunting is limited and must be stringently regulated, because for many centuries man has abused the animals and their habitat.

The decline of game is not precipitated by regulated hunting. It results from the destruction of the natural environment and the wanton extermination of wildlife. Industry is rapidly pre-empting vast expanses of swamp, savanna, delta, prairie, tundra, taiga, and even the most productive habitat of all, the rain forests. The African veldt and the North and South American plains are being plowed and fenced. Asian and Mediterranean wetlands are being dredged for commercial navigation or filled and paved for factories. All of these ecosystems are crucial for the survival of wildlife.

Today, industry—the word was once associated with personal skill and diligence—touches every land and all bodies of water on earth, even those unsuitable for agriculture. It is able to modify environments that the farmer cannot use. Tracts of land in the far North, in the deserts, on remote islands, or in the mountains—where hunting peoples had until recently seemed to be beyond the grasp of industry—are now exploited by corporations whose executives may never visit any of these places. The resources they want are not those that the local people need.

Especially hard-hit is the Eskimo. The culture of this quintessential hunter was safe so long as there was nothing known to be commercially useful in the Arctic wastes. Now the industrial world's thirst for oil has sent the shadow of civilization across even the stark, white lands of the North. Traditional skills and perceptions seem meagre beside the world of the computer, kayaks are traded for outboard-powered skiffs, and sled dogs are replaced by snowmobiles. Chickens grown thousands of miles to the south now feed men who once hunted walrus and seal from fragile boats made from the hides of the hunted.

Still, there are a few who cling to a way of life and an understanding of nature more ancient than the oldest wheel. "There is only one great thing," sings an Eskimo hunter, "to live, to see the great day dawning and the light that fills the world."

Yet there are also people from the industrialized world who are working diligently to protect fragments of these distinct and diminishing habitats on the plains, prairies, and deserts; in the rain forests and mountains; and along the rivers and coasts. They are carrying on the work begun more than a century ago in Europe and North America by sportsmen/naturalists, who began to attempt to preserve portions of their vanishing wilderness.

Natural diversity is not just a fashionable phrase. It is essential to man's continued well-being and possibly to his existence as a species. Hunters learn the value of diversity, and the rules of conservation which guard diversity, at such an early age that they often assume that the world already knows what the hunter perceives.

But the civilized world has largely forgotten the lessons of the hunt.

While extinction has always been part of the pattern of evolution, in recent industrialized centuries, the pace of wildlife extinction has accelerated alarmingly. In the nineteenth century, 75 bird and 27 mammal species vanished. So far in the twentieth century, 53 bird and 68 mammal species are gone, and there are 345 bird, 200 mammal, 80 amphibian and reptile, and an incredible 20,000 to 25,000 plant species currently threatened with extinction.

Some hunting peoples have had a little, but not much, to do with this. We know, for instance, that after the Polynesians came to New Zealand about the tenth century, their descendants, the Maori, had killed the last indigenous swan (*Cygnus sumnerensis*) by the fifteenth century, and had also killed the last moa some two or three hundred years later.

American Indians always killed animals for food but may have contributed to the extinction of the mammoth and the mastodon by driving them over cliffs, killing many more animals than could be utilized. They may also have contributed to the extinction of several other species that were failing to adapt to new environmental conditions following the withdrawal of the Laurentide glacier after the last periodic Ice Age. They hunted bison, too, but killed only for need. It was not until the beginning of the 1870s that the railroad opened up the plains of North America to market hunters. They shot the bison and sold the meat (often

In the rain forests, the abundant natural growth of trees, bushes, other plants, and seemingly parasitical vegetation allows virtually no space for deliberate cultivation. The peoples that make the forests their home do so only by sharing them with a huge range of fauna—birds, beasts, reptiles, insects, and fish—and by finding or hunting whatever they need for their survival. Shown below is a man of the Vedda tribe, Sri Lanka.

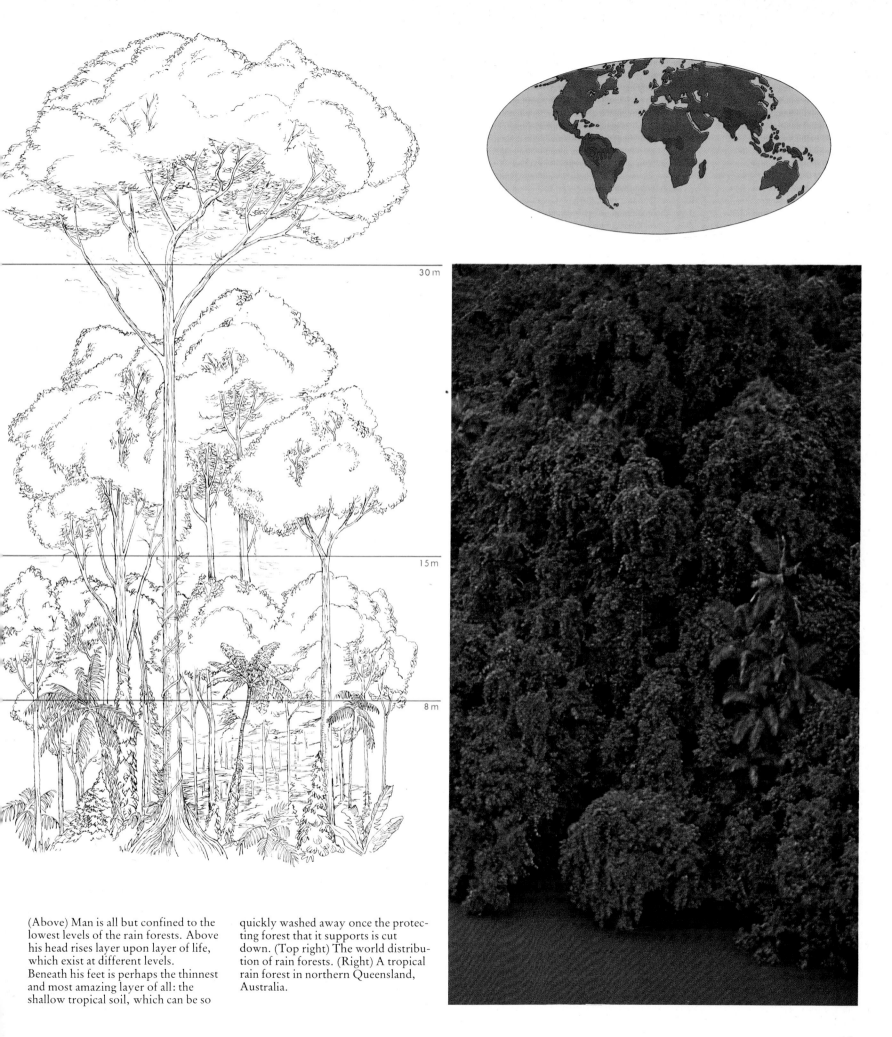

(Above) Man is all but confined to the lowest levels of the rain forests. Above his head rises layer upon layer of life, which exist at different levels. Beneath his feet is perhaps the thinnest and most amazing layer of all: the shallow tropical soil, which can be so quickly washed away once the protecting forest that it supports is cut down. (Top right) The world distribution of rain forests. (Right) A tropical rain forest in northern Queensland, Australia.

30 m

15 m

8 m

Of the main types of vegetation in the world, illustrated below, the tundra *(1)* produces least growth per unit of area per year (see diagram, right). The tropical rain forests *(8)* produce more than eighteen times as much. Between these two extremes lie the coniferous forests *(2)*, the deciduous forests *(3)*, the steppes *(4)*, the subtropical forests *(5)*, the deserts *(6)*, and the savannas *(7)*.

When the annual growth of each zone is compared with its standing crop, a different picture emerges. On the arctic tundra, the annual growth accounts for no less than twenty percent of the total standing crop. In the tropical rain forests, the figure is just under seven percent; in the coniferous forests of the middle taiga, just over three percent; and in the proverbially slow-growing oak forests, just over two percent. On the temperate steppes, by contrast, the annual growth is as much as forty-five percent of the standing crop, and in the subtropical deserts only a little less, at forty-two percent.

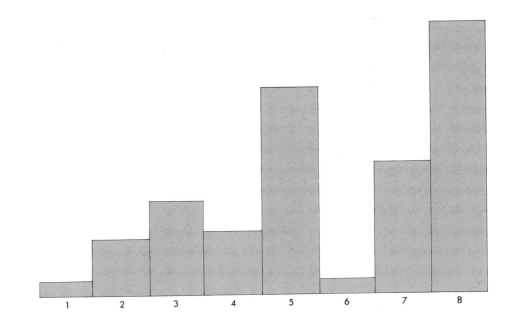

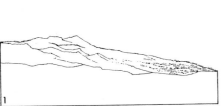

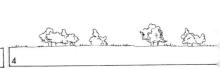

only the choicest parts) to frontier settlements, railroad camps, and army garrisons. Bison skins were sold for tanning and the bones for fertilizer. Furthermore, huge hunts were organized for the recreational hunters that helped further to destroy the great herds.

Yet, during the nineteenth century, *recreational* hunters had begun the revolutionary task of preserving wild and scenic areas as a means of preserving threatened fish and wildlife species. Their start in North America would have been more difficult, were it not for the fact that, as a class, sportsmen were, and are, largely members of the industrial elite that earns profits from the development and exploitation, ironically enough, of many of the very wildernesses they seek to set aside. In the ranks of these early preservationists were many cultural and political leaders, which meant that the word *conservation* became respectable far sooner than it would have if the revolution in environmental appreciation had been led by intellectuals alone.

In the British Isles and continental Europe, recreational hunters were mostly of the landowning class, who hunted, shot, and fished on great estates—privately-held tracts of woods, fields, waters, and mountains. Those who owned the land and the game on it were, very largely, of the aristocracy that had once been feudal. For the landed gentry, conservation was not a new concept but merely an aspect of land ownership with a tradition already centuries old. It was obviously a facet of managing one's property adequately to pay competent gamekeepers and to manage the habitat and the game as renewable and profitable resources.

Habitat improvement, selective shooting, supplemental breeding and feeding of game when necessary, predator control (including ferocious

laws against poaching), closed seasons, and other techniques of conservation all contributed to the tradition of private ownership that has ensured that game is still available in Europe, despite its ever-growing, ever more urbanized populations.

In Africa and Asia, recreational hunters, regardless of whether they were of the landed gentry or not, were members of the exploiting class; some were empire-builders, but all saw what seemed an infinite wilderness—limitless game in unbelievably productive habitats. They saw no need for management of the game or the land, and so African and Asian wildlife diminished at an astonishing and steadily accelerating rate.

The crumbling of European empires did not reverse the trend, for the remaining game was regarded by the peoples of the emerging nations as sorely needed food or detrimental to agriculture—or both.

Only very recently have strenuous efforts been made by a few African and Asian governments to conserve the wildlife of the savannas, the plains, and the rain forests of these continents. Here, too, as in North America, enlightened self-interest has at last spawned a conservation ethic, for wildlife is a tourist attraction, and tourism has been touted as a salvation for the economies of some African and Asian nations.

In North America, most of the land was obtained by treaty from the Indians and, as in Africa, its resources seemed limitless. In the decades after the Civil War, a few far-sighted visionaries who fortunately wielded enormous influence sparked off a concern for conservation in their writings and legislative proposals.

For some creatures, the effort was not in time. The cutting of the vast forests in the eastern half of the United States was probably the most

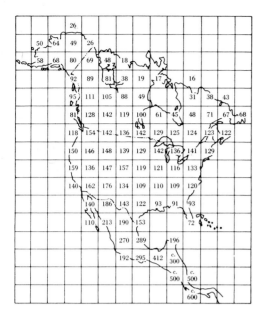

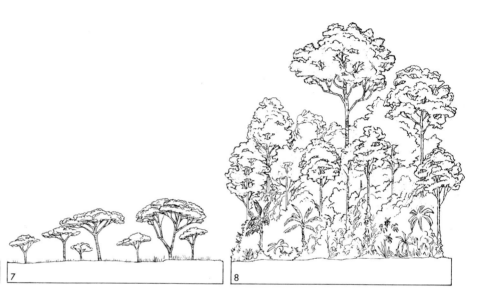

(Left) The grid imposed over the map of North and Central America shows the numbers of breeding land-bird species in different parts of the continent. This shows a range from only 16 in the north of the Northwestern Territories of Canada, to over 400 in southern Mexico; in Ecuador, on the northwest coast of the South American continent, there are seven times the number of bird species as are found in New England, or over 800.

The same pattern may be observed for other creatures and plants in other parts: Europe has 192 species of fish, while over 1,000 have been recorded in the Amazon basin. A deciduous forest of 4 acres in Michigan will contain 10 to 15 species of trees, while the same area of tropical rain forest in Malaya may contain up to 227 different species. (Krebs, *Ecology*. New York, 1972.)

significant factor in the demise of both the passenger pigeon and the Carolina parakeet. Neither species was an important target for sportsmen. The passenger pigeon was mostly shot in large numbers by commercial gunners and pioneers, and the parakeet was usually the victim of angry fruit growers whose crops were ravaged by this beautiful bird when it switched its diet from acorns to apples.

The essential habitat of both species had been the great deciduous canopy stretching from the Atlantic to the Mississippi and from upland Georgia to New England. Once that was cut into patch-quilt remnants of its former ubiquity, there was no way the passenger pigeon and the Carolina parakeet could survive.

A similar process involving many more species is seen today in tropical rain forests. The recreational hunter has long been intrigued by what he loosely calls "the jungle," and former American president Theodore Roosevelt was, in 1914, not the first sportsman to explore the rivers of Brazil and to hunt for jaguar, tapir, and other game.

Partly because of Roosevelt's concern, Barro Colorado Island, created by flooding associated with the construction of the Panama Canal, was made a sanctuary and a scientific research preserve. The island is nearly 3,000 acres (1,200 hectares) in area, with a sizable tract of rain forest. Yet the island is apparently not large enough, for its list of unique flora and fauna has been shrinking steadily for over half a century.

Every minute of every hour of every day in the year, about 50 acres (20.5 hectares) of tropical rain forest are being destroyed. The original area of rain forest on earth was roughly 6.2 million square miles (15.9 million square kilometers). By 1975, this area had been reduced to 3.6 million square miles (9.3 million square kilometers), and at the present attrition of 92,500 square miles (245,000 square kilometers) per year, our grandchildren will never be able to visit a tropical rain forest.

Although such conservation groups as the World Wildlife Fund, supported in part with sportsmen's money, are making every effort to set aside representative tracts of rain forest before it is all gone, the vital question is: how much is enough?

Rain forests contain more species than any other ecosystem on earth. Between twenty-five and fifty percent of all plant and animal species on earth are found in this environment. Yet no tropical rain forest is older than about 10,000 years.

How did this incredible diversity of life develop so rapidly? Do creatures in the rain forest have a low extinction rate, or are rain forests just amazingly conducive to the emergence of new species? Perhaps both are true, for certainly rain forests permit more species to live in harmony with one another than any other environment (except the somewhat comparable oceanic "kelp forests").

Even though we have barely begun to study such phenomena, we are losing rain forests faster than even our best instruments can collect data about them. The red soil of the tropics is curiously infertile, and the farmer who clears a tract in the jungle must abandon the land within a few years unless the soil is reinforced annually with chemical fertilizers (a cost beyond the reach of most subsistence farmers). Furthermore, such red soil does not easily reproduce the lost rain forest. We do not know how rain forests came into being, and we are unable to reproduce them (except at fantastic cost) once they are gone.

15

The grasslands of Africa cover a large part of the continent from below the Sahara to South Africa. The type of grassland varies from semi-desert and torrid steppe (on the periphery of the Kalahari and Sahara deserts) to the savanna of the equatorial regions to the veld of South Africa. The annual rainfall and the periods during which the rain falls are major factors in deciding what type of grassland an area will have. The savanna supports a wide variety of herbivorous animals that live together in relative harmony, as each species has its own food patterns and/or eats at levels that the other species cannot reach. Highest up comes the giraffe, and then comes the

elephant. The gerenuk (1) stretches up on its hind legs to reach the intermediary levels. The gazelle (2) and the topi (3) crop at the grass at its lowest level; the zebra (4), the gnu (5), the white rhino (6), and the Cape buffalo (7) are all grazers; some crop close, others crop at the tops of the various grasses. The black rhino (8) prefers twigs and bark, while the dik-dik (9) eats the lowest leaves on bushes. These herbivorous animals support predators, such as lions (a lioness is shown here with a newly killed gazelle), and scavengers, such as vultures and hyenas, shown here eating carrion. The hyena is also a predator.

(Right) This savanna has recently received an abundant fall of rain. Trees and grasses are flourishing, and the area is capable of supporting a wide variety of animals. The flat-topped acacia trees are a familiar sight on savanna grasslands.

A major question involving this destruction of the world's rain forests is the effect on the earth's climate and geography as the estimated 340 billion metric tons of carbon stored in the wood fiber of rain forests are released through cutting and burning. Even cautious scientists speculate that, in addition to warming world temperatures so that the polar ice caps will shrink and the oceans rise by many meters, the grain-producing potential of western North America will vanish due to generally drier summers. In addition, the forests absorb carbon dioxide and give off oxygen to an extent that might make our survival somewhat dependent upon theirs. Therefore, we can say without any hesitation that the preservation of natural environments is considerably more important than merely being a nice way for wealthy sportsmen to make tax-deductible, charitable donations.

Major and permanent alterations in the world's climate are too much like science fiction for most people to take them seriously. However, wildlife and habitat preservation can be put in another, more immediate context. For example, when people learn that the armadillo is currently being studied as part of man's search for a cure for leprosy, that the albatross may provide a cure for heart disease, the black bear for kidney failure, and the manatee for hemophilia, wildlife conservation makes the most urgent kind of sense.

Furthermore, a wild flowering plant called the foxglove, found in Europe and Morocco, is the sole source of the drug digitalis. Without it, between 10 and 20 million people would die within seventy-two hours of heart failure. People are less inclined to shrug at the idea of endangered plants. And when you ask why fewer than 20 plant species produce ninety percent of the world's food, when nearly 80,000 plant species are edible and nutritious for man, you may start a few wheels turning in the minds of people who had, perhaps, taken a high-protein diet too much for granted.

During the past century alone, many species have become extinct, and although people nowadays are more aware of the importance of conservation, there are many other, once-plentiful species that are now rare or even in danger of extinction. Illustrated here is the now-extinct passenger pigeon, which once existed in millions in North America.

Chapter 2

The Hunter's Role in Habitat Preservation

George Reiger

The musk-ox is an animal of the arctic regions. Originating in Asia, it wandered over the land bridge that once connected Alaska and Siberia. Protected since 1917 in Canada and 1950 in Greenland, it now appears to have a secure future, although recent Norwegian attempts to implant the animal in Spitsbergen have failed.

In 1978, in the over-populated state of Jalisco, Mexico, a unique species of corn was discovered to have the same number of chromosomes as our domestic variety. Its uniqueness lies in the fact that it is a perennial plant; it does not wither and die with the coming of winter, but from year to year produces tiny ears of corn on stalks. When this species is crossbred with our larger hybrid species, corn on the cob can be harvested from plants tended much like blueberries and pineapples, which are grown without the increasing annual expense of spring planting.

This fabulous discovery was made in an area where the plant was assumed to be just another weed. In fact, this area of scrubland, host to dozens of bird species and several non-migratory mammals, was slated for clearing and development. Had that happened without a proper analysis of the area's resources, all mankind would have lost infinitely more than could have been satisfied by building a few more housing units for Mexico's ever-burgeoning human population.

Even after we have domesticated or synthetized a product of nature, we are foolish to turn our backs on its origins. This happened during the 1960s after pharmaceutical firms had become over-confident that the malarial preventive they were marketing in substitution for natural quinine, which is derived from the bark of South America's cinchona tree, was sufficient for any malarial threat. However, when warfare escalated in Southeast Asia, the *falciparum* malarias of that region took an increasing toll—until natural quinine was reintroduced as a more potent antidote than its imitation.

The world is running out of petroleum, and the price per barrel keeps rising. This has set off a frantic search for natural and artificial substitutes. Several plants, among them the widespread euphorbia tree of equatorial latitudes, may provide some relief. An acre of euphorbia trees, under which other plants grow and wild game grazes, will yield ten to fifty barrels of oil per year at a cost that may be economic or even profitable.

How is all this related to hunting? Simply and directly. Just as primitive peoples in South America had known about the curative powers of quinine long before they were discovered by civilized Europeans, equally primitive people of Africa and Australia taught modern scientists about oil in the euphorbia, a characteristic which makes this tree superb for starting campfires but almost too rich and smoky for cooking.

These examples are further related to hunting because sportsmen were among the first to perceive that an arboretum doth not a forest make, and wild creatures in a zoo are no longer wild.

Since, in hunting, the act of killing is momentary compared with coming close to the animal in its own environment, the recreational hunter has always been concerned more with the perpetuation of species as a whole than with the artificial propagation of remnant individuals in zoos. The hunter knows that *habitat preservation is central, not just to the perpetuation of wildlife, but to the preservation of his own well-being.*

An example of wildlife preservation is the North American pronghorn antelope. Pre-Columbus, the pronghorn and the bison together dominated the ecosystems of the western prairies and plains. Each numbered perhaps 30 or 40 million. Their food and water requirements differed subtly enough for them to complement each other. Yet by the turn of the twentieth century, the pronghorn is estimated to have numbered only some 13,000 animals. By 1927, it was being hunted in only three states.

Wildlife management since then, however, has ensured a stable population today of some 400,000, with hunting seasons for *Antilocapra americana* in sixteen western American states, two Canadian provinces, and one Mexican state. Nearly 2 million head of pronghorn have been shot since 1927 without jeopardizing the species.

Today, cattle have replaced the bison on the grasslands, and there is little likelihood that bison will be restored beyond the relatively few token herds that exist, since the environmental needs of cattle and bison are identical. However, pronghorn occupy a niche in no way competitive with cattle, and as ranchers have gradually come to appreciate this fact, the pronghorn has flourished.

The comeback of the American elk, or wapiti (to distinguish this member of the deer family from the European elk, or moose), has been more limited than the pronghorn's, because the wapiti's habitat requirements make it impossible for the species to adapt to life with man in so many regions preferred by both them and us. Although small herds exist in Michigan, Pennsylvania, and Virginia—all part of the wapiti's historic range—the subspecies that used to roam through these states, *Cervus canadensis canadensis*, is now extinct.

However, in the West, wherever room still exists, the wapiti thrives. It is presently hunted in nine American states and three Canadian provinces. Colorado alone estimates that wapiti hunters contribute more than $40 million to the state economy. License fees account for one-tenth of this total and go directly into wildlife management and research programs.

Although the dollar value of the wapiti harvest is a fraction of that of the whitetail-deer, cottontail-rabbit, or mourning-dove harvest in the United States, just seventy-five years ago, there were probably fewer than 25,000 wapiti in existence. That population figure now represents less than one-fourth of the annual harvest.

Unfortunately, we may be at the apogee of wapiti restoration. This animal is essentially a creature of the wilderness. With the current boom in backpacking and camping, non-hunters are inadvertently forcing wapiti out of many favored summer ranges. In addition, increasing numbers of hunters indicate an interest in shooting at least one "elk" in their lifetime. However, this commitment is casual, and hunting pressure continues to build only in the most easily accessible parts of the wapiti's range—a factor detrimental to the quality of local herds—while, on the other hand, there is insufficient hunting for wapiti in more remote areas, a factor equally detrimental to the quality of remote herds. North American advances in game management are admired by wildlife authorities throughout the world; yet here is a case in which the Americans might do well to emulate the selective-shooting system of game management that has long been in force in Europe.

Increased logging poses yet another threat to big game, and habitat acquisition is becoming increasingly expensive. Finally, wildlife management itself is belittled by many people who are opposed to hunting, and research is discouraged or extremely difficult in officially designated American Wilderness Areas.

At one time, the wapiti was approaching extinction because the animal was slain for a pair of incisiform canine teeth in the forward part of the upper jaw. These "whistlers," "buglers," or "elk teeth" were especially prized by members of the Benevolent and Protective Order of Elk (BPOE), an American social fraternity, which paid such high prices for

(Right) Wide, seemingly empty stretches of undisturbed countryside, far from urban and industrial concentrations: such is the typical national park. Shown is a national park in northern Sweden. Human activity here has been largely organic and has consisted of reindeer herding and subsistence fishing by the Lapps.

(Below) No matter how remote or undisturbed a wilderness is, it is accessible to modern methods of transportation, for instance the helicopter *(1)*. With energy at a premium nowadays, an undisturbed waterfall *(2)*, even in a national park, can be exploited for electricity, permanent means of access *(3)* being built. Soon, another part of the wilderness will have vanished beneath the waters of a hydroelectric dam *(4)*.

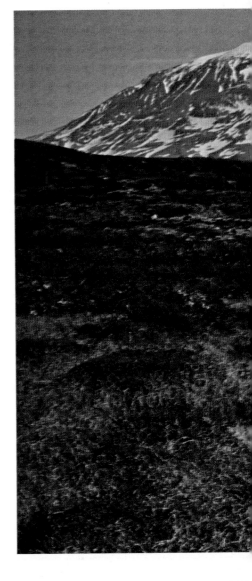

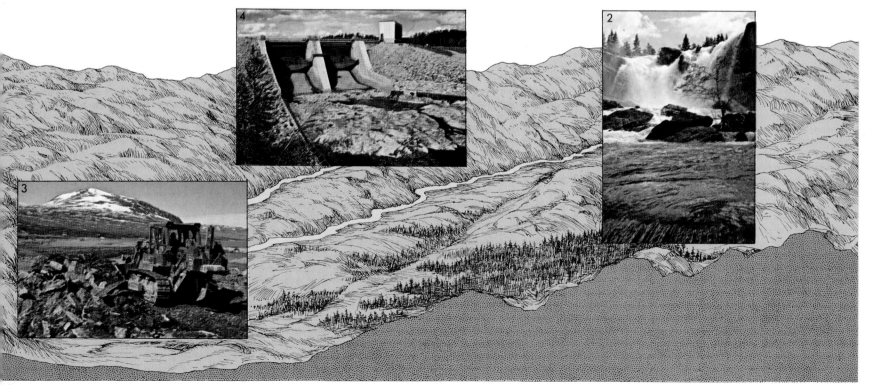

Breeding only once in about every four years, the Indian rhinoceros *(1)* is perhaps typical of the four other surviving species: the black rhinoceros *(2)*, the white rhinoceros *(3)*, the Java rhinoceros *(4)*, and the Sumatra rhinoceros *(5)*. While these unurgent reproductive habits suggest a long evolution into a peaceful, unthreatened existence, they can hardly explain the attribution of sexual potency to rhinoceros horn. It is a grotesque irony that this belief should combine with human population growth to threaten all species of rhino with extinction.

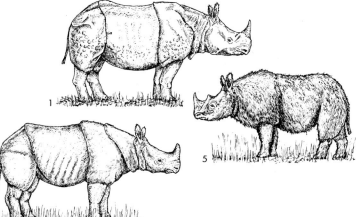

(Right) The anatomy of an Indian rhinoceros: *(1)* the "horn" is, in fact, a growth of hair-like material, supported on a structure extending forward above the upper jaw. The upper lip *(2)* projects in a finger-like extension similar to that on the extremity of an elephant's trunk.

these biological anomalies that wapiti were slain by the hundred for their teeth alone.

Equally bizarre is the current slaughter of rhinoceros for their horns. While the rhino was always considered to be a trophy animal because of its size and the danger inherent in collecting a specimen, trophy hunting *per se* was never a threat to the survival of the various rhino subspecies. Habitat destruction and horn hunting have become such a threat today.

Rhino horn is now literally worth its weight in gold. Whereas a decade ago there were 20,000 black rhino in Kenya, there are presently fewer than 2,000.

The horn is normally powdered and used in potions alleged to cure everything from leprosy to impotency. In north Yemen, it is carved into dagger handles, for which wealthy Arab sheiks pay $10,000 (£5,000) each. Poachers run enormous risks by sneaking into national parks, tracking the animals at night, spearing them, sawing off the horn, and escaping before dawn—risks far too great to be worth taking for the relatively little money they are paid for the contraband by middlemen, who buy and sell the horn several times before it reaches the consumer as an alleged aphrodisiac or as a decorative item.

Still, a Kenyan park ranger earns only $56 (£28) a month, while a poacher is paid over $100 (£50) per lb (0.5 kg) for a horn that averages nearly 8 lb (almost 4 kg). The risks notwithstanding, it is a wonder that more rangers do not become part-time poachers! Perhaps the fact that some illegal buyers in Nairobi pay nearly $400 *per ounce* for rhino horn shames the rangers into trying to purge this scandal from their land.

Their efforts to date, while often more risk-filled than those of the poachers, have not been enough, although recent reports indicate that black rhino numbers are at last beginning to grow. Although Kenya is a signatory to the international treaty banning trade in endangered species and their products, fourteen of the eighteen African nations where the rhino survives have *not* signed the treaty; and China, a principal market for rhino-horn powder, has only recently agreed to sign.

In the Ngorongoro Crater in Tanzania, there were 76 black rhinos in 1978; 26 in 1979; and possibly none today. In all of Africa, there are only an estimated 10,000 to 20,000 black rhinos; approximately 3,000 southern white rhinos; and less than 500 northern white rhinos.

In Asia, barely 1,135 Indian rhinos survive, and increased poaching and habitat conflicts between man and rhino threaten even this small number. Sumatra may have 225 rhinos left, and Java maybe about 50. Since a female rhinoceros produces only one calf every four years, there is no way normal procreation can keep pace with the poaching.

One of the ironies of the East African problem is that it has become so much worse since regulated recreational hunting was outlawed some years ago. Not only were rhinos worth many times more to local economies when hunted as trophies than their horns alone are worth today, but the presence of recreational hunters on safari helped to prevent much of the poaching that is currently possible, because there is no way for the meager East African game-protection staffs to patrol all the areas where rhinos are in jeopardy. In bygone days, every "white hunter"—that is, professional hunter/guide—was also a deputy warden, and poachers were more afraid of them and their camp staffs than they are of the vague and arbitrary justice of Kenyan or Ugandan law today.

Despite the fact that it is unlikely that this generation of sportsmen will have the opportunity to hunt rhino, sportsmen continue to give generously of their time and money to preserve this marvelous species which, after the elephant, is the largest of all land animals. Wildlife enthusiasts who are not hunters themselves are eager to contribute to saving "Flipper" the dolphin and "Blubber" the whale, but there is no such popular

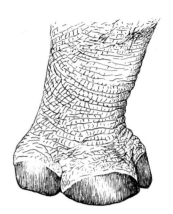

(Below) The rhinoceros is a three-toed animal. Much of the bearing surface of the foot comprises the thick horn that protects an elastic pad in the foot, which cushions the impact of the animal's weight.

upsurge of feeling for the rhinoceros. It is a magnificent brute, but its magnificence can best be perceived by those who have hunted it.

Thus, it is not surprising to learn that the World Wildlife Fund is funding the effort to save the rhino from extinction. Since its founding in 1961, the Fund has allocated over $40 million (£20 million) to 1,800 wildlife research and habitat preservation projects in 131 countries. It has helped to create or support 260 national parks on five continents and has helped to save 33 endangered species of mammals and birds from extinction. Let us hope its drive on behalf of the rhino comes in time.

Most people still see the preservation of wildlife as a matter of maintaining threatened or endangered species in small parks and zoos. They confuse the salvation of a few token individuals with the general perpetuation of species. By contrast, and intrinsic to the hunter's recreation, is the understanding that a healthy population of any species is a result of natural selection, in which the weakest die of disease, parasites, or the attack of predators, leaving the strong to further the species; evolution never stands still. Natural diversity implies that there be enough food, water, and other requirements for a given species in its preferred ecosystem; but it also implies that there will be competition as well.

This is why the hunters long ago began to form habitat preservation and restoration societies. Although the American National Audubon Society is not normally regarded as either a hunter-affiliated organization or a land-preservation group, its early membership and direction were provided in large part by hunters who established the pattern for habitat preservation that makes this organization the largest non-profit and non-governmental land steward in North America.

In more recent decades, the Nature Conservancy—again, with many hunters in its leadership and ranks—has provided additional momentum to habitat protection and, most recently, has begun to focus on the dilemma of the rain forests in Central America and the Caribbean.

Although Ducks Unlimited (DU) owns no land, it has leased hundreds of thousands of acres in Canada for the protection of wetlands and the perpetuation of wildlife dependent on wetlands—including dozens of birds and mammals that will never be hunted by the waterfowling contributors of DU.

Likewise, in the British Isles, the Waterfowlers Association of Great Britain and Ireland (WAGBI) supervises not just the instruction of young hunters and the protection of game species; it is in the vanguard of efforts to save imperiled wetlands in these two nations.

Throughout the world, recreational hunters are playing a leading role in the protection of the natural environment so essential to the well-being of man as well as wildlife. Sportsmen are ridiculed or harassed by ignorant people; their importance to conservation's past, present, and future is often maligned by anti-hunters determined to rewrite history, so that the recreational hunter will have played no role at all.

But to exclude the hunter from history is to deny mankind its roots—roots which still supply us with all the vital ingredients of life and evolution. Man is a predator by ancient design. Unlike the ducks or deer he now hunts, he possesses eyes set for optimum three-dimensional vision—like those of the peregrine falcon and the great cats, our fellow predators. Our jaws and teeth were developed not for living on roots and berries alone. We were obliged by nature to be hunters, and so long as there is game to hunt, there will be hunters.

ROE DEER (*Capreolus capreolus*)

II Game

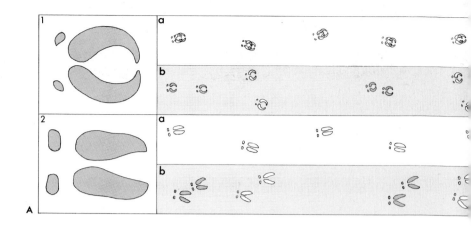

Chapter 1

European and North American Game Animals

Caribou, or Reindeer *(Rangifer tarandus)*

This is an animal of the sub-polar regions, and while there are a number of subspecies, the principal division is between animals that live above and below the tree line; the former, perhaps not surprisingly, are generally smaller. Caribou is the only species of deer of which both bulls and cows have horns of more or less the same size, those of the cows being slightly lighter than those of the bulls. Another feature, but not one so readily noticeable, is the animal's pelt, which is light, thick, an excellent insulator, and waterproof; the animals can survive winter temperatures of –40°C (–40°F) but have trouble dissipating heat in summer. Neither prolonged rain, nor even swimming, causes their skin to become soaked, while the air-retaining qualities of the pelt make it very buoyant.

Reindeer—the word derives from Old Norse—are most associated, in Europe, with the Lapps, who maintain semi-domesticated herds that range unhindered, except for human intrusions, over most of northern Scandinavia and into Russia. The animals are found all the way east through Siberia. In North America, the animal is called caribou—a word that came into English from French, and derives from an American Indian language—and has been important to some Indian peoples, and vital to the Eskimo of North America and Greenland, for food, clothing, shelter, tools, and weapons.

The woodland subspecies do not migrate or range extensively, at any rate not nearly to the same extent as the barren-ground or tundra subspecies. These move in spring and fall between winter and summer territories that may be 600 miles (1,000 km) or more apart; they do so in herds that can be enormous: as many as tens or even scores of thousands of animals. They tend to make use of the same migration routes and the same calving grounds year after year and are thus particularly, if not very apparently, sensitive to human intrusions into their territory. Any sort of permanent construction—the Alaska pipeline is the best-known recent example, but by no means the only one—may disrupt the breeding and migratory habits of the animals.

Apart from men, the reindeer's natural predators are wolves, bear, wolverine, and lynx, which prey mostly upon stragglers from the herds; weak, sick, and injured animals are thus eliminated. Calves are often taken, but they are most at danger from cold, wet weather in spring.

The mating season is in late summer and early fall, and calves are born, after a gestation time of about eight months, in late winter or early spring. Calves are usually single, but twins occur; they can follow their mothers after only some twenty-four hours.

The largest caribou in North America are the Osborne caribou (*R. t. osborni*), of the Rocky Mountains and have massive antlers. They are generally classified as a woodland species, and others, elsewhere in the world, are the woodland reindeer of Scandinavia (*R. t. fennicus*) and the

Siberian reindeer (*R. t. sibericus*). Woodland caribou are found across the whole of northern Canada, but their real stronghold is in the east, and the best trophy heads are from the interior of Newfoundland.

Barren-ground reindeer (*R. t. tarandus*) in North America and Greenland include a number of geographical subspecies. The main one is the Greenland (*R. t. groenlandicus*), found from southern Greenland to the MacKenzie River a little to the east of the Alaska border. West of the river, and westward into the Yukon and Alaska, is the home of Grant's caribou (*R. t. granti*), the largest of the barren-ground animals. To the north, across the Arctic islands, and into northern Greenland is the range of the small, pale Peary caribou (*R. t. pearyi*), and it is estimated that there are about 25,000 of them; as well as their coloration and size, their antlers are distinctive, being almost upright.

A few wild reindeer (*R. t. tarandus*) still exist in the mountains of Norway and Karelia in Finland, but most are now owned by Lapps who mark them for ownership with a complicated arrangement of cuts in the ears. [GG]

Moose, or European Elk *(Alces alces)*

These animals—the largest members of the deer family *Cervidae*—are huge, quite unmistakable beasts with immense, spreading, palmated horns, a drooping nose, and almost grotesquely long legs. In their element—the marshy forests of the north—these great deer move like shadows, specters of a seemingly vanished past. Their American name, moose, derives from the Narragansett name for them—moos.

They have a circumpolar range, like the reindeer, but further south. The European species (*A. a. alces*) is now found chiefly in Scandinavia, where it is known as elk; it can weigh up to about 1,200 lb (540 kg). Further east is the Siberian species (*A. a. pfizenmayeri*) of northern Russia, and it is comparable in size to the Alaskan moose. A smaller subspecies, the Manchurian moose (*A. a. cameloides*), is found in eastern Asia.

The North American species is led, in size, by the Alaskan moose (*A. a. gigas*), which is almost black, can stand 7½ feet (230 cm) at the shoulder and weighs up to 1,800 lb (800 kg); its horns are proportionately large and are therefore the most sought-after trophy. It ranges through the wooded regions of Alaska, the western Yukon, and northwest British Columbia. A much smaller, pale variety occurs in the Rockies, the Shiras moose (*A. a. shirasi*), which only seldom exceeds 1,000 lb (450 kg) in weight.

Elsewhere in North America, moose are either of the eastern or northwestern subspecies, respectively *A. a. americanus* and *A. a. andersoni*. Bulls weigh about 1,000 lb (450 kg), but the average is lower; the northwestern is slightly larger, and ranges through Canada from western Ontario to the Pacific and north to the Beaufort Sea above Alaska, and

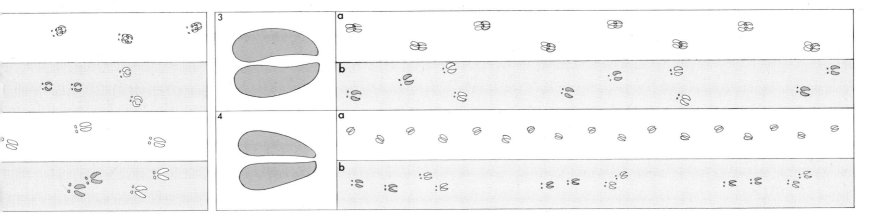

across the northern parts of Wisconsin, Michigan, Minnesota, and North Dakota. It overlaps with the eastern moose, which inhabits the forests of eastern Canada, and, in very small numbers, those of remote areas of the northeastern United States.

All moose need woodlands with bogs and marshes and, while they prefer deciduous trees for food, they will also eat coniferous shoots and buds. If these are scarce, as often may be the case in spring, moose will graze on early spring crops. In warm weather, they eat aquatic grasses and other such vegetation and can sometimes be seen flank-deep in lakes or even submerged, like a hippo. They can swim well, too.

They mate in September and October, the cows calling to the bulls with a loud, bawling noise. The bulls fight, sometimes with fatal results, but do not maintain harems. They shed their antlers during the winter, growing new ones during the spring and summer. Gestation takes some eight or nine months, and calves are thus born mostly in May; twins are common, and calves remain with their mothers for a year. While the cows are hornless, their size makes them formidable, and they resent intruders when they are with very young calves. Bulls in rut become blindly furious and commonly work off their rage on trees: they have been known to charge locomotives. While hunters might shoot them at this time, perhaps in self-defence, the flesh of a bull in rut is not good to eat. At other times, by contrast, it is prized, being tender and succulent, and, of course, there is a great deal of it. In the far north of North America, and in much of Scandinavia, the meat is a significant part of a winter's food supply; the annual legal cull in Sweden, for example, is nearly 100,000 elk of an estimated population of over 300,000. Many are killed on the roads there, too, and their very bulk and dark coloration make them a deadly menace for motorists at night. While the Scandinavian population of elk has been growing steadily for some years, as towns absorb more and more people, in North America the southern parts of the moose's range have shrunk from the intrusion of human activity. [GG; TT]

Red Deer *(Cervus elaphus)*

The red deer stag is the pre-eminent hunting trophy of Europe and, as such, has been celebrated for centuries in art, literature, and music. Called *Hirsch* in German, the animal was formerly reserved for noblemen only on the continent of Europe, while, in Britain, its strictly legal status was vague until after World War II. The North American red deer (*C. e. canadensis*) is known as the wapiti, or elk.

Red deer now occur westward across Europe from the British Isles to Russia, wherever there are the deep forests that the animals like. The exception is the treeless forests of Scotland that still hold many red deer; these areas were still heavily wooded in the first half of the eighteenth century, and have retained their deer and names, but not their trees.

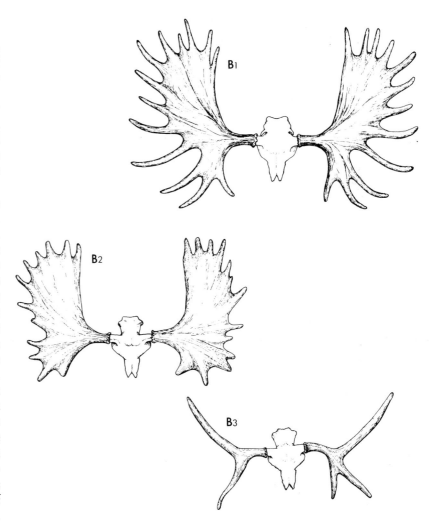

A Deer tracks in soft earth or thin snow can be distinguished from one another. *(1)* Caribou have markedly rounded hoof-prints: *(a)* walking, *(b)* running. *(2)* Moose have asymmetrical hooves that are roughly parallel when the animal is walking *(a)* but spread out when it is running *(b)*. *(3)* Red deer tracks. *(a)* When the animal is walking, the hind feet overprint the marks of the front feet. *(b)* When running, the dewclaws, or lateral hooves, leave clearly visible marks. *(4)* Roe deer tracks are similar to, but smaller than, those of red deer. *(a)* Walking. *(b)* Running.

B The horns of moose and European elk are of different sizes and forms. *(1)* Moose's are generally larger; this is an example of the palmated type, with "fingers" spreading out from a "palm." *(2)* European elk, palmated form. *(3)* European elk, cervina form. All sorts of variations between palmated and cervina types occur.

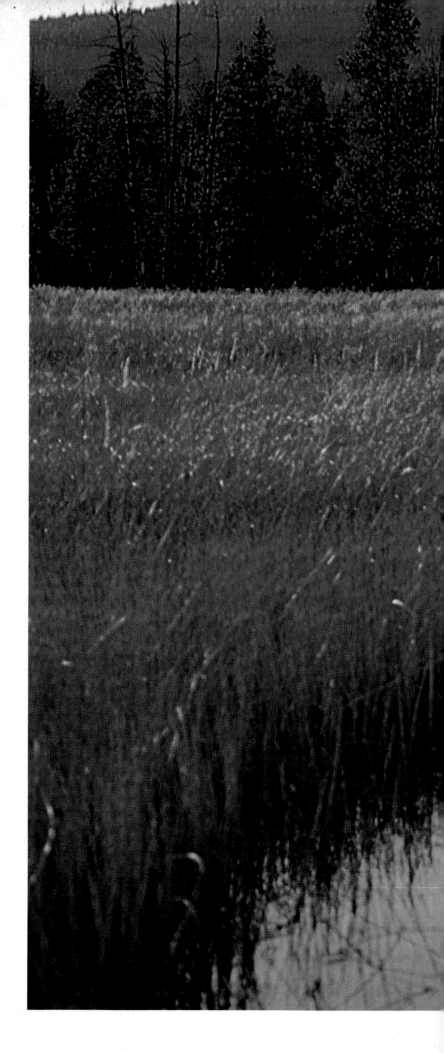

(Above) **FALLOW DEER** (*Dama dama*).
(Center) **MOOSE** (*Alces alces*).
(Below) **CARIBOU, or REIN-DEER** (*Rangifer tarandus*).

(Right) **WAPITI** (*Cervus elaphus canadensis*).

An average red deer stag of central Europe weighs about 275 to 300 lb (125 to 135 kg), stands about 4 feet (120 cm) at the shoulder, and measures about 6 feet (180 cm) in total length. A pair of antlers—a head—may have up to twelve points; it is then called a royal. Exceptionally, an eighteen-pointer head has been known. Red deer are larger in Eastern Europe than anywhere else, while those of Scotland, which live on exceptionally poor land, considered agriculturally, are smaller. Hungary, Czechoslovakia, and Yugoslavia all have good populations of large deer. Those of West Germany are smaller in average size, but their numbers are impressive, having been maintained by that country's superb game-management endeavors.

Red deer can adapt to new habitat and have done well in numerous transplantations. New Zealand, for example, now has a large population in isolated areas, and there are healthy herds in parts of South America and Asia. A few red deer have been imported into North America, perhaps inadvisedly, for they have competed with domestic species—whitetail and mule deer, and wapiti—for browse and cover in habitat continually being reduced by human activities.

Red deer are gregarious and form large groups, normally led by an old hind and consisting of hinds, calves, and young stags; the older stags usually congregate in smaller bachelor herds throughout much of the year. The rut—the breeding season—begins towards the end of September, being heralded by the roaring of the stags as they identify and challenge one another; the sound resembles that of a roaring lion. The stags fight by butting one another; curiously, stags with antlers having only a single point, or altogether without antlers, are most likely to overcome their rivals. Well-developed heads of horns seem superfluous in these rutting struggles and, if they become entangled and locked together, the stags can starve to death. [TT]

Roe Deer (*Capreolus capreolus*)

Roe deer, compared with red deer, are diminutive: a mature buck weighs about 50 to 65 lb (23 to 30 kg) and stands about 28 inches (70 cm) at the shoulder. Bucks have antlers that have at most six points; does rarely have horns, which are always small. Bucks and does have a rich foxy-red coat in summer; in winter, it turns grayish and can be flecked with yellow. There can be many color variations while, in the Netherlands and northwestern Germany, melanistic—i.e., black—roe deer can occur. In winter, a white rump patch develops, and the species has special muscles that can cause the patch to expand into a disk, to form an alarm signal. The tail is very small, hardly visible. In winter, the does develop a tuft of long hair, called the anal tush, which is sometimes mistaken for a tail; it can be a useful way of distinguishing does from bucks that have shed their antlers.

There are two types of roe deer, the field roe and the forest roe, and the latter is far more common. It prefers small woods, ideally those that are bordered by meadows or fields, for this habitat provides ample shelter and an optimum food supply. The field roe prefers open fields and can obtain the shelter it needs from even the most meager thickets and brush. Even in heavily populated countries, the deer population can be considerable. In West Germany, for example, some 60,000 deer a year are killed accidentally on the roads.

Distribution elsewhere in Europe is southward from Norway, Sweden, and southern Finland to Spain, Portugal, and Greece; the species stretches eastward to Iran and the Ural Mountains. In the British Isles, the species was at one time nearly extinct but is now abundant, having been extensively introduced out of its original areas. East of the Urals and throughout much of Asia, the European roe is replaced by a somewhat larger subspecies, the Siberian roe (*C. c. pygargus*), while another subspecies, the Chinese roe (*C. c. bedfordi*), is found in China and most of the Korean peninsula. [TT]

(Above) The development of the roe deer's horns. (1) Winter months. (2) February. (3) March-April. (4) June-September. (a) First point. (b) Second. (c) Third.
(Below) The red deer's antlers. (1) First or second year. (2) Second year. (3) Third year. (4) Fourth year. (5) Fourth or fifth year. The ten-pointer. (a) Brow antler. (b) Bay. (c) Tray. (d) Fork. (6) The twelve-pointer, or royal. (a) Pedicle. (b) Brow. (c) Bay. (d) Tray. (e) Tine. (f) Palm. (g) Top. (7) The fourteen-pointer. The crown (a) may develop several more points. (8) The sixteen-pointer. After this, the antlers will almost certainly go back, although eighteen-pointers have been recorded.

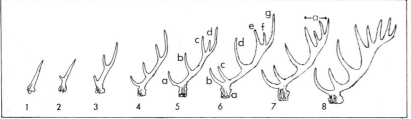

Fallow Deer *(Dama dama)*

Originally a native of Mesopotamia, in the valleys of the Tigris and the Euphrates, the fallow deer has been successfully introduced into many other parts of Europe. It now occurs in the wild in virtually all European countries apart from some—Belgium, Holland, Italy, Norway, Portugal, and Switzerland—where it is preserved in parks and private estates. Transplanted herds thrive in the wilds of New Zealand, on private hunting preserves in North America, and in the wild in eastern Kentucky and in other parts of the southeastern United States, where wildlife agencies have studied the possibility of establishing fallow deer in huntable numbers.

Smaller than the red deer, a mature fallow stag weighs about 200 lb (90 kg) and stands about 3 feet (90 cm) at the shoulder. Unlike almost all other deer, fallow deer have spots on their pelts when mature, a feature that is particularly noticeable when their pelts take on their characteristic reddish-brown summer coloration. Fallow deer exhibit a much wider range of color variation than do most species of deer: from almost black to a light yellowish-brown. Wholly white and wholly black specimens have been observed. The common name of the species—fallow—indicates what must have once been its predominant color, a pale brownish or reddish yellow.

Only the bucks have antlers and—another unusual feature of the species—they are palmated, like those of the European elk. Perhaps semi-palmated would be a more accurate description, for the horns grow from the head in the normal, unpalmated fashion, but on mature bucks, definite palms do develop at the top of the antlers.

Typically for European deer and some other animals, fallow deer are larger in size (and antler dimensions) the further east they live; the best heads and the largest deer are to be seen in Czechoslovakia, Rumania, and Russia. There is a subspecies known as the Persian or Mesopotamian fallow deer, which occurs in southern Iran; as this is the area from which fallow deer were first transplanted, by the Romans, these deer may be the only examples of the original form still existing in the wild.

Fallow deer are less sensitive to the presence and activities of people than are red deer, for fallow deer are usually satisfied with small woodlots and sparsely forested areas, even in areas of high human population density. While they are often found living together with populations of red deer and roe deer, they seem for some reason—perhaps competition for mast and other foods—to avoid areas with a high boar population. Fallow deer have been suggested as "the deer of the future" for Western Europe, but it is unlikely to become as popular with hunters as the red deer. [TT]

Whitetail Deer *(Odocoileus virginianus)*

These deer range in size from bucks of 200 lb (90 kg) and more in the upper Northeast and Midwest of the United States, to the tiny Florida Keys whitetail (*O. v. clavium*), which would be exceptionally large at 80 lb (36 kg). An even smaller variety is reported from Coiba Island, off Panama. Apart from these two small subspecies, whitetails are much alike, despite having been divided by taxonomists into some thirty subspecies, of which seventeen are found in the United States.

The deer now occur in North America east of the Rocky Mountains. Their northern limits are determined by winter cold and snow conditions. While their gray-brown pelts give good protection against cold, snow deeper than about 3 feet (1 m) is really too much for them, but they have, in fact, reached the James Bay area at the south of Hudson Bay and the Peace River Valley of Alberta, a bare 400 miles (640 km) south of the Arctic Circle.

They flourish on the abandoned farms of the northeastern United States, where their population has been reckoned to be as high as fourteen deer to the square mile. More southerly states, such as Alabama

The antler development in the wapiti, the North American red deer. *(1)* In March, the pedicles are just visible. *(2)* After three months, the budding horns are covered with velvet. *(3)* In August when the antlers are fully grown, the velvet covering becomes itchy, and the bull rubs it off on trees and bushes.
The tracks made by a wapiti in flight are also shown. They are similar to those of the whitetail deer.

and Texas, have high populations, and various subspecies range through Mexico and into Central America.

Whitetails do well in immature wooded areas, for these provide the food and cover they need; historically, they have spread with the cutting of the mature forests of the eastern United States, for these lacked brushy undergrowth and branches low enough for the deer to graze on. They eat practically anything vegetable and, on cultivated land, will dig up root crops such as beets and carrots and will enter orchards to eat the apples off the trees. With this adaptability, it is hardly surprising that their population in North America is as high as 10 million.

During the warm summer months, the deer grow fat, the fawns gather strength, and the antlers of the bucks develop. By late October, when the rut begins, their antlers have been scrubbed clean of velvet on bushes. Bucks do fight among themselves, but only briefly and without harming each other; their antlers can, however, lock together and then both bucks will starve to death.

The species is polygamous, and bucks attract does by establishing a series of "scrapes." They scratch the earth clean of leaves and vegetation, then scent it with urine and musk from the tarsal glands. Each buck may have several secluded scrapes and, at the peak of the rut, he will visit them regularly.

Shortly after the rut, whitetails start a gradual migration to their wintering areas. This can entail a move of anything from a mile to a hundred miles or more (2 to 160 km); distances tend to be short in the south and long in the north.

In the south, wintering areas are loosely defined or not defined at all, whereas in the north, where snow can drift to depths exceeding three feet (1 m), the deer depend on "yards" for survival and trample out deep runways to and from food and shelter through drifts that would hopelessly bog down a single animal. A "yard" is an easily recognized wintering area, usually on a south-facing slope, in a valley, or in some other sheltered spot. A yard that is overcrowded can provide insufficient food if the weather turns severe; even if many deer die, the remainder seem unwilling to move on as a group or to disperse.

By March, the strains of winter begin to show, for the deer that survive become gaunt and ragged by early spring; this is especially marked with the yearling fawns, which are too short to reach such food as is available, and, during the most severe winters, all the yearling fawns may not survive.

By April, the snow banks melt, and the survivors can begin to roam and gorge themselves. The fawns are born, spotted and almost scentless. [GG]

Mule Deer (Odocoileus hemionus)

From Mexico to Alaska, Rocky Mountains mule deer (O. h. hemionus) or one of its ten subspecies are found just about everywhere in the western half of North America. Each of them is adapted to its own particular niche—from the arid Mexican plains to the windswept ridges of southeastern Alaska—and, with the exception of the two races known as blacktail deer (see below), all have about the same life pattern.

A distinguishing characteristic of all mule deer is their large ears and, on a big buck, they can be as long as 12 inches (30 cm), measured from their base. Some experts maintain that the ears serve to dissipate excess body heat. The animals are typically barrel-bodied with stocky legs; they have short white tails tipped with black. Their antlers are formed of a number of branches, rather than a single branch with spikes growing off it. Of all mule deer, the Rocky Mountains "muley," as they are affectionately called, has the largest spread of antlers and is the most prized trophy. An adult buck will weigh about 400 lb (180 kg).

These deer are migratory, spending summers at altitudes sometimes exceeding 8,000 feet (2,400 m). From about the middle of September, the

deer descend along well-worn trails of their own making to winter pastures; the deer in the southern part of the range do not migrate, however.

Breeding takes place toward the end of October and, while the deer congregate in groups of bucks and does, they do not form harems, as some other species do, nor do the bucks fight as much. Fawns are born after a gestation period of about seven months; does produce single fawns in their early breeding seasons but, later, commonly produce twins or even triplets. The fawns are born when the deer have returned to their summer pastures; the bucks move there first, followed shortly afterward by the does heavy with young.

Mule deer may live as long as twenty years, although the average life span is about ten years. They were formerly much preyed on by cougars and wolves, but these predators are now scarce. Coyotes, bears, and lynx may take an occasional deer, but the adult mule deer are large and formidable antagonists. [GG]

Blacktail Deer *(Odocoileus hemionus columbianus)*
(O. h. sitkensis)

These two subspecies of mule deer inhabit the Pacific coastal forests of

(Below) The mule deer. Movements of the black tip against the contrasting white of the rump make a vivid signal that is visible at a great distance. The species got its common name from the animals' huge ears.

(Below, inset) The blacktail buck stretching up to browse can be identified by the large extent of black on its tail.

North America, ranging from southern California to Vancouver Island—the Columbian Blacktail—and thence northward through the vast off-shore archipelago of Queen Charlotte Islands and into the Alaskan Panhandle—the Sitka blacktail. They differ in a number of respects from the mule deer.

Their tails appear black—they have a white underside—and are flared, while those of the typical mule deer are cylindrical. The Columbian is slightly darker and slightly smaller than the average mule deer, while the Sitka is darker and smaller still. A pale brownish-yellow variety occurs in the deserts of the Southwest, but, otherwise, blacktails are deer of the forests and mountainous brush country.

Like whitetails, they are elusive and crafty and, when they do not flee, running flat-out, they can "freeze" into immobility, even when a hunter or his dog is in the neighborhood, or move noiselessly away. While mule deer typically run with a bounding motion, blacktails bound only occasionally.

They swim well and have thus spread out over the British Columbian and Alaskan archipelago, which is now over-populated with them. Once, cougar, wolves, and lynx kept down their numbers, so that the deer did not exhaust their own food supplies, but this is now what curtails populations, especially in severe winters, when many blacktails can starve to death.

They thrive best in areas of new growth, such as may be found after forest fires or lumbering operations. Although they have been observed to be faithful to a given territory, despite pressures of hunting, the biggest concentrations of deer occur in these new growth areas.

Their breeding season begins in mid-September in the south of their range and in November in the north. Fawns are born after a gestation time of about seven months and twins are so common that this is really the rule. [GG]

Pronghorn *(Antilocapra americana)*

A mature buck weighs up to 145 lb (65 kg) and will then stand 41 inches (105 cm) at the shoulder. Both sexes are horned, and the bucks' horns may grow to a length of 20 inches (50 cm), but 12 inches (30 cm) is the average. One peculiar feature of the bifurcated horns is that they consist of an inner core and an outer sheath, the latter shed annually. The horns of the females rarely exceed a length of 3 inches (8 cm).

Pronghorns are russet to dark brown and have white underparts. The face and front of the neck are patterned in black, brown, and white. If it is scared, the animal erects the long, white hair on its rump patch.

Pronghorns belong to the western parts of North America, where they occur from southern Alberta to northern Mexico. During the winter, they live in large herds, which break up into smaller ones in spring. A herd of the smaller type usually consists of an old buck with up to eight hinds and their young. The younger mature bucks then congregate in bachelor herds. The rut takes place in September-October, and the gestation period lasts eight months. The hinds commonly give birth to one or two young. Pronghorns generally live in open, dry grassland and avoid forests. They mainly eat grass, herbs, moss, and lichen. [RE]

Mountain Goat *(Oreamnos americanus)*

This animal is an antelope and is distantly related to the antelopes of Asia and Africa but does its best to live up to its name: it looks and acts like a goat, and lives in the mountains like one, and so acquired its name from the first Europeans who saw it.

It is found only in North America, occurring in the high mountain peaks of southern Alaska, the Yukon, and the Northwest Territories south through British Columbia and Alberta into Washington, Montana, and Idaho. There are small herds in Wyoming and the Black Hills of South Dakota.

It has a strikingly thick, white coat with long guard hairs. The males, or billies, weigh from 200 to 300 lb (90 to 135 kg), and the females, or nannies, are slightly less heavy. Both are horned, and while the horns of some nannies are longer, those of the billies are thicker and more massive.

Mountain goats can keep their footing on almost imperceptible small ledges, outcroppings, and bumps as they cross practically vertical cliffs. They appear to be able to walk up vertical rock walls and successfully to defy gravity. Their hooves are unique in that they have a spongy portion that grips almost like a suction cup, but, despite this, occasional mishaps do occur. Indeed, falls from heights, and rockslides, account for a far greater number of fatalities than all other causes combined—predators, disease, hunting, and shortages of winter food.

Nannies and kids stay together in herds of up to a dozen animals, while the billies are solitary, or gather in small bachelor groups, except in November, which is the start of the mating season, and in winter. They feed principally on grass from high mountain meadows.

Billies become pugnacious in the mating season. Kids are born from April to June and, while single births are most common, twins do occur.

During winter, the goats seek lower elevations on southerly exposed hills, where the wind has swept away the snow; in spring, they move back into the peaks. [JK]

Bighorn Sheep *(Ovis canadensis)*

Bighorn sheep have spectacular, heavy, curving horns and inhabit high mountain country that is as magnificent as the sheep and that would seem barren without them. The bighorn is North America's most coveted trophy.

Bighorns are divided, for purposes of scoring trophies and establishing records, into two classes: Rocky Mountains bighorn and desert bighorn. There are, a little confusingly, different geographical variations, too, for example, the Californian bighorn.

The animal's range extends from central British Columbia and Alberta south through the western mountains into northern Mexico and Baja California. The arid hills of Nevada, California, New Mexico, Arizona, and northern Mexico, including the Baja, comprise the habitats of the desert bighorn, which is less numerous and slightly smaller than the mountain bighorn.

Both rams and ewes have horns, but the ewes' are smaller, lighter, and lack the complete "curl" of the rams'. Mature mountain rams may weigh up to 300 lb (135 kg), but 250 lb (113 kg) is a more usual weight; the ewes are about three-quarters the size of the rams.

Bighorns are generally brown with pale snouts, rump patches, and bellies. Mountain bighorns tend to be dark brown, while the desert variation may be as dark, but is mostly a lighter tawny or buff color that blends well with its surroundings.

The breeding season is in late October and November. The rams mate with as many ewes as possible. The older, stronger rams keep the younger ones away from the ewes. Spectacular butting jousts are common between antagonistic old rams. These battles are almost a ritual. Accidents do occur in which one of the opponents is hurt, but this is rare. After the breeding season, the rams lose their jealousy and antagonism for one another and form bachelor herds apart from the ewes.

Winter is a hard time for sheep. As the first snows come, the sheep move down from the high mountain meadows of 9,000 to 10,000 feet (2,700 to 3,000 m) to pasture at 2,000 to 3,000 feet (600 to 900 m). The better winter ranges always have southern exposures and are regularly swept free of snow by the wind. In the spring, the sheep return high into the mountains.

One of the problems that affect bighorn sheep is that their winter pastures are frequently grazed over by domestic sheep and cattle in the

(Above) The sure-footed mountain goat in a typical hump-backed stance. (Left) Tracks of a mountain goat walking in snow. Its hooves have a sort of suction-pad action that helps them to adhere to hard, rocky surfaces.

(Left) **BIGHORN SHEEP** (*Ovis canadensis*).
(Left below) **MOUNTAIN GOAT** (*Oreamnos americanus*).
(Far right) **DALL SHEEP** (*Ovis dalli*).
(Below) **MOUFLON** (*Ovis musimon*).

summer months. When the bighorns descend into lower elevations in the winter, they must contend with overgrazed pastures. [JK]

Dall Sheep *(Ovis dalli)*

The Dall sheep is a wild sheep of Alaska, the Yukon, and the Northwest Territories, while its subspecies, the Stone sheep (*O. d. stonei*), is found in the mountains of northern British Columbia.

The coat of the Dall is white, and its horns are thinner in structure than those of the bighorn, and they flare out at their tips. Like the Stone, the Dall is sometimes referred to as a "thinhorn."

The Stone sheep is dark gray to almost black, and its horns are somewhat heavier than those of the Dall, while having the same shape and structure. Stone sheep horns are separately classified in the trophy records, and it is worth noting that the biggest wild-sheep horns, the famous Chadwick head, are of a Stone sheep.

Both Dall and Stone sheep have essentially the same life history as the bighorn, although Dalls do not seem to make so great a seasonal migration as do bighorn sheep. After the rut, the rams and ewes stay more or less together for the entire winter, and, when spring comes, the rams separate into bachelor groups.

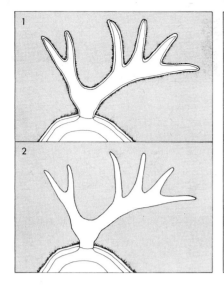
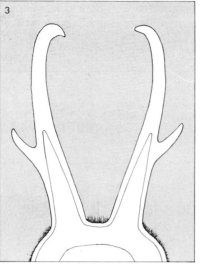
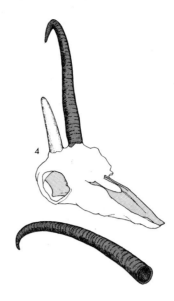

Some horned animals—red deer, for example—grow and shed their horns annually. *(1)* During the period of growth, the horns, which grow out from the skull, are covered with skin. *(2)* Later, this falls away or is rubbed off against trees and saplings. *(3)* Bovids—cows and antelopes are of this class—have hollow horns that grow around a core of bone. These horns are not shed, and grow longer year by year. Shown are an exception, the horns of the pronghorn, which sheds its horns, but not their cores, annually. *(4)* The skull of a chamois, showing the core of bone protruding from the skull.

Dall sheep have less trouble in winter than bighorns, for they live in more remote areas and seldom have to compete with domestic livestock for winter grazing. Their population is greater, too, and the number of hunting licences issued annually is greater. [JK]

Mouflon *(Ovis musimon)*

A relatively rare animal on the continent of Europe, the mouflon was introduced there from Sardinia and Corsica. It has adapted successfully to the hilly hardwood forests of Central Europe, particularly in areas of dry rocky terrain. It has also been successfully established on the Hawaiian island of Lanai. Like red deer, mouflon require a fairly large area within which they can satisfy their instinct to roam.

Mouflon are in many ways similar to the bighorn sheep of North America, but they are considerably smaller, an average German specimen weighing only about 100 lb (45 kg). They stand about 30 inches (76 cm) high at the shoulder. In winter, they are dark brown, with parts of their bodies being almost black.

They feed primarily on herbs and grasses, and cause practically no damage to trees or crops. They roam as they feed, returning to particularly favored meadows in the late afternoon.

Ewes and lambs herd together, being led by an old ewe. Rams, on the other hand, are solitary. Mature rams may, however, band together for a time, but not during the rut. This occurs in November and December; then, the rams rejoin the herd and battle with one another for possession of harems. Those that are unsuccessful roam restlessly during this time.

The distinguishing feature of the mouflon is, of course, its horns; this is so for all species of wild sheep. As many mouflon rams do not develop horns with a spiral, only really good trophies closely resemble those of the bighorn sheep. A common, and so less desirable, type is of horns curving in a long graceful sweep outward from the head, then in toward the neck. [TT]

Chamois *(Rupicapra rupicapra)*

Related to, but smaller than, the North American mountain goat, the chamois is an antelope which is found in similarly high terrain, primarily in the Alpine region but also, in smaller concentrations, in other, lesser mountain ranges. It is only sometimes found below the timberline.

It stands about 2½ feet (76 cm) high at the shoulder and is about 3½ feet (107 cm) long. A mature male weighs about 75 lb (34 kg) and a mature doe some ten percent less. In winter, both are dark brown to black, but, in summer, somewhat lighter brown. The face is yellowish-white, marked with a dark stripe from the ear to the nose, over the eye.

Bucks and does are horned, and both are hunted as trophy animals. They are among Europe's most sought-after game animals. The horns, which are never shed, curve rearward toward the head, the buck's with a pronounced hook. The doe's are somewhat smaller.

The German for the animal is *Gams*, thus giving the name *Gamsbart* to the highly prized trophy consisting of a thick brush of the hair from the spine of a mature chamois. This hair is plucked, not cut, and formed into a fan or mushroom-shaped brush which adorns the hat, forming part of the traditional dress of the inhabitants of the Alpine region. No self-respecting Bavarian seems to feel that his or her wardrobe is complete without one such hat. [TT]

Ibex *(Capra)*

This is a family of European wild goat, of which there are two species, the Alpine ibex (*C. ibex*) and the Spanish or Iberian ibex (*C. pyrenaica*). Some eight varieties exist and differ chiefly in the size and shape of their horns. However, it is only in the Pyrenees and in Spain that sufficient numbers of ibex exist to make hunting practicable; some 30,000 Spanish ibex are said to inhabit the Pyrenees and the central mountainous region of Spain.

Through intensive game-management programs, the Alpine ibex, or *Steinbock*, as it is known in the German-speaking parts of Europe, has been re-introduced into the Alpine regions of Switzerland, Austria, Germany, Italy, and Yugoslavia. Before this was undertaken, the animal had been reduced to near-extinction, with a small colony remaining in the Italian Alps, and another, smaller one in the mountains around Salzburg.

Both species of ibex are short and stocky, and males reach a weight of 230 to 240 lb (105 to 110 kg). Their horns are so large in proportion to their bodies that they seem ungainly. Those of the Alpine ibex are the longer, attain a length of nearly 40 inches (100 cm), are set close together on the animal's head, and curve back in a simple arc; they have a triangular cross-section and heavy knobs or ribs on the front-facing surface. The horns of the Spanish ibex are slightly shorter, tend to a lyre shape with a slight curve towards the tips, and lack the knobs of the Alpine ibex.

Ibex are proverbially agile climbers, and this goes for the newborn kids, too; they can follow their mothers without difficulty only a few hours after birth. In summer, ibex graze on high-altitude mountain vegetation, and they move down the mountains when snowfalls begin, to feed on whatever grasses and lichens there are.

Ibex breed from about October to December, during which time the billies fight furiously among themselves. A gestation period of some five months causes kids—almost invariably single—to be born in spring. [TT]

Wild Boar (Sus scrofa)

Wild boar are still found in Europe eastward from West Germany and, like the red deer, the animals become generally bigger as one goes eastward. The average weight of males in West Germany, for example, is about 200 lb (90 kg), while in Turkey, it is almost 400 lb (180 kg). Wild boar are not only omnivorous, but destructive, too, and the damage that a herd can do to a grain or potato field in only a single night is almost unbelievable. In the more densely populated agricultural areas of Europe, they have, therefore, been hunted relentlessly, but the species is by no means near extinction.

They are also nomadic, so much so that they are omitted from the annual game census required by West German law. They usually keep close to heavy thickets that provide escape routes, if need be, and while they will cross open, dry areas, it will only be when they are moving from one place to another. They forage at night, and the chances of seeing wild boar by chance during the day are slim. They are, therefore, usually driven when hunted.

Wild boar are armed with formidable tusks, protruding for up to 8 inches (20 cm) from either side of the snout. When charging, boar do not detour round anything, not even a hunter. Their tusks are very sharp, and hunters have been known to take refuge in handy trees to avoid them. It has been debated whether or not boar are naturally aggressive, or "only" given to trying to escape as fast as they can on such occasions but, in the field, it is probably advisable to jump first and debate later.

Wild boar were transplanted to North America first in the 1890s, again in 1910 and 1912, and yet again in 1925. Naturally, some of the animals escaped and spread out into the surrounding countryside, often interbreeding with stray domestic pigs or their feral relatives, so the coloration of wild boar in North America is now more variable than that of their European cousins. Weights vary from about 200 to about 350 lb (90 to 160 kg), with the heavier animals being generally of the least intermixed wild strains. [TT]

Brown, or Grizzly, Bear (Ursus arctos)

In Europe, the brown bear exists in small numbers in the Pyrenees, the Alps, the Balkans, and northern Scandinavia; it is also found in Russia and Asia. In North America, despite the diminishing areas of wilderness available, there are healthy numbers of grizzly and Alaskan brown bears. Scientists now classify all of these bears as the same species, but of different geographical races. This is not entirely satisfactory from the North American point of view, as no one knows where the grizzly's range ends and the Alaskan brown's range begins, and the best way to distinguish between these two may be to speak of the grizzly as the inland bear and of the Alaskan brown as the coastal bear.

The range of the inland (grizzly) bear extends from the mountains of Wyoming, Montana, and Idaho north through British Columbia and western Alberta, and through the western part of the Northwest Territories, the Yukon, and the interior of Alaska. The Alaskan Brown (coastal) bear ranges from southern Alaska—including, of course, Kodiak Island, which is famous for the size of its bears—southward into British Columbia. The coastal bear is bigger than the grizzly because it eats more protein and fat. It is famous for catching and eating salmon, both live fish on their way up the coastal rivers to spawn, and dead fish that fail to survive spawning. The female coastal bear—female bears are known as sows—weighs between 500 and 800 lb (230 and 360 kg); fully grown males—boars—range from 800 to 1,200 lb (360 to 540 kg) and can exceed that, too. One of the largest on record weighed over 1,600 lb (752 kg) and was nearly 9 feet (274 cm) long. Incidentally, it is the skulls of bears, not the skins, that are used to rank them in the famous Boone and Crocket Club trophy records, as skull dimensions are a reasonably reliable indicator of a bear's size, whereas skins can be stretched.

The inland bear does not have access to such large quantities of rich food as the coastal, and it is consequently smaller: sows weigh from 400 to 600 lb (180 to 270 kg) and boars from 500 to 800 lb (230 to 360 kg).

The pelt of U. arctos varies in color from dark brown to almost blond or russet. Inland bears frequently have white-tipped guard hairs, hence the name "grizzly."

Brown bears are omnivorous. Apart from fish, they eat all kinds of vegetation, wild fruits, berries, grass which they graze like cows, and all sorts of small animals—rodents, birds, reptiles—which they catch or dig out of their holes. They eat insects, too, and have been observed swimming, mouth open, in streams where water-borne larvae were plentiful. Bees, grubs, and the proverbial honey need scarcely be mentioned. Bears will kill and eat larger animals, and eat carrion: moose, deer, caribou, elk, wild sheep. Old boars have been known to eat even bear cubs.

Salmon of five different species spawn in the rivers of the Pacific Northwest and, as they spawn at different times, it is possible for bears to eat salmon most of the summer. Even inland bears eat fish when spawning runs occur in inland rivers and streams; their other food is most abundant in late summer and early fall, and it is then that they are most likely to be seen by the hunter, for they are active then and spend much time above the timberline, foraging for food in order to accumulate fat for their winter dormancy.

The first big snow of late fall or early winter drives them to their dens. They do not hibernate in the strict sense of the word, as their body temperature does not fall. In the early spring, the bears emerge from their winter dormancy. The adult boars are the first to emerge. Sows with cubs, which are born during the dormancy or which are from the previous year's dormancy, come out last.

On emerging in spring, bears still have rich and glossy pelts, with no patches of hair rubbed out. At first, they feed on grass, so the place to hunt them is on grassy hillsides and mountain meadows. Most bears shot in the spring are shot by hunters who have packed into the mountains with pack horses or have scouted from boats along coastal inlets and rivers.

The brown bear is an animal of the wilderness. Its continued existence depends, therefore, on there being enough wilderness available for it; undeniably, its range is on the decrease. [JK]

Black Bear (Ursus americanus)

There are some twenty recognized subspecies of black bear, but most are similar enough to make the differences between them of academic importance only. Northern British Columbia is the home of U. a. kermodei—the Kermode bear—which is gray-white, and of U. a. emmonsii—the Glacier bear—which is bluish in color and occurs also in southern Alaska. Apart from these two, there are black bears, ranging in color from jet black to honey blond, from central Mexico to the northern tip of Alaska, and from the Atlantic to the Pacific. In the eastern part of North America, most are black, usually with a tan or grizzled snout and often with a white chest blaze.

They are much smaller than *U. arctos*—the brown or grizzly bear—with weights usually between 200 and 400 lb (90 and 180 kg). They can be very much larger; in 1885, a Wisconsin bear was weighed at 802 lb (364 kg), and nearly seventy years later, in 1953, another Wisconsin bear had a dressed weight of 585 lb (265 kg), representing a live weight of 735 lb (333 kg). On its skull measurement, it is the biggest black bear trophy on record.

Black bears thrive in heavy brushwood and mixed deciduous and coniferous forests, and they are omnivorous, eating whatever they can get. This includes all sorts of vegetable and animal food, and the gleanings of garbage dumps and edibles in hunting cabins and tents. When hungry, black bears are recklessly intrusive and very dangerous, and, at all times of year, they are unpredictable.

There was still a bounty for killing bears in the 1950s, but they are now accorded the status of game animals, and so, bear hunting is regulated. They are protected in national parks, and elsewhere may not be hunted over carrion bait nor, in many regions of the United States, may they be tracked with dogs.

Like *U. arctos*, black bears do not hibernate entirely but seek dens in fall or early winter. A sow either gives birth to cubs in the den, usually in January or February, or has the previous year's cubs with her; in either event, she is unlikely to sleep undisturbed. Both boars and sows are sometimes found in the vicinity of their dens, even in the middle of winter. The length of their usage of dens depends on the local availability of vegetation to eat, so that in the south of their range, where the growing period is long, bears scarcely use a den at all, while in the north they may be in it for more than six months a year.

A usual litter is two cubs, but more occur; a litter of six was observed in 1947, but this must be exceptional. The cubs weigh about ½ lb (225 g) at birth but weigh about 75 lb (34 kg) at the end of their first year. They are usually driven off during their second year, become sexually active at three or four years of age, are full-grown by seven, and may live to thirty. [GG]

Polar Bear *(Ursus maritimus)*

The polar bear is a magnificent animal of the snow, ice, and water of the Arctic. Apart from man, the polar bear's only enemy is the killer whale, which occasionally takes a polar bear.

Polar bears are circumpolar, being found around the entire fringe of the Arctic. This includes the whole arctic coastline of North America, Greenland, and the arctic islands. Bears sometimes wander as far south as James Bay, at the south of Hudson Bay in Canada.

Polar bears are, on average, the largest bears of North America, being generally larger than the brown bears of the northwest Pacific coast. Polar bears weighing over 1,600 lb (725 kg) have been shot, although the average is around 1,000 lb (450 kg). The sows are slightly smaller. The polar bear's color is yellowish-white, and its body is somewhat pear-shaped, for ease in swimming.

Like all bears, polar bears are solitary, although the sows and their partly grown cubs travel together, but once the cubs reach sub-adulthood, they must cope on their own. The only time polar bears are sociable is during their breeding season, which lasts for a short time in early summer. They are polygamous.

Cubs are born after a gestation period of about 240 days. The sows give birth in a den found, perhaps, among jumbles of pressure ice; the cubs are seemingly very small, weighing only about 2 lb (1 kg), or about 0.2 percent of their mature weight. They begin to travel with their mother a few months after they are born and remain with her for two years.

Polar bears eat mostly meat, seal being the main quarry, which the bears can stalk with great skill. They can wait for hours at a breathing

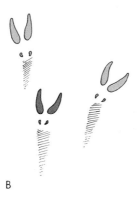

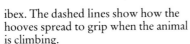

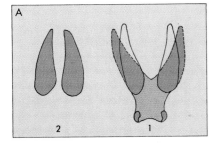

(Opposite) **ALPINE IBEX** (*Capra ibex*).
(Above) **CHAMOIS** (*Rupicapra rupicapra*).
A The hind *(1)* and fore *(2)* hoof of the

ibex. The dashed lines show how the hooves spread to grip when the animal is climbing.
B The ibex's tracks when it is moving at speed.

hole to claw out an unwary seal, much as a domestic cat claws out field mice. They eat carrion, too, such as the carcasses of beached whales, and will remain in the vicinity until the meat is consumed. They will eat fish, particularly spawning char and salmon, and will take ground-nesting birds and their eggs, lemmings, and even mice. They have been known to kill musk-ox and walrus, but walrus can put up a formidable resistance.

The United States Marine Mammal Protection Act protects the polar bear from being hunted in the territories of the United States, the only exception being native peoples—i.e., American Indians and Eskimos—who, if they still live in their traditional ways, may hunt polar bears. [JK]

Cottontail Rabbits *(Sylvilagus)*

Cottontail rabbits are among the most popular game animals in North America, not least because they are at home in many different habitats; farms and farm-edges are favorites, in addition to woodlots, old grown-up fields, brushy cutovers, and even swamps. Except for the Pacific coast and the northern parts of New England, they are found everywhere in the United States.

While the common, or eastern, cottontail inhabits most of this range, three subspecies occur in parts of it. The mountain cottontail (*S. nuttalli*) predominates in the Rocky Mountains region, the desert cottontail (*S. auduboni*) predominates in the more arid regions of the West, and the New England cottontail (*S. transitionalis*) predominates through the Appalachians and southern New England.

The eastern cottontail is about 17 inches (43 cm) long and weighs up to a maximum of about 4 lb (1.8 kg). It is brownish-gray, whereas the mountain and desert cottontails are yellowish, and the New England cottontail is reddish-gray, with a vague blackish patch between ears, during the hunting season. The tail, which appears white and cottony when the animal runs, has given a name to the species.

The eastern cottontail is normally most active early in the morning and late in the evening; when subjected to heavy hunting, it may become nocturnal. It does not dig burrows but makes use of holes dug by woodchucks. Like hares, cottontails tend to circle back to their territory when pursued; the New England cottontail tends to describe larger circles than the eastern. [NS]

Swamp Rabbit *(Sylvilagus aquaticus)*

Swamp Rabbits can weigh up to 6 lb (2.6 kg) and are found in the southern states of the central United States in swamps and marshes. Their hair is coarser than that of the cottontail, and the characteristic nape patch is dark and distinct.

When bolted by hounds, swamp rabbits run in wide circles and do not seek shelter underground, but will swim if pressed. They are plentiful in south-central Tennessee, and chases can last up to an hour, for this rabbit seems to know how to avoid detection and can creep through thick undergrowth when in the vicinity of a hunter. [NS]

Hares *(Lepus)*

A number of hares are found in North America, but not all of them are called hares. The whitetail jackrabbit (*L. townsendii*), which inhabits the northern Rocky Mountains and Great Plains, is one of them; another is

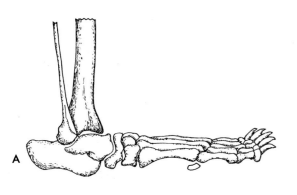

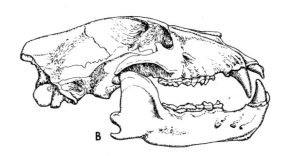

(Left) **POLAR BEAR** (*Ursus maritimus*).
(Below) **BROWN, or GRIZZLY, BEAR** (*Ursus arctos*).
A The bones of the foot of a black bear. The animal walks on the sole of the foot.
B The skull of a brown bear, showing the prominent canine and molar teeth.
C The track of a brown bear; the larger imprints are those of the hind feet.

the blacktail jackrabbit (*L. californicus*), which inhabits the southern part of the Rockies and the Plains. The arctic hare (*L. arcticus*), the tundra hare (*L. othus*), and the snowshoe, or varying, hare (*L. americanus*) are other species. The snowshoe is found across the northern part of the United States, well south through the Rocky Mountains in the West and in the Appalachians in the East, and over almost all of Canada. The tundra hare inhabits the tundra coastal region of Alaska.

All hares have long ears and very long back legs, hear and see excellently, and can run fast and with stamina, preferring to run uphill when pursued or in danger. Being strongly territorial, hares run in a wide circle when hunted by dogs, and will eventually try to return to their own familiar area. They live above ground and, unlike rabbits, do not seek shelter in holes.

Both the tundra and the snowshoe have coats that change from brown in summer to white in winter. The whitetail jackrabbit may change its coat in the northern part of its range, but the blacktail jackrabbit does not. [NS]

Brown Hare (*Lepus europaeus*)

This is the most hunted, but not the only, hare in Europe. The Alpine hare (*L. timidus*) inhabits the Alps and the Scandinavian mountains, and a subspecies occurs in Scotland, where it is called the blue hare (*L. t. scoticus*), for, in spring and fall, its coat has a bluish cast because the brown fur of summer is mingled with the white hairs of winter. Smaller than the brown hare, with longer legs and longer ears, it prefers high, rocky terrain. Ireland has its own subspecies, the Irish hare (*L. t. hibernicus*), which looks like the blue hare but has a proportionately larger head and shorter ears; it does not turn white as regularly as the blue hare, and its winter coat is often white patched with russet. In general, though, the brown hare has a white coat in winter.

Regional variations occur, the British subspecies being darker brown than the hares on the continent of Europe, while there are slight differences in average size, with hares from the north being generally larger than those from the south.

The continents of Asia and Africa have each their local race and,

together, some seven subspecies, each more or less resembling the brown hare, but differing in details such as skull structure.

The brown hare has been transplanted to North America, where it now ranges from the Great Lakes region through much of the State of New York and into western New England. It overlaps with the cottontail rabbit and the snowshoe hare.

The brown hare has an average length of about 25 inches (64 cm) and an average weight of about 9 lb (4 kg). It is a close relative of the North American jackrabbit, which is a hare, and not a rabbit, despite its name.

Brown hare live above ground, out in the open at all times of year. They rely on their ability to detect visible or audible danger, and to hide or to run so as to escape it: their sight and hearing are excellent, they can crouch down and become all but invisible but, when they run, they run extremely fast and strongly, preferring to run uphill, when their long, powerful back legs are of great advantage. Their numbers can be considerable, so much so as to constitute a menace to crops: perhaps, on good agricultural land, in excess of one hare to every 3 acres (1 hectare).

Hares form an important link in the food chain, for foxes, the larger hawks and eagles, and other predators depend on them for their own survival. [TT]

Gray Fox (*Urocyon cinereoargentatus*)

The gray fox is indigenous only to North America, chiefly to the eastern United States. It is the same size as the red fox but not usually as luxuriously furred. Its color is mostly peppery gray, but with some rust, white underparts, and a black brush tip.

It is hunted by the same methods as the red fox (see below). Unlike the red, it uses dens in winter—most often in rocky crevices or other hollows in sloping woodlands. It is more shy of open fields than the red fox. At one time, ferrets were sometimes used (as they have been used to hunt European red foxes) to move them from their dens. In the United States, ferreting is generally illegal, but small dogs are used for the same purpose by a few hunters. This is not, however, a common method.

When pursued by hounds, the gray fox is neither as fast nor as long-running as the red fox, for it has smaller lungs and slightly shorter legs. However, it provides good sport, and good practice for hounds. When tracked without hounds or enticed by a predator call, it is as canny and difficult to take as the red fox. Moreover, it has a unique ability that it exhibits when pursued. It can climb trees. The only American canine species with real tree-climbing ability, it readily scrambles up a leaning or thickly branched tree when pressed, or it eludes hounds and hunter by plunging into very thick, tangled cover and then "holing," climbing, backtracking, or employing some other maneuver to lose its pursuers. [RE]

Red Fox (*Vulpes fulva*)

At one time, the Eurasian and North American red foxes were thought to be separate species, but they are one and the same. In North America alone, there are probably a dozen subspecies of red fox, the number being uncertain because of range overlap, interbreeding, and color and size variations that do not qualify local populations for the status of a distinct race. Additional subspecies inhabit virtually all of Europe and much of Asia and Africa.

In the British Isles and Continental Europe, the typical hunter who carries a gun may shoot any fox he encounters as vermin—a game- and poultry-destroying pest. In that part of the world (indeed, in most parts) the red fox is not considered game by riflemen or shotgunners. It is game only for those equestrian sportsmen who ride to hounds. In North America, however, it is shot as game, and in many regions has legal game status—with seasons and limits. Wildlife managers in the United States, though they are not equally progressive with regard to all species, have

(Above) **SNOWSHOE HARE** (*Lepus americanus*).
(Left) **BROWN HARE** (*Lepus europaeus*).

(Below) **COTTONTAIL RABBIT** (*Sylvilagus*).

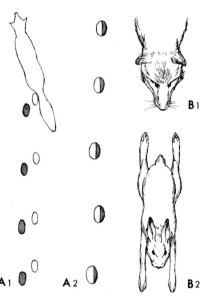

proved that the fox rarely causes any serious depletion of poultry or other farm stock and is not detrimental to rabbits, ground-nesting game birds, or other wildlife populations if its own population is kept in balance.

An average adult red fox weighs no more than 7 to 12 lb (3 to 7 kg). Its fur makes it look bigger, but it is the size of a house cat or small dog. Its color is generally coppery or rusty, with some peppering, white underparts, and black feet, but there are wide variations. The tip of the copiously furred tail, or brush, is white. America has another important species, the gray fox, and some color variations of the two species can cause confusion, but a white tail tip always marks the red fox. That of the gray fox is always black.

Red foxes den for whelping and rearing their young but, unlike grays, they do not normally den for shelter in the winter. They like mixed, brushy habitat and fields where they can have a good view of potential enemies and good hunting for rodents, rabbits, and other small prey.

The traditional American method of hunting them is with hounds. Sometimes, the hunters take all their enjoyment from watching or hearing their dogs work and do not bother to shoot the quarry. Sometimes, however, they try to intercept the line of chase or wait at likely openings and crossings in the cover, using shotguns to kill the fast-fleeing fox. A second method, which employs smallbore centerfire rifles more often than shotguns, is to track and scout for foxes on snow, without the aid of hounds. A red fox generally naps after mousing or taking other game. He is likely to do so on a small hummock or rise with a good view. He curls up but faces his back trail and frequently raises his head to look for danger. He does not sleep soundly but only "cat-naps." Getting within range and getting a clear shot before the fox detects intrusion and escapes is therefore a challenging sport.

Another method, and one steadily increasing in popularity, is to conceal oneself and attract a fox within rifle or shotgun range by sounding a predator call. In some states, phonographic calls are legal for predators (including not only fox but bobcat, coyote, raccoon, and cougar), but a mouth-blown call is more challenging. Its sound usually imitates the squeal of an injured or terrified rabbit. Some predator calls mimic the sounds of injured birds or other creatures. [RE]

Gray Squirrel *(Sciurus carolinensis)*

The gray squirrel is one of the most sought-after game animals in North America. The species ranges through the United States and southern Canada from the middle of the Great Plains eastward to the Atlantic Ocean. The western gray squirrel (*S. griseus*) is found from the nut groves of southern California to the slopes of Mount Rainier in Washington.

Gray squirrels weigh on average about 1 lb (0.5 kg), but older animals can weigh fifty percent more. Their tails are long and bushy, hence their common name of "bushytail." They are a grizzled gray with a whitish underside. They inhabit large woods, especially those containing trees producing ample supplies of acorns, beechmast, hickory nuts, hazelnuts, and walnuts. In the south, they eat pecans, and, in the west, almonds. If such foods are scarce, gray squirrels will also eat corn. [NS]

Fox Squirrel *(Sciurus niger)*

This squirrel is found in the same parts of the United States and Canada as the gray, with the exception of New England, where it is seldom seen. It is slightly bigger than the gray, with an average weight of $1\frac{1}{2}$ lb (0.65 kg), and up to 3 lb (1.3 kg) for older animals.

It is a rusty yellow with some gray markings and has an orange belly. In some parts of its range—especially in the Carolinas—it is typically black with white facial markings.

The fox squirrel is at home in woodlots where mast- and nut-producing trees are close to farm-field openings. It often ventures into grain fields, eating especially corn. [NS]

Raccoon (*Procyon lotor*)

The raccoon is a grayish-brown, thick-furred nocturnal carnivore with a bushy, ring-marked tail, and a characteristically masked face. Raccoons weigh between about 12 and 35 lb (5.4 and 15.9 kg) as adults and can weigh even more. They are found near water all over North and Central America in wooded areas (but not in the Rocky Mountains), where they survive by eating omnivorously.

Related to the panda, raccoons, including here the coati species of the southwestern United States and Central and South America, are agile and climb trees easily, which is how most raccoon hunts end, with the animal "treed." Like foxes, they are intelligent, if not so fast over the ground. They can also swim; in water, a large raccoon is a match for a hound and can even kill it. [NS]

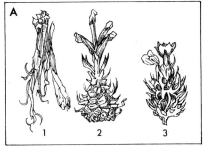

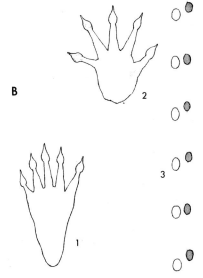

(Top) **GRAY SQUIRREL** (*Sciurus carolinensis*).
(Left) **RACCOON** (*Procyon lotor*).
A Signs that squirrels have been feeding. *(1)* Remains of an unripe pine cone. *(2)* Remains of a ripe cone. *(3)* Remains of a larch cone.
B The raccoon's rear footprint *(1)*, front footprint *(2)*, and tracks *(3)*.

(Above) **EURASIAN WOOD-COCK** (*Scolopax rusticola*).
(Left) **COMMON SNIPE** (*Gallinago gallinago*).

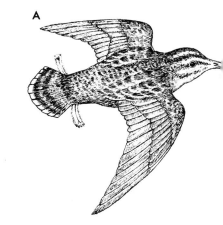

A

A Snipe "drum" as their outer tail feathers vibrate during their mating display.
B Woodcock have eyes so placed as to give binocular backward vision, a vital facility when the bird is probing in deep, soft soil.

48

Chapter 2
Upland Fowl

Eurasian Woodcock *(Scolopax rusticola)*

The Eurasian, or European, woodcock is closely related to the American variety and resembles it closely, but it is a bit bigger—13 to 14 inches (33 to 36 cm) as against 10 to 12 inches (25 to 30 cm). Its bill is proportionately bigger, too. Close relatives of snipe, but rounder in the body, both species of woodcock belong to the sandpiper family, being essentially long-legged small shorebirds that have some characteristics in common with upland birds.

They like moist habitat, however, though not so boggy as that favored by snipe, for they probe for earthworms, which are their principal food, as well as for grubs and insects. They are found in wet deciduous, coniferous, or mixed woodlands, scrub, and even on the edges of moorland, where they may occur together with grouse. Their chalky-white droppings, and the round holes caused by their probing for food, indicate their presence.

Their coloration is generally dark, while their underparts are barred with light and dark brown. Their legs and bills are a dull fleshy or fleshy-gray color. Their wings are rounded, and their large eyes are set far back in the head.

They are crepuscular. At dawn and dusk, they fly in courtship displays that are known, in Britain, as roding. A roding woodcock flies a regular course at 20 to 30 feet (6 to 9 m) with slow, owlish wingbeats, usually at sunset, sometimes in the early morning. Roding may last an hour. Since a roding male is indicating his territory, other woodcock will be chased away; especially during roding, the male may utter a high-pitched sneezing cry or a croak that may be produced by a rush of air through the primaries. Woodcock have a fairly elaborate courtship display, which takes place as early as March (in the southern part of their range, which borders on the Mediterranean countries). A hen with a brood of young will feign injury if disturbed; woodcock have often been observed to carry their chicks from one place to another, by flying for short distances with them usually between their feet.

They hold tight for pointing dogs, and they will usually let a flushing dog approach quite close before flushing into the air; they may, however, scurry or skulk off through ground cover before rising. Cocker spaniels got their name from their use in flushing woodcock.

Their range is extensive, stretching across Europe eastward from the British Isles, excluding only the sub-Arctic north and the dry Mediterranean region, through the whole of Asia to Japan. [RE]

American Woodcock *(Philohela minor)*

Despite the total difference of their Latin names, the American and the Eurasian woodcock are essentially the same species in general appearance and habits. A dark, plump bird of wet and swampy woods, with rounded wings, an extremely long bill, and capable of producing a whistling noise in flight (made by the action of its wings), the American woodcock has spread in recent years from the Maritime Provinces of Canada as far away as the American Midwest.

The woodcock's presence may be detected by the round drill holes it leaves in soft ground, in which it probes for earthworms, its principal food, and by the chalky-white splashes of its droppings, which are a more noticeable sign. The woodcock is migratory, being forced to move when the first frosts harden the ground, but it is a species that returns unerringly to the same fields on its return migration.

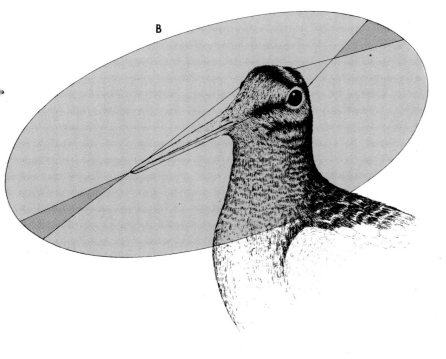

(Below) **CALIFORNIA QUAIL**
(*Lophortyx californicus*).
(Opposite, top) **BOBWHITE
QUAIL** (*Colinus virginanus*).
(Opposite, lower) **SCALED QUAIL**
(*Callipepla squamata*).
A Only one species of North Ameri-
can quail has a long, erect head plume:
the mountain quail (*Oreortyx pictus*).
B Two North American species of
quail have rounded, forward-inclining
plumes, and, of these, one has a dis-
tinctive black patch on its belly: Gam-
bel's quail (*Lophortyx gambelii*).
**C MEARNS', or HARLEQUIN,
QUAIL** (*Cyrtonyx montezumae*).

Breeding is preceded by an elaborate courting ritual in which the male flies vertically up from the ground, uttering a sound that can be represented as a deep, guttural "peent." The ritual takes place at dawn or dusk, and the bird can disappear in the dim light, only to descend again, uttering the same cry. This can continue for twenty to thirty minutes.

Woodcock are now found over the entire eastern United States, plus southern Ontario, Quebec, and the Maritime Provinces. They generally nest from Pennsylvania and Ohio northward to the limits of their range; they winter mainly along the delta of the Mississippi and elsewhere in the Deep South. [NS]

Common Snipe (*Capella gallinago* or *Gallinago gallinago*)

There are large numbers of species and subspecies of snipe in various parts of the world, where there exist the marshes and bogs that provide the right environmental conditions. The various species encompass several genera, but all belong to the family of wading birds, the *Scolopacidae*, and all have similar habits.

Some—the European jack snipe, for example—are smaller than the common snipe; some—the great snipe of Scandinavia and northeastern Europe is one—are larger. The New Zealand snipe has the odd habit of nesting in the deserted underground burrows of other birds, whereas all other snipe nest above ground, employing a grass-lined hollow. The great snipe is alone in having a communal courtship display. Whatever its Latin or common name, it is probably safe to say that—to a hunter—a snipe is a snipe, and that a description of the common snipe will suffice for all.

This bird looks rather like the woodcock but is smaller and not so bulky. It is usually about 10½ inches (27 cm) long, with long legs and a long, slender bill. It has mottled brown plumage, horizontally barred with black, and it has black stripes through the eyes.

As with those of woodcock, snipe droppings look like chalky spatters on the ground, while the snipe's feeding habits of probing in soft ground leave round holes. Snipe feed in boggier ground, however, and rely less on earthworms than do woodcock.

Snipe are difficult to observe on the ground, but they can be flushed from marsh plants such as sedges and bullrushes, when they will rise with their characteristic zigzag flight and hoarse cry. Their flight straightens after some 30 feet (9 m), a fact well known to experienced hunters, who prefer to wait out their snipe before firing. Snipe fly into the wind and generally return to the spot from which they were flushed. [RE]

Wilson's Snipe (*Capella gallinago delicata*)

When flushed, this American snipe, like snipe elsewhere in the world, flies in a characteristic zigzag and is, therefore, a challenge for even an expert shot. It is called jack or common snipe in North America, but these are the names of two separate species in Europe; *Lymnocryptes minima* and *Gallinago gallinago*. It is very slightly smaller than the American woodcock, which flies straighter when flushed, and has rounded wings, not pointed ones. In addition, the woodcock inhabits swampy woody ground, whereas the Wilson's snipe is found in open swamps, bogs, boggy meadows, and pastures.

Within North America, this snipe breeds all across Canada and over much of the northern United States, and winters practically anywhere in the United States and northern Mexico where the terrain is suitable; some snipe migrate further south, reaching as far as Brazil. [NS]

Bobwhite Quail (*Colinus virginianus*)

This is the classic bird of American upland hunting. Small grain fields and wide fencerows maintained large populations of bobwhites, but this type of agriculture has given way to one demanding huge open fields. Some landowners have, however, continued to manage their land with an eye to hunting bobwhites, and the birds also occur on some state-owned lands managed with the purpose of keeping up populations of these and other upland birds.

These quail are small ($8\frac{1}{2}$ to $10\frac{1}{2}$ inches/22 to 27 cm) and generally brownish with light and dark reddish tints in some feathers. They gather in bevies of a dozen up to thirty. [NS]

Scaled Quail (*Callipepla squamata*)

This quail is indigenous to the arid country of western Texas, New Mexico, southeastern Arizona, and Mexico.

Its breast feathers have the appearance of scales and give the bird its name. Its back is gray, and its upper back, upper breast, and neck have a bluish cast. Both males and females have a white, cottony crest, which is more pronounced on males. The bird is also known as the "cottontop" and as the blue quail.

These quail gather in bevies of up to one hundred birds, but most commonly, numbers in a bevy do not exceed twenty. They run rather than fly, unless forcefully flushed. [NS]

Gambel's Quail (*Lophortyx gambelii*)

Gambel's quail, like the scaled, prefers dry country and occurs in Arizona, western New Mexico, southern California, and in Mexico south of the Arizona border, but less profusely there than in the United States.

This quail and the California quail have a black head plume that bends forward; the mountain quail also has a black head plume, but it is upright. The Gambel's is distinguished from the California by a black belly spot; otherwise, the two species are similar, with faces and necks outlined in white, reddish crowns, chestnut sides, and brownish backs. Like scaled quail, Gambel's prefer to run before they fly. [NS]

California Quail (*Lophortyx californicus*)

This quail occurs on the west coast of the United States, from southern California to Washington. It prefers mixed woodlands in valleys and foothills but will move onto farmland and has been known to gorge on grapes in the wine country in California.

The males of the species are similar to those of the Gambel's quail. The females are also similar, but the California hen has a light throat.

California quail sometimes flock together in huge bevies, but most contain about twenty-five to sixty birds. Several such bevies may be found close to one another. Like most quail, this one runs strongly before it flies.

The species is also known as the valley quail, to differentiate it from the mountain quail. [NS]

Mountain Quail (*Oreortyx pictus*)

This quail occurs in the same geographical regions as the California, or valley, quail but is found most commonly in the mountainous regions and chaparral, often adjoining small streams. It can be distinguished from the California quail by its long straight head plume, and by white bars on its sides. The sexes are similar, although the female is duller in color.

Like other quail, the mountain quail runs strongly and is reluctant to fly; it must, therefore, be flushed vigorously if the hunter is to get a shot at it in the air. [NS]

Mearns', or Harlequin, Quail (*Cyrtonyx montezumae*)

This is a bird of the mountainous country between 4,000 and 6,000 feet (1,200 and 1,800 m) in southeastern Arizona in the United States and in the states of Chihuahua, Coahuila, and Sonora in Mexico.

It has a plump shape and is slightly smaller than the other quail noted here. Its second name is derived from the black and white pattern of the feathers on its face; the females are brownish, while the males are more a reddish-gray.

This quail, like all the others of the arid regions of North America, fluctuates in numbers in proportion to the annual rainfall. [NS]

Crested Quail (*Colinus cristatus*)

This is the quail of northern South America and is especially prevalent in Columbia. Its crest is similar to that of American plumed quail but, when pointed by a dog, it does not flush wildly as they do, but sits tightly, hiding like the bobwhite and the Mearns' quail. It flocks in coveys and occurs around cattle pastures; it eats principally weed seeds. [NS]

Chachalaca (*Ortalis vetula*)

This is an unusual game bird of northeastern Mexico, found around openings in woodlands and thickets. Its name derives from its loud raucous call. It is about 20 to 24 inches (51 to 61 cm) long.

It has a long tail and a small head. Its general coloration is brownish, but the tail, which is rounded and tipped with white, has a greenish sheen. [NS]

Wild Turkey (*Meleagris gallopavo*)

There are at least half a dozen subspecies of the wild turkey which, itself, looks very much like a slim version of the farmyard bird. The males are much larger than the females and have more intensely colored red wattles. All mature males and—confusingly—some females develop "beards" comprised of a hanging tuft of feathers on the breast.

Of the subspecies, the eastern is the most numerous, having been introduced most successfully throughout the east, south, and midwest of the United States, after a period of continuous decline caused by the felling of the forests that had been the turkey's natural habitat. The rehabilitation of the wild turkey is one of the big success stories of North American game preservation.

The bird needs mature forests providing acorns, walnuts, hickory nuts, hazelnuts, beechmast, and the like, especially in winter when abundant food is essential to its survival.

Turkeys roost in trees, staying in the same place all night. They are very wary and have good eyesight, and are thus difficult to approach.

All the subspecies have essentially the same general form as the principal species, but they vary in size and, to some degree, in coloration, too. Starting with the largest, the Florida, or osceola, turkey can weigh up to 22 lb (10 kg) and is found chiefly in central Florida, but it can occur further north, where intergrading may occur; it is lighter than the eastern turkey. The Merriam turkey is close in size and appearance to the eastern turkey, and it is, in effect, the wild turkey of the Rocky Mountains region, occurring in large numbers in Colorado, Arizona, parts of New Mexico, and in California, Wyoming, Montana, and parts of some other western states. The Rio Grande turkey is smaller, weighing about 10 lb (4 kg) on average and is relatively pale; it is a native of Mexico and the lower southwestern United States and has been successfully introduced into Oklahoma and Kansas. Gould's turkey and the Mexican turkey are so much alike that there is disagreement as to whether or not they are separate subspecies; they are small, leggy birds, but, despite this, they are the ancestors of the now much larger domestic turkey. Finally, the ocellated turkey of the jungles of Central America and the Yucatan Peninsula in Mexico: it is slightly smaller than the eastern and Merriam turkeys, and is a separate species (*Agriocharis ocellata*). [NS]

Tinamous (*Tinamidae*)

There are at least forty-five different species of tinamous, a family of Central and South American birds, of which most are jungle birds and,

(Left) **WILD TURKEY** (*Meleagris gallopavo*).
(Above) **CHACHALACA** (*Ortalis vetula*).
(Center) The wild turkey in flight.

therefore, seldom hunted; only a few species—those found principally on the pampas of Uruguay and Argentina, and one on the plateaux of Ecuador—are frequently shot.

Tinamous vary in size, with the larger species being about the size of a cock pheasant and the smaller about that of a partridge. Their general form is rounded, with a very short tail almost completely covered by the wings when they are folded; the head and neck are slender, the beak is down-curving. Their legs are strong, being typical of a bird that spends much time on the ground.

Remarkable in a number of respects, tinamous are perhaps strangest in that only the male birds incubate the eggs. The females, moreover, usually lay two or three eggs in each of a number of nests. The eggs themselves are all manner of colors: green, turquoise, purple, wine-red, chocolate, slate-gray, even black. The young are precocious, being ready to feed with the parent birds almost immediately after hatching; the eggs are, significantly, exceptionally large, at least in some species, weighing up to ten or eleven percent of the weight of the hen bird.

On the pampas, the hunter can expect to encounter three species, the spotted, the martineta, or crested, and the red-winged tinamous, respectively *Nothura maculosa*, *Eudromia elegans*, and *Rhynchotus rufescens*. The spotted is the most abundant and is about the size of a partridge. The martineta is a beautiful pheasant-sized bird with black and white barred feathers (excellent for trout flies), and a long, slender crest on its head. The red-winged, named for its characteristic appearance, is scarce compared with either of the other two species and is wary, flushing usually at nearly maximum shotgun range on almost every encounter. Its local name is *perdiz colorado*.

Both the spotted and the martineta are found in coveys, but do not flush together; the martineta, particularly, flushes one at a time, giving the hunter little time to reload when the covey numbers ten or twelve birds. When flushed, they fly like pheasants, with furious wing beats followed by glides. Although shooting is sporting, in the almost total absence of cover—which must be seen to be believed—it is nowhere as difficult as with grouse or woodcock.

Shooting in Ecuador is quite another matter, for the birds, of the genus *Nothoprocta* and called partridge tinamous, are at home on the high plateaux of the Andes, at 10,000 to 12,000 feet (3,000 to 4,000 m); the hunter, and his dogs, must accustom themselves to these conditions. These birds are hardly gregarious, like the tinamous of the pampas, and usually flush one at a time. [AL & NS]

(Above left) **TINAMOUS** (*Nothura maculosa*).
(Above) **MOURNING DOVE** (*Zenaidura macroura*).
(Opposite, above) **ROCK DOVE, or DOMESTIC PIGEON** (*Columba livia*).

PIGEONS AND DOVES

These names are confusingly interchangeable, particularly when it is remembered that, in Britain, doves are protected while the woodpigeon (*Columba palumbus*) is not and may, therefore, be shot as a pest. *Columba livia* is called either rock dove or domestic pigeon in North America, but rock dove in Britain.

Rock Dove, or Domestic Pigeon *(Columbia livia)*

This bird is very common in practically every urban area of the United States; in Europe, it occurs only in the Mediterranean countries and round the coasts of Scotland and Ireland.

It has a white patch at the base of the tail, two dark stripes on its wings, and a dark band on its tail. The British woodpigeon, *Columba palumbus*, is larger and has a conspicuous white marking on its neck and on the wings. When they fly up in alarm, both species make a loud clapping noise, caused by their wings striking together.

C. livia is a hardy bird, perhaps because it rarely has trouble in finding food. It is tame in the parks and city squares of North America, but it is very wary in the countryside, where it is regarded as a pest. [NS]

Scaled Pigeon *(Columbigallina passerina)*

This is a small, fast-flying bird found in many areas, but perhaps most in the mountains of Central and northern South America. Its name derives

from the appearance of its breast feathers; the scaled quail is so named for the same reason. [NS]

Band-tailed Pigeon *(Columba fasciata)*

This bird summers in the mountains of Nicaragua, Costa Rica, and northern Panama, and migrates northward to breed in northern Mexico, New Mexico, Texas, Arizona, and parts of Colorado, and along the coast of California, and even of Oregon and Washington.

Slightly bigger than a rock dove, the band-tailed pigeon gets its name from the gray band on its broad tail. Other distinguishing features include a bright yellow bill, bright yellow feet, and a semi-circular white ring on the nape of its neck. It flies fast and uses thermal air currents.

In the Central American mountains, the band-tailed pigeon feeds mainly on a grape-like berry that abounds in the trees that shade the coffee plantations.[NS]

White-crowned Pigeon *(Columba leucocephala)*

This American bird gets its name from its shining white crown, for it is otherwise completely dark. It nests in the Florida Keys and often migrates to Cuba during the summer. It used to be hunted there, before the Revolution, and may one day be accessible again to visiting hunters. [NS]

Sand-grouse (*Pteroclidae*)

This family of birds includes several species, but they are pigeons, despite a number of resemblances to grouse. For example, they have short, feathered legs, grouse-like beaks, stout bodies, nest on the ground, and do not perch. Like pigeons, however, they lay few eggs per clutch, and their young are precocious and fast-growing. Sand-grouse look like doves in flight and are about the same size as a rock dove, but their coloration is like that of a partridge.

They like dry desert country and so occur rarely in Europe but more commonly in Africa, Asia Minor, Asia proper, and parts of India. They feed on seeds and fruit, and the birds can often be observed flying down to water-holes, for example in safari-country in Africa. [NS]

Mourning Dove (*Zenaidura macroura*)

This dove nests in eastern Canada, the eastern United States, and even in Mexico; it migrates to the south of its nesting grounds, and so can be found in the eastern United States for most of the year. It is a common species, being smaller and slimmer than the domestic pigeon (or rock dove), and with a brownish or grayish coloration and a pointed tail. The mourning dove flies fast but can change direction easily. In some of the

(Top) **VARIEGATED SAND-GROUSE** (*Pterocles burchelli*).
(Center) **WHITE-WINGED DOVE** (*Zenaida asiatica*).
(Right) **CHESTNUT-BELLIED SAND-GROUSE** (*Pterocles exustus*).

56

states it is classified as a song bird, and protected accordingly; not entirely paradoxically, the states in which it enjoys most protection are those in which it is scarcest.

Mourning doves flock together, often to grain fields after the harvest. Modern agricultural machinery leaves plenty of gleanings behind and the doves gorge themselves. They can do some crop damage, too, but this can be kept down by shooting. There seems to be little pattern to their migration, perhaps because—according to estimates—the annual mortality of this species is sixty to eighty percent. [NS]

White-winged Dove *(Zenaida asiatica)*

This dove is just about the same size as the mourning dove (11 to 12 inches/28 to 30 cm) but has conspicuous white patches on its wings. Its tail is rounded and has white "corners." Like most doves, it is a strong flier. It has a strong, rather owlish call note that contrasts with the melancholy call of the mourning dove and the purring coo of the European turtle dove.

White-wings tolerate, or even favor, more arid climes than those that suit the mourning dove, but in other respects their habitats are similar. Like all doves, the white-wing thrives in good agricultural land and seems to do especially well in farm country that has been newly converted to small grain crops. This has been observed on the west coast of Mexico, where irrigation has caused the former desert to bloom, and in the Mexican state of Campeche, in southwestern Yucatan, where the jungle has been cut and replaced by rice fields.

White-wings and mourning doves occur together in southwestern Texas and northeastern Mexico, and on some Caribbean islands, notably Cuba. The white-winged dove's nesting range in the United States includes southwest Texas, southern New Mexico, Arizona, and California; it nests in northern Mexico, too. It is hunted in these states, and the other areas mentioned, and in a number of central American countries—Guatemala, Honduras, El Salvador, Nicaragua, Costa Rica, and Panama—to which it migrates. It only sometimes reaches as far south as Panama, doing so only when food is scarce in countries further to the north. [NS]

Columbian, or White-tailed, Dove *(Zenaida auriculata caucae)*

This dove looks very much like the mourning dove but has perhaps more white in its tail, which is shorter and less pointed. Also, the white-tail has

dark iridescent blue, rather than black, facial markings. A similar species, found in the West Indies, lacks the white tail markings; it is sometimes called the eared dove.

There are some white-tailed doves in Panama, but they are overwhelmingly abundant in Columbia. They nest all the year round, but with a concentration into three major breeding periods. The young birds are sexually mature at the age of four months.

A further factor that has contributed to the enormous numbers of white-tails is the change in farming methods in Columbia. The jungles have been cut, and farmland has been given over to small grains—rice, wheat, and sorghum. The doves feed on these, being estimated to consume about twenty percent of the entire crop, and glean the fields in the fifteen-day period between harvest and replanting. The birds have become a major pest, and hunting is unrestricted. [NS]

Ptarmigan *(Lagopus)*

This family of birds is circumpolar in range, occurring on the Arctic tundra of North America, Greenland, Iceland, the Scandinavian mountains, and Siberia. Their southern limits in North America extend to British Columbia and the Rockies, northern Minnesota, Maine, and the Adirondack Mountains of New York State. In Europe, ptarmigan are found on the hills of northern Scotland, in the Alps, in the Pyrenees, and in Scandinavia.

Ptarmigan are about the same size as partridge, or a bit bigger. In winter, they are white, with black markings that vary from subspecies to subspecies; in summer, they are generally brown, with white wings. Subspecies overlap in range to some extent, and it can be difficult to distinguish one from another.

In North America, the rock (*L. mutus*) and willow (*L. lagopus*) ptarmigan are very similar, for their summer plumage is generally brown with white wings, and their winter plumage white with black tails. The willow is a darker brown in summer, while the rock can be grayish. In winter, the rock has a black streak from the bill, which is smaller and more slender, to the eye. The rock ptarmigan prefers the most exposed and barren hills, while the willow prefers sheltered ground. A third species, the white-tailed ptarmigan (*L. leucurus*), has a white tail at all times of year.

In Europe, the ptarmigan (*L. mutus*) is the bird known in North America as the rock ptarmigan. In Scotland, it occurs together with the red grouse (*L. l. scoticus*), and in Scandinavia with the willow grouse (*L. lagopus*); these grouse are regarded as conspecific. They are slightly larger than the ptarmigan (15 to 16 inches/38 to 41 cm, as against about

14 inches/36 cm). They differ in appearance from the ptarmigan very much as the North American ptarmigan do from one another. The ptarmigan occupies higher ground than do either of the grouse.

The red grouse is described separately (below). A little confusingly, in the British Isles, ptarmigan are sometimes regarded as species of grouse, whereas the opposite view is generally held elsewhere. A partial explanation may be that the red grouse was known, in Gaelic, as *tármachan*, before it got the name of grouse.

Most ptarmigan and grouse are virtually inaccessible to man during winter, when they live much of the time in burrows and tunnels under the snow. Some are trapped in winter, for example in Swedish Lapland, where winter temperatures can be as low as –40°C (–40°F).

The willow ptarmigan of North America is an exception, for it can be found in winter on the shores of bays and rivers in the more wooded sections of the north. The birds can be seen on the tidal flats, at the high tide mark, and in the stands of small willow and other bushes that afford shelter and food.

Ptarmigan in North America are relatively unwary birds for, where they have not been hunted, they are unafraid of man. For this reason, they are sometimes known as "fool hens," together with western ruffed grouse and spruce grouse. [NK]

Red Grouse *(Lagopus scoticus)*

This is the grouse of the British Isles, where it occurs on the high hills of Scotland, northern England, and Wales. There have been red grouse on high ground in southwestern England, and a small number have been introduced into the Ardennes in Belgium.

They are plump, reddish-brown birds, about 15 to 16 inches (38 to 41 cm) long; in winter, their plumage changes to white and can cause confusion with ptarmigan (see above). They have a loud crowing call and, in the breeding season, a call often rendered as "go-back, go-back, go-back."

They inhabit hills above the treeline. Their principal food is heather which, in Scotland, has traditionally been burned off, in the practice known as "muirburn," which allows young shoots to grow, while fertilizing the ground with ashes. While grouse became of sporting (and commercial) interest in the nineteenth century, sheep have been grazed in the Scottish highlands since at least the eighteenth century. Both eat heather, however, but in Britain of the last quarter of the twentieth century, grouse are perhaps the more valuable of the two animals.

Populations of grouse vary from year to year, depending in part on the weather in spring after eggs have hatched, when the young birds are vulnerable to exceptional wet and cold. Apart from muirburn, grouse can be supported by draining bogs, and by plowing up grit, which these birds eat, as do many grouse and ptarmigan. [NS]

Ruffed Grouse *(Bonasa umbellus)*

This North American grouse is a bird of the briars, brambles, and early new growth that flourishes after woods and forests have been cut. Ruffed grouse are rarely seen on the ground, for they like to stay in thick cover. When they do fly up, it is very suddenly and with an explosive whirring of wings.

The cocks and the hens are about the same size (16 to 19 inches/41 to 50 cm) and with a prominent dark-barred fantail. In the hen, the barring may be broken in the center, whereas that on the cock is unbroken. The birds from the Pacific states are typically reddish-brown, while those from the Rockies are grayish. They have, however, a wide distribution across North America, occurring through most of Canada and the Pacific Northwest, and from the Midwest to the Atlantic: in Minnesota, Wisconsin, Michigan, Ohio, Pennsylvania, New York, all of New England, the Maritime Provinces of Canada, and in Quebec and Ontario.

(Opposite) **WILLOW PTARMI-GAN** *(Lagopus lagopus)* in summer plumage.
(Top) **RED GROUSE** *(Lagopus scoticus)*.

(Center) **ROCK PTARMIGAN** *(Lagopus mutus)*.
(Below) The rock ptarmigan in winter plumage.

The male of the species has an identifiable "drumming" display, which produces a characteristic noise like the roll of a drum or a muffled thumping. This is caused by the cock beating its wings fiercely while standing erect, sometimes on an old log or some other low perch. The birds do this most before and during mating, but also at other times of year, if not so frequently.

It has been discovered that ruffed grouse do exceptionally well in aspen woods and forests in which trees are at stages of growth from seedlings up to forty-year-old trees. Timber and wildlife managers have been taking advantage of this; ruffed grouse have responded by developing high populations, using the newly cut areas for cover, nesting in the slightly more developed areas, and feeding on the buds produced by the mature trees. Ruffed grouse lay up to about twenty eggs and are capable of increasing rapidly in population; cold, wet weather after chicks hatch causes a dearth of insects, on which the young feed, and, later, a fall in the overall population. [NS]

Spruce Grouse *(Canachites canadensis)*
This is a bird of the deep wet forests of Canada and Alaska. It is about the same size as the ruffed grouse, darker, and unwary, tending to perch in trees undisturbed by the presence of hunters. This is why it—like the ruffed grouse and ptarmigan in an unhunted area—is known as the "fool hen."

In addition to in Canada and Alaska, it occurs locally in the northern parts of some of the United States: New York, Michigan, and Minnesota. [NS]

Sharptailed Grouse *(Pedioecetes phasianellus)*
This bird's most distinctive feature is its short, pointed tail, which appears white in flight. The sharptailed grouse is distinguished from the prairie chicken (see below), which shares the same habitat of brushland bordering on farmland, by its lack of the prairie chicken's feather tufts, which hang down noticeably on either side of the neck, and by the fact that it does not have the rounded, dark tail of the prairie chicken. The two birds are about the same size (17 to 18 inches/43 to 46 cm).

Sharptailed grouse occur in the upper midwestern United States and in the prairie provinces of Canada. [NS]

Greater Prairie Chicken *(Tympanuchus cupido)*
This North American bird was once plentiful in the extreme, for it

flourished in the fencerows that were maintained to border grain and pasture fields on the midwestern prairies; these fencerows have been eliminated in the interests of creating larger and larger fields and with them have gone all but relatively few prairie chickens. These are now found together with sharptailed grouse and with the gray or Hungarian partridges that have been introduced into North America.

Prairie chicken have a characteristic group courtship ritual, in which the males produce a hollow booming call, similar to the noise generated by blowing across the top of a bottle.

They are about the same size as the sharptailed grouse and have a short, dark, rounded tail; they are brownish in color. [NS]

Lesser Prairie Chicken (*Tympanuchus pallidicinctus*)

This bird is like a small, pale prairie chicken. It has a restricted range and is perhaps most numerous in Kansas and Oklahoma, for both of these states have hunting seasons for the bird.

It prefers a more arid climate than the greater prairie chicken but is otherwise similar, having even much the same courtship display. [NS]

Blue Grouse (*Dendragapus obscurus*)

Also known as the dusky grouse, the blue grouse is a relatively big bird, averaging 22 inches (56 cm) in length. It occurs in the Rocky Mountains, from Colorado north to British Columbia.

It has salty black upper parts and slate blue underparts. The cock has an orange or yellow comb over the eye; the hens are of a variegated brown color. [NS]

Sage Grouse (*Centrocerus urophasianus*)

This is a large, grayish bird, the cocks of which can be nearly as big as a small turkey (26 to 30 inches/66 to 76 cm), while the hens are smaller. Both cocks and hens have a tail that is long, but not as long as that of the ring-necked pheasant. Their general coloration is brown with a black underbelly; the cocks have a white breast.

The sage grouse inhabits open sagebrush plains in the western United States and eats insects and vegetation, including sagebrush. [NS]

Capercaillie (*Tetrao urogallus*)

The capercaillie, or capercailzie as it is sometimes called in English, is the largest species of European grouse; the cock weighs, on average, between 8 and 12 lb (3.5 and 5.5 kg). It has a wingspan of approximately 50 inches (125 cm) and is some 38 inches (96 cm) long. The hen is much smaller, weighing about half as much as the cock. The capercaillie is a dark bird, ranging from brown to black on its head. Its underside has a dark gray coloration, and its belly is speckled with black and white. There is a bright red spot of naked skin above each eye, and the breast and neck have a dark green metallic look.

It inhabits remote hilly or mountainous areas that are forested, from Scotland and Scandinavia in the north and the Pyrenees in the south, eastward to Mongolia. It lives on a variety of foods, including buds, leaves, pine needles, berries, insects, and grasses.

The mating season starts in late winter and continues until early summer, the exact time being determined more by the weather than by anything else. If warm weather comes early, then the breeding season begins early, too. The mating cock noisily tries to attract the hens in an elaborate ritual that starts about an hour and a half before sunrise.

He begins his song in a favored tree that is used year after year. The song consists of four "verses:" a snapping, a warbling, a sharp popping like the sound of a champagne cork being released, and a hissing. While the bird is hissing, it is deaf to all other sounds, and it can be approached during these few seconds. If undisturbed, the cock repeats his song over and over again until sunrise, when he flies to the ground, and performs a dance for the benefit of the hens he may have attracted.

The bird is known as *Auerhahn* in German. Its name in English derives from the Gaelic *capall coille*, meaning horse of the woods. [TT]

Black Grouse (*Lyrurus tetrix*)

This large grouse is indigenous to most of northern Europe, including southern Scandinavia, and also occurs across Russia and northern Asia to the Pacific Ocean. It is larger than the North American grouse, with cocks being larger than hens: about 2.6 lb (1.2 kg) to 1.8 lb (0.8 kg).

Males are black or bluish-black with a metallic sheen. Their wings are marked with an oblique white bar. The tail feathers are curved in the shape of a lyre, and their underside is white. The hen bird is gray.

Black grouse are found in and at the edges of forests, a type of habitat that intensive farming continues to eliminate. Populations of black grouse have declined recently.

The black grouse, like the capercaillie (see above), has an impressive courtship display: males gobble furiously, beating their wings and extending the head and neck. Nests usually contain eight eggs. [NS]

Hazel Grouse *(Tetrastes bonasia)*

This is a grouse of coniferous woods with a range similar to that of the black grouse. It is about 14 inches (36 cm) long, typically grouse-shaped, but with a longish tail and a slightly crested head. Its head and neck are brownish-red, the underside of its neck is noticeably black bordered with white, its back is a bluish-gray, and its tail is marked with one black and one gray band which show conspicuously in flight. It has a camouflaged appearance and tends to rely on this, rather than on flight, when preyed on by animals and birds. It often perches in trees.

It likes a fairly specific mixture of forest, of which the principal ingredient must be conifer, with admixtures of aspen or alder, birch, and even some juniper; it needs thick undergrowth, too. This habitat occurs over the whole of Europe, with the exception of the British Isles, Denmark, parts of France, and much of the Balkans. Altogether, there are half a dozen subspecies that collectively extend the bird's range right across the Eurasian land-mass to Korea; it is known in Japan, too.

Hazel grouse are monogamous and form pairs without any elaborate ritual in the autumn. When they pair in spring, the cock attracts the hen by emitting a piping sound that can be—and often is—imitated by hunters. [NS]

Ring-necked Pheasant *(Phasianus colchicus)*

This is the pheasant of the Old World. Long-tailed and brilliantly colored, the cock pheasant has a characteristic white ring round its neck, while the hen is smaller, brownish, and has a tail that is longer than that of various grouse, with members of which species it is sometimes confused.

The ring-necked pheasant, which was indigenous to Asia Minor, was introduced into much of Europe by the Romans. There are many species still indigenous to Asia, including China, Mongolia, and Korea. The ring-necked pheasant was introduced into North America in the 1880s, and it is now well-established in many parts of the continent.

It is a bird that prefers to run to cover rather than fly but, when flushed into flight, it utters hoarse croaks and flies strongly, with bursts of wing-beats alternating with glides. It crows when roosting at night.

It is one of several species that have suffered, in North America, from changing farming practices that have reduced the cover it needs, "clean-farming" methods having decimated its population in some areas. Many feel that pen-raised pheasants have diluted the gene pool of once-wild and virile birds. [NS]

Partridge *(European)*

Gray, or Hungarian, Partridge *(North American)*
(Perdix perdix)

Partridge are found from the northern Iberian coast eastward to Russia, through virtually the whole of Europe, including the British Isles, and north to Scandinavia. Three subspecies carry the range across Asia.

Birds from Hungary were introduced into North America, and there are now large populations in Oregon, Idaho, Washington, Montana, and North and South Dakota, smaller but still thriving populations in the Great Lakes states, and still smaller but no less healthy populations in upper New England. In Canada, there are large populations in Alberta, Saskatchewan, Manitoba, and the eastern part of Ontario.

"Gray" partridge is a somewhat misleading name, although the birds have a grey neck and upper breast. They have a pale orange-chestnut colored face and a conspicuous, horseshoe-shaped dark-brown mark on

(Left) **CAPERCAILLIE** (*Tetrao urogallus*).
(Right) **HAZEL GROUSE** (*Tetrastes bonasia*).
(Below left and far right) **BLACK GROUSE** (*Lyrurus tetrix*).
(Below right) Tracks of *(1)* ring-necked pheasant and *(2)* capercaillie.

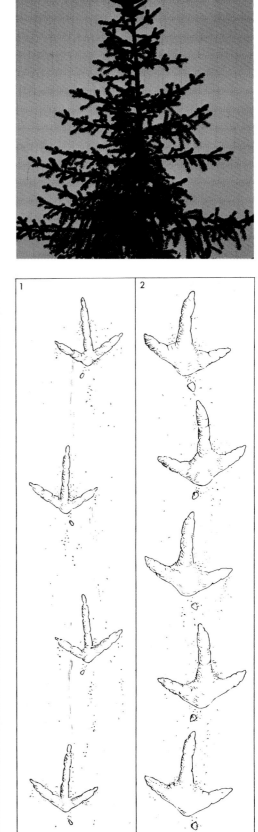

(Above) **RING-NECKED PHEAS-
ANT** (*Phasianus colchicus*). The male
bird.
(Right) **RING-NECKED PHEAS-
ANT** (*Phasianus colchicus*). The
female bird.

the lower breast. They are shorter-tailed than the pheasant and much larger than the European quail. The average length is 12 to 14 inches (30 to 36 cm).

Partridge love stubble and grain fields, both for roosting and feeding, and the same parts of fields, plains, or prairies are used year after year. A flushed covey tends to return to the same spot. Coveys normally number up to about twenty birds in late fall or winter, and a covey of this size would include the birds from two nests; this facilitates breeding, for partridge do not breed with siblings. [NS]

Chukar Partridge *(Alectoris graeca & A. chukar)*

These species, which have been introduced into the United States, are called rock partridge and chukar, respectively, in Europe; they occur in Italy, Greece, Turkey, and eastward into Asia, on stony and rocky slopes and wooded ground. This corresponds to their habitat in the United States, in the lowland mountains of Idaho, Utah, Nevada, Washington, and Oregon.

Chukars are much smaller than prairie chicken, being only about 13 inches (33 cm) long. The sexes are similar, with an olive-brown back, a white underface patch outlined in black, and buffish flanks marked with eight to thirteen vertical bars of black and chestnut. The chukar gets its name from the sound of its call.

Several species of chukar have a fairly wide range across Asia and are also native to southern Europe. Those in North America are descended from Himalayan and Turkish stock. The European rock partridge utters a ringing whistle rather than clucks and cackles. The chukar requires rather specialized habitat for, while it can withstand cold, it cannot cope with much snow and is therefore most successful in fairly arid or warm regions. In Europe, the chukar is closely related to the red-legged partridge (see below). [NS]

Red-legged Partridge *(Alectoris rufa)*

This bird is native to southwestern Europe, occurring in Portugal, Spain, and southwestern France. It has been introduced to the Azores, Madeira, the Canary Islands, and southern Britain, where it seems to fare best on relatively dry cultivated lands and amid sand dunes. It is slightly larger than the partridge, and the young birds of the two species are very similar.

The adult birds can be identified by a red bill and legs, heavily barred flanks, and a long white stripe above the eye, as against the pale orange-chestnut colored face of the gray partridge, which also has a conspicuous dark-brown horse-shoe mark on its lower breast. The red-legged runs more swiftly. Both species prefer to run than to fly.

When this bird flies, however, it is one of the fastest and, for the shooter, most challenging of the European upland birds. [NS]

Chapter 3
Waterfowl

Canada Goose *(Branta canadensis)*

The most common of all North American geese, with a population well over two million, the Canada Goose is known as the honker, for its habitual call is a loud, resonant honking; this can usually be heard before the birds are in sight when they are migrating. They fly in V-formation.

Canada geese can be easily identified by sight, too, for they have a very conspicuous white patch under their chins, the remainder of their heads and necks being black. Their wings and backs are a dark gray-brown, and their breasts, flanks, and under-tail coverts are white.

Canada geese have been introduced into Europe and New Zealand, but wild flocks appear only in North America. They nest in the northern part of the continent, as far south as the northern United States; most of them winter from the mid-United States to the Gulf of Mexico.

In some regions of North America, they have become troublesome to farmers, for they feed in corn and wheat fields, sometimes in very considerable numbers. [NS]

Snow Goose *(Chen caerulescens)*

This is a white goose with black wing tips. It weighs about 7 lb (3.2 kg) and nests in the extreme north of the American continent and on Greenland, and it winters over much of the eastern United States; some vagrants occur in Europe.

The lesser snow goose (*C. c. caerulescens*) winters mainly along the delta of the Mississippi, on the Gulf coast, in scattered areas of Mexico, and in a few parts of California. The greater snow goose (*C. c. atlantica*) winters along the Atlantic coast, mainly in Delaware, Maryland, Virginia, and southward.

The lesser snow goose can also be of a blue phase—known as the blue goose—when their bodies are a slate-gray; the immature birds are a brownish-gray.

When migrating, the snow goose is noted for long flights and a minimum of stops. These usually occur at staging areas. The geese glean grain fields after the harvest but, in some areas of central Canada, which they traverse before the harvest, they can do considerable damage to the crops. [NS]

Ross' Goose *(Chen rossi)*

Ross' goose is a miniature of the snow goose (see above), being wholly white with black wing tips, a shorter neck, and, in flight, more rapid wing-beats.

It nests in northern Canada (Southampton Island) and winters mainly in the San Joaquin Valley in west-central California, and in some other western states, and in western and central Canada. [NS]

Emperor Goose *(Philacte canagica)*

One of the most beautiful species of geese, adult emperor geese have blue-gray backs edged with black, and then white. Their heads are white, and their bills and legs are pink; immature birds are generally darker.

The emperor goose nests at the extreme east of the Eurasian land mass and in western Alaska, and winters in the Aleutian Islands, on Kodiak Island, and on the Kamchatka peninsula, in Russia. [NS]

(Below) **CANADA GOOSE** (*Branta canadensis*).

Subspecies of the Canada goose. *(1)* Cackling Canada goose (*B. c. minima*). *(2)* Lesser Canada goose (*B. c. parvipes*). *(3)* Vancouver Canada goose (*B. c. fulva*). *(4)* Atlantic Canada goose (*B. c. canadensis*).

(Above left) **BEAN GOOSE** (*Anser fabalis*).
(Left) **BARNACLE GOOSE** (*Branta leucopsis*).
(Above right) **GRAYLAG GOOSE** (*Anser anser*).

White-fronted Goose *(Anser albifrons)*

This goose can be distinguished by its white facial patch round a pink bill, irregular black and brown markings on its belly, and orange legs; immature birds have yellow legs, and lack the facial patch and the markings on the belly. On the adult birds, the rest of the head and neck, and much of the body, are a grayish-brown. This goose is known to North American and British wildfowlers as the specklebelly.

It has a global distribution, with a breeding range that is circumpolar, except for a few small gaps in the Canadian Northwest Territories, one of which is occupied by the much larger tule goose (*A. a. gambelli*), a subspecies.

White-fronted geese winter on the coasts of North America from southern California, round Mexico, to the Gulf coast and the marshes of Texas and Louisiana, but they are rare on the East coast. In Europe, they winter round the British Isles, the coasts of northwestern Europe from France to Denmark, and eastward in the Mediterranean from Italy. Elsewhere, they are found on the coasts of the Black and Caspian seas, Asia Minor, India, China, parts of Southeast Asia, and Japan. Like other gray geese, they migrate in large flocks, travelling in lines or chevron formation.

It is said that it was geese of this species that alerted the Roman garrison to an incursion of Gauls in 390 BC. [NS]

Magellan Goose *(Chloephaga picta)*

While not a true goose—the sexes being unalike—but a species of shelduck, the Magellan is the major goose-like bird of South America, with a range extending over the lower part of the continent, and stretching out to include the Falkland Islands. The males are white with black wing tips, and their white back feathers are tipped with black; their feet are black. The females have barred light- and dark-brown breasts and necks, and russet heads; their wings are white below and black above but have white edges at the tips. Their feet are yellow or orange.

They winter in southwestern Argentina but, because they are numerous and grass-eaters, they are unwelcome to the farmers of the region, whose cattle and sheep are thus deprived of food. [NS]

Ashy-headed Goose *(Chloephaga poliocephala)*

This bird inhabits the same range of South America as the Magellan goose (see above) but is smaller. The two species sometimes fly in formation together but are easily distinguished, for their coloration differs considerably: an ash-gray head and a russet neck and dark chest identify this species, which also has dark, almost black wings with a white leading edge. [NS]

Graylag Goose *(Anser anser)*

This is a goose of the Eurasian landmass and does not occur in North America. It is one of the largest and strongest of the wild geese. Its coloration is predominately gray, and its head and neck are not darker than the rest of its body. In addition to these characteristics, it can be distinguished from other "gray" geese by its pinkish-gray feet and bill. On long flights, it travels in V-formations, and honks while in flight.

The western (European) race has a thick orange bill. It breeds mostly in Iceland and across the Palaearctic region, and it winters in Britain, the Netherlands, France, Spain, and North Africa.

The eastern race has a thick pink bill and looks lighter, for its feathers have a light edge. It breeds across northern Asia and winters from the eastern Mediterranean to China. An intermediate form is found in western Russia and the Balkans.

Graylags, like many geese, are grass eaters and fly at dawn to their feeding grounds. [RE]

Bean Goose *(Anser fabalis)*
Pink-footed Goose *(A. f. brachyrhynchus)*

The bean goose is a Eurasian bird, breeding from Greenland to eastern Siberia and wintering over a large part of Europe and Asia, with a few strays occurring over the Alaskan islands. It is a gray goose and can be distinguished from the graylag, for example, by its yellow feet and its black and yellow bill (those of the graylag are, respectively, pinkish-gray and orange or pink). It is a rather large goose.

In fall and winter, it feeds heavily in grain-stubble fields, favoring barley, but it also eats a wide variety of other vegetable food.

The pink-footed goose is another gray goose, but slightly smaller than the bean. It has a very dark head, a small pink beak, a relatively light toned body, and pink legs. It has a more restricted range than the bean goose, breeding in Greenland, Iceland, and Spitzbergen, and wintering mostly in the British Isles, northern France, Belgium, Holland, and Germany. Pink-footed geese occasionally appear in other parts of Europe, including Russia. They rest in the Faeroes and Shetlands en route to Scandinavia. They fly in skeins of over 1,000 birds, with family groups of adults and goslings keeping together, a habit common to a number of species of geese. Pink-footed geese gather in large flocks on moors, sandbanks, marshes, estuaries and other coastal lands. Except when hungry, as on arrival from migration, they are difficult to approach, being very wary. [RE]

Barnacle Goose *(Branta leucopsis)*

Smaller than the Canada goose, and white-faced while the Canada goose is white only under the chin, the barnacle goose is predominately a European bird; it occasionally appears on the Atlantic coast of North America. It is markedly a black-and-white bird, with the black of its neck extending down to its breast, and with black feet and bill; its upper parts are a lavender gray. Its call is a short, shrill, repeated bark.

It winters mainly in Denmark, on the German coast, in the Netherlands, and in Ireland and Scotland. It nests in the high Arctic.

While it is known as the "little nun" in France, on account of its coloration, it was once believed, according to a Welsh writer in 1187, to grow on trees and, in Ireland, to be a sort of fish, being eaten as such on fast days. [NS]

Brant, or Brent, Goose *(Branta bernicla)*

This is a small dark goose, hardly bigger than a mallard drake. There are three distinct races that differ from one another in their range and degree of darkness of plumage. Brant geese of all species have black heads, necks, and chests, and brilliant white rear-parts. Their total range encompasses the entire Arctic, while they migrate southward in winter and appear in northern Europe and Asia, and in North America.

The dark-bellied, or Russian, brant (*B. b. bernicla*) has a dark gray-brown belly; it nests to the north of Europe and Asia, and migrates along the coastlines in winter. The light-bellied, or Atlantic, brant has much paler under-parts that contrast strongly with the relatively darker upper-parts; it breeds in eastern Canada, Greenland, Spitzbergen, and the Franz Josef archipelago, and migrates southward in winter along the Atlantic shores. The dark- and light-bellied brants can occur in the same flocks, or gaggles. The third subspecies is the black, or Pacific, brant (*B. b. nigricans* or *B. b. orientalis*). It is much darker than the other two. It breeds on the islands and coasts of Siberia, Alaska, and western Canada, and winters on the Pacific coast from southwestern British Columbia to Baja California.

Brants are more maritime in their habits than most geese, resting on the water, and feeding in shallow coastal waters, often up-ending to do so. On short foraging flights, they often fly in low, ragged flocks and on longer flights form wavering lines, but not regular formations. [RE]

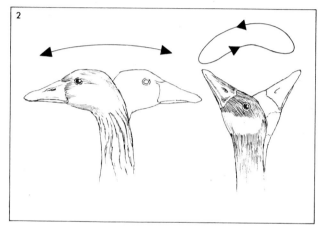

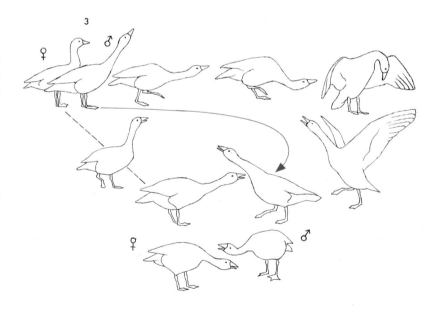

A Communication among geese is well-developed. *(1)* When a goose prepares to fly, it signals to others of the same species in the flock. *(2)* A graylag goose shakes its head from side to side so that its red beak is noticeable; a Canada goose raises its head so as to display the conspicuous white patch on its cheeks and neck. *(3)* An intruding goose is seen off: a gander advances with its head extended and held successively lower. The intruder, head drooping and with wings spread as if protectively, turns away. The triumphant male "goose-steps," flaps its wings, and stretches out its neck exultingly. As he rejoins the female, she trusts her head forward toward him, but lower than his. (Right) **BRANT, or BRENT, GOOSE** *(Branta bernicla)*.

(Above and opposite, top left) **SHOVELER** (*Anas clypeata*).
(Below) **MALLARD** (*Anas platyrhynchos*).
(Opposite, top right) **COMMON, or NORTHERN, SHELDUCK** (*Tadorna tadorna*).

(Opposite, center) Surface-feeding ducks, such as the mallard *(1)*, have their legs placed centrally under the body; the legs of diving ducks *(2)* are to the rear. Surface-feeding ducks fly up from the water with a spring *(3)*, while diving ducks patter along the surface for some distance before becoming airborne *(4)*.

Other Geese

There are a number of species of geese in various parts of the world, of which one—the Hawaiian nene goose—is recovering from a condition of near-extinction. Other species include the swan-goose, the bar-headed goose, and the red-breasted goose of Asia; the Cape Barren goose of Australia; an African sheldgoose known as the Egyptian goose, which is actually a sort of long-legged duck; and three sheldgeese of South America—the ruddy-headed goose, the Orinoco goose, which is a forest dweller, and the maritime kelp goose. [RE]

Shelducks (Tadornini)

Shelducks have short, narrow, goose-like bills, and most species have white upper and under wing coverts and iridescent green specula, and their downy plumage is strongly patterned.

Probably the most abundant and widespread is the common, or northern, shelduck (Tadorna tadorna), which breeds from the coast of western Europe eastward through much of Asia. This species is slightly larger than a mallard. The sexes are colored alike, but the male is larger and has a large frontal knob on his bill; at a distance, the birds appear black and white. Their heads and necks are a dark, metallic green, bills are bright red, and bodies mostly white but with a broad brown band across the breast. The legs are orange. The tip of the tail, the wing tips, and a broad band along the rear edges of the wings are black.

The ruddy shelduck (T. ferruginea) has a breeding range that covers small parts of southern Europe, northernmost Africa, and much of Central Asia. It migrates deep into Africa and down the southern coasts of Asia, but unlike the common shelduck, it is an inland bird. Almost uniformly rusty or orange-brown in coloration, its head is pale, its bill and legs are black, and its wings and tail are marked with black; there is

white on its wing coverts. The male has a small black neck-ring.

Other species of shelduck include the Cape shelduck of South Africa, the New Zealand shelduck, the Australian shelduck, and the radjah shelduck, which is an Australian species, but occurs also in the East Indies. [RE]

Mallard (Anas platyrhynchos)

This is the common bird of the entire northern hemisphere—the brightly colored drake with his cocky, curled rump feathers, and the brown, comparatively drab duck. They breed over virtually all their range, and they migrate as far south as North Africa, Southeast Asia, and southern Mexico. There are Hawaiian and Laysan Island races, too.

Mallard have adapted to human settlement about as well as pigeons and are thoroughly at home in cities and urban parks—fat, comfortable, nearly domesticated birds that occasionally breed with domestic strains.

Nevertheless, truly wild mallard are wary and shy of man, particularly hunting man. [NS]

Shoveler (Anas clypeata)

The common, or northern, shoveler is found throughout North America, Europe, and Asia, and it occasionally visits South America, Africa, and even Australia.

While it is a small duck, a little smaller than a mallard, it can be identified, even in flight, by its disproportionately large, spatulate bill, which is widest near its rounded tip. When migrating, both sexes are brownish, the male being in molt and thus hardly brighter than the female; they can then be mistaken for teal or, later, for small mallards. The male is otherwise colorful, with a green head, like that of a mallard, a

Pintail (*Anas acuta*) in flight. Their slender, pointed bodies are a distinguishing mark even at a distance. Of the pair to the left, the male bird has a predominantly white body and a dark head and rear part.

white breast, reddish-brown flanks and belly, a black rump with a sooty tail with whitish outers, and a slaty brown back. Both sexes have orange feet, a blue wing patch, and green specula.

Shovelers are found in fresh, brackish, and salty shallows. In some North American regions—notably California, Louisiana, and northern Mexico—there are large wintering populations; some birds fly to Hawaii from breeding grounds in Alaska. They breed over much of Europe, but not in Italy or Spain. [RE]

Gadwall (*Anas strepera*)

Gadwall of both sexes are sometimes taken for female mallard, although the male gadwall is predominantly grey but with a black rump, while the female has a yellowish-orange bill with dark markings (the female mallard's is orange); both sexes show a white patch on the wing in flight, whereas the female mallard has white-bordered blue specula. Mallards have less pointed wings.

While found all over the world except in South America and Australasia, gadwall are nowhere very abundant. They migrate early in fall, like some species of teal, and their passage is usually over by the end of October. [NS]

Pintail (*Anas acuta*)

Pintail are second only to mallard in numbers, and the northern species of pintail breeds round the entire arctic region, from Iceland through Scandinavia, the northern parts of Russia to Siberia, and through Alaska and much of Canada to Greenland. Pintail migrate southward into large parts of Africa, lower Asia, and South America; some winter on Pacific islands. An antarctic species is found on the islands in the south of the Indian Ocean; other species are native to the West Indies, to South America, and Africa.

The male of the northern pintail is characterized by white sides and a white front to its neck, a brown head, and a long pointed tail. The female is brownish, with a less markedly pointed tail, and otherwise looks rather like a female mallard, but without the wing specula. Pintail are about the same size as mallard, but slimmer, and with longer necks. In flight, while the mallard male's white neck ring is noticeable, the pintail male has a white streak running up toward its head from its under-parts.

Pintail fly extremely fast and tend to fly higher than most ducks, even when approaching a resting or feeding place. On short flights, they fly in small ragged groups, in twos or threes, or singly. On longer flights, they fly in large skeins, sometimes breaking into rippling arcs or ellipses.

Their wings are raked and pointed, and their bodies streamlined. They are far more wary than mallards. [NS]

Black Duck (*Anas rubripes*)

This duck is not really black, but dark brown, stippled with buff or creamy white on the feather edges; in winter plumage, adult males have a U-shaped line, adult females a V-shaped line, on the small feathers on the sides of the chest. In the air, black ducks appear, to experienced observers, like dark, very large female mallards, but with long sooty, flat-bellied profiles, large heads, a moderate wing-beat, and wide, only moderately curving wings.

Their major breeding grounds extend across eastern Canada but stretch to include part of the eastern United States and, to the west, the prairie provinces of Canada and the adjacent parts of the United States. The birds that breed in the west of this range migrate south along the Mississippi valley, but the rest, the majority, winter from New England down through the coastal states to North Carolina; the greatest concentration occurs on the Delmarva Peninsula at the junction of Delaware, Maryland, and Virginia.

The black duck is diminishing in number, for it is shyer and less adaptable than a mallard, for example, and cannot adjust to human disturbance of its environment. [NS]

Duck species are far too numerous for all to be given space here or even named; those that are mentioned are the most commonly hunted over the widest areas. Other duck of hunting interest include the torrent duck of the Andes; the blue, or mountain, duck of New Zealand; the falcated duck of eastern Asia; the mallard-like yellow-billed duck of Africa; the Australasian spot-billed duck; the Philippine duck, another mallard-like species; several shoveler or shoveler-like species occurring in South America, Africa, and Asia; the harlequin, the oldsquaw or long-tailed, and the goldeneye or whistler duck—all of them widely distributed sea ducks, but often found on inland waters; and the bufflehead. There are, too, localized races of the mallard, known by various names in the areas where they occur. [RE]

Wood Duck (*Aix sponsa*)

Smaller than the mallard, the male wood duck is, perhaps, the most strikingly colored of all North American waterfowl; it can also be identified by its head-crest, which slopes down from the back of its head. The female is without brilliant markings but has a darkish, crested head

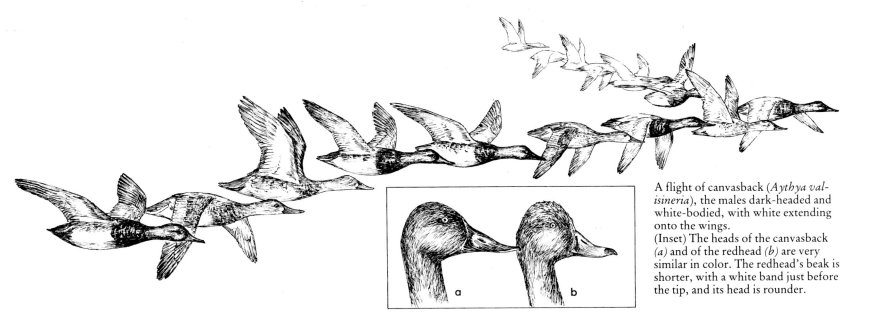

A flight of canvasback (*Aythya valisineria*), the males dark-headed and white-bodied, with white extending onto the wings.
(Inset) The heads of the canvasback *(a)* and of the redhead *(b)* are very similar in color. The redhead's beak is shorter, with a white band just before the tip, and its head is rounder.

with a conspicuous white patch round the eye. It is brownish, with light flanks contrasting with darker wings. In the air, wood duck show a contrast between a white belly and darker wings and breast; their square tails are noticeable, too. On land, they have a markedly upright stance, like all tree ducks.

They inhabit wooded, swampy country over most of the eastern United States northward to Canada and, in the west, from central California to southern British Columbia. A major wintering area is the valley of the Mississippi southward of Illinois to the coastal marshes of the Gulf of Mexico; others are the marshes and tidal rivers of the Atlantic and Pacific coasts.

Wood duck nested, until comparatively recently, only in hollow trees, but human destruction and management of woodlands have made these scarce. The ducks have adapted, however, to the specially designed nesting boxes provided by conservationists, game managers, and others, and wood duck populations, which at one time had fallen to dangerously low levels, have made a remarkable comeback.

A number of other species, similar in some respects to the wood duck, are occasionally hunted in widely separated parts of the world. Among the more significant of these are the mandarin duck of east Asia, the males of which are even more highly colored than the male wood duck; the Australian wood duck, or maned goose, of which the males are more dully colored than the females; the Brazilian teal, a small South American percher; the ringed teal of the southeastern part of South America; the wild form of the muscovy duck, with a range from Mexico to southern Brazil; and the white-winged wood duck of southeast Asia. [NS]

Fulvous Tree-duck *(Dendrocygna bicolor)*

This is a brownish, long-necked, almost goose-like duck, of which the sexes are alike. Its long legs are noticeable, both when it is on the ground and in the air, when they trail beyond the tail. A white stripe along its side separates the darker wings from the lighter flanks. In the Americas, it is common from Mexico to northern Argentina, and extends northward only to the southwestern United States. It occurs also throughout most of eastern Africa, on Madagascar, in India, and in some other parts of Asia.

In its Central and South American range, it occurs together with another tree-duck, the red-billed, or black-bellied, which is less common than the fulvous. Both species are also known as whistling ducks, the fulvous having a squealing, whistling call that can perhaps be rendered as "chee-weee."

There are six other species of tree-duck and, like the two mentioned here, they fly with slow wing beats, but they are so trusting that they circle round hunters, for whom they represent very poor sport. One of them, the lesser whistling duck of India and southern Asia (*D. javanica*), is additionally not only small and drab in appearance, but unpalatable too, having a downright unpleasant taste. [NS]

Canvasback *(Aythya valisineria)*

Slightly smaller than a mallard, the canvasback male is a white-bodied duck with head patterning like that of the pochard and redhead (see below), but with a distinctive long bill that gives its head a sloping profile. The female shares this profile but has a grayish hue, although with about the same patterning.

Canvasback breed in the prairie provinces of Canada, in the Yukon, in Alaska, and in a few parts of the upper United States. They winter in considerable numbers in the area of Chesapeake Bay on the East coast, in San Francisco Bay in slightly less substantial numbers, and also along the coasts of the gulfs of California and Mexico.

At one time, canvasback were extremely plentiful, but they declined significantly under the impact of market shooting, drought, and the draining of wetlands, and have never really recovered. Their favorite food, the wild celery, grows in fresh or brackish, but not salt, water, and it, too, has declined. To make matters worse, the closely related redhead duck (see below) sometimes lays its eggs in canvasback nests, thereby reducing the chances of survival for the eggs and ducklings of both species. [RE]

Redhead *(Aythya americana)*

A North American pochard, this bird is similar in appearance to the European pochard, except that the female has an indistinct face patch and is uniformly brownish (the female of the European pochard shows a contrast between a darker head and a lighter body). The ring-necked duck (*A. collaris*), a slightly smaller bird, can be confused with the redhead but has (in the male) a black head and back and (in the female) a dark back and darker head; ring-necked ducks have shorter bills than redheads.

Redhead breed primarily on the potholed prairies of central Canada and the Bear Lake region of northern Utah. They migrate along all the major American flyways, some reaching central Mexico, but with large numbers staying on Chesapeake Bay and the sounds inside the Outer Banks of North Carolina. Sometimes, eighty percent of the redhead population winters along the Gulf coast, from Florida to Yucatan.

Like the canvasback, the redhead has suffered from the effects of industrial activity on wetlands, and its total numbers have declined. [RE]

European, or Common, Pochard *(Aythya ferina)*

Pochards are diving ducks that are fast in the air, flying with a quick wing-beat, but they are poor walkers. One of the more common species is the European pochard, which ranges from Britain across Europe and through much of Asia.

It is about the size of a mallard. Both sexes have grayish wings and dark-gray feet; the male's head is dark reddish-brown, the female's is brown or grayish-brown. The male's breast is black, the female's colored like her head. Their bodies are, respectively, grayish and brownish.

Pochard breed in freshwater regions, but during migration and in winter, some species, including this one, are also to be found in brackish estuaries, tending to gather in large flocks.

Pochard are wary and difficult to approach. Like all diving ducks, they run over the water to gather speed for flight, for their wings are short. [RE]

Greater Scaup *(Aythya marila)*

A bit smaller than the mallard, the male of the greater scaup (the North American name) has black fore-parts, a black head with a greenish sheen, a dark rump and tail, and a light gray back; its under-parts are white. Virtually the only difference between it and the male of the ring-necked duck is that the latter has no white stripe showing through the wing primaries. The males of greater and lesser scaup are virtually impossible to distinguish apart in the air, for they are almost the same size, but the male of the lesser scaup has a purplish head, and a crown that is more pronounced and is almost a tuft.

The female greater scaup is a brownish duck with a clear white patch round the base of its bill; this and the white wing stripe are the only features by which it can easily be distinguished from the female of lesser scaup, ring-necked duck, and redhead.

Greater scaup have a nearly circumpolar breeding range, perhaps the most famous nesting grounds being those on the tundra ponds and potholes of Alaska; there are other nesting grounds in Canada, northern Europe, and Asia. Some of the birds remain surprisingly far north in winter, but other migrate along the sea coasts of Europe, Asia, and North America; they prefer maritime wintering habitats, where they sometimes gather in enormous flocks, feeding near shore in the early morning or near dusk. They are inquisitive and may approach a strange moving object that is not recognizably human. [RE]

Lesser Scaup *(Aythya affinis)*

This is a North American species. It is essentially a pochard of the interior of the continent, for it winters more over inland waters than the greater scaup (see above). It looks almost exactly like the greater scaup, and the differences between the two species, such as they are, are noted above.

Lesser scaup nest from Alaska through central Canada, and in some of the upper central and western United States. They migrate southward as far as Panama, but some remain relatively far north.

Lesser scaup eat more vegetation than do greater scaup; another difference is that the lesser is a decidedly more wary and suspicious bird than the greater. [RE]

The species of *Aythyinae* named above are the most commonly hunted diving ducks, the group which includes goldeneyes and pochards. Other in the group are the southern pochard of South America and Africa; the rosy-billed pochard of lower South America; the red-crested pochard,

(Above) **GOLDENEYE** (*Bucephala clangula*).
(Opposite, top) The goldeneye's typical mating display.
(Opposite, center) **PINTAIL** (*Anas acuta*).
(Opposite, bottom) **BLUE-WINGED TEAL** (*Anas discors*).
(Right) Duck species in flight may be distinguished by the coloration of their wings and specula. *(1)* Cinnamon teal; *(2)* blue-winged teal; *(3)* green-winged teal; *(4)* common teal; *(5)* mallard; and *(6)* black duck.

with a range from southern and eastern Europe through Central Asia; the Australasian white-eye; the ferruginous white-eye of southern Eurasia; the Baer's pochard of eastern Siberia; the New Zealand scaup; and the Eurasian tufted duck, which resembles the ring-necked duck mentioned above. [RE]

Sea Ducks

Sea ducks include mergansers, eiders, and scoters. In general, merganser are less maritime than other sea ducks but still rely heavily on fish and other aquatic animals for food, and share some other characteristics with sea ducks.

Merganser have long, narrow, almost cylindrical, sawtoothed bills, in contrast to the heavy bills typical of other sea ducks. Some merganser are crested, some are quite colorful. The common merganser (*Mergus merganser*) of Eurasia and North America is known to many European hunters as the goosander.

Eider (*Somateria mollissima*) are larger, more arctic, and far more maritime ducks. The females are brownish, the drakes generally patterned in black and white, though the heads of some species are colorful. Most species have black wings with white covert patches; some have colorful bills. Typical of eiders is a leathery bill extension, or shield, which runs up onto the forehead. They tend to fly low, usually in a line. The scooter is closely related to the eider. The drakes are black or nearly so, the females are a dark, grayish brown. The white-winged scoter (*Melanitta fusca*) has a white speculum and is the most widely distributed scoter, being found in North America, especially across Canada, and along the coast of Europe from Portugal to Scandinavia. [RE]

Common Teal (*Anas crecca*)

Called simply teal in Britain, this bird is a little more than half the length of a mallard; it is the smallest European duck, and one of the smallest in North America, where it can occur on the East coast.

Both sexes have a green and black speculum pattern and gray feet. The female looks like a very small mallard female—a mottled brown bird with a pale or white belly. The drake has a black bill and a chestnut head with a broad, curving, green eye stripe with a narrow light or white outline that is faint or absent in the American green-winged teal (see below), which also lacks the common teal's horizontal black and white stripe above the wing. The green-winged teal, however, has a vertical white stripe between flank and breast—the common teal lacks this.

Both species sometimes occur together on the Atlantic coast of North America. The common teal breeds in Iceland and over much of Europe and Asia; it migrates far to the south, reaching as far as a line between the Gulf of Guinea in the west to the Gulf of Aden in the east in Africa, and reaching as far south as Sri Lanka and Malaya in Asia. [NS]

Green-winged Teal (*Anas carolinensis*)

A very small duck, about half the size of the mallard, the green-winged teal breeds in Alaska, Canada, and the upper United States, the most productive nesting area lying between the Mississippi River and the Pacific coast. It migrates as far south as Central America, though the greatest wintering concentrations are in upper Mexico and along the Gulf coast of the United States.

Green-winged teal are hardy birds which, in some parts of their range, are among the very late migrants, but they seldom linger at waystops where they rest and feed.

The green-winged is hard to distinguish from the common teal (see above, where both are described). In flight, both appear dark-headed, small, and white-bellied. They feed in the water, up-ending to reach bottom growth, and sometimes feed on land. A characteristic call by the male is a whistling. [NS]

Blue-winged Teal (*Anas discors*)

The blue-winged teal is a purely American species. It is slightly larger than the green-winged or common teals (see above), and both sexes have brownish wings with green specula and a large, unmistakable light-blue patch formed by the upper coverts; in bright sunlight, this patch can appear white. The male has a bluish-gray head with a conspicuous, white facial crescent in front of, and extending back over, the eye. In dim light, it is hard to distinguish this teal from either the green-winged or the cinnamon teal (see below).

Blue-winged teal nest in the greatest numbers in the area between the Great Lakes and the Pacific. They migrate as far south as Chile and Argentina, with a major concentration gathering in Columbia on the marshes at the mouth of the Magdalena River, which lies to the northeast of Panama. Other concentrations are found in Florida, the coastal marshes of Louisiana and Texas, and, in Mexico, in Culican and the Yucatan Peninsula. They also winter on Cuba and in Guyana.

Blue-winged teal feed on flooded rice fields, freshwater marshes, ponds, sloughs, and creeks; they eat mostly vegetation. They fly low, fast, and erratically, often in tight clusters. [NS]

Cinnamon Teal (*Anas cyanoptera*)

Like the blue-winged teal, the cinnamon teal is an American species. The two species are about the same size, have about the same behavior, and occupy the same habitat.

The cinnamon teal has the same blue wing patch as the blue-winged teal, but the male is a rich cinnamon brown, with a black rump, while the female is slightly more rusty in color, and has a longer, wider bill. While all ducks occasionally dive to escape danger, the cinnamon teal is among the most adept at swimming long distances underwater.

Major breeding grounds are in the states of Washington, Idaho, and Utah, and the largest wintering concentration gathers in Mexico. Several subspecies occur in South America. [NS]

Baikal Teal (*Anas formosa*)

This species breeds mainly in Siberia, migrating and wintering throughout much of eastern Asia, with a few accidentals straggling into Alaska. Major wintering grounds include southern Siberia, eastern China, Japan, Mongolia, and Korea.

The female has brown and buff plumage and looks rather like a female green-winged teal (see above), except that she has a conspicuous pale buff cheek mark. The male is one of the most handsome of ducks, having a unique head pattern of buff-yellow, green, and black, with each of these colors trimmed with white. The sides and breast are spotted, and the wings are brown with green specula.

In behavior and habitat, this teal resembles the more common varieties described above. [NS]

South American Green-winged, or Speckled, Teal (*Anas flavirostris*)

Both sexes of this teal are pale-brownish and speckled with darker brown heads (there are teal from the northern Andes, however, with quite gray heads). The speculum is like that of the common teal (see above); the bill is sometimes yellow and sometimes as dark as that of the green-winged teal of North America.

The South American species occurs in various parts of western and southern South America, and its habitats and behavior are roughly like those of the other teal described above. [NS]

Several other varieties of teal with limited distribution are hunted in different parts of the world. They include the silver teal (South America), the tiny Hottentot teal (Africa and Madagascar), the Cape teal (southern and central Africa), the gray teal (East Indies, Australia, and New Zealand), and the teal sometimes considered a reddish variant of the gray, the Madagascar teal. There is also the chestnut teal of Australia and Tasmania, the brown teal of New Zealand and the adjacent islands, and the marbled teal, sometimes held to be of another genus, which ranges from the Mediterranean to southwestern Asia. Finally, there is the Eurasian garganey. [RE]

Baldpate, or American Widgeon (*Anas americana*)
This is a common medium-sized dabbling duck, slightly smaller than a mallard. The male is brown and has a whitish forehead and crown, a marking often visible when the birds are in flight, or as they rise from fields or water; the female has a grayish head and a brownish body.

Baldpates nest throughout southern Canada and, in smaller numbers, in Alaska and a few states south of the Canadian border. The greatest concentrations are in Canada's central prairie-pothole region. Large wintering concentrations gather in central California, the Mississippi Delta, and on parts of the coast of the Gulf of Mexico.

Baldpates frequent freshwater ponds and marshes, and brackish and salt marshes and bays. Although they feed on crops and in gardens, they are primarily aquatic feeders; being poor divers, they feed in company with other species that dive, canvasbacks and scaup, for example, so as to feed on the vegetation that floats to the surface as these other ducks feed underwater. [NS]

European Widgeon (*Anas penelope*)
The male of the European widgeon is most readily distinguished from that of the American widgeon or baldpate (see above) by a buff, rather than a white, forehead and crown, and a bright orange-brown or chestnut face and neck, in contrast to the baldpate's green eye stripe. The females are similarly brownish, but the European widgeon is tawnier on the head, and a more dusky brown on the body. Both sexes of the European widgeon have white upper wing coverts and green specula patterns, those of the female being a dingy white or gray, with less green.

European widgeon breed on Iceland, in Scotland, in the upper parts of Scandinavia, and eastward through northern Russia. They winter over large parts of Europe and Asia; birds from Europe visit the Atlantic coast of North America with a frequency that is debated by ornithologists and wildfowlers there, and birds from the eastern end of their breeding range, in Asia, visit the Pacific coast of North America. These visits occur mostly during the fall or winter, while the interior of North America has been visited by European widgeon in spring.

European widgeon have behavior and habitats very close to those of the baldpate. [NS]

In addition to the two widgeon of the northern hemisphere described above, there is a widgeon of South America, the Chiloé (*Anas sibilatrix*), from the south of the continent. It is the only dabbling species of which the female has a brightly colored head. Both males and females have iridescent green heads, their flanks are orange-brown, and their breasts have a scaly-looking black and white pattern.

One sometimes hears of a bird called a "Cape widgeon," but this is, in fact, a misnomer for the Cape teal (*Anas capensis*), which is bigger than other teal. Both sexes of the species have pink bills, green and black specula broadly bordered with white, and are otherwise mottled gray. [RE]

Male ducks are commonly but not invariably more brightly colored or more clearly marked than the females. *(1)* European widgeon; *(2)* American widgeon; *(3)* Australian teal (*Anas gibberifrons gracilis*); and *(4)* Baikal teal.

(Opposite, top and inset) **EURO-PEAN WIDGEON** (*Anas penelope*).
(Opposite, lower) **EUROPEAN EIDER** (*Somateria mollissima mollissima*).

(Below) European eider, female on the left, male on the right.
(Left) Other eider include *(1)* American eider (*S. m. dresseri*), *(2)* King eider (*S. spectabilis*), *(3)* the female and male spectacled, or Fischer's, eider (*S. fischeri*).

Chapter 4

African Game Animals

African Lion *(Panthera leo)*

The lion is perhaps the most eagerly sought trophy in Africa. As a symbol of strength, fortitude, vigor, and dignity, the lion represents the qualities most admired by hunters.

Within historical times, lions ranged over a considerable area that extended from the Balkans and the Middle East, through north Africa and all the sub-Saharan regions, to the Indian peninsula. Their range today is very much reduced, being limited to the Gir Forest in India, where only a few lions live, and to areas south of the Sahara desert. Anthony Dyer, a professional hunter and an authority on African game, estimates that there are some 15,000 lions living in the wild in Africa, with several thousand more living in captivity.

Lions are found in a variety of terrain: plains, bush country, savanna, forest, desert, and even on the edges of swamps. They are found from sea level to montane forests at an elevation of 10,000 feet (3,048 m) or more. To the trophy hunter, however, their range is more geographically exact. Among the better lion areas are the Kalahari desert in southern Botswana, northern and central Tanzania, southern Kenya, northeastern and western Uganda, southeastern Zaire, southeastern Sudan, southeastern Chad, and the northeast of the Central African Republic.

Lions vary greatly in appearance. On the vast Serengeti Plains of Tanzania, a lion in its prime will inevitably have a large, thick mane; this can extend from his head, where it almost covers his ears, along his back behind his shoulders, and completely covers his chest between his forelegs, on the elbows of which there will be large tufts. This is what a trophy lion should look like.

The coloration of lions varies very much, from a very light yellow to a smoky gray color, while manes vary even more, even among lions in the same area. It is not uncommon to see a pair of male lions, lying side by side, that have manes of totally different hues: blond, black, ginger, rust, maybe even pepper-and-salt.

Big lions can be found in thorn desert, forest, and savanna scrubland, but their manes are seldom as impressive as those on plains lions, for the long, thick hair is torn away by thorns and scrub. These lions are certainly not inferior trophies, being, in fact, sometimes bigger than plains lions, and more difficult to hunt.

A big lion will stand almost 4 feet (126 cm) at the shoulder and measure over 10 feet (305 cm) from the nose to the tip of his tail. When standing on his hind legs, he will be over 7 feet (213 cm) tall. He will weigh up to 450 lb (204 kg).

Lions are gregarious, living in prides that vary in number from a pair of animals to over thirty. A typical pride would be a pair of males together with four or more females and cubs. It is not unusual to find a solitary male, but the chances would be that the animal had left his pride for a short period only.

Lions breed at all times of year. The gestation period is about 108 days. Cubs have a pelt that is spotted at first and very slowly changes to the typical adult appearance. Litters of two or three are normal, but up to six cubs have been recorded in a litter. They are usually weaned after three

(Above) **LION** *(Panthera leo)*.
(Right) **LEOPARD** *(Panthera pardus)*.

or four months, the process beginning when the mother brings them small pieces of meat. They are not mature until they are almost four years old, are in their prime at five or six, and begin to breed at four; lionesses produce a litter every two years for about ten years.

Lions are somewhat territorial animals, although they do wander from their territories from time to time in search of a mate or during the migration of prey animals. It is generally believed that lions occupy a territory about 40 miles (64 km) in circumference. They mark their territories by several methods, of which roaring, and urinating on bushes, are two common ones.

Lions frequently hunt in a seemingly coordinated fashion, with either males or females frightening or driving their prey so as to bring them nearer the others in the pride, that may have been waiting downwind of the prey, or merely nearby, to take advantage of the victims' panic rushes. The young animals take part in these hunts, thus learning to hunt and kill.

An experienced lion can stalk prey with great skill until it gets within range for a sudden spring, or attack over a short distance, undertaken with a tremendous burst of speed. The prey is killed with a blow of a paw, by a neck bite that may either break the neck or suffocate the victim, or by a grip on the nose, which is then twisted until the neck is broken. Lions hunt passively, too, like tame cats, waiting for their prey,

for example, at waterholes. They share the killings from a joint hunt, with the immature animals eating once the adults have eaten. A big male can devour 75 lb (34 kg) of meat in a day.

Lions hunt by day and by night, having excellent vision at all times and well-developed senses of hearing and smell. They can see well enough to watch vultures circling at considerable distances and can keep distant herds of plains animals under observation, too. When the grass is tall and obscures their view or makes it difficult to scent the wind, they may climb trees. Tree climbing is a trait that is seemingly more common in some areas than in others. Lions seem to climb habitually in Manyara in Tanzania, and on the Ishasha Flats in the Ruwenzori Park in Uganda. Trees therefore afford the threatened hunter with no reliable sanctuary.

Man is, in fact, the lion's only enemy now, for tigers, which can overpower a lion, no longer occur in the same areas as lions. Lions have always been hunted, and their numbers have been very greatly reduced in recent times. Nowadays, they are exposed to poaching in the game reserves. [BH]

Leopard *(Panthera pardus)*

The leopard is much smaller than the lion, a healthy male weighing slightly over 150 lb (70 kg), with a record of over 200 lb (91 kg). A leopard normally stands about 2 feet (61 cm) at the shoulder and

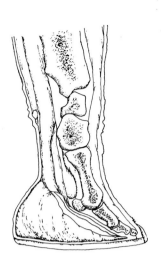

(Left) Like the rhino, the elephant has an elastic pad in its foot to cushion its weight.

(Right) The African (*Loxodonta africana*) and Indian (*Elephas maximus*) elephant are different species. The former has larger ears and a finger-like projection at the end of its trunk. The Indian elephant has a relatively upright forehead; that of the African elephant is sloping.

measures just over 7 feet (213 cm) from his nose to the tip of his tail; specimens of nearly 9 feet (274 cm) have been shot, but this size is unusual.

Leopards vary in size and coloration, depending on climatic conditions and where they live. At high altitudes—and they can live at up to 7,000 feet (2,133 m)—they tend to be larger and to have thicker, longer coats than lowland leopards, while in desert or semi-desert areas, they are much paler and smaller than those living in lush areas; an old desert male may not exceed 6 feet (183 cm) in length. In Asia, color variations in different habitats are perhaps even more marked than in Africa. Black—i.e., melanistic—leopards are very rare in Africa, seeming to occur mostly at high altitudes, but seem actually to be the dominant type in Malaysia, and to be common elsewhere in southeast Asia. The remarkable spots and rosettes are similar everywhere, but Himalayan leopards have a deep, rich coat, while dense-forest leopards have short, glossy fur and often show more reddish tones between the black markings.

There are populations of leopards in many parts of the world. In some parts of Africa, they are very scarce—in south and southwest Africa, for example—while they have been virtually exterminated in Somalia, which was once celebrated for its leopards. Elsewhere in Africa, they are found in varying numbers, but—contrary to popular belief—they are not an endangered species, although they have been unmercifully poached in some areas.

There are populations in parts of India and, to a lesser degree, also in parts of southeast Asia: leopards were abundant in Vietnam, Laos, and Cambodia before the war became widespread in the 1960s, while the more remote wilderness areas of Thailand, Burma, and Malaysia all continue to maintain good leopard populations. Safaris are difficult to organize, and hunting is restricted there, for the governments of these countries are reforming their forest and wildlife management and game regulations.

The leopard is found at all altitudes and in all climates, from sea level up almost to the timberline on the higher mountains in Africa. They are found on the plains of Africa, but only where there is thick cover. They favor thick, tree-lined gullies, riverine bush, sand rivers where there is sufficient cover, forests, and rocky kopjes (the small hills of southern Africa).

Leopards are solitary animals. Cubs are born after a gestation period of about ninety days and stay with their mother for one to two years. The usual litter comprises two cubs.

Leopards are exceptionally cunning hunters, having superb eyesight and a good sense of smell and hearing. They are, of course, extremely rapid in movement and can climb very well indeed, even when carrying prey weighing up to 200 lb (90 kg), such as an impala or a young giraffe. Leopards eat almost all sorts of other animals, and catch and kill birds, too. They habitually carry the carcasses of their prey up into trees to keep them safe from vultures. They return repeatedly to their kills, eating a bit at a time.

In the bush, a leopard can sometimes be detected by observing birds and monkeys that have been alarmed by its presence. They chatter and cry and follow the leopard about from a safe distance. Hunters can also learn to follow a leopard's tracks, but leopards are not so easily seen as lions are, for they are not to be found lolling under a thorn bush in the heat of the day but are secretive and shy if unmolested.

An exception to this behavior may be observed in the Seronera area of the Serengeti National Park in Tanzania, where leopards can be seen in relatively open woodland and can be photographed with relative ease. [BH]

Elephant *(Loxodonta africana)*

The African elephant is found very widely throughout Africa south of the Sahara, but only in national parks in South Africa. Elephants can be found in a great variety of altitudes and terrains, from tropical sea coasts to mountains in excess of 11,000 feet (3,350 m), and in rain forests, open savannas, semi-deserts, swamps, and montane forests. Just how many elephants survive in Africa is not known, but in some parts, their numbers have been falling very sharply, a trend that seems likely to continue as the requirements of human settlement and farming, and the attraction of objects carved in ivory, continue to increase their present rate.

Elephants are gregarious animals, living in herds that can, exceptionally, number more than 2,000 individuals; usually, however, the herds are very much smaller, and a mating herd consists of between 12 and 30 animals.

They spend much of their time feeding. An adult elephant needs between about 200 and 600 lb (100 and 300 kg) of vegetation daily, and a good deal of water, too—between 35 and 50 gallons (130 and 189 liters) would be a day's intake for a big bull. They feed on a variety of roots, shoots, leaves, grass, and bark that they strip from trees with the aid of their tusks—a habit that has left its mark on parts of eastern Africa,

84

where trees killed off in this way are all too common. Elephants push over large trees, too, if they cannot otherwise reach foliage that they want to eat. They are, thus, particularly destructive and demanding eaters.

This has caused the elephant to be regarded as a particular menace as the need for agricultural land has increased in the past few decades. Elephants have always been hunted, however, but while primitive methods were—and are—cruel, they have never been particularly effective and are certainly less so than shooting with modern weapons. Other than man, however, adult elephants have no natural enemies, although their young are sometimes taken by lions and leopards (and by tigers in India) that have escaped the vigilance of the herd.

Elephants mate at any time of year, and their gestation period is about twenty-one or twenty-two months; Indian elephants *(Elephas maximus)* have a slightly shorter gestation period. Calves remain with their mothers for up to ten years, so that, calving every third year, a cow may be followed by two or three calves of different ages. An elephant is mature at about the age of sixteen, and bulls are in their prime at about twenty. They may attain an age of between fifty and seventy.

While it is usually Indian elephants that have been trained, African elephants were used for a time in logging operations in what was the Belgian Congo. Their trunks, which can easily lift large logs, are used to tear branches from trees during feeding, and to discipline calves, but they can also exhibit an astonishing sensitivity: they can pick up single peanuts from the ground, pluck up and clean tusks of grass, draw up as much as 4 gallons (15 liters) of water when drinking or washing. A trunk can be employed as a sort of periscope, to sniff the wind well above ground-level. An elephant has even been observed using its trunk to pick up a piece of brush and use it to wipe one of its eyes. [BH]

Rhinoceros *(Black: Diceros bicornis. White Northern: Ceratohe-rium simum cottoni. White Southern: C. s. simum)*

These are misleading names, for rhino are not really either white or black, but while their skins are the same shade of dull gray, and their coloration that of whatever mud or soil they have wallowed or rolled in, they are distinguished, in part, by the form of their lips. The white rhino has wide (Afrikaans *wyd*) lips suitable for grazing, like a cow, while the black rhino has a finger-like prehensile protuberance on its upper lip, which it uses when browsing on vegetation, although, like the white, it will also graze on grass or growing crops.

The white is larger than the black (up to 3,500 lb or 1,590 kg, as against a maximum of 2,800 lb or 1,270 kg) and has a horn that can be as much as 5 feet (152 cm) in length, compared with some 4 feet (122 cm) for the black rhino of the rain forests and mountains, and only some 20 inches (51 cm) for the black rhino of the plains.

The white is docile, usually peaceful, and travels in herds of up to a dozen. The black, by contrast, is irritable, pugnacious, aggressive, and usually solitary: it is the species given to unprovoked attacks on objects that, to its poor eyesight, may appear to challenge it, such as trucks, railway locomotives, and hunters who, in a number of well-attested instances, have survived by choosing the right moment to sidestep out of the line of charge. A final difference is in their behavior when dropping dung: the white rhino lets it lie where it falls, whereas the black rhino scatters it with energetic kicks from its hind feet.

Both black and white rhino have exceedingly poor eyesight and seem to be unable to see clearly beyond a range of about 60 feet (18 m). They have highly developed senses of hearing and smell, and rely very largely on them to detect danger; the red-billed oxpeckers, the birds that characteristically perch on rhino and eat the parasitic insects that infest them, give out shrill cries of warning on the approach of danger, thus compensating for the rhino's poor sight. White cattle egrets also follow rhino (and buffalo and elephant), and feed on the insects that these animals disturb in grass and vegetation.

Rhino need to drink water at least once every twenty-four hours and follow well-trodden tracks to and from their drinking places, for they cover considerable distances, of up to 15 miles (24 km), from water. Unlike the Asian rhinoceros, however, specimens of which have been known to die from sunstroke, the African species are not sensitive to hot sun. Another peculiarity is their fondness for the dried-out branches of a cactus-like tree called *Euphorbia candelabra*: this tree supplies the native Africans with a white milky latex that they use to tip their hunting arrows, but while this substance is said to be capable of blinding a man for life, it is apparently not troublesome to the rhino once it has dried out.

The white rhino, in its northern form, is present in only very small numbers in southwestern Sudan and in northeastern Zaire, and is virtually extinct in northwestern Uganda. In its southern form, it is found in in South Africa in national parks, on private land, and in Zululand; it has been reintroduced into Zimbabwe-Rhodesia. The black rhino is still to be seen over a considerable range and in reasonable numbers. It occurs throughout much of Kenya, from the Aberdare Mountains and Mount Kenya through the semi-desert of the northern frontier and in much of the south, too, extending through nearly all of Tanzania in good numbers. In Zambia, it is found in the Luangwa Valley, in the Zambezi River valley below Kariba, in the Kafue National Park, and in the nearby regions. In Zimbabwe-Rhodesia, it occurs in most of the northern and northwestern regions, and in Mozambique, mostly north of the Zambezi. In Uganda, it is rare and is found only in the northern areas. There are a few in the north of the Central African Republic, and a few more in northern Cameroon. In Botswana, a very scattered, limited population inhabits the Okavango region in the northwest of the country, while in South Africa, the black rhino exists only in the national parks.

Rhinoceros have long been hunted for the sake of their upstanding horns, that are still prized, in the form of powder, in much of Asia for their supposedly aphrodisiac properties. While they are composed of closely matted hair and a bony substance that grows on the skin of the animal, and are thus not horns in scientific fact, this makes little difference to those who kill the rhino to obtain them. Unfortunately, and perhaps ironically, the rhino, as a species, cannot reproduce itself prolifically.

The gestation period is seventeen to eighteen months, and the calves, which stay with their mothers for some two years, become sexually mature at about three years. The females, however, mate only about once every fourth or fifth year, for they do not do so as long as they are accompanied by their calves. The bulls attract them by uttering high-pitched nasal calls, which are imitated by the hunters of some of the African tribes to lure rhino to within arrow range.

This slow reproductive rate suggests that the species has evolved into a state in which it has no natural enemies, but because of human depredations, its numbers have been reduced to some 20,000 black rhino, and only some 2,000 white. [BH]

African Buffalo *(Syncerus caffer)*

Several varieties of buffalo, all belonging to the genus *Syncerus*, are widely distributed throughout Africa. There is some disagreement between biologists as to the number of species and subspecies, for the Cape buffalo *(S. c. caffer)*, for example, may differ extremely in size, color, horn formation, and in other ways, too, as a result of widely differing diets and environments. The dwarf buffalo was once considered as a separate species but is now classified as a subspecies, *S. c. nanus*. The Cape, or black, buffalo is the largest and most famous form.

These many races of buffalo are collectively found in almost all types

(Opposite) **AFRICAN ELEPHANT**
(*Loxodonta africana*).
(Above) **AFRICAN BUFFALO**
(*Syncerus caffer*).

(Below) **BLACK RHINOCEROS**
(*Diceros dicornis*).

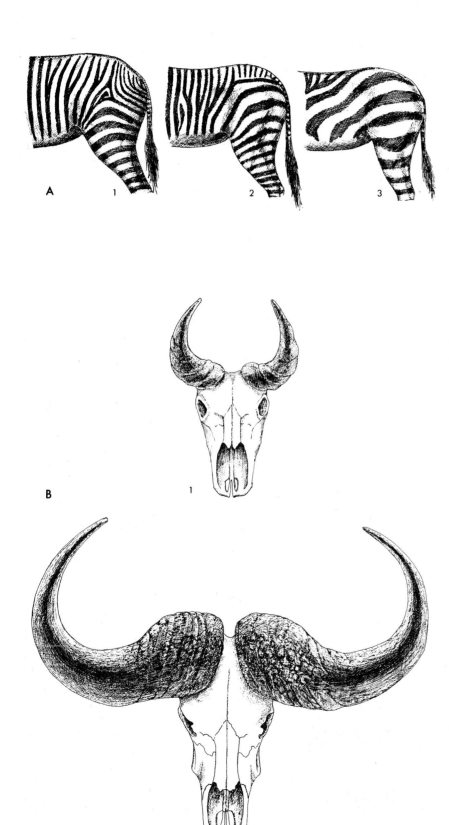

Variations between some African species.
A Zebra: *(1)* Grévy's; *(2)* Hartmann's, or mountain; and *(3)* Burchell's.
B Buffalo: *(1)* dwarf and *(2)* Cape.

of African habitat except true desert, from sea level up to the snow line of the mountains that straddle the Equator.

The Cape buffalo is most widely distributed, occurring throughout East Africa, in the eastern and southeastern parts of Zaire, in Mozambique, Zambia, Malawi, South Africa, and Botswana, and in parts of Angola. It is encountered also in Rwanda, Burundi, southern Ethiopia, and southern Somalia.

A northwestern variety is much smaller, both in body size and in its horns, and has a very narrow distribution, occurring only in the northern part of the Central African Republic, and in Chad.

A northeastern form is widely distributed. It is only slightly smaller than the Cape buffalo but has much smaller horns and varies very much in color; in some areas, in the Semliki Valley of Uganda, for example, one may see red, gray, rust, buff, chocolate, and even black buffalo together in the same herd. The same variety occurs in western Uganda, eastern Zaire, southern Sudan, and in the Omo River region of southern Ethiopia.

The dwarf buffalo is, as its name suggests, much smaller than the other buffalo: it stands about 4 feet (122 cm) at the shoulder and weighs only about 660 lb (300 kg), and its horns are smaller, too. It is usually tan or buff, although some specimens can be quite dark. The dwarf buffalo lacks the "boss" that others have; this is the heavy centerpiece of horn growing out from the skull. It is found from the Luanda area of Angola, through the equatorial rain forests of Zaire and Brazzaville Congo, and northward through a part of the Central African Republic and Cameroon, and in a good deal of West Africa: Guinea, Guinea Bissau, Sierra Leone, Liberia, the Ivory Coast, southern Senegal, and western Gabon.

It would be a mistake—and in the field, perhaps, a fatal one—to confuse the African buffalo with the water buffalo, a docile Asiatic animal that can be tamed and used as a beast of burden.

The Cape buffalo stands up to 6 feet (180 cm) at the shoulder, weighs up to three-quarters of a ton (1,650 lb/750 kg), and is possessed of exceptionally sharp sight, hearing, and sense of smell. Its curved, sharp horns can attain a length of up to 62 inches (158 cm), and it can run at a speed of up to 30 mph (48 km/h). It is cunning, unpredictable, aggressive, and very strong.

Buffalo are gregarious, living in herds of anything from a half-dozen up to several thousand, with leaders—most often an old and experienced female—and scouts. A herd will defend itself collectively, presenting an antagonist or an intruder with the formidable sight of massed horns: the buffalo protect themselves and their young with great bravery, and even a buffalo cow, with its single calf, can keep off an attacking lion.

Even though the herd is led by a cow, the bulls will fight with great ferocity to attain a sexual domination over the herd. Very old bulls are often solitary, however, or congregate with other bulls in small herds that forage together. When unmolested or undisturbed, bulls can remain within a comparatively small area, if it can provide them with their needs of ample grazing, water, and cover. Bulls may live for about thirty years, cows for about half that time. They breed at all times of year, the gestation period being about eleven months; single calves are the rule. [BH]

Bongo *(Boocercus eurycerus)*

There are two races of bongo, the western or lowland (*B. e. eurycerus*), and the eastern or mountain (*B. e. isaaci*). They are short, thick-set antelopes, and a good bull will weigh up to 400 lb (181 kg) and stand about 48 inches (127 cm) at the shoulder. Both sexes are horned, the record for a male being 39½ inches (100 cm); horns on the females are thinner than those on the males, and usually a good deal shorter.

The western bongo has a wide, if scattered, range, commencing as far west as Sierra Leone and Liberia, and extending eastward through the

Ivory Coast, Ghana, southern Nigeria, and southeastern Cameroon, southern Central African Republic, the Yambio area of southern Sudan, and northern Zaire.

The eastern bongo is found only in the high forests of Kenya—those of Mount Kenya, the Aberdares, the Mau and Cherangani hills, and the Londiani area—and only at altitudes between 6,000 and 12,000 feet (1,830 to 3,660 m), where the climate is usually cold and damp. Here the bongo lives exclusively in dense bush, forest, or bamboo, and is considered one of the most elusive and wary of game animals. It is, therefore, among the most highly prized trophies in the world.

The western bongo occupies the low-lying, tropical rain forest, but often feeds in open glades, along game trails, and in big savanna clearings where there is light or moderate bush.

They are nocturnal animals, feeding alone at night. During the day, they lie up, sometimes with one or two females. When they move, they travel easily through thick bush, walking with their heads slung low with their horns lying flat along their backs; as a result, they often have bald patches on their rumps. [BH]

Zebra *(Equus)*

There are three varieties of zebra: Grévy's, Burchell's, and Hartmann's, or mountain, zebra.

The Grévy is the largest and, some think, the most beautiful. It has a restricted range, being confined to the northern frontier of Kenya, a narrow strip of southern Ethiopia, and southern Somalia south of the Webi Shebeli, where there is a very small population. It lives in semi- and near-total desert and can go without water for considerable periods of time.

Its stripes are thin, compared to those of Burchell's zebra, so at a distance it appears gray, like a donkey. At close quarters, it can be distinguished by its massive body, its thin stripes, a broad black dorsal belt running about halfway down its back, and enormous, round, tufted ears. Herds of about thirty animals are common, and solitary males are sometimes to be seen.

Burchell's is the most common zebra, and it is often seen with other animals on the plains: wildebeest, springbok, kudu, giraffe, buffalo, and ostrich. It is an adaptable species and, in some areas, a very numerous one, usually living on the open plains within reach of water; in southern areas, it is found in miombo and mopane forest or in light bush, as well as on the plains.

Hartmann's or the mountain zebra is now very localized and scarce, occurring only in the stony hills of Namibia-Southwest Africa and southwestern Angola. It is relatively small, standing only about 4 feet (125 cm) at the shoulder. [BH]

Bushbuck *(Tragelaphus scriptus)*

Bushbuck are spiral-horned antelope of the same family as the bongo but with wide varieties of size, horn length, and range. Weights can range from 100 to 175 lb (45 to 79 kg), and the animals can stand from 30 to 38 inches (76 to 96 cm) at the shoulder. A Masai bushbuck's horns are acceptable as a trophy if they exceed 13 inches (33 cm) in length, but the record is $21\frac{5}{8}$ inches (55 cm). The horns are keeled, in some cases sharply so, and in very old animals, the tips may be whitened or "ivoried," an effect that considerably enhances their appearance and occurs with all the spiral-horned antelope: bongo, sitatunga, kudu, eland, and nyala.

Bushbuck are plentiful, and their ten different races have a range that extends from sea-level to 11,000 feet (3,350 m). They are equally partial to warm, dense coastal forest, riverine forest at higher altitudes, rain forest, swamp forest, and true equatorial or high-altitude rain forests, where they are found in dense bamboo and tall stinging nettles. The races are the Masai, Nile, giant or Barker's, harnessed, South African, Lim-

popo, Chobe, Arusi or Menelik's, Abyssinian, and Shoan bushbuck.

Bushbuck are often to be seen on forest trails and clearings during early mornings or late evenings and, unless disturbed, they are very territorial, often being seen day after day in the same area. They are most active at night, however, and lie up during the day in dense thickets. Because of this and their secretive habits, they have managed to survive in areas that are quite densely populated by man; they are commonly seen living quite close to modern cities.

They are shy, wary, and cautious, and essentially solitary animals, occasionally being seen in pairs or accompanied by a fawn. Like some other spiral-horned antelopes, they give a sharp dog-like bark or a series of barks when alarmed. For their size, they are strong and can be aggressive, and there are records of men being attacked by wounded bushbuck. [BH]

Eland *(Taurotragus)*

There are five species of the eland, which is the biggest of the African antelopes; they are the East African (*T. pattersonianus*), the Western giant, or Lord Derby's (*T. derbianus*), Livingstone's (*T. livingstonii*), the Central giant (*T. gigas*), and the Cape eland (*T. oryx*). Big bulls can weigh up to 2,000 lb (907 kg) and stand upward of 65 inches (165 cm) at the shoulder. The cows are much less massive, weigh some 800 lb (360 kg), and are a reddish-brown in color. Bulls, especially old bulls, are dark gray but are sometimes called "blue"; they have a prominent dewlap beneath the neck and a heavy, dark triangle of tufted facial hair, called the "ruff."

Both bulls and cows have spiral horns, those of the cows being very much thinner. An average for the East African eland would be upward of 25 inches (64 cm), while that for one of the giant elands would be over 38 inches (97 cm). The record size for the giant eland's horns is $47\frac{5}{8}$ inches (121 cm).

Eland are antelope of the wide open plains as well as of open woodland and scattered acacia. They are able to live in quite dry regions by obtaining the moisture they need from the vegetation they eat. They are shy, alert, and possessed of excellent senses, particularly eyesight. They are found in herds, often of 20 or more, sometimes of as many as 200. Bulls sometimes congregate in small herds, and solitary old bulls are quite common. Eland are in general peaceful animals.

The East African species has a wide range, being found in localized habitat throughout northern and southern Uganda and most of Kenya, with the exception of the far northwestern areas and the coastal belt, and in most parts of Tanzania.

Livingstone's eland is scattered through Mozambique, Botswana, Zimbabwe-Rhodesia, Angola, and southeastern Zaire, and is kept on private property in South Africa.

Lord Derby's eland is found in the woodland regions of the Central African Republic, southern Chad, southwest Sudan, and Cameroon. The Western giant eland, which was once plentiful and ranged from Senegal to northern Nigeria, is found now in the Nikola-Kobia Park and in the upper Gambia, in Senegal, in southwestern Mali, and in the Niger region. The Cape eland is to be found in the Giants Castle Game Reserve in Natal, and from the northern part of the Cape province to the Zambezi River. [BH]

Greater Kudu *(Strepsiceros strepsiceros)*

This is the second largest antelope, and the largest member of the bushbuck group. A male can stand up to 5 feet (152 cm) at the shoulder and weigh up to 500 lb (227 kg). Its horns are spiralled and spread outward; the record horns, from the Transvaal, measure $70\frac{1}{2}$ inches (179 cm). The females are hornless.

The greater kudu is gray in color, with brownish markings, and has up to thirteen vertical white stripes over the shoulders and back. It has a mane that runs down to its shoulders, giving it a slightly humped look; the male has a mane on the front of its neck, too.

The males are often solitary, but it is common to encounter a group of a dozen or more animals, accompanied by a male, although three or four is more normal with the northern and western varieties.

Greater kudu are fond of rocky hills, broken with thorn scrub and acacia woodland, and they are frequently found in hot, dry areas bordering on deserts. In the south, they are more often found on low scrub and rolling or broken flat miombo forest. They never venture onto open plains, but stay close to cover at all times. They do not move during the day but feed during the first hour of daylight and at dusk.

There are three varieties of greater kudu—the northern, southern, and western—but the only significant difference between them is the larger horns of the southern variety. Taken together, they have a wide range, being found in Chad, Sudan, Ethiopia, southern Somalia, northwestern Kenya, northeastern Uganda, most of Tanzania, Zambia (where they are plentiful), Mozambique, Botswana, Zimbabwe-Rhodesia, Namibia-Southwest Africa, Angola, and South Africa.

They can be hunted by tracking in some areas and, indeed, this is often the only way to locate them. In some types of terrain, such as the Singida district of Tanzania, they can be spotted from hillsides, or glassed at dawn and dusk, feeding on the edges of riverine bush or close-to-heavy scrub. They are alert, wary, and elegant; the greater kudu is one of the most sought-after trophies of Africa. [BH]

Lesser Kudu (*Strepsiceros imberbis*)

A big male of this antelope group weighs up to 230 lb (104 kg) and stands 40 inches (102 cm) at the shoulder. Horns are spiralled, and a good head will have horns at least 27 inches (69 cm) long; some have exceeded 30 inches (76 cm). The does have no horns.

The lesser kudu buck is slate-gray, and the doe is fawn to buff in coloration. Both usually have nine vertical white stripes over the shoulders and back.

Bucks are mostly solitary, while the females and young form small herds of up to half a dozen animals.

The species is alert and wary and, when alarmed, the lesser kudus utter a call like the bark of a dog. They are always encountered in bush or in low scrubland in semi-arid country, among rocky and broken hills, and escarpments, and they are never found on open plains. They obtain the moisture they need from the vegetation they browse on, and so can exist without access to drinking water.

The lesser kudu has a range restricted to central and southern Somalia, where it is common, southern and eastern Ethiopia, the Karamoja district of Uganda, the northern and eastern regions of Kenya, and northern Tanzania. It is best hunted in the early morning and late evening, when its movements may be observed from hilltops, using glasses. [BH]

Nyala (*Tragelaphus angasi*)

The nyala is part of the bushbuck subfamily and has many characteristics in common with the bushbuck. A mature nyala bull weighs between 250 and 300 lb (113 and 136 kg) and stands about 42 inches (107 cm) at the shoulder. Only the males have horns; a head of 28 inches (71 cm) or more would be a good trophy, while the record is $33\frac{3}{8}$ inches (85 cm). The horns are spiralled.

The males are larger than the cows, which are conspicuously marked with vertical white stripes on the shoulders and body, in a manner that resembles the kudu.

Nyala live in small family groups comprising females and young, sometimes accompanied by a bull. Bulls congregate in small groups, and

(Top) **NYALA** (*Tragelaphus angasi*).
(Lower) **CAPE ELAND** (*Taurotragus oryx*).
(Opposite) **LESSER KUDU** (*Strepsiceros imberbis*).

90

solitary bulls are common. Nyala favor thick bush and riverine forest, and they often feed in the same areas day after day, being found never far from water.

Of the two subspecies, the common nyala is found in Mozambique as far north as the Zambezi River valley, and in the Shire valley in Malawi. There are a few in the northeastern part of the Kruger National Park in South Africa, and on private property in Zululand. The mountain nyala is found only in Ethiopia, at high altitudes in western Harar Province, the northwestern Bale Provinces, in Arusi Province, and in the chain of mountains from Mount Badda toward Mount Nkolo. [BH]

Sable Antelope *(Hippotragus niger)*

Sable bulls are black, can weigh up to 500 lb (227 kg), and stand up to 54 inches (137 cm) high at the shoulder. The cows are brown and smaller. Both bulls and cows have annulated horns; the cows' are much thinner and straighter than the bulls', which have attained lengths of 52 inches (132 cm) in Zambia and 46 inches (117 cm) in Tanzania, while the East African variety has a record of only 40 inches (102 cm). The horns sweep backward in a graceful curve, their length seemingly out of proportion to the size of the animal's body.

Sable are shy and alert, congregating in herds of usually a dozen or so, sometimes up to forty or more; each herd is dominated by a bull. Two or more bulls may herd together, while big bulls are often solitary.

Sable are found near water, often in company with other animals, zebra, for example, and otherwise favor miombo-type forest, which is usually woodland.

The common sable has quite a large range, extending from southern and western Tanzania southward through southern and western Zambia, Zimbabwe-Rhodesia, northern Botswana, most of Mozambique, the Transvaal of South Africa, and the Katanga province of southeastern Zaire. The other two subspecies—the giant and the East African—are protected in reserves in, respectively, Angola and the Shimba Hills of Kenya. [BH]

Kob *(Adenota)*

From a distance, the kob resembles the impala, although the kob is much heavier; a male is mature at $2\frac{1}{2}$ years and weighs 225 lb (102 kg); a female weighs usually around 150 lb (68 kg). The male stands about 35 inches (89 cm) at the shoulder. Kob are thus not very big but are thick-set, and they have strong legs. Their coats—greasy like those of waterbuck—are a reddish-ginger, with hair about $\frac{3}{4}$ inch (2 cm) long.

The kob's lyre-shaped horns are similar to, but much thicker than, those of the impala. Twenty-two-inch (56 cm) horns make the Rowland Ward record book, while the record for the kob is $28\frac{3}{4}$ inches (73 cm).

The kob is a plains antelope, remaining out in the open even during the mid-day heat. There is no limited breeding season, fawns being seen at all times of year. Large harems congregate on the breeding grounds, which are territorial, and a single male will remain on his territory, enticing females with whistles, and fighting off other males. Occasionally, herds of up to forty males gather together and wander from one breeding ground to another.

There are three varieties of kob—the Uganda, the white-eared, and the western—and they have different ranges. The Uganda kob is confined mostly to the western areas of Uganda, although a few occur in southern Karamoja while, across the border with Kenya, there is a very limited and protected population in the Kitale district. In the west, it occurs in eastern Zaire to the Rusindi-Rutshuru plains, where it is quite plentiful.

The white-eared kob occurs in the southern Sudan, south of Malakal, along the White Nile to Bor, and also from the Bahr el Ghazal region to Gambela in Ethiopia.

The western kob occurs in southern Chad, the Central African Republic, and westward through Cameroon and all the way to Gambia. [BH]

Roan Antelope *(Hippotragus equinus)*

A good bull of this antelope species will weigh up to 600 lb (272 kg) and stand up to 54 inches (137 cm) at the shoulder. For its size, the horns of the male are disappointing, measuring anything from 24 inches (61 cm) upward for an acceptable trophy, over 30 inches (76 cm) for a good East

African head, while the record, which comes from Zimbabwe-Rhodesia, is 39 inches (99 cm). The females are smaller than the bulls and have horns which are thinner and usually, but not always, shorter than the bulls'.

The roan antelope's name well describes its coloration, which is the same for bulls and cows. They congregate in herds, usually of no more than a dozen, except in the Karamoja area of southern Uganda, where they are to be found in relatively large numbers, and where herds of up to 100 head have been recorded. They have a soundly based reputation for being aggressive and will protect themselves against predators.

They are true plains animals, found never far from water, and they frequently associate with other animals, including zebra, topi, giraffe, and even waterbuck. In some areas, they live wholly in the open, while in others, they live in open woodland or miombo forest. They graze and browse, and will browse particularly at the height of the dry season or after grass fires.

Their range is extensive, but they are not found in great numbers in any part of it, except in the Karamoja region. They are found in northeastern Zaire, northern Uganda, the Ankole district of southern Uganda, fairly commonly in parts of Tanzania, rarely in Kenya, and in scattered pockets through the Sudan in the upper Bahr el Ghazal area, the Blue Nile region, the upper Atbara, and the Setit River valley. They are found also in the Central African Republic, southern Chad to northern Cameroon, in the Ivory Coast, southern Senegal, and southwestern Mali. They are widespread in Zambia, especially in the Luangwa valley, and occur locally in Zimbabwe-Rhodesia and northern Botswana, and rarely in Mozambique. They are quite common in Angola where suitable habitat exists. [BH]

Lechwe *(Kobus leche)*

A male lechwe weighs up to 180 lb (82 kg) and stands around 37 inches (94 cm) at the shoulder. Only the males have horns, which are annulated, lyre-shaped, and often spread very wide. A head of 28 inches (71 cm) would make a good trophy, while the record is 34¼ inches (87 cm).

These beautiful antelope congregate in herds of more than fifty head, and they will happily share their environment with other species: roan antelope and reedbuck, for example, often being seen in their company. The males often form herds on their own but do not move far from the mating herds.

There are four races of lechwe: Mrs Gray's or Nile; red; Kafue; and black. Mrs Gray's is really a semi-aquatic animal and often feeds in shallow water on the flood plains it inhabits; its hooves are slightly elongated and suit its environment. It is found in the swamps and flood plains of the southern Sudan, from Tonga and Lake No along the White Nile as far south as Bor. It is also found at Lake Nyubor and the Bahr el Ghazal River, and in the Machar marshes east of Malakal.

The red lechwe is found in central and southeastern Angola, western Zambia, northwestern Botswana, and southeastern Zaire. Kafue lechwe are found only in southern Zambia on the Kafue Flats, while black lechwe are found on the flood plains southeast of Lake Bangweulu and the lower Lulimala River in Zambia. [BH]

Puku *(Adenota vardoni)*

This antelope is related to the kob, waterbuck, and lechwe, and resembles the red lechwe in many respects, being similarly colored—a bright golden yellow—with annulated horns; it is only slightly smaller in size.

They congregate in small herds, inhabiting open grassland, lightly wooded savanna, and miombo forest. They are found in southern Tanzania, along the Rufiji and Kilombero rivers and at Lake Rukwa, southward through Zambia, in the Katanga province of southeastern Zaire, in parts of Angola, and in northern Botswana. [BH]

Three types of horn on African antelopes. *(1)* Puku, seen from in front; *(2)* roan; and *(3)* sable, of which the horns are much longer, more heavily ringed, and more backward curving than those of the roan.

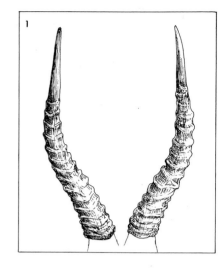

Reedbuck (Redunca)

Reedbuck together comprise three species and eight subspecies and collectively have a very wide range indeed. Their differentiation is based on variations in coloration and the size and forms of the horns.

The Bohor reedbuck stands about 30 inches (76 cm) high and weighs about 75 lb (34 kg). Only the males have horns, and a good trophy head will have horns of over 11 inches (28 cm), while the record is over 17 inches (43 cm). The southern reedbuck is the largest of the reedbucks and can weigh up to 170 lb (75 kg) and stand up to 37 inches (95 cm) at the shoulder. Horns measure 15 inches (38 cm) on average; the record is 18 inches (46 cm). The mountain reedbuck is very much smaller, usually weighing no more than 40 lb (18 kg) and standing 24 inches (61 cm), or a bit more, at the shoulder. A horn over 4 inches (10 cm) would be a good trophy.

Unlike other varieties of reedbuck, which live in open grassland and lightly wooded plains, the mountain reedbuck live on quite open hillsides, often on rocky hillocks.

Sometimes, a very large population of reedbuck is found together in one area, but these animals do not congregate in true herds. They usually travel and feed in pairs or singly.

Their range stretches from the west coast of Africa, from Senegal to Nigeria, and then through Sudan and Ethiopia, Uganda, eastern Zaire, Kenya, Tanzania, and through nearly all of southern Africa. [BH]

Hartebeest (Alcelaphus)

The hartebeest is an antelope that acquired its name in southern Africa but which has a spread over much of the continent south of the Sahara. With some variations, they are about 4 feet (125 cm) high at the shoulder, weigh about 300 to 320 lb (136 to 145 kg), and have a brownish-gingery coloration. Their horns are mounted on a pedicle and are very thick but seldom attain a length of more than 23 in (58 cm).

For the most part, hartebeest favor wide, open plains where they congregate in herds of seldom more than twenty to thirty animals, but usually much fewer. Solitary animals of either sex are common. They mix freely with other game animals and, as their alarm signal is a loud snort which alerts all other animals in the vicinity, they can pose problems for the hunter.

They have an unusual gait, and their front legs appear longer than their back legs; when not seriously alarmed, they move in a manner called "stotting"—a peculiar bouncing run characteristic of several other animals, especially the Thomson's gazelle.

Of the eight different species of hartebeest, Hunter's is exceptional in being slightly smaller (40 inches/102 cm at the shoulder) and slightly less heavy (260 lb/118 kg). Its horns resemble those of the impala. It occurs along both banks of the Tana river, east of Bura, in Kenya, but is found in heavier concentrations north of the Tana, where its range extends into Somalia, southeast of Afmadu. It is found in flat semi-desert thorn scrub, and while it is very localized, it is populous in the areas where it is at home, belying claims that it has become extinct. It is protected in Kenya.

Coke's hartebeest is found in southern Kenya, and as far south as central Tanzania. The Lelwel, or Jackson's, hartebeest is common in western and northern Uganda, but rare in central Kenya, where it has been protected for years. The Lelwel is also found in Chad and the Central African Republic.

Two rare forms are Swayne's and the Tora hartebeest. The former is found only in Ethiopia and there mostly only in the Borana region. The Tora occurs only in the border area between Ethiopia and the Sudan, as far north as the Dinder and Rahad river areas.

The Cape hartebeest is also very localized, occurring only on private estates in South Africa, and in the Wankie region of Zimbabwe-Rhodesia.

The western variety of hartebeest is found in the border area between Chad and the Central African Republic, and also in northern Cameroon, the Ivory Coast, Guinea, and Mali.

The Lichtenstein's hartebeest is mostly concentrated in southwestern Tanzania and western Zambia, but is also found in Malawi, the Katanga province of Zaire, in Mozambique, and in eastern Angola. It prefers to live in open woodland and miombo forest than in open, short-grass plains. [BH]

Wildebeest (Connochaetes)

These animals have manes and tails resembling those of a horse, a head resembling that of an ox, but horns like those of a buffalo. The name "wildebeest" is from Afrikaans, and "gnu" comes from a Hottentot language.

Gnu stand hardly higher than a hartebeest, being about 50 inches (125 cm) at the shoulder. They are considerably heavier, however, and a mature adult will weigh about 500 lb (227 kg). Both sexes are horned, the cows having horns that are much thinner than the bulls', and the record head has a spread of 33½ inches (85 cm).

About ninety-five percent of the cows calve annually, and it has been estimated that only some fifteen percent of the calves survive, most of the remainder falling prey to lions, hyenas, and other predators.

The white-tailed gnu, or black wildebeest, is now found only on private land in the Orange Free State and in parts of Natal, in South Africa.

The brindled gnu, or blue wildebeest, is found in Mozambique and westward into Zambia, Malawi, Zimbabwe-Rhodesia, Botswana, Angola, and southern Tanzania. A few occur on private land in South Africa. Neither of the two species mentioned forms herds of more than about eighty head, and the animals live in open mopane, miombo, and acacia woodland.

The most populous subspecies is the white-bearded gnu, which has a range from south-central Kenya through north-central Tanzania. Some 350,000 share the Serengeti Plains with 180,000 zebra and over a half million gazelle, not to mention other fauna. [BH]

Topi (Damaliscus korrigum)

Topi resemble hartebeest, having the same sloping back and long face, although their horns are not mounted on a pedicle. Their coloration is very distinctive: the major part of the body is a dark maroon-chocolate, the forelegs, part of the shoulders, the rear legs, and the flanks are a gunmetal blue, and the coat sometimes looks like watered silk. With a height of about 50 inches (125 cm), they are about the same size as most hartebeest, but weigh slightly less, at 300 lb (136 kg). Both sexes have horns, those of the cows being less annulated, and thinner; the record length, from Uganda, is over 28 inches (71 cm), but the average is about 20 inches (50 cm).

They are common in southwest Uganda, where they congregate in herds of up to several thousand, but elsewhere over their range, they are relatively scarce and occur in herds of no more than a dozen or so. They are animals of the short-grass plains, but in the south of their range, they may be found in light woodland and miombo forest.

Apart from in Uganda, they occur in Kenya, Senegal, Upper Volta, Niger, Nigeria, Chad, the Sudan, Ethiopia, southern Somalia, and Tanzania. [BH]

Grant's Gazelle (Gazella granti)

The largest of the five subspecies of the Grant's gazelle, the southern variety, stands about 35 inches (89 cm) at the shoulder and weighs about 165 lb (79 kg), while the horns of the bucks can reach a length of 30 inches (76 cm) or even more, making for impressive trophies.

(Above left) **TOPI** (*Damaliscus korrigum*).
(Left) **WHITE-BEARDED GNU** (*Connochaetes taurinus albojubatus*).
(Above right) **LECHWE** (*Kobus leche*).

Coloration varies only slightly among the subspecies: the face has white, black, and brown vertical markings, the upper body is short-haired and light brown, the sides are fawn, and the underbelly white. The hind quarters and the tail, which has a black tuft on it, are white, and the legs are fawn on their outer edges and white on the rest. The females, which have thin, short (maximum 14 inches/36 cm) horns, may be confused by an inexperienced observer with the Thomson's gazelle, for they have lateral broad black or dark gray stripes.

The southern Grant's gazelle congregates in herds of up to forty head, and herds of up to about a dozen bulls are fairly common. Calves are born at all times of year.

The species is totally independent of drinking water, for these gazelle obtain the moisture they need from the vegetation they eat. They are often found in the remote, dry desert country in northern Kenya east of Lake Rudolf, where no other game is to be seen at the height of the dry season. They are also found in the lush Masai highlands, though never in green forest or bush, but always out on the high, sometimes cold, windswept plains, or in light acacia woodland, dry thorn scrub, or even camifora woodland. Grant's gazelle are often seen together with giraffe, zebra, Thomson's gazelle, and wildebeest.

Within the areas they inhabit, they are one of the most common species. Taken together, the five subspecies occur in Uganda eastward from Karamoja, through northern Kenya almost to the coast, southward through northern and central Tanzania, and then again in southern Somalia as far north as the Juba River and the Borana region of southern Ethiopia, and westward into a small part of the southern Sudan.

Bright's gazelle, one of the subspecies, is found only in the Karamoja region of eastern Uganda. It is slightly smaller than the southern, with straighter, smaller horns, and a good trophy would measure 26 inches (66 cm), while one of 22 inches (56 cm) would meet Rowland Ward's entry requirements.

Two other subspecies, Peters's gazelle and the north Kenya Grant, are virtually indistinguishable to all but the expert eye. They have shorter horns than the southern subspecies, and a different coloration of the hind quarters and flanks.

Roberts's gazelle is found in the far south of Kenya and the far north of Tanzania, along the borders between the two countries. It has large, heavy horns, the tips of which veer outward at a sharp angle, almost horizontally, about halfway up the horn. The subspecies is thus easily identifiable.

The Grant from whom this gazelle takes its name is James Grant, born in Scotland in 1827, an explorer and the author of "A Walk Through Africa" (1864); he died in 1892. [BH]

Thomson's Gazelle (Gazella thomsoni)

An adult male "tommy," as these antelope are often called, weighs about 60 lb (27 kg) and stands about 24 inches (61 cm) at the shoulder. Both sexes are horned, but the horns of the females are small, often twisted or deformed, and sometimes altogether absent. Those of the males have reached a length of 17 inches (43 cm), while horns of 14 inches (36 cm) would make a respectable trophy.

Males and females have the same coloration: pronounced facial markings with vertical black, white, and light gray stripes (resembling those on the Grant's gazelle), a dark-brown dorsal area edged with a lighter shade of brown, and a white underbelly. A lateral black stripe, about 3 inches (8 cm) wide, extends from the shoulder to the front of the hind leg.

Tommys are found in herds of up to several hundred, while males that have failed to maintain a place in a breeding herd congregate with others in like condition, occasionally making attempts to gain or regain lost territories and harems. Tommys fight frequently among themselves.

Thomson's gazelles are attractive, energetic, and colorful animals, are plains antelopes, and are never found far from water; they are occasionally found in light acacia woodland. They are restless and migrate annually.

They are very populous within their range, the northern extent of which is Maralal, in central Kenya, and which stretches southward over the Laikapia Plateau, through the southern Masailand of Kenya, and the northern Masailand of Tanzania.

This gazelle is named after Joseph Thomson (1858–1895), a Scot who was already active in African exploration while still in his early twenties. [BH]

Impala (Aepyceros melampus)

These antelope, which can in a single leap cover 35 feet (11 m) or reach a height of 12 feet (3.6 m), form breeding herds several hundred strong, and all-male herds of up to fifty bucks. The breeding herds are served by, at most, a few young males, and sometimes by only one, who is constantly challenged by others in fights that, on occasion, end in the death of one of the combatants.

Only the bucks are horned, and their horns, which have an S-shape when viewed from the side, may exceed 39 inches (100 cm) in length, although 27 inches (69 cm) would still be a good trophy. A buck stands about 32 inches (81 cm) at most at the shoulder and weighs about 180 lb (82 kg).

Impala favor lightly wooded country and low thorn scrub but, sometimes, venture quite far out onto the plains. They are never found in really dry country and seldom move far from water. They are largely territorial and never move far from their home areas.

There are three subspecies, of which the East African has the largest horns. It has a very wide range, from a good part of southern Uganda, eastward into Kenya as far north as Maralal, southward and eastward toward the coast, and into northern Masailand in Tanzania.

The southern impala is found in the eastern part of South Africa, right through Mozambique, Zimbabwe-Rhodesia, Botswana, southeastern Angola, Zambia, the Katanga province of Zaire, Malawi, and southern Tanzania.

The third subspecies, the Angolan or black-faced impala, is distinguished from the other two by its black face. It is found in southwestern Angola and over the border in Namibia-Southwest Africa.

The common name of the species derives from Zulu. [BH]

Springbok (Antidorcas marsupialis)

This pseudo-gazelle now has an extremely limited range on private land in South Africa and Namibia-Southwest Africa. It was once exceedingly numerous and, in herds of hundreds of thousands, would eat everything in its path. It is larger than the Thomson's gazelle, which it resembles in coloration and habits. It prefers short-grass plains.

The record for springbok horns is over 19 inches (48 cm), but any trophy over 17 inches (43 cm) would be considered a very good one. [BH]

Duiker (Cephalophus & Sylvicapra)

This antelope family acquired its common name from the South African Dutch word meaning "diver," used to describe the animals' habit of disappearing into thickets at any sign of danger. There are no fewer than twenty-one subspecies or varieties of duiker, and their collective range covers the whole of Africa, except for the countries north of the Sahara.

All duikers are small: most stand about 20 inches (51 cm) at the shoulder, while one subspecies, the yellow-backed, can be as much as 26 inches (66 cm), and another, the blue, not more than 10 inches (25 cm). Most subspecies have arched backs, but the four bush subspecies have straight.

One subspecies, the red duiker, has horns on both sexes. Otherwise, only bucks have horns: most have horns that slope backward, but the bush subspecies have straight horns. [BH]

Oribi (Ourebia ourebi)

These are diminutive antelope standing up to 26 inches (66 cm) at the shoulder and weighing around 38 lb (17 kg). The record horns come from Uganda and measure $7\frac{5}{8}$ inches (19 cm). The females are hornless.

In addition to the animal known simply as the oribi, there are two varieties, Haggard's oribi and the Kenya oribi; together, they have a very wide range throughout sub-Saharan Africa. They are found from northern Ethiopia southward through the eastern Sudan, Uganda, Kenya, Tanzania, and all the way to South Africa, and westward from Ethiopia to Senegal.

They live on open grassland, seldom far from water, and their only refuge is usually tall grass, where they lie up during the heat of the day. They run for cover when alarmed, first emitting a high-pitched whistle.

They do not form herds but stay in pairs or family groups of three; in some areas, it is possible to see several hundred sharing an area of short grass. [BH]

Klipspringer (Oreotragus oreotragus)

These small antelope of the rocky hills, cliffs, escarpments, and kopjes (small rocky hillocks of South Africa) are goat-like in their surefootedness on even the most precarious rock ledges. They stand a mere 22 inches (56 cm) at the shoulder, weigh up to 40 lb (18 kg), and are usually a dull gray in color; they blend in well against backgrounds of rocky hillsides and outcrops. Their hair is coarse, spiny, and falls out readily. Horns are usually, but not always, absent in the females; the record is $6\frac{1}{4}$ inches (16 cm), and a reasonable trophy would measure about 4 inches (10 cm) or more.

Klipspringer are territorial and are usually seen singly or in family groups of three or four. For the most part, they are browsers and, while able to do without water if juicy leaves can be had, will drink if it is available.

They are not particularly numerous but, within their very specialized habitat, they have a very wide range—from northern Ethiopia to South Africa, and westward through sub-Saharan Africa to northern Nigeria.

The name of the species is from Afrikaans: "klip" meaning rock and "springer" meaning jumper. [BH]

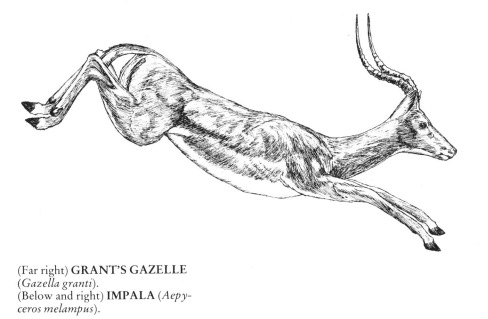

(Far right) **GRANT'S GAZELLE**
(*Gazella granti*).
(Below and right) **IMPALA** (*Aepy-ceros melampus*).

(Above) **SPRINGBOK** (*Antidorcas marsupialis*).
(Right) **ORIBI** (*Ourebia ourebi*).
(Far right) **WATERBUCK** (*Kobus ellipsiprymnus*).

Waterbuck *(Kobus ellipsiprymnus & K. defassa)*

The waterbuck is a stocky, heavily built animal, rather slow on its feet. The bulls weigh up to 470 lb (213 kg) and stand 50 inches (127 cm) at the shoulder. They are usually a gray-buff color, and the females are often reddish-brown, but sometimes a light gray. The hindquarters are marked with a white ring (common waterbuck) or a white patch (Defassa). The waterbuck's coat is long, shaggy, and very greasy.

The bulls have horns, which are annulated and curve forward slightly. The record, on a head from Uganda, is 39 inches (99 cm).

Waterbuck are never found far from water but, on the other hand, are rarely to be seen actually in water. They like swampy areas and riverine forest, and they graze or browse in the open, in light woodland or in very open savanna. They are most active early in the morning or in the late evening, and spend the day in light shade, not necessarily in a thicket.

Large herds are common—up to fifty or sixty animals—but smaller herds of around a dozen, containing a single bull, are most common. Bulls sometimes congregate in small herds, and single bulls are common.

There are six varieties of the two species: the common, Sing-Sing, and Rhodesian waterbucks, and the Defassa, Uganda Defassa, and Angolan Defassa waterbucks. Their collective range is very great. It extends from South Africa through Mozambique, Zimbabwe-Rhodesia, northern Botswana, Zambia, Malawi, Tanzania, Somalia, southeastern Ethiopia, Zaire, Uganda, Rwanda, Burundi, the Central African Republic, southern Chad, Cameroon, the Ivory Coast, Guinea, Sierra Leone, Mali, Senegal, and most of Angola. [BH]

Warthog *(Phacochœrus aethiopicus)*

This animal gets its name from the large, bulbous, wart-like bumps on its face. It is dull gray in color and has a thick mane from the back of the head down its spine, but has otherwise little hair. A big hog will weigh up to 170 lb (77 kg), although the average weight is less, while a good pair of trophy-size tusks will measure 10 inches (25 cm) or more; tusks of over 23 inches (58 cm) have been collected. Sows have tusks that are usually much shorter and thinner, but tusks of over 10 inches (25 cm) have been recorded. The lower tusks are razor-sharp, being constantly honed against the upper tusks as the animal eats. The animal uses the lower ones to dig with, grubbing up roots and grass, and kneels to do so.

Warthogs are sometimes seen in sounders—the group term for swine of all sorts—or in family groups of three or four. They are found all over sub-Saharan Africa in a variety of climates and terrain, from the intense heat of low desert scrub to the bitter cold of highland plains, and from the edges of tropical rain forests to thick scrubland and savanna.

They often inhabit holes or burrows, sometimes those that ant bears have abandoned or been ejected from. Warthogs enter their holes by backing into them, the better to be able to come charging out, head first. When hurt or threatened, they are fearless and have been known to attack hunters; they are very quick on their feet and are brave, hardy, and very intelligent. [BH]

Bush Pig, or Red River Hog *(Potamochoerus porcus)*

This diminutive pig, which weighs around 50 lb (23 kg), has a wide distribution throughout the equatorial rain and riverine forests of sub-Saharan Africa, all the way from west to east, and southward as far as South Africa.

Its reddish hair covers its entire body, while its long, semi-pointed ears are topped with a small tuft of hair. Its tusks are small, usually not exceeding 2 inches (5 cm).

Bush pigs are solitary or live in small family groups. They can be encountered on game trails and in small glades in the early morning or evening, when they can be hunted on foot. [BH]

Following page: (Opposite) **WART HOG** *(Phacochœrus aethiopicus)*. (Inset) **BUSH PIG, or RED RIVER HOG** *(Potamochoerus porcus)*.

Giant Forest Hog *(Hylochoerus meinertzhageni)*

The giant forest hog is related to the wild boar of Europe. A large male stands some 36 inches (91 cm) at the shoulder and can weigh over 400 lb (181 kg). It has a coat of coarse black hair and has unimpressive tusks. If wounded or cornered, it will not hesitate to attack. It can make for an interesting hunt.

It occurs in West Africa, Zaire, Uganda, Kenya, southern Ethiopia, and southwestern Sudan. In the western part of this range, its habitat is equatorial rain forest at relatively low elevations while, in Uganda, it includes both equatorial rain forest and riverine bush at elevations of between 2,000 and 3,000 feet (609 and 914 m); in Kenya, it is found in higher rain forests, generally over 6,000 feet (1,829 m) in the large mountain ranges. [BH]

Addax *(Addax nasomaculatus)*

Addax are among the few antelope that are true desert dwellers. They live in hostile, waterless country southward from the Atlas mountains. They are fairly plentiful in the Faya and Mourdi depression areas of northern Chad and are also found in north-central Niger and the northwest of the Sudan. The rainfall in the Sahara region is, at best, 10 inches (25 cm) a year, but over much of the range of the addax, there is no rainfall whatever.

They survive by eating hardy desert vegetation, which grows very quickly once there is any rain, and addax are adept at finding it. When conditions are exceptionally dry, the herds of addax that normally number about forty animals—although they can be as much as several hundred—break up into smaller groups to seek forage.

Addax have largely white coats, with a tinge of fawn commencing in front of the hind legs, running laterally forward to the neck and chest, where the coloration darkens to brown. The face is divided by a white band below, above, and between the eyes. The forehead is dark brown.

They have hooves well adapted for walking on loose sand, for they can splay out (as the sitatunga's can), but this is a handicap on firm ground, such as roads built in the desert: large numbers of addax have been run down by vehicles.

A mature male addax weighs about 270 lb (122 kg) and stands about 40 inches (100 cm) at the shoulder. Both sexes have horns that are annulated and spiralled: the record is 43 inches (108 cm) measured along the spiral. They make magnificent trophies, and the animal is worthy of being hunted in its hostile environment by sporting means. [BH]

Scimitar-horned Oryx *(Oryx algazel)*

The range of this oryx is limited to the peripheral grassland that extends from Mauretania south of the Sahara eastward through northern Mali and southern Algeria to central and northern Niger, Chad, and the northwestern Sudan.

Scimitar-horned oryx are able to exist without water to drink, for they rely on desert plants and grasses to provide the moisture they need. While they sometimes run in herds of up to about fifty animals, during exceptionally dry conditions they will disperse into smaller groups—as addax do—in search of grazing. Solitary animals are most unusual.

This is the only oryx to have backward-curving horns: these are very beautiful and long, with a record of just over 50 inches (127 cm) and an average of upward of 40 inches (102 cm). A good male is similar in size to the Beisa and fringe-eared oryx, standing about 48 inches (122 cm) at the shoulder, and weighing from about 380 to 400 lb (172 to 181 kg). Very few sportsmen, but altogether too many illegal hunters, have collected this species, so that in some areas its numbers have been sadly depleted. [BH]

101

Gemsbok *(Oryx gazella)*

This is the southern variety, and the largest, of the oryx: a mature male gemsbok can weigh up to 500 lb (227 kg) and stand over 48 inches (122 cm) at the shoulder. The females often have longer, but thinner, horns than the males—a characteristic of oryx. Their horns can reach a length of 48 inches (122 cm), although 40 inches (102 cm) would be a good trophy.

Gemsbok live, but are scarce, in the dry deserts of the Karoo, north of the Orange River; however, they have their strongholds in the Kalahari desert of Botswana and on private lands in Namibia-Southwest Africa. A subspecies, called the Angola gemsbok, is found in the Mocamedes area of southwestern Angola.

Gemsbok have black-and-white heads, black flank strips, and black patches on rumps and hind legs. They can exist indefinitely without water to drink, for they can derive enough from Tsama melons and succulent desert bulbs. Herds of twenty animals are not uncommon, although a more usual herd numbers about six or more. Solitary bulls are sometimes seen. [BH]

Beisa & Fringe-eared Oryx *(Oryx beisa beisa & O. b. callotis)*

These are two varieties of East African oryx, only one of which has fringes on its ears; otherwise, they are almost the same, having the same tan coloration, the same distinctive black-on-white facial markings, the same size, and the same horn formation (although the horns of the Beisa oryx tend to be the smaller). Big bulls weigh up to 450 lb (204 kg) and, like other species of oryx, they stand about 48 inches (122 cm) at the shoulder. A good set of horns from a bull will measure upward of 27 inches (69 cm), but cows will often have longer horns.

These oryx are animals of the dry bush country and its scattered acacia scrubland, and of country that is seasonally a desert. They can exist with little or no drinking water for long periods, although they will drink readily if water is available.

The fringe-eared oryx inhabits the low bush country of southern Kenya, northern Tanzania, and central Masailand.

The Beisa is found more widely, from northwestern Uganda (in Karamoja, where it is almost exclusively confined to the Matheniko plains), eastward and northward into southern Ethiopia (in the Omo River region), and southward into the northern Frontier District of central Kenya and the Rift Valley. It occurs also in southern Somalia.

Oryx are alert, wary antelope that congregate in herds of up to 100 animals; solitary bulls are common, but herds of bulls are not. They have excellent senses, particularly eyesight, and flee at the first sign of danger. They have great stamina and can provide good hunting.

They are often hunted at quite long ranges, sometimes over 450 feet (140 m), and it should be noted that the skin in their neck region is exceptionally thick—over an inch (2.5 cm) in most cases—affording them protection when bulls fight for possession of the herd. [BH]

Gerenuk *(Litocranius walleri)*

The gerenuk, or Waller's gazelle, is an exclusively East African animal, inhabiting arid thorn scrub and semi-desert brushland. It has a slender body and a long neck, and while it is called "swala twiga" in Swahili, or "giraffe antelope", it has an awkward gait resembling that of a camel, and when it runs through the brush, it stretches its neck out straight, parallel to the ground.

It has spindly, long legs, is reddish-brown, and weighs less than 90 lb (41 kg) as a rule; a bull stands up to 40 inches (101 cm) at the shoulder. The horns are fine for so small an antelope, being thick, annulated, and lyre-shaped, and a good head will exceed 12 inches (30 cm); the record is $17\frac{1}{8}$ inches (43.5 cm). The females are hornless.

(Below) **ADDAX** (*Addax nasomaculatus*).
(Opposite, top) **GERENUK** (*Litocranius walleri*).
(Opposite, lower) **GEMSBOK** (*Oryx gazella*).

The gerenuk's range is limited, but it is by no means scarce. It occurs from southern Ethiopia southward into Kenya east of Lake Rudolf, throughout northern Kenya, and through central Kenya into northern Tanzania. There is also a large population in southern Somalia.

Gerenuk are totally independent of drinking water; they browse on thorn scrub and can stand on their hind legs to reach it at a height of 8 feet (2.4 m), thus giving them access to a source of food not otherwise eaten by browsers.

They are often found in herds of a dozen or more, and while smaller family groups containing two or more adult males are common, solitary males are rare. Gerenuk feed and move until quite late in the morning, when they retire into the cover of the thorn scrub to emerge again from 5 o'clock onward. [BH]

Dik-dik *(Madoqua* & *Rhynchotragus)*

Dik-dik are tiny antelope that stand no more than 14 inches (36 cm) high at the shoulder and usually weigh less than 10 lb (4.5 kg). They are very territorial, and the males fight aggressively in defence of their territories. They use the same places time and time again to deposit their droppings, which accumulate in small mounds. When frightened or distressed, dik-dik utter a high-pitched sound of alarm.

They lie up in the heat of the day, emerging late in the evening to browse through the night; they are still active in the early morning. They are most often found in dry lowland semi-desert and thorn scrub and, being totally independent of drinking water, are often found in areas where other game is scarce or absent. They are not confined solely to

(Left) **NILE CROCODILE**
(*Crocodylus niloticus*).
(Below) **HIPPOPOTAMUS** (*Hippopotamus amphibius*).
A Two beasts with three senses above the water: hearing, sight, and smell.

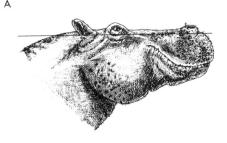

A

desert areas, for they are found on the high, windswept, short-grass plateaux of southern Kenya and north-central Tanzania; here, and in the lowlands, they are found in scrub, along dry watercourses, and near rocky foothills where there is suitable cover.

There are no less than eight species of dik-dik in Africa, with the biggest concentration in East Africa, where they are common. The two most common species are Grant's and Guenther's dik-dik. The former has a range that stretches from central and southern Somalia westward to southern Ethiopia, southeastern Uganda, and eastward throughout Kenya (except in the central highlands and the Lake Victoria district), then southward into northern and central Tanzania. Guenther's dik-dik is found only in central Somalia and westward through southern Ethiopia and southward through the northern regions of Kenya. [BH]

Hippopotamus (Hippopotamus amphibius)

While hippos occur in almost all the swamps, rivers, and lakes of Africa south of the Sahara, and are relentlessly hunted for food in many parts of Africa, there is absolutely no sport in shooting them in the water, where they spend most of the day resting. They lie submerged during the heat of the day, with only their noses and eyes above water.

In areas where they have been persecuted, they will seek the shelter of papyrus swamps during daylight hours. They emerge at night to feed on land and move great distances from water, sometimes as much as five miles (8 km), in search of food. Their primary food is grass, which is not bitten off by the teeth, but clipped off by the lips which are squarish, coarse, very tough, and have quite sharp edges.

Hippos often establish their own roads, very well-trodden paths, quite smooth, with a ridge of grass along the center, as if made by a narrow-wheeled vehicle, for they (unlike elephants) walk with their feet slightly apart.

People often—mistakenly—think that hippos are sluggish because they are fat, but they are exceptionally fast on their feet on dry land, being able to run faster than an elephant and nearly as fast as a rhino or buffalo, and they are far more nimble than any of these species. They weigh up to 4 tons (9,000 lb/4,000 kg), can exceed 13 feet (c. 4 m) in length, and have a hide that is as thick as that of a rhino. They have been known to attack cars, and a hippo can be expected to charge if trapped out of water, or on finding that a man has carelessly interposed himself between the hippo and the water.

They have massive teeth. The lower incisors, which can achieve incredible lengths of up to 4 feet (122 cm), are curved and sharp, being constantly honed against the round, pointed upper tusks that are small only by comparison. They are used occasionally for ripping up aquatic vegetation, but their primary function is for fighting. Hippos fight savagely among themselves, often killing each other; fights commonly take place at night and are usually prompted by mating urges.

They breed throughout the year, sometimes collecting in schools of up to sixty. Cows give birth to single calves and use shallow water as a nursery. In the water, hippos can float or sink at will, and so can walk along the bed of a river or lake, although they must surface to breathe. [BH]

Crocodile (Crocodylus niloticus)

Crocodiles are found in the rivers, swamps, and lakes of Africa south of the Sahara, where they live mostly on fish, being extremely swift swimmers. Crocodiles leave the water to bask in the sun, to move to another locality, or to nest. Females bury their eggs in sand, and remain close by to guard them from the many predators that take the eggs or eat the young: baboons and monitor lizards eat the eggs, and hawks and eagles take the young, which make for the water as soon as possible after the hatching.

Although crocodiles do not hunt on land, they have exceedingly good reflexes and senses, and are not especially easy to approach. It is sometimes presumed that, because crocodiles are reptiles and have very small brains, they must therefore be of a low order of intelligence. [BH]

Sitatunga (Limnotragus spekei)

This unusual antelope ranges through the swamps and river-systems of western and central Africa, and through those of Uganda, southern Tanzania, Zambia, Mozambique, Botswana, and Angola. There are four varieties: the western, northern, Zambezi, and Island sitatunga.

Sitatunga are unusual in that they are very strong swimmers and have a hoof structure adapted for walking on thin layers of floating swamp vegetation; the hoof is elongated, being over 6 inches (15 cm) long, and can be splayed out. Sitatunga seldom venture far onto dry land, to which their hooves are unsuited, but spend most of their time either in the water or in swamps, where they are agile. They often immerse themselves until only their heads remain above water, doing so either to rest for brief intervals during the day when the weather is hot, or to avoid detection.

Their coats are long and silky. The males, which at maturity will stand up to 48 inches (123 cm) at the shoulder and weigh between 200 and 240 lb (91 to 109 kg), are a deep chestnut color, sometimes very dark, have a white chevron between the eyes, white on the insides of the ears and between the forelegs, and a stripe on the throat. Females are paler, often a dark red, and much smaller than the males.

Horns on the males (the females have no horns) are spiralled, keeled, and frequently, on old specimens, "ivoried." Each variety of sitatunga has a different maximum horn length, but any male with horns over 24 inches (61 cm) is a very good trophy.

They are solitary animals, but pairs, accompanied by a single off-spring, do occur. They possess many of the traits of the bushbuck, their alarm signal being a similar bark, or series of barks.

Contrary to popular belief, sitatunga often feed in swamps during the day. They feed at night, too, and sometimes on firm ground. In their environment of swamps, tall papyrus, and watery marshlands, they are not easy animals to hunt, within the rules of fair chase. [BH]

Chapter 5

Asian Game Animals

(Opposite, top left) **JAPANESE SEROW** (*Capricornis c. crispus*). (Opposite, top right) **TAHR** (*Hemitragus jemlahicus*). (Opposite, lower) **MARKHOR** (*Capra falconeri*).

Tahr *(Hemitragus jemlahicus)*

Tahr and blue sheep (see below) are Asian members of the goat-sheep group: they are neither true goats nor true sheep but have some characteristics of both. The tahr is similar to such wild goats as the markhor (see below) and the Siberian ibex (see below).

There are four subspecies of tahr, of which three are endangered; these are the Arabian, the Sikkim, and the Nilgiri tahr. The fourth is the Himalayan tahr, of which a healthy population inhabits the Himalayas; it has been successfully introduced into New Zealand. The subspecies can survive in extremely rugged and rocky terrain where few game species can find food or even move about.

Tahr are goat-like in appearance; an adult male may stand 40 inches (100 cm) at the shoulder and weigh 240 lb (110 kg), while the females are about three-quarters of this size. The male has a strong collared mane on the shoulders, neck, and chest, which is a paler shade of the browns and gray-blacks of the body color; the mane can be almost golden in color. In winter, tahr develop spectacular coats, for their colors deepen to match the contrasts of sunlight on snow. Their ears are small and pointed. Their underparts are hairless.

Both males and females have horns, the form of which varies somewhat among the different subspecies; their general pattern, however, is close set at the base, curving outward and downward, with a sharp front edge. The males' horns grow to a length of about 16 to 18 inches (40 to 45 cm), the females' being perhaps about 4 inches (10 cm) less.

In the Himalayas, one finds tahr within and just above the timberlines, where the beautiful monal pheasants and markhor are also to be found. This can be as high as 10,000 feet (3,000 m) in winter and 13,000 feet (4,000 m) in summer. Tahr move over these steep, rocky hillsides with a sure-footed rapidity that seems reckless to the human observer, but they can survive in this terrain, and find food, for all that they prefer the greater abundance to be found at the timberline. [GY]

Blue Sheep *(Pseudois nayaur)*

By contrast to the tahr, the blue sheep is more sheep than goat and, of its three subspecies, the Himalayan is the best known and most abundant; for ardent sheep hunters, it is also a highly prized trophy.

Body heights of adult rams are about 36 inches (90 cm), and their weights are about 175 lb (90 kg); the ewes are smaller by about one-third or one-quarter. The blue coloration of the species is seen only in the winter coats of yearling sheep, for fully grown adult sheep have darker gray-brown fleeces that are heavy in winter.

The horns on older rams are shaped somewhat like those of the tahr. They can reach a length of about 30 inches (80 cm); the ewes have horns that are at most about a quarter this size.

The Himalayan blue sheep inhabit open slopes at elevations of between 9,000 and 16,500 feet (3,000 and 5,000 m) in Tibet and Nepal. Most hunters who get access to blue sheep do so in Nepal, although it is now becoming possible to visit the People's Republic of China and travel to the western provinces, where subspecies of blue sheep can be hunted.

The Szechwan subspecies seems to exist in considerable numbers in the extremely rugged and sparsely populated region of northwestern Szechwan, and in the Tsinghai province, and southward into the Ning Ching Shan mountain range and over the border into northernmost Burma. A pygmy subspecies is fairly well distributed along the middle Salween and Mekong gorges, as far south as the Yunnan province of the Republic, which borders on Vietnam. [GY]

Takin *(Budorcas taxicolor)*

The takin, serow (see below), and goral (see below) are usually classified in a special group known as goat-antelopes; takin are the largest and, for the last thirty or forty years, have been among the rarest of Asian big game, for they inhabit the bamboo and rhododendron forests of the rugged mountainous region at the eastern end of the Himalayas, where China, Burma, and Tibet meet.

Takin have a heavy, ox-like build, with a head that, in profile, slightly resembles that of a moose or European elk, for it is large, with a humped nose and a broad muzzle. The horns rise flatly from the skull and curve outward at an angle from a bulky base. The hooves are very broad and powerful, and long pseudo-claws are prominent behind them. Males stand up to about 50 inches (130 cm) at the shoulders, females about 10 inches (25 cm) less. Males weigh up to 750 lb (350 kg).

The Szechwan subspecies, which is also found in northernmost Burma, has a strikingly golden or reddish-brown fleece, and a pleasant legend claims it as the animal whose golden fleece was sought by Jason and the Argonauts. Another subspecies, the Mishmi takin, is found in the high forests of Burma; it has a darker coat, but otherwise resembles the Szechwan subspecies.

Takin establish well-trodden trails along the mountain slopes and move in large herds in the areas where they are still undisturbed. When threatened, they prefer not to move, even when approached by men. In winter, when the snowfalls are heavy, they may descend to bamboo forest at elevations of about 6,500 feet (2,000 m), while, at other times of year, they can be found at elevations of 15,000 feet (4,500 m) or even more. [GY]

Serow *(Capricornis)*

The serow's fourteen subspecies have a collective range from the higher Himalayas and their eastern reaches into northern Southeast Asia and southward as far as Malaysia and Sumatra. About half of the subspecies are endangered but, of the remainder, some have maintained good numbers and comprise important big game in many areas.

Adult male serow stand about 40 inches (100 cm) or a little more at the shoulder, which appears to be slightly humped, and weigh between 285 and 330 lb (130 and 150 kg). The sexes are alike in coloration; tropical and sub-tropical serow are very dark, almost black, with hair that is silvery-gray at its base, while the Himalayan forms are more brownish, have silvery to bluish hues on their winter coats, and have a light fleece under the hair. Most subspecies have a neck crest of bristly hair that can

MALAY BEAR (*Helarctos malayanus*).

be described as a short mane. Both sexes are horned, the males having rounded, thick-based horns up to 10 inches (25 cm) long, which rise in a gentle backward curve from the animal's flattened skull.

Typical serow habitat features rugged cliffs together with dense brush or forest, where the animals can browse. Serow are not found on open grasslands. They have a remarkable ability to withstand drought.

Serow are sedentary and establish permanent bedding places that are usually difficult of access, even for leopards, being placed under rocky overhangs or in the entrances to shallow caves. Serow may use these locations for life. Their habits are so regular that certain trees, for example, become daily horn rubbing posts, while serow trails become deep with dust and droppings.

Serow—and goral, a related species—have an alarm cry that sounds like a human sneeze repeated at brief intervals. This sound, heard from some hidden location, may be the first clue to an animal's presence. Serow are not gregarious and do not form herds, but keep in small family groups that are rearing young. They tend to feed alone but may bed fairly close to one another. [GY]

Goral *(Nemorhaedus goral)*

The goral is another of the Asian goat-antelopes. Adult males stand about 30 inches (75 cm) at the shoulder and weigh about 65 to 75 lb (30 to 35 kg). Goral look rather like miniature serow, for they have a neck crest of bristly hair, and horns with the same gentle backward curve. Those that inhabit high, cold habitat may have coats that are fleece-like, but, at lower elevations, their coats are less thick, even sparse. The color is brown with tinges of gray, a black tail, a strikingly white throat patch, and a white chin. Against a background of drying grass or weathered rock, goral are extremely well camouflaged.

Goral cannot tolerate humid air and need more specialized habitat than serow. Unlike serow, goral are animals of temperate zones and grasslands, grazing on mountain meadows at elevations of up to, and a bit more than, 8,000 feet (2,500 m); in some parts of the Himalayas, goral tend to bed just inside the timberline and to graze on the slopes above, but they are both gregarious and without the rigid habits of serow and may bed in different places. They can adapt to cliff-dwelling where terrain and natural enemies compel this, and, when this occurs, they become more like serow in their habits.

Goral are to be found grazing late into the morning and again in the early evening, and their preference for grazing, rather than browsing, tends to keep them out on open slopes during their feeding periods. But like serow, goral get most of the water they need from dew and succulent vegetation, and therefore do not frequent watering places. [GY]

Tibetan Black Bear *(Selenarctos thibetanus)*

This bear has an all-black coat, except for a distinctive white "V" on the chest, which is absent on the subspecies from Laos. The ears are rather long and protrude stiffly; they are squared rather than pointed at their tips. Males have heavy manes which accentuate the apparent size of the head and neck. The claws are strong and sickle-shaped.

The Tibetan black bear has a wide distribution, from the western extremes of the Himalayas through South and Southeast Asia. The high rain forests, notably those of Southeast Asia, are the homes of the largest subspecies; males from Burma and northern Thailand have weighed more than 550 lb (250 kg) and, while this may be about average for large bears from a number of Himalayan habitats, a majority of black bears from drier regions such as India or southern China weigh about half this: 275 lb (125 kg).

Tibetan black bears are, like most bears, omnivorous, eating fruits, nuts, vegetation, honey, ants, small animals such as voles and hares, but only in exceptional cases will they take sheep, goats, or yaks. They hibernate wholly or partly from about November to April. During the rest of the year, they bed at the foot of large trees in the deep forests, in rocky hollows at the base of cliffs, or at forest edges.

When aroused or surprised, Tibetan black bears become very temperamental, and sows with cubs can be especially dangerous, while the boars are unpredictable at all times. Most of these bears will retreat from a man, if they get the opportunity to identify him as such, a "whoof" or snort being a signal of retreat. A clacking of teeth or a chomping sound, by contrast, indicates that the animal is about to attack, although some bears will not give any such warning at all. They can become man-killers, and the writer once shot one in northern Thailand that had killed six people by charging at them without warning from an ambush. [GY]

Sloth Bear (Melursus ursinus)

The sloth bear is one of nature's oddities. Its face, accentuated by a wild mane, is a rude caricature of a true bear's, its nostrils are concave, with a deep groove over the upper lip, while the lower lip protrudes well forward of the upper. Its snout is gray-white, its head and body black, and it has a white or brownish-white "U" mark on its chest. It has long and coarse fur. The bear's tongue is long and narrow, and can be flicked out—snake-like—for some 6 inches (15 cm) beyond the lower lip: the animal uses it to eat termites and honey.

Sloth bears are short-legged and walk awkwardly, being hampered in movement by their very long, sickle-shaped claws. A large male weighs about 300 lb (135 kg).

Sloth bears are found in Sri Lanka and in parts of eastern India, where they inhabit lowland forests. Their sloth-like behavior in trees induced early European observers to the erroneous belief that they are sloths. Like bears, however, they are omnivorous and are adept at and well equipped for opening termite colonies and bees' nests.

They are less alert than other bears and, if taken by surprise, can become alarmed and excitedly defensive, but their apparent local reputation for aggressive behavior seems to be undeserved. Their long claws, which are useful when climbing or digging, prevent them from running when chased but can be used defensively, for the bears adopt an almost crablike stance, and rake about threateningly with their claws. [GY]

Malay Bear (Helarctos malayanus)

Popularly called the sun-bear, the Malay is a compact, thickset bear with short, dense fur that looks as if it has been sheared, and with ears that look clipped. It is black, with a broad brown or yellow muzzle and—on most subspecies—a yellowish "U" on the chest. It has very strong sickle-shaped claws, using them to tear open bees' nests, which it robs expertly, using its long tongue to reach deep down inside them.

Fully mature males can reach nearly 220 lb (100 kg) on a length of about 60 inches (160 cm), but averages would be considerably less in habitat other than the mountain forests that are this bear's ideal. The species is found in southern China, Laos, Burma, Malaysia, Sumatra, and Borneo and, while it prefers untouched forests, it has learned to adapt to second-growth and more open forests.

Mountain tribesmen call this bear "man-bear," but this has no affectionate connotations, for the species is often curiously quick to investigate human intrusion, often with serious results. Although a Malay may seem to be tumbling and rolling playfully down slopes after a retreating man, many people who have survived the resulting mauling can attest to the species' aggressive nature. This bear is more feared by the local people than is the Tibetan bear. In Laos, the Malay has been reported to be the most frequent cause of wild-animal killings of human beings. [GY]

Markhor (Capra falconeri)

The markhor and the ibex (see below) are the two wild species of true goats in Asia, and both have large and beautiful horns, and are challenging animals to hunt, as they provide justifiably prized trophies.

Among wild goats, the markhor is second in size only to the Siberian ibex. An adult markhor buck weighs about 240 lb (110 kg) and stands about 44 inches (110 cm) at the shoulder. Its body is about 60 inches (165 cm) long. The horns are unique in being twisted in tight spirals, that on the right twisting to the left and vice versa, and the two together forming a characteristic "V"; some subspecies exhibit horns that spiral less tightly than those of the Suleiman markhor, a subspecies that typifies the species.

Markhor have summer coats that are light brown and winter coats that turn paler or acquire shades of gray. On their throats, chests, and shanks, adult animals have strong beards, manes, and fringes; these are dark brown to almost black and give the animals a shaggy appearance. Females have beards and, sometimes, short fringes. Tails are black, and knees have dark or black markings. Subspecies inhabiting higher elevations may acquire a pelt that is rather deeply fleeced, while at lower elevations, and especially in Baluchistan and parts of Afghanistan, markhor have heavy hair rather than a fleece.

There are reasonable opportunities to hunt markhor on either side of the border between India and Pakistan in Kashmir and, while markhor occur in Afghanistan and in neighboring Russia, there is no hunting to be had in either country for visiting sportsmen. [GY]

Siberian Ibex (Capra ibex siberica)

The ibex, like the markhor, is a true goat, being *the* classic mountain goat; it has an affinity for rocky terrain in all parts of the world. Even when ibex can live on lush grassy steppes, for example those in Mongolia, they prefer to remain close to rocky outcrops. The largest of the ibex, which is itself the largest of the wild goats, is the Siberian ibex, a subspecies found from Mongolia through western China to the western Himalayas, Afghanistan, and Iran.

Despite this wide range, the Siberian ibex exhibits little variation from region to region and—apart from size—has close similarities with all other subspecies except the Spanish ibex. There are, however, subtle differences between eastern and western Caucasian forms, and more obvious differences between the Siberian and the Nubian, Abyssinian, and Alpine subspecies.

An adult male Siberian ibex weighs about 330 lb (150 kg), stands about 40 inches (110 cm) at the shoulder, and has a body length that may reach 65 inches (170 cm). The males have impressive, back-curving horns that bulge forward, then arch backward. They are notched at intervals of about 2 inches (5 cm) and have a total length that has reached 61 inches (155 cm); the horns usually reach the animal's rump when it tilts its head backward. The horns of the females are usually under 16 inches (40 cm) long.

Ibex have coats that vary from region to region and from season to season. The Siberian ibex has a summer coat that can exhibit shades of gray-brown, brown, or reddish-brown, and a winter coat that may be paler brown or, on animals from the highest elevations, a mouse-gray. The fronts of the feet are patched with black, and the back legs may be nearly white. Both sexes have beards.

Ibex are found in their rocky environments at heights above sea-level of between 1,500 and 16,000 feet (500 to 5,000 m). Ideally, they choose rocky cliffs that adjoin slopes with vegetation on which they can browse or graze, while the cliffs afford bedding places or retreats. They are among the hardiest of the cold-region ungulates, being well able to tolerate freezing conditions and strong winds.

Over much of their range, predators such as wolves and snow leopards are more of a menace to ibex than is man, for example in the Afghanistan and Russian Pamirs and on the Tibetan plateau. Tehri and western Nepal

(Above upper) **CHITAL DEER** (*Axis axis*).
(Above left) **MUNTJAC, or BARK-ING DEER** (*Muntiacus muntjac*).
(Above right) **HOG DEER** (*Axis porcinus*).
(Opposite) **TIGER** (*Panthera tigris*).

along the Himalayas were once ideal environment for ibex at elevations from 9,000 to over 25,000 feet (2,800 to 7,500 m), but few are to be found there now. Russia has closed vast areas of the mountainous parts of eastern and southeastern Uzbekistan to hunting, but there are said to be many ibex there.

Persian and Siberian ibex have been introduced into the southwestern United States and Mexico, where they have been adapting very well in a totally new environment. There are also ibex in Iran. [GY]

Muntjac, or Barking Deer (Muntiacus muntjac)

This is one of the smaller species of Asian deer. It is found widely throughout southern and southeastern Asian forests, from lowlands up to mountains nearly 10,000 feet (3,000 m) in height. About twenty subspecies are recognized and include forms from India, China, Java, and other islands. A feral population has established itself in the British Isles, where escapees from wild-life parks have bred in the woods preserved for pheasant shooting.

Muntjac vary considerably in size and coloration. Bucks of the larger subspecies from highland forests can weigh up to 75 lb (35 kg) and have a height at the shoulder of about 25 inches (65 cm). Body lengths of up to 42 inches (105 cm) are found on black muntjacs and the Tenasserim or Burmese forms; Chinese and Indian forms are close to this size, while the island forms are somewhat smaller. Muntjac have plumply rounded bodies; their rumps are higher than their withers.

Muntjac are among the most red-colored of deer, but some subspecies are darker and can be almost black, while muntjac from open and grassy environments can be much paler shades of reddish-brown. Their tails are fairly long and white underneath, and are exhibited as flags when the animals are running. The throat and belly are light tan, and the inside of the thighs is white.

Only the bucks have antlers, which grow from raised, hair-covered pedicles; they are shed annually. The antlers are usually two-pronged with a very short lower prong. They are very sharp-edged, and hooked. Only exceptionally do the antlers exceed a length of about 5 inches (13 cm). The bucks' canine fangs may be hidden by the upper lips or may slightly protrude; they measure not more than about 1½ inches (3 cm) on the external curve.

Muntjac venture cautiously into open meadows and onto grassy slopes to graze in the early mornings and evenings; during the day, they spend most of the time in dense brush or jungle, and thus cannot easily be seen. Their alarm call, however, is very distinctive and has given the species its popular name: it sounds like the barking of a dog.

Muntjac bucks can defend themselves effectively with their horns, for they can fatally injure dogs—either from a hunting pack or from a pack of wild dogs—and are thought by some observers to constitute a check on the numbers of wild dogs. It seems unlikely, however, that they could "see off" hounds of a size and determination typical of those in a trained hunting pack in the British Isles. [GY]

Hog Deer (Axis porcinus)

Hog deer have bodies that are plumply rounded, their withers are slightly lower than their shoulders, and their coats are mainly brown or dark brown with paler underparts. The bucks, which are larger than the hinds, have a shoulder height of about 28 inches (72 cm), while their horns, which are six-pointers, are usually between about 20 and 24 inches (50 to 60 cm) in length, although exceptional horns can be as long

as 32 inches (80 cm). Bucks weigh up to about 110 lb (50 kg).

In much of Southeast Asia—Assam, Burma, and what was Indochina—hog deer inhabit the higher mountains and the deep rain forest as well as more low-lying land. They get their name from their habit of "hogging" their way through the undergrowth by means of tunnels or trails; their survival has had much to do with their ability to evade predators in this way. Their habit of running with their heads sunk toward the ground has also contributed to their name.

They are relatively asocial and seldom associate in groups of more than two or three. They used to be common over their range—from northern India to Vietnam—where they inhabited the river valleys, but they are not so common now. In India, they tend to be valley animals still and have taken to swampy habitats. [GY]

Chital Deer (Axis axis)

This is the only species of deer that normally has white spots at all ages and on both sexes (the fallow deer, Dama dama, is spotted in summer and, at most, inconspicuously spotted in winter). It is reddish-brown to tan over much of its body, with a white belly. The lowest row of spots on the side describes a horizontal line, while the black of the nose and muzzle tip is accentuated by a surrounding white patch. The rather brushy tail is white underneath.

Adult bucks stand 30 to 38 inches (75 to 97 cm) at the shoulder, with a body length of 43 to 55 inches (110 to 140 cm); their average weight is about 220 lb (100 kg). The hinds are about one-third smaller than the bucks.

Only the bucks have antlers, which have three points a side and are thin, bending back sharply before rising into the fork; the base prong at the front dips forward, as does the main branch. The larger bucks may have antlers of about 40 inches (100 cm). Chital antlers tend to be less symmetrical than those of hog deer and sambar, for they are easily modified when still in velvet, being then still soft. They reach a maximum in size just before the rainy season, when they are shed.

Chital are found in the deciduous forests and the savanna regions of India and Sri Lanka; the two Indian subspecies have been introduced into game parks in Australia, New Zealand, Hawaii, and South America.

They herd in groups of five to ten, demanding little more than water, shade, and grazing grass; when the grass becomes lush in the monsoon season, chital may herd together in large groups. They prefer the peripheries of denser forests for bedding down and, being more diurnal than most deer, spend much of their time in open meadows and grasslands between sparse forests. [GY]

Tiger (Panthera tigris)

The tiger is the largest—and perhaps most threatened—of the big cats, with a population in the wild estimated to be around 5,000; only fifty years ago, it is estimated that there were twenty times as many. These were spread over much of Asia, but, today, tigers are living in the wild only in the Siberian-Manchurian region and in some parts of southern Asia. There are some in game preserves.

Hunting of tiger will remain illegal until the numbers of wild tiger in game sanctuaries overwhelm the game supplies there. Efforts are under way to restore tiger populations in India, Nepal, Bangladesh, Burma, Thailand, and Malaysia, and, while the Russian authorities do not publish the results of their efforts in Siberia, programs to protect tigers there do appear to be a reality. The deep forests of Vietnam, Laos, and

Cambodia used to shelter vast numbers of tigers, but the wars of the 1960s and 1970s have greatly reduced them.

Provided prey and cover exist, tigers can inhabit almost any climate or environment: snowy heights, tall grasslands, dry or wet forests, marshlands or rocky mountains have all had populations of tigers, but whatever the terrain, they must have shade and shadows. They avoid wide open areas by day. They live as close to rivers as possible, being often in the water; they swim as readily as jaguars, and they hunt along river banks.

Despite their great size—Siberian tigers weigh up to 650 lb (300 kg)—and apparent sluggishness, tigers are capable of moving with amazing swiftness and agility; they can leap straight up in the air to a height of 15 feet (4.5 m) or spring 30 feet (9 m) at a bound. They attack prey from an ambush, bounding out to take horned prey by the rump and throwing it to the ground, or striking hornless prey directly, often at the throat, with tremendous blows of the paws with claws extended, and with the dewclaw acting as a knife. A tiger will drag the carcass of its prey to a secluded spot; water buffalo or wild cattle, which weigh more than a tiger itself, are moved with ease. A tiger will gorge itself on a kill, perhaps eating up to 50 lb (23 kg) of meat, and will then sleep this off for several days, maybe for as much as a week. Several tigers may share a kill, and they are not unsociable when they meet, for they exchange rubs of recognition.

When prey is scarce, tiger may cover a circuit of more than 100 miles (160 km), but they will also follow shorter circuits, passing the same spots within a few days, provided that an important kill has not been made.

A tigress will mate first when more than about 3½ years old. One to six cubs are born after a gestation period of about 100 days; they stay with their mother for some two years, and, before they have learned to hunt, the tigress kills a variety of animals that she might not otherwise touch. Among them are porcupines, whose spines can cause persistent, crippling pain and frustration to such an extent that tigers so injured lose their instinctive fear of man and become dangerous in the extreme. Such cases are, fortunately, rare, just as the menace of man-eating tigers has diminished as tigers themselves have diminished in number. Today, they are an endangered species. [GY]

Nilgai, or Blue Bull (Boselaphus tragocamelus)

Adult bulls weigh 450 lb (200 kg) or more and have a body height of 60 inches (150 cm) and a body length of about 80 inches (200 cm) from nose to rump; cows are somewhat smaller and lack horns. Those of the bulls are short, usually under 6 inches (15 cm). Nilgai are high at the withers, have sloping backs and, as their legs are long, have a slightly giraffe-like gait when running.

The older bulls become a blue-gray in color, and have a fringe of hair at the throat, just below a white patch; they have a loose mane from mid-neck to the withers. Their under-thighs are white, and they have a white ring just above the hooves. The younger bulls and the cows have the same white markings, but their overall color is a reddish-brown.

Nilgai live on the plains of India and Pakistan. In Hindu communities they can become a serious menace, for only non-Hindus may shoot them, and there is no other practical way of preventing them from grazing on farmers' crops.

The species is the sole surviving remnant of the prehistoric *Tragocerinae*. [GY]

Sambar (Cervus unicolor)

A large bull sambar weighs about 700 lb (320 kg), stands about 60 inches (150 cm) at the shoulder, and has a body length of about 106 inches (270 cm). Sambar are found in lowland forests, grassy second-growth swamps, or high mountain forests up to an elevation of about 8,200 feet (2,500 m). The largest animals come from the high forests, but sambar, of which there are six subspecies, also occur in India, Sri Lanka, the Nepal Terai, Assam, Burma, and much of Southeast Asia, including the islands of the East Indies, where they usually weigh not more than about 130 lb (60 kg). However much sambar differ in size, their coloring is much the same: a dark to light brown body with paler underparts, and the same long, brushy tail. The neck ruff of the bulls may be deep and shaggy.

Only the bulls have antlers, which they shed annually. Those of the mountain sambar become massive and, with a lesser spread than those of American elk, or wapiti, and with fewer points, they have an external circumference of about 50 inches (125 cm). Typical antlers have three points a side.

Despite such antlers, sambar move easily through the thick bamboos and undergrowth of the dense forests they inhabit. They seek out mineral—especially sulphur—licks and, in hotter, drier environments, tend to seek out mud wallows daily, and may stay close to swamps and watercourses. They are alert and wary at all times, except just before and during the rut, and they are usually difficult to approach. Their alarm call, a single high-pitched "kleenk" sounded at intervals, sounds like that of the American elk. [GY]

Barasingha (Cervus duvauseli)

Tha barasingha is a deer with a range now confined to the lower forested or swampy regions of the Nepal Terai and north-central India to Assam, and the northwestern part of Burma. Substantial herds are still to be seen in the Sarda River valley in western Nepal.

Rather large and heavily set, a barasingha stag has typically a height of about 45 to 48 inches (115 to 120 cm), a length of about 70 inches (180 cm), and a weight of some 580 lb (265 kg). The dark or reddish-brown hair is thicker than that of the sambar; it is water-repellant, too, and barasingha can adapt with ease to swampy conditions. They are, in fact, sometimes known as swamp deer. [GY]

Blackbuck Antelope (Antilope cervicapra)

Blackbuck have horns that grow in spirals of up to four complete twists, measuring altogether up to about 40 inches (100 cm); hinds are hornless. Mature bucks stand about 33 inches (85 cm) at the shoulder and weigh about 100 lb (45 kg). The older bucks have an almost black coat, while the hinds and fawns are a light tan or tawny; all blackbuck have white underparts, and their legs are dark on the outside and white on the inside. Their coats are, in general, as sleek as those of ponies. Their eyes are ringed with white "spectacles," and their chins are also white.

Blackbuck inhabit plains, where their resistance to heat and lack of water enables them to go without drinking for two or three days at a time. Their eyesight and sense of smell are excellent, and they can identify human beings at considerable distances.

They are found in India and Pakistan and are among the most huntable antelopes in Asia. [GY]

115

Chapter 6
South American Game Animals

Jaguar *(Panthera onca)*

A mature male jaguar can measure up to 100 inches (2.8 m) in length, of which about one-third is tail, and can weigh up to about 250 lb (115 kg). The females are somewhat smaller. Despite this weight, the animal climbs well; it can swim, too.

It has been called South America's tiger, but it is not striped, its leather-gold pelt being flecked with dark rosettes or roughly four-sided markings. Locally, the jaguar may be called *tigre*, or *leopardo*.

There are jaguar in most (if not all) South American countries, with a distribution southward from Mexico in Central America, down through the rain forests, jungles, and tropical areas of the continent, with the largest concentration in the Amazon Basin. Its local range is often circumscribed by the presence of man, especially near fairly large communities and in cattle areas.

It takes animals of all sorts, including cattle, but it is wary of bulls, and of herds of tapir (see below). Among smaller animals, it preys upon not-fully grown crocodiles and caymans, turtles, and fish; it eats reptile eggs, too.

As is well known, the jaguar's beautiful pelt has led to its being hunted nearly to extinction, and the species is one of those that have attracted the interest of the World Wildlife Fund. [JR]

Puma *(Felis concolor)*

This is the cougar, or mountain lion, of North and Central America. It is found throughout South America in rain forest and jungle, and in arid and mountainous regions, but it has become scarce because many have been shot by hunters and farmers. Its habitat has also been encroached upon.

It is a tawny color that ranges from a fairly light brown to a dark or reddish brown; its underside is pale brown or white, and its ears and tail have dark tips. Its coat is not marked or patterned in any way. An average male weighs between 100 and 160 lb (45 and 73 kg) and is between 70 and 95 inches (180 and 240 cm) long, of which about one-third is tail. The females are smaller by about one-third.

The puma is active at dawn and dusk, and during the night in areas where it has been much disturbed; in undisturbed areas, it hunts by day. It climbs readily and often lies in ambush for its prey, leaping down upon it from a branch or an outcrop of rock. Puma seem to take the most varied prey, from quail to cows and from domestic cats to wapiti. Wounded puma have been known to attack man. [JR]

Ocelot *(Felis pardalis)*

The ocelot is much smaller than the jaguar, being about 60 inches (1.5 m) in length overall, of which about one-third is tail; it has a weight of about 25 lb (11 kg).

It is a nocturnal animal that keeps to thick forest, lying up during the day in thick vegetation or in a tree. It climbs excellently, catching birds and monkeys in trees at night, but it also eats rodents of all sizes—the capybara, which is the largest, can weigh up to 100 lb (45 kg)—as well as snakes and lizards.

It occurs southward from the United States—Mexican border to northern Argentina; this is more or less the same range as the jaguar's, and the two animals are often found in the same area.

Ecologically, it is probably valuable as a control on the populations of the species on which it feeds. Nevertheless, it is trapped and shot by farmers and ranchers but, like the African leopard, it may on balance be better to tolerate it than to kill it. Like most other large cats, its pelt has been too attractive for the good of the species, the survival of which is now a matter of international concern. [JR]

Marsh Deer *(Blastocerus dichotomus)*

This is the largest South American deer; it can grow as big as a red deer, or up to a weight of some 440 lb (200 kg). Its horns have a double fork and are thus very similar to those of the North American mule deer (see p. 32). It is reddish-brown in color, brightening in summer and becoming duller in winter in those parts of its range where the seasons are marked.

It is found in wooded areas adjacent to water and has therefore an extensive range, from the Guianas southward through Brazil to northern Argentina. [JR]

Guemal *(Hippocamelus)*

These are small deer of the high Andes, where they are found at heights of 11,500 feet (3,500 m) or more, from Ecuador to Chile. They are generally brown, with coarse coats and with horns forming a simple fork.

One variety (*H. bisulcus*) is called *huemul* in the mountains of southwest Argentina and southern Chile. It is about 30 to 40 inches (75 to 100 cm) in height, and its general form resembles that of the roe deer (see p. 30), but the *huemul* is more heavily built and is stronger. It features a black facial stripe that runs from between its eyes and along its nose.

A Peruvian variety (*H. antisensis*), locally called *taruga*, is smaller. [JR]

Savanna Deer *(Odocoileus gymnotis)*

This is a small white-tailed species, similar in coloration to the white-tailed deer (see p. 31) of North America, but a bit smaller, and with smaller antlers. It is found on the tropical and sub-tropical treeless grasslands of the Guianas, Venezuela, and south of the Amazon Basin, where the local populations shoot it for food. [JR]

Peccary *(Tayassu)*

This is a pig-like species that occurs only in the New World, where its range extends from the southwestern United States southward to Patagonia. The peccary has a thick skin covered with a bristly thick coat that is long on all parts of its body and mane-like on its head. It has very

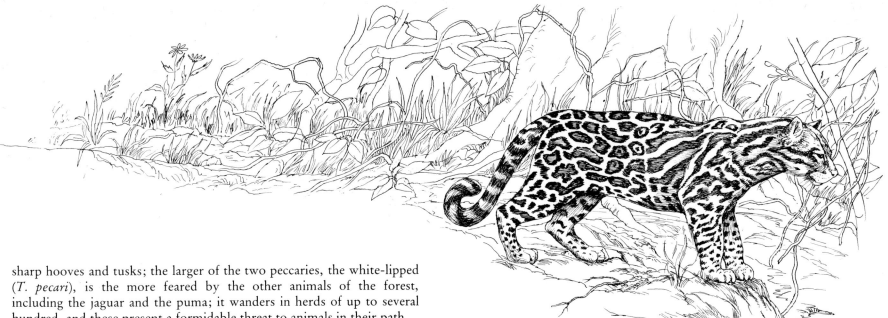

sharp hooves and tusks; the larger of the two peccaries, the white-lipped (*T. pecari*), is the more feared by the other animals of the forest, including the jaguar and the puma; it wanders in herds of up to several hundred, and these present a formidable threat to animals in their path.

The white-lipped peccary is so called because it has a white patch of hair on its lower jaw, which contrasts with the dark-gray coat of the boars and the dark-brown of the sows. The boars stand up to about 18 inches (45 cm) at the shoulder and are about 40 inches (100 cm) long. The collared peccary (*T. tajacu*) is perhaps 2 inches (5 cm) lower and 4 inches (10 cm) shorter; it gets its name from the pale or white band that usually encircles its neck and shoulders; its general coloration is much as the white-lipped peccary's, but slightly lighter.

Only the collared peccary occurs over the northern and southern extremities of the range: in the southern United States and Argentina and southern Chile. Both varieties eat the usual foods of wild pigs: roots, bulbs, shoots, and all sorts of small vertebrates and invertebrates, including even snakes. They have been observed to challenge rattlesnakes to strike, whereupon they leap up above the snake to land with all four hooves together on its back, thus killing or maiming it.

Its flesh, although it can taste of musk, is much prized. There is, however, no danger of the species being made extinct.

Both peccaries are locally called *javelina* or *jabalí*; the white-lipped is also called *senso* or *marina*. [JR]

Tapir *(Tapirus)*

There are three species of these pig-like animals in South America; all are characterized by an elongated prehensile snout. The most widely spread is the lowland tapir (*T. terrestris*), which can reach a length of about 80 inches (200 cm). It has short thick hair on its body and a short brush-like mane on its neck. The boars are smaller than the sows, which can be fierce in their own defence and that of their young. The animals are otherwise shy. They have extremely tough hides and, in thick jungle undergrowth, can rush unhindered through tangles that can easily stop a dog; on open plains, however, they fall easy prey to their pursuers. They are good swimmers and can swim for long distances underwater; they surface with a sort of sneezing.

Lowland tapirs occur from the north of South America down through southern Brazil, Paraguay, and northern Argentina.

The mountain tapir (*T. pinchacus*) has a thicker pelt and stronger legs and hooves than its relatives; it has white-tipped ears and feet. It lives in the Andes of Columbia, Ecuador, and northern Peru at heights of between 7,000 and 13,000 feet (2,100 and 4,000 m).

The Central American, or Baird's, tapir (*T. bairdi*) occurs only on the western side of the Andes in Ecuador and Columbia, and in Central America from southern Mexico to Panama. It is about the same size as the lowland tapir; its snout is the most elongated of those of the tapirs, with the possible exception of the Asian species (*T. indicus*). [JR]

(Opposite) Female and young of the **LOWLAND TAPIR** (*Tapirus terrestris*).
(Top) **OCELOT** (*Felis pardalis*).
(Lower) **HUEMUL** (*Hippocamelus bisulcus*).

(Opposite, top) **WHITE-LIPPED PECCARY** (*Tayassu pecari*).
(Opposite, lower) **MARSH DEER** (*Blastocerus dichotomus*).
(Above) **PUMA** (*Felis concolor*).

119

Guanaco *(Lama glama huanachus)*

This animal is related to the camel and has a similar body form but, of course, without the camel's hump. It is smaller than a camel, however; males stand about 45 inches (115 cm) at the shoulder and weigh about 165 lb (75 kg). The females are smaller and weigh less. Guanacos can close their noses as camels can, their coats are woolier than those of camels, their hooves are more deeply cloven, their ears are larger, and their tails longer.

The guanaco is one of the two wild species of the llama family, the other being the vicuña, which is celebrated for its fine wool. The guanaco is found in the Andes of the southern part of South America—southern Peru, Bolivia, Patagonia, and the archipelago of Tierra del Fuego—and inhabits the mountains from the snowline downward; it occurs also further north, in tropical South America, but not below an elevation of some 4,500 feet (2,000 m), on account of its inability to sustain great heat. [JR]

Species Introduced into South America

A number of species of game have been introduced into South America or, more accurately, Argentina. The red deer is described, as a European animal, on p. 27. The other introduced species, and the page references of their main descriptions, are fallow deer (p. 31), chital deer (p. 112), blackbuck, or Indian, antelope (p. 113), and wild boar (p. 39). [JR]

III The History of Hunting

Chapter 1

The First Recreational Hunters

John F. Reiger

Throughout almost all of man's evolution as a species, he has been a hunter. Only yesterday, after more than a million years, did he emerge as a "modern" being: urban, industrialized, and cut off from his natural habitat and the creatures he used to hunt. "The exciting life of the Stone Age hunter still survives in our social dreams, as an expression of our biological past," writes René Dubos, the eminent French-born American biologist.

After many decades of a seeming bias of scholars against the qualities of the primitive hunting and gathering peoples—savages who had preceded the "advanced" farmer—a new interpretation has been offered by a growing number of anthropologists and prehistorians. Indeed, one could almost say that the earlier interpretation of man's development has been turned on its head. Now some scholars suggest that man's undoing began when he became a farmer, and that he not only lost much in a psychic and spiritual sense, but that it was then that his war on the environment began in earnest. As a hunter, he had learned to be alert, self-reliant, and ingenious in outwitting the craftiest game. He had also learned how to cooperate in group activity and how to share the kill. Virtually every physical and mental development that supported the survival of the "naked ape" derived from the hunting life.

In prehistory, the change from a hunting–gathering economy to tillage and domestication of beasts is the beginning of settlement and "civilization." According to the traditional scenario of historical events, man now had a predictable food supply, and therefore he could devote more time to leisure and creativity. He now developed cultures with social stratification, complex religions, large-scale building projects and, finally, the written word or symbol that marks the transition from prehistory to history.

There are, of course, many exceptions to this tidy format. At least two North American Indian peoples, for example, developed social stratification and a rich artistic life, but exceptions notwithstanding, man became settled and "civilized" after he took on the role of the farmer, and not before. Some recent scholars argue that civilization had its price. Man now saw the creatures sanctified by hunting ritual as predators on his crops. Indeed, every living thing that failed to fit into the microcosm which agricultural man had designed for himself was, if possible, ruthlessly eliminated.

The farmer became a prisoner of the weather and the land that had once nurtured his spirit as well as his body. Instead of being able to wander with the tribal group, the individual and the group were now tied to a tiny parcel of land, the constant worry being that natural forces could, in a single stroke, wipe out an entire year's work. In short, agriculture may have marked the rise of what is generally accepted as civilization, but it also signaled the beginning of man's enslavement to given place.

However uncomfortable the life of the Stone Age hunter, his days were filled with *meaningful* activity. His hunting was part subsistence

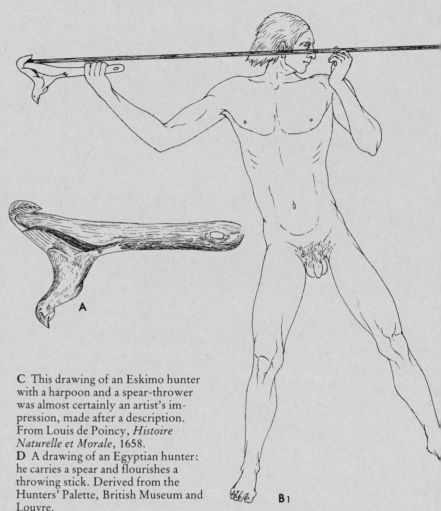

C This drawing of an Eskimo hunter with a harpoon and a spear-thrower was almost certainly an artist's impression, made after a description. From Louis de Poincy, *Histoire Naturelle et Morale*, 1658.
D A drawing of an Egyptian hunter: he carries a spear and flourishes a throwing stick. Derived from the Hunters' Palette, British Museum and Louvre.

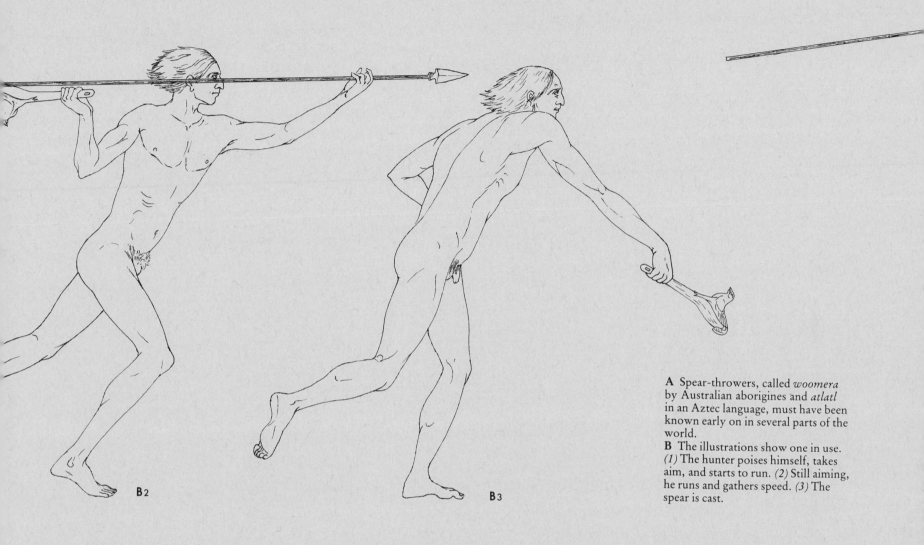

A Spear-throwers, called *woomera* by Australian aborigines and *atlatl* in an Aztec language, must have been known early on in several parts of the world.
B The illustrations show one in use. *(1)* The hunter poises himself, takes aim, and starts to run. *(2)* Still aiming, he runs and gathers speed. *(3)* The spear is cast.

B2

B3

and part religion, part work and part pleasure. Historians of hunting generally draw a sharp distinction between the chase as recreation and the subsistence hunting of prehistoric or primitive societies. Although there are obvious reasons for the distinction, it may be more revealing to base a history of hunting on the thesis that, even for Stone Age man, the subsistence hunt was also a form of recreation—an activity that elicited pleasure apart from providing food.

That his hunting could have been *more* than a chore required for survival is suggested by the magical feeling which radiates from the paintings in the famous caves at Lascaux and Font-de-Gaume in France and Altamira in Spain. I first saw the masterpieces of Font-de-Gaume in the summer of 1964. Their aesthetic effect and the response they aroused in me, a modern recreational hunter, may be inferred from my diary entry for 25 August of that year:

"The entrance to the cave is on a hillside, and looks exactly like every painting or drawing I have ever seen that has endeavored to reproduce what life must have been like in that prehistoric period.... Most of the paintings, or I should really call them sketches, were of bison, horses, great stags... smaller deer, and mammoths.... The paintings were mostly done by Cro-Magnon people and were of two major periods; one group was from about 17,000 years ago, the other from over 25,000 years ago. Evidently, the cave was used by one band of people for a time,

deserted, and later discovered by another, totally different group, who added their artistic endeavors to another section of the cave.

"The artists were clever in that they incorporated the contours of the cave walls into the painting itself in order to give the subject more of a feeling of movement and life—this attempt at realistic depiction is clearly preconceived and not the least bit accidental.

"It was appreciation and affinity that I felt for these primitive human beings and their evidently unquenchable desire to recreate their environment. Imagine two or three of those element beings crouched next to that same cave wall 20,000 years ago, with one or more holding a torch, while the respected artist traced his wet, stained finger over the surface and created something very much like the bison the family group killed the day before. Perhaps, when the artist was finished, the entire group came nearer, holding their torches ever closer to the masterpiece, and they all grunted with satisfaction and, undoubtedly, joy."

Despite their antiquity, these Cro-Magnon peoples were among the first of our own species, *Homo sapiens* ("wise man"). Their wisdom developed out of surviving the challenges of a demanding environment; they had already displaced the first real hunter, the Neanderthal man, and refined the latter's hunting tools and methods.

Perhaps the earliest hunting implement was a club, one of the large bones of a prey animal killed by disease, accident, or predators. At some

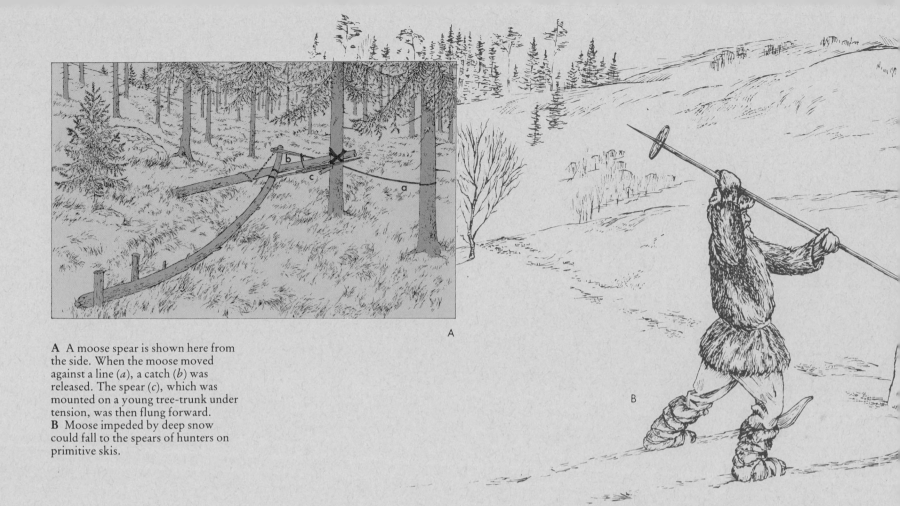

A A moose spear is shown here from the side. When the moose moved against a line (*a*), a catch (*b*) was released. The spear (*c*), which was mounted on a young tree-trunk under tension, was then flung forward.
B Moose impeded by deep snow could fall to the spears of hunters on primitive skis.

point, a man-like creature must have wielded a large bone as a club and realized how useful it could be when facing beasts which had such formidable weapons as bone-like horns, hooves, and teeth. Utilized (as distinct from made) bone clubs were possibly the first hunting weapons.

The only other real contender for this honor would have been a heavy stone, simply picked up and thrown at an animal or bird. Even the giant cave bears of Europe were killed or disabled by boulders cast down on them from fairly high elevations by the later Neanderthal hunters.

Here, the tendency to imitate nature would probably have come into play. After seeing the results of an avalanche that trapped and killed animals, the earliest man-like beings may have endeavored to duplicate, in a small way, the deadliness of a hurtling projectile.

At this point, one might ask if the early hunters pursued the bigger mammals instead of the smaller, less dangerous, species, and if so, why? Hunting bands probably found it easier (and relatively more rewarding) to trap large, slow-moving beasts, such as mammoths, rather than the smaller, quicker animals. This is particularly true of large animals like the bison, which can be driven into snow and rendered almost helpless. Interestingly, this technique of catching and killing game "mired down" in snow was a hunting technique used in North America and Europe as late as the early years of the twentieth century.

Another likely reason for pursuing large game animals in the Pleistocene epoch, but one overlooked often, was the need for one-piece furs to cover an individual's body. In the intense cold of the Ice Ages and before man learned to sew, the largest mammals with the thickest coats may well have been even more important for clothing than for food.

Once again, the development of man's reason and spirit of cooperation made up for his vulnerability. The same two traits would also allow him to fashion hunting weapons and methods that would eventually make him the most formidable animal of the Pleistocene.

The cave bear had once been an important quarry of Stone Age

hunters, but when climatic changes transformed the ecosystems of Central Europe, the mammoth became the major source of food there and, according to recent archeological work, in North America as well. The ancestors of the American Indians crossed the Bering Strait (a land bridge when glaciation had drastically lowered the water level) between Siberia and Alaska in a series of migrations that took place about 25,000 years ago.

Both in Europe and North America, the mammoth was probably pursued into deep snow or muddy swamps, where it mired down and could be killed. One scholar suggests that they might also have been taken in huge "deadfalls," a sort of trap that would have killed or disabled an animal after it sprang the "trigger." On entering the deadfall and springing the trap, the mammoth was apparently knocked down by heavy logs. The scholar does not suggest how such heavy logs could be lifted so high, however. Another probable trapping technique was the use of pitfalls, deep holes dug in the ground and thinly covered with branches and leaves as camouflage.

Enough social organization would have been achieved by this time for us to hypothesize the technique of using beaters to drive the animal toward the trap or pit, or to the place where it would mire down. Archeological excavations have revealed that, in some regions, the hunters worked together to drive large game animals over cliffs. Even when trapped in a deadfall or pit, the beast would usually have to be killed by spears or other tipped weapons.

The horse became extinct in North America before the appearance of the first human, but it was to succeed the mammoth in Central Europe as the major prey species of the Stone Age. Wild horses traveled in great herds, and their gregariousness and speed proved to be their undoing. Initially, fires were set to drive the animals in the general direction of a cliff, and beaters and obstructions were placed along the sides to keep the animals running in the desired direction toward the precipice. The

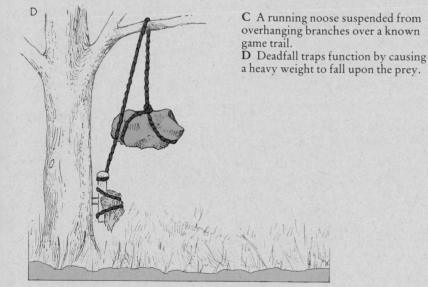

C A running noose suspended from overhanging branches over a known game trail.
D Deadfall traps function by causing a heavy weight to fall upon the prey.

momentum of the animals behind pushed the ones in front over the edge.

At Solutré, near Lyons, is a famous horse-hunting site with the remains of over 10,000 horses at the base of a precipice. One estimate puts the total number of horses killed there at over 100,000. Used for centuries, the site reached the peak of its usage about 40,000 years ago.

Just as the cave bear had been replaced by the mammoth, and the mammoth by the horse, now the horse was to be replaced by the reindeer as the major prey species of the later Stone Age hunters of Central Europe. Although the animal had been occasionally hunted as far back as Neanderthal times, it was only with the last great period of glaciation that the reindeer would become the primary game animal.

Reindeer grazed in huge herds as the horses had, and the Stone Age people pursued them with the same techniques as those they had found so useful in bringing down horses. They used fire and beaters to drive the reindeer, but not over precipices, for the most common method seems to have been to drive the animals into rivers, where they became all but helpless. North American Indians used similar methods in hunting deer, and even as recently as the late nineteenth century, Indian hunters in New York State used hounds to drive whitetail deer into lakes where they were killed from canoes.

By the time the reindeer became the chief quarry of the late Stone Age people, European hunters were using weapons that made them most accomplished predators. Chief among these were the bow and arrow and the spear-thrower, or *atlatl*. The latter weapon is a short stick with a notch or cup at one end in which the spear end is placed. The atlatl, of course, is not thrown with the spear but is retained in the hand. The device gives the thrower added leverage by acting as an extension of the hunter's arm and has been shown to add as much as sixty percent to the distance attained by a hand-thrown spear. Recorded in Europe, North America, and Australia, it was used also by the Eskimo, as it is useful when hunting in a boat, because one hand can be used to steady the craft.

Along with the advances in weaponry in the late Stone Age came the beginnings of agriculture and animal domestication. The latter may have begun when the young of quarry that had been killed were caught and preserved. Dogs must first have appeared as scavengers about the hunters' encampments and, although they were eaten until prehistoric times, they were among the first animals to be utilized as hunting allies.

While hunting and food-gathering were the exclusive sources of food in the early Stone Age, they must have become less important later. Kitchen middens of the later Stone Age from sites in Europe warrant this conclusion, for only a relatively small proportion of the bones identified by archeologists are of wild species, all the rest being of domesticated animals.

With the "Great Change" of the beginnings of settled agriculture, man would begin to try to transform the natural world rather than endeavor to live off it. His life would become less unpredictable and his chances of survival less uncertain. For these reasons, no doubt, he was willing to settle for the drudgery and boredom of a largely agricultural existence.

Hunting bands would become small settlements, of which the population grew with the food supply. The settled tribes defended their agricultural and grazing lands against other tribes. But people must still have been able to move on to other territory for, during thousands of years, the overall population density remained extremely low. The richest and most easily used farming and grazing lands were limited, existing only in certain types of ecosystems, and competition for these favored localities must have been great.

Before the change, the strongest and most athletic members of the group were the most active hunters. After it, they became warriors when necessary, either providing protection for the rest of the tribe or harrying its neighbors. The strongest of these warriors became chiefs, and the seeds of a stratified social society were sown.

Chiefs and perhaps their descendants came to be accorded, or to acquire, certain privileges, none more inviolate than that of hunting wild animals. Larger areas of land were tilled, and larger herds of domesticated animals were grazed. Hunting lands gradually shrank and came eventually to be monopolized and protected so the game on them could survive. This development must have taken several thousand years. Hunting, once a necessity for survival, and as such permeated with sympathetic magic and religion in the minds of Stone Age hunters, had become a symbol of social status, being, for the first time in history, *purely* a recreation—a sport.

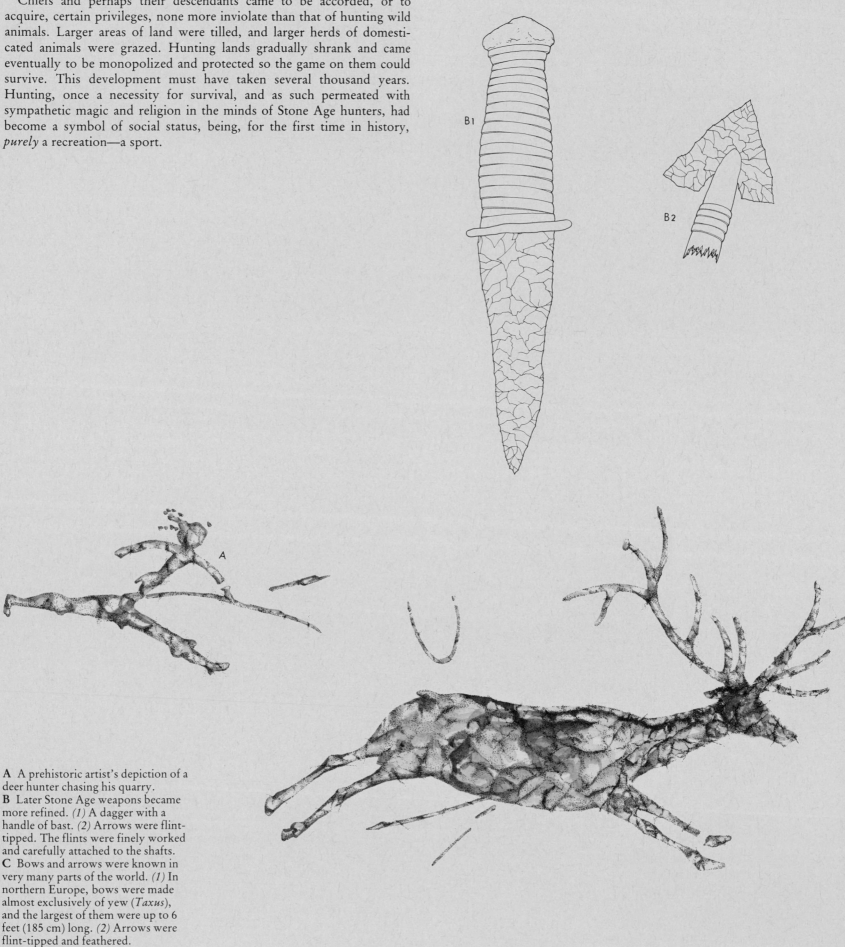

A A prehistoric artist's depiction of a deer hunter chasing his quarry.
B Later Stone Age weapons became more refined. *(1)* A dagger with a handle of bast. *(2)* Arrows were flint-tipped. The flints were finely worked and carefully attached to the shafts.
C Bows and arrows were known in very many parts of the world. *(1)* In northern Europe, bows were made almost exclusively of yew (*Taxus*), and the largest of them were up to 6 feet (185 cm) long. *(2)* Arrows were flint-tipped and feathered.

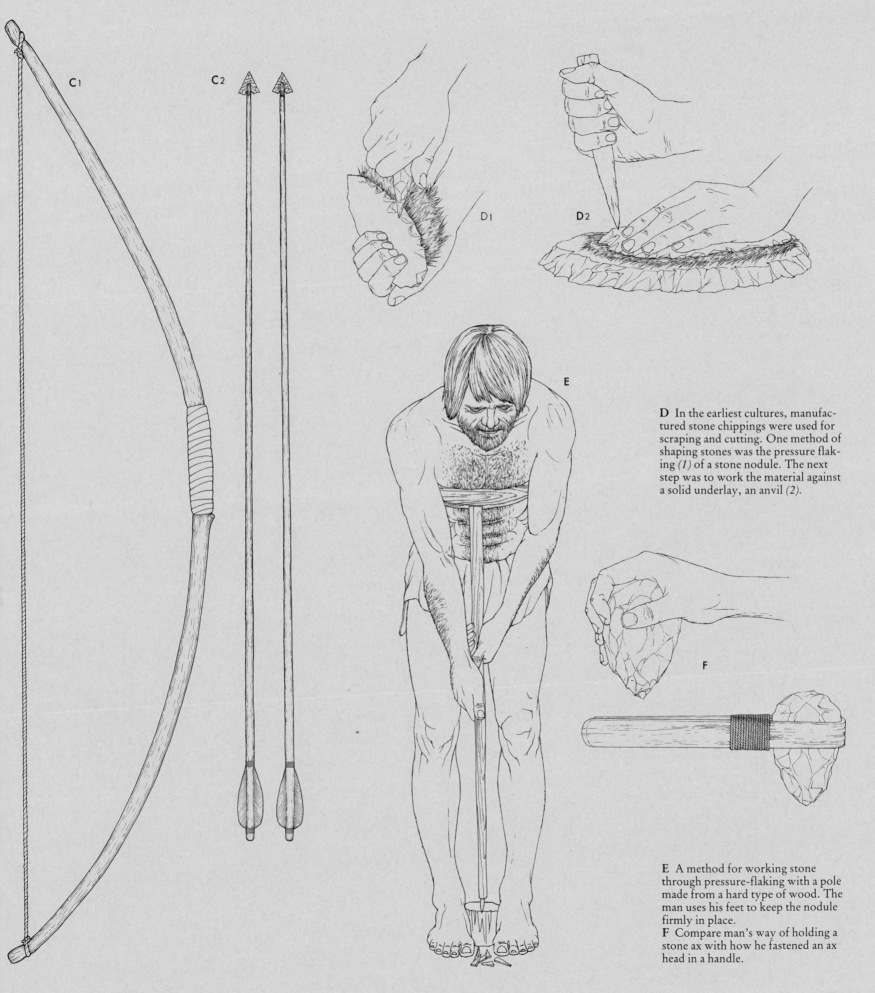

D In the earliest cultures, manufactured stone chippings were used for scraping and cutting. One method of shaping stones was the pressure flaking *(1)* of a stone nodule. The next step was to work the material against a solid underlay, an anvil *(2)*.

E A method for working stone through pressure-flaking with a pole made from a hard type of wood. The man uses his feet to keep the nodule firmly in place.

F Compare man's way of holding a stone ax with how he fastened an ax head in a handle.

127

Chapter 2

Hunting from Early Times to the Middle Ages

John F. Reiger

Many non-hunters might say that, when hunting became unnecessary for survival, it became a "mere" recreation and thus decadent, but they would fail to understand that there is nothing more important in life than recreation. According to *Webster's New International Dictionary,* "to recreate" is "to cheer ... renew or enliven ... refresh after wearying toil or anxiety ... give fresh life to." Hunters have always been fortunate in that their favorite recreation is as significant for them as their vocations. For many, it is more significant.

For these hunters, it has not been enough to live comfortably. One must live with vitality and dedication. In his *Meditations on Hunting* (1942), the Spanish philosopher José Ortega y Gasset wrote: "Other living beings simply live. Man, on the other hand, is not given the option of simply living; he can and must dedicate himself to living. ... And it happens that many men of our time have dedicated themselves to the sport of hunting. Furthermore, throughout universal history, from Sumeria and Acadia, Assyria and the First Empire of Egypt, up until the present now unraveling, there have always been men, many men ... who dedicated themselves to hunting out of pleasure, will, or affection."

The symbolic importance of hunting to the rulers of the great ancient civilizations is obvious if one scans art-history volumes. It is little short of amazing how many of the illustrations depict hunting scenes. Just a few examples are the wild-oxen hunt on the Egyptian temple of Rameses III (1195–1164 B.C.) at Thebes and the famous fowling scene from another Theban tomb; the Assyrian king hunting lions, from the palace of Assurbanipal (669–626 B.C.) at Nineveh, and the magnificent "Dying Lioness" at Nineveh, showing a lioness pierced with arrows, rearing up for a last attack; and, finally, the Persian king Chosroes I (531–570 A.D.) hunting ibex from horseback—the creation of a silversmith in the sixth century A.D.

Though from different periods and places, what all of these art works have in common is vigor and visual reality. As one art historian observed, "natural forms have been recorded with the same keenness of observation we noted in prehistoric cave paintings."

After studying the hunting art of the great ancient civilizations, one is compelled to agree with Ortega y Gasset that the hunter is, perhaps more than others, the "alert man," for "only the hunter, imitating the perpetual alertness of the wild animal, sees everything."

From the historian's point of view, the pictures of hunting are, perhaps, most important for their depiction of what was hunted and how.

Although the ancient Egyptian peasantry hunted for food, the pharaohs and their courts hunted for pleasure, sometimes employing coursing dogs that looked like the modern greyhound. A scene from King Tutankhamun's bow case shows one of these dogs running alongside a gazelle-like animal, while seizing one of the animal's front legs in his jaws. The young pharaoh rides behind in his chariot, about to loose an arrow at the animal his dog is slowing down for him.

Hunting from a chariot pulled by two speedy horses seems to have

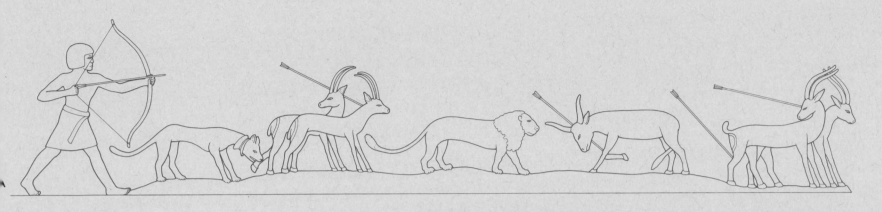

A Part of a painted relief from Ti's tomb in Sakkara, Fifth Dynasty, 2563-2423 B.C. In addition to the long-tailed hunting dogs shown here, the relief depicts some short-tailed hunting dogs of about the same size, and one much smaller dog, seemingly herding a bull. Among other animals shown is a rabbit and what looks like a pair of hedgehogs.

B Reality or a hunter's dream? Tutankhamun and dog despatching five lions and two lionesses. The pharaoh, who may be drawing his bow left-handed, has three full quivers in reserve, after loosing off fifteen arrows. From a painted wooden chest in the tomb of Tutankhamun at Thebes.

B

been the preferred method of pursuing big game. The bow and arrow was widely used for less dangerous prey, while the spear was more often reserved for formidable beasts such as lions and wild oxen.

Small game was also widely hunted by the Egyptian rulers. Among the most famous examples of all Egyptian tomb art is the wildfowl-hunting scene from Thebes already mentioned. The hunter stands in his boat as it moves deep into a swamp filled with very tall papyrus, and he apparently knocks down pintails and other ducks as they are flushed ahead of the craft. The weapon used is a long, S-shaped throwing-stick. In one hand he holds three fluttering ducks by the feet. It is not certain whether they are game, just taken, for they may be live decoys used to attract passing flocks.

One thing is certain, however. Given the abundance of waterfowl then on the Nile and the flocks of ducks that must have risen in front of the hunter's boat, his heavy throwing-stick was an effective weapon when hurled into their midst. As strange as it may seem to us, it appears that the waterfowler's *cat*, and not a dog, retrieved the downed birds.

The ancient Assyrians, too, hunted big game from chariots, but they seem to have preferred the bow and arrow, even for the fiercest animals. One famous scene shows an enraged lion, already pierced with several arrows, climbing into the back of the king's chariot, while, at point-blank range, he shoots an arrow at it.

That the Assyrians liked their hunting dangerous is shown by another work of art. At Nineveh, it depicts the king hunting lions on horseback. This time he is using a spear, which he is thrusting down a lion's throat while the beast stands on its hind legs, apparently ready to pull the king out of the saddle. Behind the hunter, a second horse is being attacked on its flanks by a lion with three arrows in it, probably shot earlier by the king.

Both the Assyrians and the ancient Persians loved hunting so much that they built huge walled enclosures where game was kept until the king and his party were ready to pursue it. In a single hunt, one Assyrian ruler claimed to have killed 450 lions, 390 wild oxen, 200 ostriches, and 30 elephants, while capturing scores of other animals that would be put into the enclosure and pursued another time. It should be noted that the word "paradise" comes from the ancient Persian and refers to a hunting park or enclosure.

With the rise of classical Greece and Rome, hunting was followed as eagerly as before, the main difference being that we know far more about it as a result of greater surviving documentation. Both pictorial art and classical literature convey the popularity of hunting for sport, at least among the upper classes.

But hunting was more than popular; increasingly, it came to be seen as an all-important part of the training for manhood, both physically and symbolically.

In Plato's *Republic*, Socrates, Plato's former teacher, says to a fellow philosopher: "Now then, Glaucon, we must post ourselves like a ring of huntsmen around the thicket, with very alert minds, so that justice does not escape us ... Look out then and do your best to get a glimpse of it before me and drive it toward me."

Plato ends his hunting metaphor by having Socrates exclaim: "By the devil! I think we have a track, and I don't think it will escape us now."

Clearly, Plato is telling the reader that the philosopher, seeking justice, should aspire to the same habits of mind that the good hunter possesses.

While Plato and other philosophers and their students were familiar with hunting, the Greek soldier-historian, Xenophon, lauded it for its physical and military influences. In his *Cynegeticus*, the first known handbook on hunting, he states: "Men who love sports [hunting] will reap therefrom no small advantage, for they will gain bodily health, better sight, better hearing, and a later old age. Above all, it is an excellent training for war."

The way the chase was practiced at this time seems to indicate that Xenophon was correct in his high estimation of its physical benefits to the hunter. While the bow and arrow may still have been used in utilitarian hunting, the spear seems to have been the most commonly employed sporting weapon. Spears were of two types: light javelins for throwing and heavy spears for jabbing at close range. One can believe that hunting encouraged mental and physical alertness in those who, armed only with a spear, struggled with an enraged wild boar!

(Hunting boar with only a spear, or with a spear and a short game sword, was an honored custom in Europe for hundreds of years; and as late as the twentieth century, several daring sportsmen both in Europe and North America briefly revived the tradition. Though the practice is far too dangerous to be recommended, the bravery inherent in it commands admiration.)

Boar were invariably hunted with dogs, the idea being to drive them into nets where they became entangled and could be dispatched with spears. Xenophon tells us, however, that the plan sometimes failed, and hunters then found themselves alone, at least for a time, with free-ranging boars.

Perhaps the most significant fact about the chase in this period is that it was a sport and not degenerate butchery. Boar hunters, for example, were on foot, armed only with spears. Their main objective seems to have been to work the dogs, some of which were almost as large as wolves, and to outwit the boar by maneuvering it into the net.

While the weapons of European hunters would change radically in the future, the *essence* of the hunt remained the same: there would be no true sport unless the animals had a fair chance of escaping, unless dogs participated in the chase, and unless there was at least some risk to one's person, however theoretical that risk might be. As the eminent Swedish historian of hunting, Gunnar Brusewitz, states, "it is certainly no exaggeration to say that the European sport of hunting has its roots in Rome and Greece."

According to Brusewitz, hare hunting in ancient Greece is an excellent example of "the show's the thing"—that the chase, rather than the kill, is what makes the hunt. For example, Xenophon recommends that, when a hare is being pursued by hounds, it should be allowed to get away "for the glory of the goddess of hunting." Two thousand years later, the French scientist-philosopher Pascal put it another way: "The virtue of the hare is not in having it but in the pursuit of it."

It should also be mentioned that hare hunting along the Danube, the northern border of the Roman Empire, exemplifies the still-current notion that only the "better class" can fully appreciate the hunt, for the rich rode after the hounds on horseback, while the poor followed on foot. The English sport of fox hunting, later brought to the American colonies, emphasizes the glories of the chase, while playing down the kill; it certainly has the same concern for social distinctions.

Along with some other components of classical Greek culture, the Romans retained Greek ideas concerning the hunt. Xenophon was especially influential. But with the spread of decadence in the Empire, hunting, too, began to suffer.

Even those who have not visited the Colosseum, built between 72 and 80 A.D. and capable then of holding 50,000 spectators, have heard seemingly lurid tales of gladiators fighting lions and slave girls being torn apart by starved crocodiles. What is remarkable is how many of these stories are uncomfortably close to the truth. Animals were brought to the Colosseum and other arenas from the corners of the Empire, and whole provinces were depleted of the larger mammal forms. Hunting had degenerated into bloodletting.

It was the fall of the Western Roman Empire in 476, some tidy-minded historians argue, that signaled the beginning of the Middle Ages in Europe. Whatever the exact date for its inception, the period continued through the Reformation and the Renaissance until the Age of Discovery. Of all the forms of hunting widely practiced in medieval times, the one that left an indelible mark is falconry, which had been practiced in Asia long before the Middle Ages began in Europe. Known for centuries on the steppes of Turkistan, an area today divided by the Russian-Chinese frontier, the sport spread east and west with the movements of conquerors and migrating peoples. After knowledge of the sport was introduced, its popularity increased apace as long as two requirements were met: a steady supply of falcons and open country in which to enjoy the aerial spectacle.

Once again, we have an excellent example of the belief that sport, and not bloodletting, is what is important. In falconry, the hawk sometimes released its prey unharmed after forcing it to the ground.

A common prey in Europe were herons. The falconer would fly his hawk at the large, slow-moving herons while they flew between their fishing areas and their rookeries.

Falconry was once open to all, but it soon came to be a pastime reserved only for the upper ranks of society. An emperor alone was entitled to fly a golden eagle or a kite, while medieval English law specified that a king was entitled to a white Greenland falcon, naturally considered the next best, a duke to a peregrine, and a knight to a goshawk. The falcon became a badge of rank, and themes relating to falconry permeated art and literature.

Printed in 1486, the first book on hunting in England is the "Boke of St. Albans," which thoroughly discusses falconry. A persistent, but seemingly groundless, legend connects the book with a Dame Julians Barnes, who is said to have been born in 1388. The book, however, reveals that the clergy—notwithstanding their official condemnation of falconry—were as much interested in the sport as were the laity outside the church.

Despite the fame of European falconry, we should not forget that the East was where the sport was born, and at the same time that Europeans were enjoying their "aerial ballets," the great Kublai Khan was enjoying his—and on a somewhat larger scale. When Marco Polo visited the Chinese ruler in the thirteenth century, he reported that the Khan went hunting with "10,000 falconers and some 500 gyrfalcons, besides peregrines . . . and other hawks in great numbers, and goshawks able to fly at the water-fowl . . . . "

The devotion of European nobility to the ancient sport of falconry failed to prevent its decline, which was hastened as more and more land came under the plow, and as shooting, and game preservation, became more widespread. Along with the Industrial Revolution and the spread of towns, these trends hampered the falconer and his bird, because they no longer had the unrestricted use they had once enjoyed of the still-remaining great expanses of open, park-like country.

Like falconry, other forms of hunting in the Middle Ages were seen by the aristocracy as their special prerogatives. King Dagobert, a Frankish ruler, was the first to establish regulations for hunting game in Europe. Under his seventh-century "forest laws," only the king and his nobles had the right to hunt. Later, in 1016, King Canute enacted the first game law in England, which prescribed the penalty of death for anyone hunting in the king's forests.

"Under Canute," according to hunting historian Michael Brander, "the old Saxon way of hunting with hayes, or hedges laid in funnel shape, through which the game was driven to the waiting hunters, was still the principal method used." The object was to kill the beasts with arrows or spears as they ran past.

After the Norman conquest in 1066, hunting methods radically changed, as did much else in England. Now, instead of driving the game to waiting hunters, the usual technique was to hunt the prey on horseback, with dogs.

A bloodhound was employed to track a stag to its bed. Once the animal was alerted, other hounds were brought up and released, with the horsemen galloping behind as best they could. Horns were sounded to keep the hunters in touch with each other until the dogs brought the stag to bay.

It is not difficult to see the close evolutionary relationship between this kind of hunting and later British and North American fox hunting. In fact, the patrons of this sport on both sides of the Atlantic often use the term "hunting" to mean this form of the chase, and no other. Even a dilettante in the sport has heard of the hunting cry of "Tally-ho!", which is a corruption of the Norman cry of "*Thialau!*".

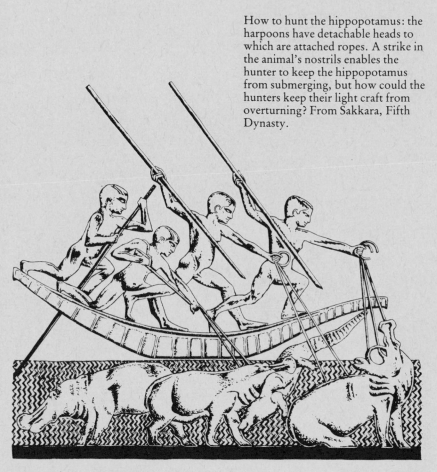

How to hunt the hippopotamus: the harpoons have detachable heads to which are attached ropes. A strike in the animal's nostrils enables the hunter to keep the hippopotamus from submerging, but how could the hunters keep their light craft from overturning? From Sakkara, Fifth Dynasty.

A1

A A peregrine falcon *(1)* waiting for quarry and *(2)* at the end of her stoop, where she has killed a cock pheasant. On the ground, a falconer has just sent off a falcon. A further four birds, all hooded to prevent them from seeing quarry too soon, perch on the frame—a cadge—borne by the cadger. In the background, a mounted falconer is having trouble keeping his bird on his wrist.

The falconer wears a heavy gauntlet, usually on the left hand. The bird perches on it and is prevented from flying away by the jesses, which the falconer holds in his left hand. With the bird so held, the falconer must be dextrous in manipulating the hood and in leashing and unleashing the bird.

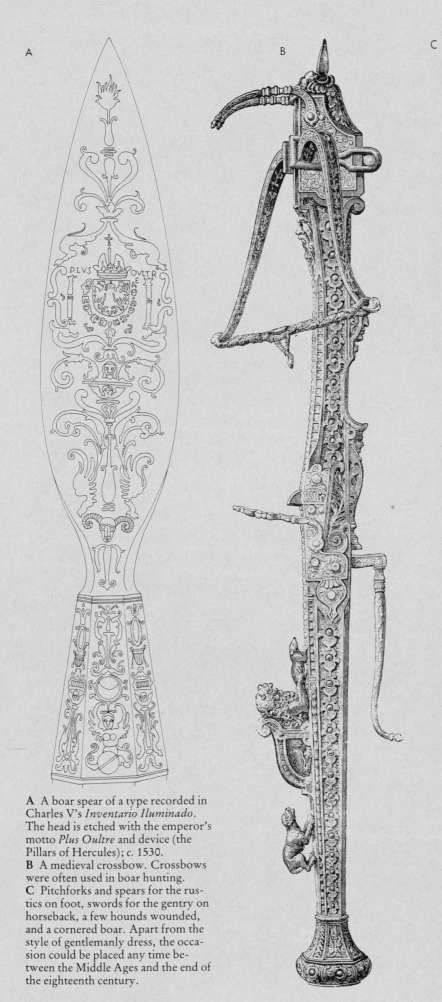

A A boar spear of a type recorded in Charles V's *Inventario Iluminado*. The head is etched with the emperor's motto *Plus Oultre* and device (the Pillars of Hercules); *c.* 1530.
B A medieval crossbow. Crossbows were often used in boar hunting.
C Pitchforks and spears for the rustics on foot, swords for the gentry on horseback, a few hounds wounded, and a cornered boar. Apart from the style of gentlemanly dress, the occasion could be placed any time between the Middle Ages and the end of the eighteenth century.

Chapter 3
The Age of Firearms

John F. Reiger

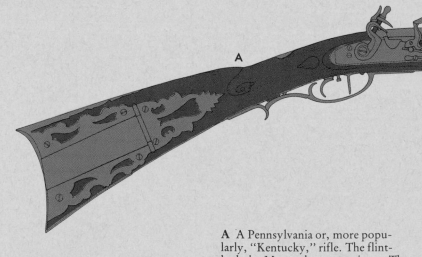

W̶hile the Norman conquest of England produced great changes in that country, a far larger change was in the making as the ships of Christopher Columbus left the Spanish coast behind them. More than any other event, Columbus's first voyage in 1492 signaled the end of the Middle Ages. Indeed, the single most important theme in world history from the beginning of the sixteenth century to the beginning of the twentieth was the movement of European peoples and cultures into every corner of the globe.

At the time of the early explorations, eastern North America was not a howling wilderness, as many still believe. Rather, it was a land already modified by the agricultural and hunting practices of an Indian population far greater than was believed even a few years ago. Most of the Eastern Woodland Indians had economies based partly on agriculture and partly on hunting-gathering traditions.

Trees were girdled and then burned off to create open spaces for the growing of crops of corn and beans, and fire was used to drive deer and other game ahead to waiting hunters. The resulting open areas in the woods, which later developed into second-growth forest, were responsible for the great abundance of species like whitetail deer, ruffed grouse, and turkey, which the Europeans found on penetrating the wilds. If the woods had been unmodified first-growth forests, with a thick canopy of branches overhead and little or no ground cover, the specific wildlife the Europeans encountered would have been nonexistent or in far smaller supply. The three species cited above all require variety in their habitats, particularly "edges" where woods and fields come together.

Many of the basic hunting techniques used by the Indians were precisely those employed by the Stone Age ancestors of the European invaders. And while Indians sometimes hunted for sport, they specialized in trapping many animals at one time, the object being to obtain as much meat as possible. Deer were driven into stockade-like enclosures or into water or deep snow, where they became virtually helpless. As already noted, fire was often employed to move the game in the desired direction.

Though the European settlers and explorers seldom used the Indians' techniques of mass slaughter, they did adopt some of their methods when pursuing individual animals. In central Europe during the Middle Ages (and as late as the Renaissance), hounds had sometimes been used to drive stags into ponds or rivers where mounted lancers speared the game. In eastern North America, this method was revived in a modified form based on the Indian practice of using dogs to drive deer into lakes, where they were killed from canoes. This cruel "sport" was not halted until the late nineteenth century.

Another type of hunting learned from the Indians was "jacklighting," sometimes called "firelighting," a nighttime endeavor. One man held a torch behind the hunter as the two men moved slowly through the woods. Stunned by the illumination, the game would freeze in its tracks, and the hunter aimed at the light reflected by the animal's eyes.

While this technique was most commonly employed in deer hunting, it

A A Pennsylvania or, more popularly, "Kentucky," rifle. The flintlock, by Moore, has a set-trigger. The 42-inch (107 cm) barrel of .44-inch (11 mm) caliber is marked N KILE—1817.
B Handgunners shooting at birds. From Tartaglia, *Three bookes of Colloquies...*

C Side-section view of a matchlock *(1),* showing the spring-and-tumbler system which activates the serpentine. *(2)* Top view of the matchlock, showing how the pancover is opened before firing.
D A seemingly ingenious means of stalking. Early eighteenth century.
E A beautifully engraved French wheel-lock, 1665.

also proved to be deadly to waterfowl. Commercial hunters, in particular, frequently mounted a light in the bow of a skiff and, with muffled oars, rowed slowly down on rafts of ducks and geese. On dark, calm nights, the birds would hardly move until the gunner behind the light was at point-blank range.

This form of unsportsmanlike hunting is by no means dead. With the coming of automobiles in the twentieth century, the ancient method has been revived by poachers, who blind deer with their headlights. This activity is still all too common in many parts of America.

It may seem strange to some that the Europeans should adopt Indian hunting techniques, when the Indians had "primitive" weapons and the whites firearms. Though gunpowder was probably known in ninth-century China and came into use in Europe in the fourteenth century, the development of guns suitable for hunting was not particularly rapid. The first portable guns, made around the middle of the fourteenth century, were dangerous to handle and required a support when fired. Although the early "hand cannon" was unwieldy and inaccurate, it was sufficiently useful in warfare to prompt further experimentation with improvements in mechanism and design. Some of the soldiers who accompanied Columbus were armed with an early, rather crude form of matchlock harquebus, but this, too, was better suited to warfare than to hunting, and the Columbus expedition carried additional small arms, including crossbows.

One of the earliest designs for a wheel-lock firearm was drawn by Leonardo da Vinci. Wheel-lock guns, which were an enormous improvement, began to appear at about the beginning of the sixteenth century. They provided faster, surer ignition than the matchlock, of which the match could sputter and die, and they were easier to aim.

Wheel-locks were sometimes used in Europe for hunting. They were gradually replaced by snaphaunces, miquelets, doglocks, and other early versions of the flintlock, and firearms came into wider and wider sporting use. One must bear in mind, however, that flintlocks were cumbersome, heavy, and unreliable by modern standards.

The eighteenth century had nearly ended before the great English gunsmiths—particularly Henry Nock—succeeded in improving the ignition system sufficiently to achieve a full, efficient burning of the powder charge in a relatively short barrel. In 1786, Nock perfected a breech that transmitted the flash from the priming pan to the charge in the barrel much more rapidly. It was chiefly this improvement that brought about a transition in smoothbores from long, heavy fowling pieces to light, graceful shotguns and thus led to the acceptance of the double-barreled gun that was to become classic.

Among rifles, one early type was far superior to the rest. This was the *Jäger* rifle—the "huntsman's rifle"—chiefly a German design wedded to the excellent French flintlock and destined to become popular throughout much of continental Europe. It was used for early target competitions, and in warfare as well as for hunting. A full-stocked, relatively short-barreled rifle, it was characterized by a rather large bore and extremely fine crafting of the lock, sights, rifling, and stock contours. Typically, it had a box with a sliding lid recessed into the buttstock for carrying small tools, flints, and greased patches.

This box was to survive into the percussion period—usually as a compartment with a hinged lid—for carrying percussion caps and patches. The *Jäger* was the direct antecedent of many fine European and English hunting rifles. It was also an important forerunner of the sporting carbine. It came to the New World in the eighteenth century with German and Swiss emigrants, and there it was gradually transformed into a lighter, much slimmer, longer-barreled, smaller-bored, graceful firearm that was at first known as the American rifle.

The *Jäger* had been designed specifically for hunting deer, boar, and chamois. The American rifle was more versatile. Because of its smaller

A A Parisian gunsmith's workshop at the end of the seventeenth century. On the left, the young apprentice learns from the master gunmaker. On the right, a journeyman removes the breech plug from a barrel. In the window hang pistols, guns, and holsters. From Nicolas Guérard, *Diverses Pièces d'Arquebuserie* (Paris, *c.* 1720).
B A silver-gilt trigger guard from a flintlock sporting gun which was made at Versailles, under Boutet, for King Charles IV of Spain, *c.* 1803.
C Two seventeenth-century shooters using matchlocks.

bore, enough powder and balls could be conveniently carried for long hunting excursions (and this had additional importance in a land where powder and lead were often hard to obtain). Moreover, it was accurate enough for squirrel shooting and powerful enough to kill deer or bears. Although it was developed chiefly in Pennsylvania, it became most famous as the "Kentucky rifle."

But during the early years of New World exploration and colonization, no *Jägers* had yet been brought to America, no light, double-barreled fowling pieces had yet been perfected, and the Pennsylvania/Kentucky rifle had not been developed. Some of the guns that first crossed the Atlantic were deadly on massed waterfowl and for jack-lighted deer, but few of them were much more effective than the long bow at moderate to long range. They were not much good, to cite an important example, for "still-hunting" deer—that is, moving through the forest silently and alertly in search of prey.

The Indian bows were vastly inferior to European and English long bows, which were already going out of use in the Old World, yet the Indian weapons had at least one advantage over the first firearms to arrive in America. Because the bow is nearly silent, if the first arrow misses, the animal will often remain still long enough for a second shot to be made.

The European crossbow was powerful and accurate but difficult to handle skillfully and, since a mechanical windlass with a series of pulleys or a gear-and-rack device (a "crannequin") was required to bend a really powerful crossbow, these arms were much slower to operate than a long bow. Moreover, powerful crossbows were costly and difficult to build. The simple bow, European or Indian, thus had hunting advantages that have been slighted by some historians.

The Indians, then, had rapid-fire "repeaters," while the Europeans were limited to single-shot guns and slow-loading crossbows. The Spanish in sixteenth-century Florida discovered that, once the Indians' initial awe of the "thunder sticks" had passed, their arrows were often more than a match for European weaponry.

This was particularly true in the American West before the arrival of repeating firearms in the nineteenth century. Riding the descendants of horses that had been introduced into New Spain or Mexico by the Spanish, the Plains Indian could loose off one arrow after another, while his white opponent struggled to prepare his muzzleloader for a second shot.

In hunting, the Western Indians used methods that would have been familiar to Stone Age Europeans. For thousands of years, at least two species of bison (the earlier, now extinct, form was larger) were driven off the edge of cliffs, just as the Europeans had done with the wild horse.

Before the horse was available to the Indians, they had only dogs to help them carry their belongings on sleds. With little mobility, because they traveled on foot, survival was of paramount importance, and hunting would have been only for food.

When the Plains Indians began to make use of the horse in earnest, at about the end of the eighteenth century, their lives were progressively revolutionized. Within hardly more than one hundred years, they had been overwhelmed by the Frontier but had first reached the apex of their development. With the horse came mobility and security from hunger, a refined system of warfare based on horse-stealing raids, and wide-ranging hunting, possibly partly for pleasure.

They now had the means of galloping alongside a rushing bison and of shooting it with bow and arrow. He who could do this, and speedily bring down the prey, was esteemed by his fellows as a great hunter.

Today, hunting buffalo in preserves with modern guns is held by many to be an unsporting contest, for the animals are slow, whereas on the Plains, where they were hunted on horseback, they were powerful, fast, and capable of turning on a rider and his horse and of killing both of them. Moreover, the abundance of prairie-dog holes added to the risks,

but the exhilaration of galloping over the Plains in the midst of a herd of buffalo was such that, in the period from the 1830s to the 1870s, Americans—and frequently European noblemen, too—traveled long distances to engage in it. This type of hunting had been begun by the Indians, who had, however, used only bows and arrows.

Most often, as a herd of bison milled or stampeded about them, these mounted sportsmen used pistols to bring down the great beasts. The American writer Washington Irving wielded a single-shot percussion pistol on such a hunt and afterward wrote of his experience in *A Tour on the Prairies*. The painter George Catlin depicted himself "running buffalo" with a Colt revolver—an obvious choice of arms, since Samuel Colt had commissioned the painting for advertising purposes. In 1837, Captain William Drummond Stewart, a wealthy and famous Scottish sportsman and explorer, who is now remembered chiefly as patron of the painter Alfred Jacob Miller, toured the Great Plains and the Rocky Mountains. On this journey Captain Stewart, too, rode among the bison with a single-shot percussion pistol.

In 1872, Grand Duke Alexis of Russia visited the United States as a diplomatic guest of President Ulysses S. Grant. One objective of his visit was the testing and purchase of .44-caliber Smith & Wesson revolvers for Russian army units. Like so many other wealthy Europeans, he longed to gallop among the thundering bison, and for a man of his rank, such a hunt was easy to arrange. He tested the revolvers by shooting bison with them. His companions on the hunt were Generals George A. Custer and Philip Sheridan. His guides were the celebrated Colonel "Buffalo Bill" Cody and "Texas Jack" Omohundro. Within about fifteen years, the buffalo had vanished from the Plains...

While western sport hunting, at least for whites, awaited the nineteenth century, eastern sport hunting developed as quickly as desire and technology allowed. The early Virginians, ever anxious to emulate the society of their mother country, were early devotees of "riding to the hounds." George Washington was one of the greatest enthusiasts of fox hunting.

America had, of course, also been blessed with a fantastic abundance of wildfowl. But as long as deer remained common, most hunters scorned smaller game. Still, in one region after another, it did not take long for deer to be overhunted to the point of nonexistence, for venison was a staple food. Virtually every effort to pass regulations was thwarted, for "game laws" were a vestige of English "tyranny," which the colonials believed they had left behind in the Old World.

When deer had become difficult or impossible to obtain, colonials looked to smaller game, and when they lived near large bodies of water, they soon discovered that, for a good part of the year, they might obtain more meat from ducks and geese than they formerly had from deer. In the 1630s, less than twenty years after Plymouth, Massachusetts, was founded, Edward Winslow, governor of the Plymouth colony, wrote about shooting waterfowl from blinds with heavy smoothbore muskets, probably mounted or rested when fired at sitting ducks.

Whether shooting upland birds or waterfowl, the most common American method well into the nineteenth century was to shoot the game sitting. Even after the double-barreled shotgun was introduced, one was expected to take the first shot on the water or on the ground, while the second shot—seen by many as almost a desperation effort—was taken as the game flushed.

The tardy adoption of "shooting flying" was the result of America's frontier heritage and a mentality that viewed hunting for sport, as distinct from hunting for meat, as an attempt to "put on airs," something that an egalitarian democracy despised. Given these and other anti-British traditions, it is hardly surprising that it took a long time for Americans to take to the "flying shooting" that had been known in Spain by the 1640s and, after the political turmoils of the intervening years, by the 1680s in

England. In *The Gentleman's Recreation*, published in England in 1686, the author Richard Blome notes: "It is now the Mode to shoot flying as being by Experience found the best and surest Way; for when your Game is on the Wing, it is more exposed to Danger; for if but one shot hits any Part of the Wings so expanded, it will occasion its Fall, altho' not to kill it: so that your Spaniel will soon be its Victor, and, if well disciplined to the Sport, will bring it to you."

Those Americans who wanted to learn the mysteries of shooting birds on the wing could have turned to *The Sportsman's Companion* (1783), which one hunting authority has called "the first real sporting book published in America." Written by an anonymous sportsman, probably a British officer stationed in what by then had been the colonies, it portrays the latest English methods of hunting wildfowl, gives hints on the use of pointers and retrievers, and even reminds the reader that he has a responsibility not to overexploit the wildlife resource.

Though Americans of that era seem to have had little interest in sporting literature, Englishmen were of exactly the opposite viewpoint. For example, Gaston de Foix's fourteenth-century *Livre de la Chasse*—which has been called "the first full-length work on hunting in Europe"—was translated into English between 1406 and 1413 by Edward, Second Duke of York. Called *The Master of Game*, it remained a standard work for centuries.

Other volumes also found ready acceptance. Among these are Sir Thomas Cockaine's *Short Treatise on Hunting* (1581), and Gervase Markham's *Country Contentments* (1615) and *Hunger's Prevention* (1621). With the rise of mercantilism, a relatively affluent middle class developed and embraced the hunt, no longer to obtain food but to emulate the aristocracy. Among such newly landed gentry, Markham's works were immensely popular.

But while Englishmen's interest in sport grew markedly in this period, their willingness to adopt superior technology and techniques stopped short of accepting the fact that gunmaking on the Continent, in Spain, France, and Germany, was far ahead of theirs. And, as we have seen, they were slow to practice "shooting flying," even after it had been in vogue for many years in Spain and France. Of course, one issue was related to the other, and poor guns made wingshooting less feasible.

Toward the end of the seventeenth century, they did enter the rather competitive business of gunmaking (with no little encouragement from their government, which took a natural interest in superior arms), and they did so with a rush. They imported the latest Continental inventions, and the great diarist Samuel Pepys, among others, wrote admiringly of European gadgets, including a couple of the earliest repeating firearms. In the eighteenth and early nineteenth centuries, the English not only took to the sport of "shooting flying" but became the finest makers of guns for the purpose. And the first truly successful percussion lock—the famous "scent-bottle" lock—was devised in 1807 by a Scottish clergyman, Alexander John Forsyth, who was an avid wildfowler.

It is odd that Great Britain, having become a nation of wingshooting enthusiasts as well as the source of the world's finest double-barreled shotguns in the nineteenth century—and of a people renowned for sportsmanship—continued to be the nation most devoted to shooting sitting ducks. This developed into a very specialized sport-within-a-sport, involving the use of enormous smoothbores, commonly called punt guns, mounted like cannon in the prows of duck boats. In the United States, punt gunning had become unfashionable among sportsmen by the late nineteenth century, although it was common among commercial market gunners for many years more, until it was stopped by law. In Great Britain, punt gunning has survived into the 1980s, with a small coterie of enthusiasts who feel that the sport lies partly in the handling of boat and gun, and partly in the challenge of paddling close enough to a large raft of waterfowl without alarming them into prema-

A self-spanning wheel-lock with a totally enclosed action, by Jacob Zimmerman, signed and dated 1646. The movement of the cock, holding the pyrites, compresses the spring which drives the wheel when the trigger is pressed.

ture flight. To be fair, this is not shooting at sitting ducks, for the ideal, most deadly shot is fired when the birds have risen a little off the water, making timing crucial.

While the Continent was moving ahead in gunmaking and techniques for wildfowl shooting, it was in a state of decadence when it came to big-game hunting. Not since the days of the Roman arena had Europe witnessed such joy in bloodletting. During the seventeenth and eighteenth centuries, in Spain, France, and what is now Germany, the most bizarre spectacles imaginable took place that had nothing to do with "hunting," though that term was used for them.

In one version of this pastime, deer were rounded up and herded down narrow alleys made of canvas screens and were wrestled to the ground and killed in front of spectators, many of whom were court ladies. In another version, deer were rounded up and forced through a "triumphal arch," down a hill, and into water, where they were shot by the "hunters." Ultimate decadence was achieved, however, when the game animals were dressed in bizarre clothing before being sent forward to be slaughtered.

Chapter 4

From the Golden Age to the Present

John F. Reiger

With the opening of the nineteenth century, great changes in sport occurred on both sides of the Atlantic. In Europe, the aristocratic liking for blood sports was eventually played down, as political, social, and philosophical ideas changed. In North America, new ideas about hunting began slowly to take root. For the first few decades, there was little sign that anything would ever change there. Game laws were abhorred as a vestige of Old World feudalism; every male believed he had the right to hunt all year long, and game was considered limitless.

One man would do more than anyone else to initiate a change in these sentiments. He was Henry William Herbert, an English aristocrat who arrived in the United States in the summer of 1831. He began writing sporting sketches in 1839 and continued until 1858, when he committed suicide.

Writing under the pseudonym of Frank Forester, he introduced into the United States gentlemanly concepts that may be called the code of the sportsman. Reading books like *Frank Forester's Field Sports* (1849), *American Game in Its Seasons* (1853), and *The Complete Manual for Young Sportsmen* (1856), American hunters learned that there was only one correct way to take game and that all other methods were "common," or even immoral. The basic idea was "fair play"—the game must be given a reasonable chance to escape; otherwise, no real sport was possible. Just as importantly, a "true sportsman" must hunt for esthetic reasons and not for meat or economic profit.

What Dame Julians Barnes and Izaak Walton had been to English angling, Herbert was to American hunting. He became the model for the rising generation of American sportsmen. And not the least of his accomplishments was to drive a wedge between sport and commercial hunters.

No code of any sportsman restrained the latter group. The sale of game has always been a part of European hunting, but there the game is sold by the owners or lessees of the hunting land, who are also the owners of the game and are responsible for maintaining it as a renewable resource. Retailing, at least in Great Britain, is also strictly licensed. It is in their own interest to prevent the depletion of wildlife. The marketing of game in Europe, therefore, has never encouraged the wholesale destruction perpetrated by the "market gunners" of nineteenth-century America.

The professional hunters argued, with some justice, that they were resented simply because they were better at taking game than the "amateurs." In any case, their argument continued, "fashion" demanded unlimited slaughter. If they did not kill and sell the game to the restaurants, hotels, and markets, someone else would. As if to encourage them, a writer in the popular, multi-volume *Cabinet of Natural History and American Rural Sports* observed in the early 1830s: "The Canvas-back [duck], in the rich juicy tenderness of its flesh, and its delicacy and flavour, stands unrivalled by the whole of its tribe, in this or perhaps any other quarter of the world ... At our public dinners, hotels, and particular entertainments, the Canvas-backs are universal favourites. They not only grace but dignify the table, and their very name conveys to

Decoy making has a long history in North America. (Above) Three decoys, found in 1911 in Nevada; they were made well over a thousand years ago by the Tule Eater Indians, ancestors of the Northern Paiutes. Two of the decoys are made of tule reeds, and the third is a canvasback's head, skin, and feathers mounted over tule reeds. (Center) Goose hunters in a pit blind, using flat, painted decoys. By Charles A. Zimmerman, nineteenth century. (Below) The frame for a modern goose decoy.

the imagination of the eager epicure, the most comfortable and exhilarating ideas. Hence on such occasions, it has not been uncommon to pay from one to three dollars a pair for these Ducks; and, indeed, at such times, if they can they must be had, whatever may be the price."

In the early part of the nineteenth century, both sportsmen and market gunners shot waterfowl such as canvasbacks from blinds, located on the end of points far out in tidal bays and rivers. Decoys were rare or unknown at first. As time went by, decoys, both live and wooden, came into wider use. While one authority after another has claimed that the employment of wooden decoys was copied from the Indians, no real proof has been offered to document this assertion. Archeologists have found cleverly made Indian decoys thousands of years old. These were generally fashioned of woven and bound reeds, and one surviving specimen has part of a duck's skin and plumage stretched over it. Decoys were seldom if ever used in Europe, but neither were they in wide use by Indians in the nineteenth century. Perhaps their development by American hunters arose out of the long practice of keeping "wing-tipped" (shot, but only slightly crippled) birds as barnyard fowl and live decoys. In order to "round out" a flock of tethered, captive birds, wooden dummies were anchored alongside. Wooden birds required far less care than live ones.

Though wooden decoys were developed independently in Scandinavia for hunting species (scoters, goldeneyes, and old-squaws) that were hunted also on the western side of the Atlantic, the folk art of the decoy achieved its highest development by far in the United States and southeastern Canada. Often a single hunter might use several hundred diving-duck decoys in conjunction with a "sink-box" (also called a "battery"). The latter looked something like a coffin with its top off. With weighted "wings" to keep the water from coming in, and anchored out in a calm sound, the device would be almost invisible to incoming waterfowl, which habitually fly low over the water when traveling in their feeding areas. With decoys completely surrounding the "box," and the hunter lying back with just his eyes peering over the edge, the ducks witnessed the incredible sight of a man doing a "sit-up" in ten feet of water as he fired at them from virtually point-blank range.

Sink-boxes proved disastrous for waterfowl populations because they led to huge bags of birds wherever they were used, and they were used in virtually every major waterfowl area along the Atlantic coast.

In Europe, duck traps were used instead. Known, interestingly enough, as "decoys," these ancient traps came in various shapes, but their general form was a huge netted funnel with the end closed off and the mouth situated in a baited pond or marsh. If the trap was of the kind used since the Middle Ages on the North Sea and Baltic coasts, the game was attracted by live decoy ducks and gently herded into the pipe by a slowly swimming dog. In England, the technique was to entice the birds inside the tunnel with a reddish-colored dog similar to a fox, and trained to appear and disappear in sight of the ducks. They became curious and followed it.

This use of a brightly colored dog with the English decoys probably has an evolutionary relationship to another hunting practice called "hunting with a red dog" in Europe and "tolling" in Canada and the United States. The dog is trained to scamper back and forth on a beach in sight of rafted ducks. Curious, they swim close enough to shore to be shot by hunters in blinds. Before about 1840, when sink-boxes were introduced into the Chesapeake Bay area by New York gunners, tolling had been one of the most popular methods for taking canvasbacks and other diving ducks. Gradually, the practice died out in the South but was still common in Nova Scotia as late as the 1930s.

By the last third of the nineteenth century, affluent sportsmen on both sides of the Atlantic were entering a "golden age" of hunting. New breechloading double-barreled shotguns had replaced the old muzzleloaders, and repeating rifles had supplanted the muzzleloading rifle and rifled musket, at least for small and medium game. Towards the end of the century, repeating shotguns would appear in America, where they were eagerly adopted, particularly by market hunters. The English and many continental Europeans, however, still seem to believe that a gun firing more than two shots is not quite sporting, and repeaters have never been popular on the eastern side of the Atlantic.

Advances in gunmaking (and ammunition) combined with new developments in transportation and communications to present a unique opportunity to sportsmen of the period 1870–1914. These were the years of the New Imperialism, when European countries were struggling with one another to occupy every last blank spot on the map, and the West was being won. The "natives" were generally docile, the ecosystems as yet relatively undamaged, and the shooting unlimited for the hunter who had the money to outfit an expedition into the wilds.

When one thinks of big-game hunting in these years, the first place that usually comes to mind is sub-Saharan Africa. Because the Boer farmers had trekked into the interior by the 1840s, the southern portion of the continent was the first to feel the unrelenting hand of the hunter. By the 1870s, much of the game had been killed off. The Boers wanted meat, protection for their crops and stock, and skins, which found a ready market in Europe. Some also killed elephants for ivory.

In the early 1870s, however, game was still abundant over the rest of the African continent. The Van Zyl family, for example, killed a herd of over one hundred elephants in one day near Lake Ngami! Early in the nineteenth century, the Boers were able to stop elephants with sixteen-pound smoothbores loaded with 4-ounce balls backed by seventeen drams of black powder. Later, breechloading double-barreled rifles were introduced that made elephant hunting somewhat less hazardous.

If sportsmen in Africa, and Asia as well, were unmindful of game depletion, it must be said in fairness to them that the game seemed limitless, and also that, quite often, they were equally unmindful of the danger to themselves. Just as they had enjoyed "running buffalo" in North America, they enjoyed facing charging African and Asian game at close quarters, sometimes with surprisingly small arms. A "howdah" pistol was, for instance, developed for shooting Indian tigers from the back of an elephant.

As with the slaughter taking place on the Western Plains of the United States in the same period, there seemed to be little restraint on the part of the hunters. Visiting Europeans and Englishmen always spoke in the most glowing terms of enormous bags. What Sir John Willoughby and Sir Robert Harvey started in Kenya in the 1880s continued until World War 1. "A continuous procession," as one writer described it, of wealthy sportsmen and sportswomen came to East Africa in quest of limitless shooting and trophy heads. Soon it was East Africa's turn to witness the sad decline of its great herds, just as South Africa had done years before. By 1910, former big-game hunters were lamenting the barren, monotonous wastes, stretching mile after mile, that once teemed with life.

While Africa was *the* place to go for a fashionable hunt in the period 1870–1914, other areas also won adherents. Australia and New Zealand had little to offer in the way of native big game, but North America was still popular. And for many, there was no area quite so exotic and appealing as the Far East.

Though the European presence in India goes back to the Portuguese in the sixteenth century, the first book on sport in that part of the world was Captain Thomas Williamson's *Oriental Field Sports* (1807). In it, the British officer describes the hunting in Bengal in the last twenty years of the eighteenth century. The book documents the devotion of Indian princes to the chase and their hunting methods, later to be employed by Western sportsmen in pursuing the incredible diversity of game available in India.

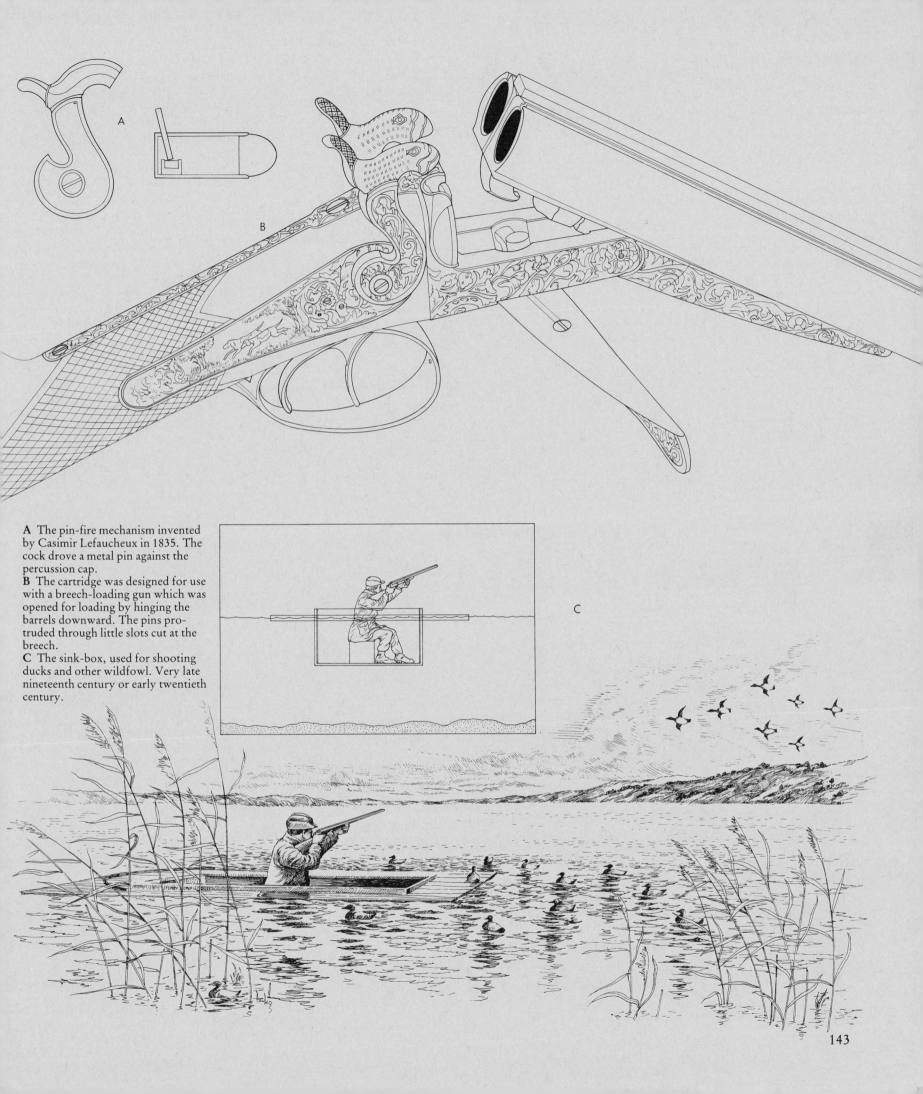

A The pin-fire mechanism invented by Casimir Lefaucheux in 1835. The cock drove a metal pin against the percussion cap.
B The cartridge was designed for use with a breech-loading gun which was opened for loading by hinging the barrels downward. The pins protruded through little slots cut at the breech.
C The sink-box, used for shooting ducks and other wildfowl. Very late nineteenth century or early twentieth century.

Like the earlier Kublai Khan, the Eastern aristocracy liked hunting spectacles. Williamson cites, for example, the use of two or three thousand trained elephants accompanying a prince on a hunt!

The British captain also discusses bear and boar hunting with lances, the hunters usually being mounted on horseback—another instance of the sportsman courting danger (and, perhaps, unconsciously making contact with his Stone Age heritage). One authority who has analyzed Williamson's work believes that the nineteenth-century English sport of "pig sticking" developed when bears proved to be too scarce to hunt with any certain success of finding the quarry. Thus, the hunters transferred the method of lancing bears to the more common wild boars. Certainly there was nothing "decadent" about facing the tusks of a boar armed only with a lance. In a fair number of cases, the hunter was dismounted and hurt.

It was only natural that coursing, too, would find a place in nineteenth-century India. After all, coursing was popular for hares in Europe, emu in Australia, and jackrabbits in the western United States. The game in India was hare, gazelle, and jackal, and was coursed with greyhounds.

Other small game included the many bird species, even peacock. These were frequently shot by sportsmen over English pointers brought especially for that purpose!

Of course, the most glamorous and dangerous game were the large mammals: elephant, tiger, leopard, and even rhinoceros. The subconti-

nent had these and many others in good numbers until well into this century. Unlike that of Africa—with its plains and savannas—much of the game country of India was thick rain forest, where the wildlife was difficult to approach. Game, therefore, was not as quickly overexploited.

The favorite way to hunt tigers, until rather recently, was to have beaters drive the game toward the hunter, who sat in a howdah, a partly enclosed platform mounted on an elephant's back. Tigers have killed and eaten enough Indians over the centuries to indicate that, even unprovoked, they are among the world's most dangerous beasts. One that was enraged enough to leap up into the howdah must have provided exhilarating moments for the tiger hunter.

With the exception of improved weaponry and, perhaps, the introduction of certain breeds of hunting dog, eighteenth-century hunting methods remained unchanged into the twentieth century. Times, however, were rapidly changing, not just for India, but for Europe and the Americas as well. Human population explosions, industrial expansion, and independence movements were all undercutting the unique set of circumstances that had created the "golden age" of hunting in the late nineteenth and early twentieth centuries. In one area of the world after another, frantic, last-minute efforts would be made to manage what little wildlife was left; but in much of the "third world," the efforts seem to have been in vain. Only in Great Britain and parts of Europe and North America, where strict regulations were passed and enforced, have species been restored to the abundance of the "golden age."

IV Hunting Arms

Chapter 1

Shotguns

ENGLISH SHOTGUNS

J.A. Maxtone Graham

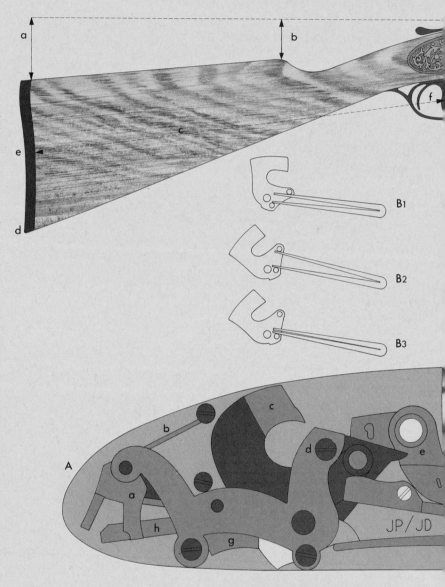

In discussing the firearms popular among European hunters, it is necessary to explain briefly what is meant by sportsmen when they speak—with some reverence—of "English guns."

In Continental Europe, as in the British Isles, double-barreled shotguns are far more popular than smoothbore repeaters. Double-barreled guns are, in fact, the rule and tradition for hunting in all of Europe. Some firms manufacture repeaters, but this is chiefly for export. However, there is an increasingly wide gap between the double guns most popular on the Continent and those most popular in Britain. In recent years, over-and-under guns have won a great many Continental admirers, whereas in Britain, the side-by-side configuration is most admired now, as it always has been.

The side-by-side is the "classic" shotgun. In the nineteenth century, this design was developed to perfection in Britain, and it alone is still closely associated with bird shooting in the British Isles. There are objective reasons why a shooter might prefer either an over-and-under or a side-by-side; these are discussed in the section on shotguns for American hunting. However, tradition and appearance of the side-by-side double are sufficient to explain the continuing British preference.

Britain imports a great many more sporting firearms of all types and levels of quality than she exports. There is a relatively new type of British shooter to be supplied: the small farmer, factory worker, businessman, and craftsman. Typically, such shooters do a bit of wildfowling now and then but never take part in grouse shoots and cannot afford the kind of double gun favored by the old aristocracy. Not even newly-rich businessmen account for many sales of the highest-quality, traditional, hand-made double guns. A man with a recently accumulated fortune, perhaps indulging for the first time in the hunting sports, is unlikely to have the patience (or intensity of interest, appreciation of the tradition, or whatever one may want to call it) to wait for a couple of seasons or more for the completion of a truly custom-built, hand-made gun.

Yet it is just such a gun that symbolizes traditional British bird shooting: a side-by-side double gun of the sort called "best" gun. This term does not mean what it might appear to mean. The finest double gun made in the United States, for example, the Winchester Model 21, is a truly excellent firearm but, in British parlance, certainly not a "best" gun; the term is used not only to specify a manufacturer's top grade—as names are used elsewhere for various grades of gun, or levels of quality—but also to specify a gun very carefully fitted to the individual buyer, and made entirely by hand. Thus, a British maker might build very fine guns and yet offer no best gun.

London has always been the center of the best-gun trade. At the end of the nineteenth century, some twenty-five makers had their shops in London, and several others were to be found in other parts of Britain.

The gunmaking firm of James Purdey and Sons was founded in London during the reign of George III. A Purdey gun is custom-made to suit the especial requirements of the individual. We show here a Purdey side-by-side shotgun to demonstrate shotgun terminology.
(a) Drop at heel. *(b)* Drop at comb. *(c)* Length of pull. *(d)* Toe. *(e)* Recoil pad. *(f)* Triggers. *(g)* Trigger guard.

(h) Receiver. *(i)* Fore-end, or forearm. *(j)* Barrels. *(k)* Muzzle. *(l)* Sight.
A The famous Purdey action. *(a)* Locking sear. *(b)* Locking sear spring. *(c)* Hammer. *(d)* Bridle. *(e)* Lock lifter. *(f)* Main spring. *(g)* Main sear. *(h)* Main sear spring.
B The working principle of the action. *(1)* Gun fired and closed. *(2)* Gun open and cocked. *(3)* Gun ready to fire.

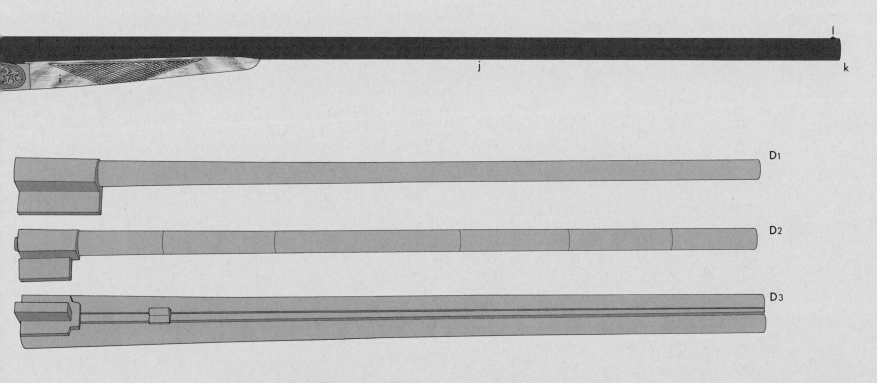

i   j   k   l

D1

D2

D3

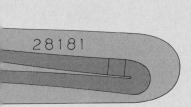

28181

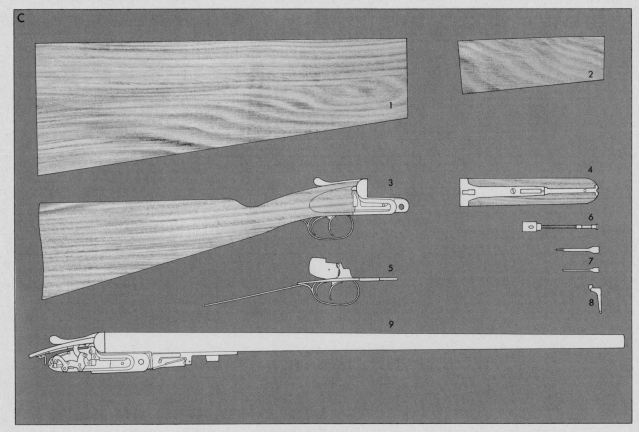

C The parts of a Purdey. *(1)* Stock blank. *(2)* Fore-end blank. *(3)* Rough-stocked gun. *(4)* The fore-end. *(5)* The furniture: trigger-plate, triggers, and trigger guard. *(6)* Fore-end snap. *(7)* Breech pin and hand pin. *(8)* Fore-end tip. *(9)* Barrels and action.

D The rough barrels *(1)* are machined from forgings of best steel. *(2)* Machined for jointing. *(3)* The barrels are brazed together and the ribs fitted.

Today, only five makers remain in the British Isles, all in London. Probably the one with the greatest reputation is James Purdey and Sons, but for reasons of tact, the following list is given in alphabetical order, and no value judgments are implied by it: Boss, Churchill, Holland & Holland, Purdey, and Rigby. During the past fifteen years, three venerable names have gone from the list: John Dickson, an old Scottish firm, have stopped making best guns; Atkin, Grant & Lang have been taken over by Churchill; and W.W. Greener have been swallowed up by Webley & Scott, who make airguns.

Best-gun makers numbers have fallen for a reason more complex than mere decline in demand. Indeed, the makers report a greater demand than they can handle: there is always a waiting list of customers, and a buyer can seldom hope to have his best gun in less than two years. Part of the reason is that the makers have always chosen to keep their best-gun operations small, almost on the scale of a cottage industry; indeed, some of the craftsmen take their work home. If the manufacture were to expand, it would no longer be elite. Another part of the reason is the difficulty and expense of obtaining some raw materials: walnut stock blanks obtained by Purdey from the Dordogne forest in France are very costly, even before they have been shaped.

Most important of all, highly skilled hand-craftsmen are in terribly short supply, and new men cannot be found or trained to replace those who retire or die. This is not an age for hand-craftsmanship. The total number of best guns produced annually does not exceed 300, and manufacturers engaged in this trade are primarily dependent for their income on guns graded as "good" guns: one without frills may be purchased for $1,000 (£500) or less, but a best gun, secondhand and in less than perfect condition, would cost much more than that, while a new one costs between $15,000 and $20,000 (£7,500 and £10,000).

Manufacture begins with a very careful fitting of the buyer, using a "try gun" which has an adjustable stock to accommodate a shooter's height, physical build, and shooting style. (Some makers have been known to send a customer to a shooting school rather than accommodate a poor shooting style.) In more than half a century, there has been little

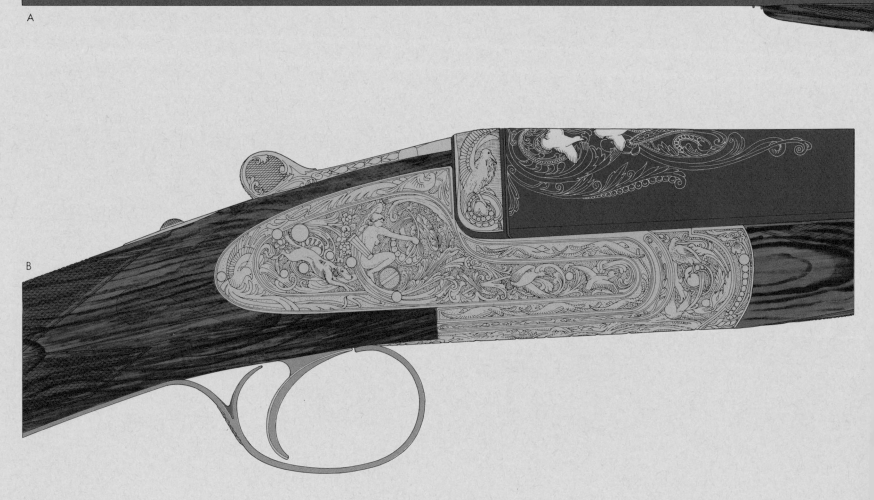

A

B

change in the manufacturing technique: after fitting, the making of a best gun is basically a matter of a lot of craftsmen wearing out a lot of tools and files, for, except for boring the barrels and rough initial work, everything is done by hand.

No one would want a best gun without suitably fine engraving, nor would a maker want to diminish his reputation by releasing a gun without proper engraving. Skilled engravers are hard to find, and their work is among the most time-consuming; one estimates that his work on a gun entails 22,000 separate strokes. The actual building of a best gun—exclusive of the waiting time before the customer's name comes to the top of the list—can require a year and a half.

At one time, those who bought such guns bought them in matched pairs, and some customers still do; the sort of driven-bird shooting that demands an extra gun and a loader is now costing over $200 (£100) a day, excluding the cost of a loader and the ammunition. King George V, whose shooting career began in the 1880s, was one of the quickest and most accurate of driven-bird shots, and he used *three* matched guns and two loaders in the butts when he shot grouse. However, more and more shooters now order guns singly.

Probably at least half of these hand-made guns are still built for the "traditional" class in Britain, but the export trade has changed. At one time, it came from maharajahs and sultans, but, in recent years, American sportsmen and industrialists have become increasingly important customers, alongside such celebrated names as Nikita Krushchev, Peter Sellers, and Lord Snowdon.

For those who lack the patience to wait for a new best gun, or the money to buy it, second-hand specimens in fine condition are sometimes sold in the same shops; some are advertised by the estates of deceased sportsmen. Such guns are still costly, but not nearly as expensive as new ones, and they can be altered (without any long wait) to fit the customer—though perhaps not quite so precisely as a new one can be fitted.

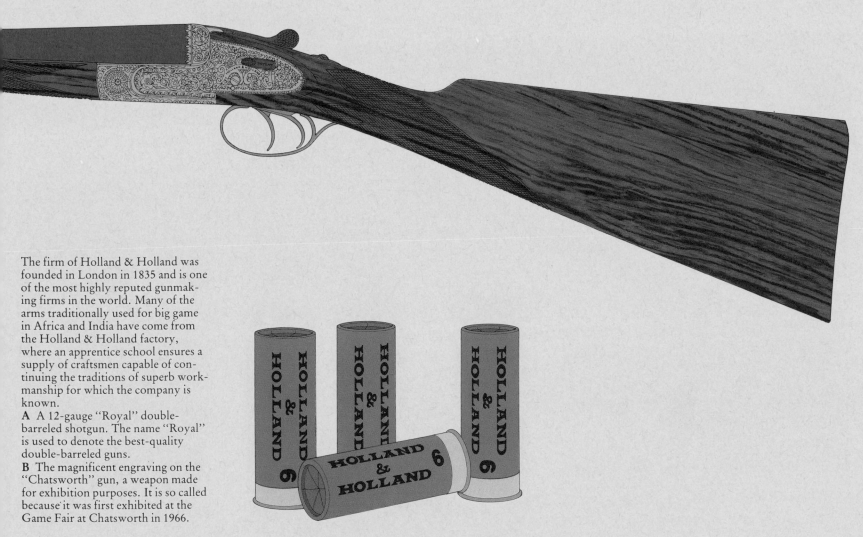

The firm of Holland & Holland was founded in London in 1835 and is one of the most highly reputed gunmaking firms in the world. Many of the arms traditionally used for big game in Africa and India have come from the Holland & Holland factory, where an apprentice school ensures a supply of craftsmen capable of continuing the traditions of superb workmanship for which the company is known.
A A 12-gauge "Royal" double-barreled shotgun. The name "Royal" is used to denote the best-quality double-barreled guns.
B The magnificent engraving on the "Chatsworth" gun, a weapon made for exhibition purposes. It is so called because it was first exhibited at the Game Fair at Chatsworth in 1966.

SHOTGUNS FOR AMERICAN HUNTING

Nick Sisley

While precision is the cornerstone of basic riflemanship, shotgunning is more like an art form. Firing almost exclusively at moving targets, shotgunners must take their shots instantly. There is never any time to lie prone, take a solid rest, carefully estimate the range, or think about ballistics tables and trajectories. Among the prerequisites for an expert shotgunner are constant practice, experience, perfect stock fit, and lead judgment.

The four important types of shotguns are the slide-action, or pump, gun; the autoloader; the traditional side-by-side double; and the increasingly popular over-and-under double. In addition to these, there are two of lesser importance—the bolt-action and the break-open single-barrel types; both have limited value and merit no detailed discussion here.

Slide-action, or Pump, Guns

The double guns of Europe have never lent themselves to the mass-production techniques favored by American manufacturers. Besides, these guns hold only two shots, and, in North America, there has always been a great interest in repeat firepower in guns.

These two problems (the need for mass production in order to reduce costs and the desire for repeat firepower) were solved by the invention of the slide action, which, because of the way it works, is also known as the pump action. It worked reliably, it did not require an excessively oversized action and receiver, and it held extra shots in a tubular magazine beneath the barrel. Furthermore, its construction was such that the action could be mass produced. Winchester's Model 97 was not the first of that basic design, but it was the first really successful slide-action shotgun—an immediate hit with hunters all over the continent, and especially with wildfowlers, who could now fire at least five shots without reloading. Some market hunters even built long magazine extensions that held as many as eleven shots (this practice was later prohibited). Fowling pieces with such long magazines were poorly balanced, especially when filled to capacity; despite this, they bagged enormous numbers of ducks and geese.

Although most Europeans disdain the slide-action shotgun, it is excellent in the field. With a semiautomatic or a double-barreled gun, a shooter sometimes takes that all-important second shot too quickly, and the result is almost always a miss—or tail feathers. With the slide-action gun, however, a split second of physical activity is required to work the action, and this effectively requires the shooter to reswing the gun for the second shot, thus giving himself a much better chance of a hit.

The slide-action gun is also the least expensive shotgun that is effective on almost any moving target. It is mechanically reliable and safe. John Moses Browning designed most of the slide-action guns that were made around the turn of the century. Exposed-hammer actions came first, followed a few years later by the internal-hammer action. All of today's slide-actions are of the latter type.

The slide-action gun's tubular magazine is quickly loaded at the receiver end. A generously proportioned fore-end of wood wraps round the magazine and serves as the pump handle, or slide. Using the non-shooting hand, the shooter quickly moves this handle rearward and then forward. This extracts and ejects a fired cartridge, feeds in a fresh one, and cocks the gun. The safety catch is usually a button on the trigger guard or a slide on the top tang. The simplicity of the action and of the feeding mechanism is a blessing, especially when one is hunting in rough upland or waterfowling country. A good slide-action gun will continue to work even with bits of sand or mud in the action, whereas this would cause a semiautomatic to malfunction. Moreover, the slide-action is a

A The Ithaca Model 37 Standard Vent Rib slide-action shotgun. The ventilated rib is a raised sighting plane that allows air to disperse the distorting hot air that rises from a hot barrel.
B The Remington Model 870 slide-action.
C The Italian gunmaker Beretta's RS 200 slide-action is now being marketed in North America. As well as their two factories in Italy, Beretta have one in Brazil.

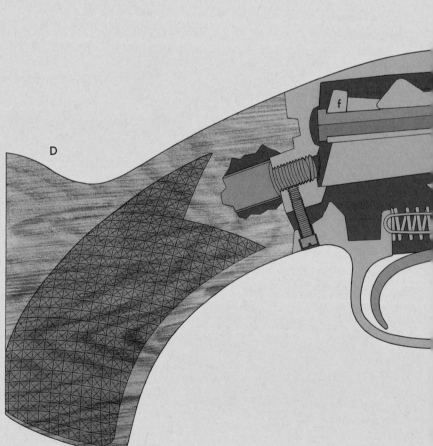

D How the slide action works. When the fore-end (a) is pulled back, the bolt assembly (b) moves into its rearmost position and the fired shell is ejected. This also feeds a new shell (c) from the magazine (d) onto the carrier (e), and the carrier is swung up into the loading position. When the fore-end is pushed forward, the bolt assembly moves forward and pushes the shell into the chamber. In the final part of the forward movement, a locking block (f) engages a lip (g) in the action housing to hold the shell firmly in the chamber, and the action cocks, ready for firing.

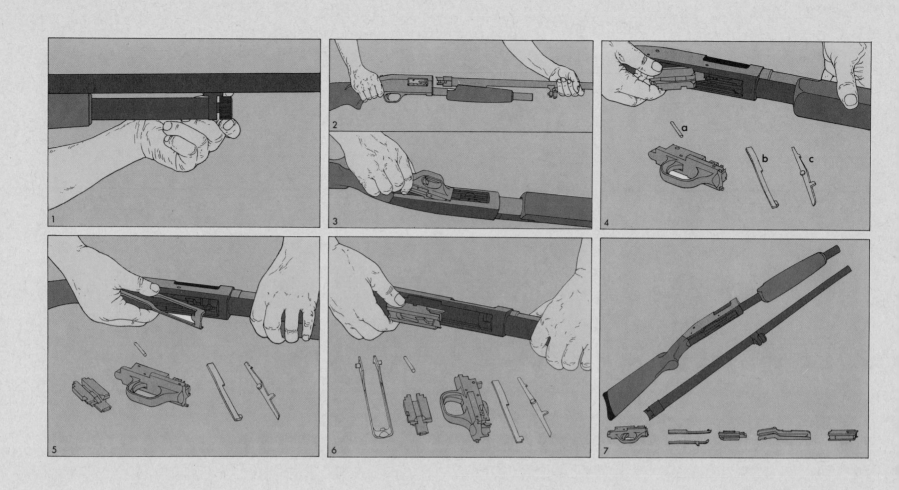

(Above) How to take the Mossberg 500 slide-action shotgun apart. *(1)* Push the fore-end forward about an inch (2.5 cm). Unscrew the takedown screw. *(2)* Remove the barrel. *(3)* Remove the trigger-housing pin and lift out the trigger housing. *(4)* Remove the bolt slide *(a)*, the cartridge stop *(b)*, and the cartridge interrupter *(c)*. *(5)* Compress and remove the carrier. *(6)* Remove the bolt assembly. *(7)* To reassemble, replace the parts in the reverse order.

(Right) The choke of a shotgun controls the spread of the shot after it is fired from the barrel. A constriction near the end of the barrel causes the shot to spread with a certain intensity. Mechanical chokes that can be fitted to a gun barrel are available now, and this means that a shotgun's choke can quickly be adapted to the game being shot at. Three different chokes: *(1)* improved cylinder choke, for shooting grouse, dove, and quail at 20 to 30 yards (17 to 27 m); *(2)* modified choke, for pheasant, rabbit, and squirrel at ranges of 25 to 56 yards (23 to 41 m); *(3)* full choke, for duck and geese at 35 to 50 yards (32 to 46 m).

versatile field gun, as its interchangeable barrels require no special fitting and can be switched very easily. Today, the slide-action shotgun is probably the most popular shotgun in the United States and, perhaps, in Canada as well.

The Semiautomatic, or Autoloader, Gun

Originally, the semiautomatic shotgun, another design by John Browning, employed the long-recoil system. Guns with this system (the Browning Auto-5 type) are still popular, although during the last few decades, the gas-operated semiautomatic has largely superseded the recoil-operated. Gas operation has proved exceedingly reliable, as well as easier and cheaper to manufacture, but its greatest advantage is a significant reduction in felt recoil.

The average shooter does not realize how sensitive to recoil he is, although the experienced man will go to great lengths to reduce it. Light recoil reduces the tendency of a shooter to flinch after a shot. Thus, the gas-operated semiautomatic provides for very fast repeat shots without significantly reducing accuracy.

Some semiautomatics tend to be a little heavier than slide-action and double-barreled field guns. This extra weight helps to absorb recoil, but it can make a gun burdensome in the field. The lightest semiautomatic currently produced is the Franchi 48/AL—a recoil-operated gun. It is a 12-gauge and weighs only 6 lb (2.7 kg) with a 24-inch (61 cm) barrel. Remington is now making a lightweight 20-gauge version of its gas-operated, mild-recoiling Model 1100.

Semiautomatics are noted for breaking down in the field. However, the reason can usually be traced to the shooter, not the action. Gas-operated guns will simply not work well if they are not clean—the action, the slide, the gas ports, and the all-important chamber. In this respect, they can never be as reliable as slide-action or double-barreled guns. However, a good gas-operated semiautomatic will function reliably to almost one hundred percent of the time if the owner makes gun maintenance a priority.

This means taking down the gun after every shooting day. To do this, one must remove the fore-end, the action bar, the rings, and the bolt. All surfaces should be sprayed with a powder solvent and then wiped off after a couple of minutes. While the barrel is off, it should be cleaned with a patch and then with a wire brush; finally, it should be swabbed dry. Plastic shotshells leave a great deal of residue in the chamber area, so it should be scrubbed with steel wool wrapped round a brass brush. If the residue is not removed, fired shells will be too difficult to pull out of the chamber. As there is only a certain amount of gas available to work the action on each occasion, there is little chance that there will be enough left to perform the other functions, if the first function (pulling the spent shell out of the chamber) requires too much energy.

Semiautomatics are generally a little more expensive to produce than slide-action guns, but somewhat less expensive than double-barreled guns. They are popular in the field only in North America, but they are made in Europe and the Orient as well as in the United States, and some Europeans are beginning to use them for clay-target shooting, because of their low recoil.

The Side-by-side Double

This is the classic game gun. For years, famous gunmakers in England have produced very limited numbers of best guns, but their prices have been so high that their market has always been an exclusive one. Excellent side-by-sides are now being made in Italy, and a few in Spain. In the United States, only the special-order Winchester Model 21 approaches the standards of a best British gun. Less expensive models are reliable but lack the careful fit, smoothness, and fine appearance of costly doubles.

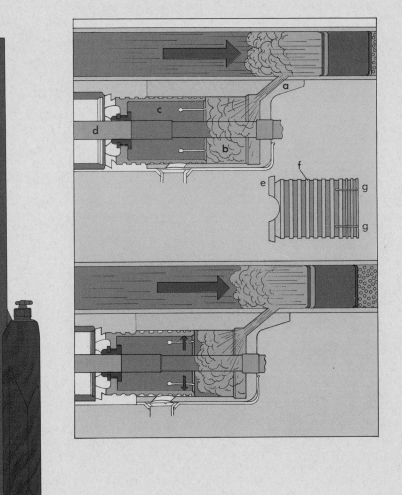

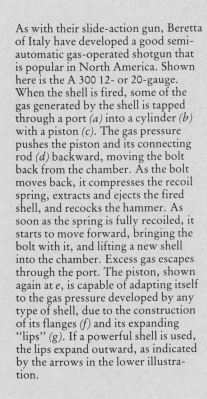

As with their slide-action gun, Beretta of Italy have developed a good semi-automatic gas-operated shotgun that is popular in North America. Shown here is the A 300 12- or 20-gauge. When the shell is fired, some of the gas generated by the shell is tapped through a port *(a)* into a cylinder *(b)* with a piston *(c)*. The gas pressure pushes the piston and its connecting rod *(d)* backward, moving the bolt back from the chamber. As the bolt moves back, it compresses the recoil spring, extracts and ejects the fired shell, and recocks the hammer. As soon as the spring is fully recoiled, it starts to move forward, bringing the bolt with it, and lifting a new shell into the chamber. Excess gas escapes through the port. The piston, shown again at *e*, is capable of adapting itself to the gas pressure developed by any type of shell, due to the construction of its flanges *(f)* and its expanding "lips" *(g)*. If a powerful shell is used, the lips expand outward, as indicated by the arrows in the lower illustration.

Gas-operated shotguns are popular on the North American continent but are frowned upon—and in some countries even forbidden—in Europe, although several European gunmakers produce such guns for export and for trap and skeet shooting.
A The Remington Model 1100.
B The Ithaca Model XL 300 Standard.
C The Weatherby Deluxe Model Centurion.
D The inside diameter of a shotgun's bore is designated by the number of perfect spheres fitting the bore that may be obtained from 1 lb of lead, e.g., a lead sphere that would fit the bore of a 12-gauge gun would weigh $\frac{1}{12}$ lb. A shotgun's gauge, or bore (as it is known in Britain), is usually marked on the barrel, and the shell's gauge is always marked on the shell. This Fiocchi shell (1), for instance, is a 12-gauge shell. The Remington shell (2) and the Winchester (3) can be loaded with shot of different size, depending on the game hunted, the range, and the pattern required. (a) Metal head. (b) Primer. (c) Powder. (d) Wad. (e) Shot. (f) Plastic collar, to protect the shot as it goes through the barrel and to provide evenly distributed patterns. (g) Plastic hull.

E The Browning 2000. Loading is carried out through the loading port. The loading capacity can be varied to suit local hunting laws—two, three, or five rounds. (Inset) The Browning's internal gas-bleed system vents surplus gas through a hole in the fore-end cap. This minimises the accumulation of powder residue.

E

155

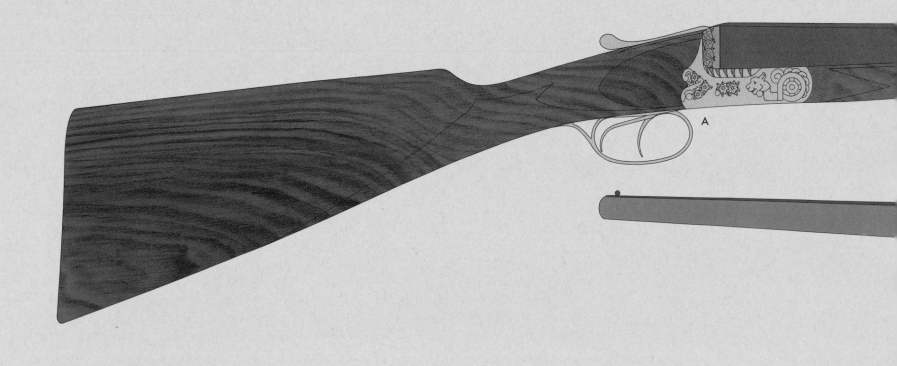

A double gun has a number of advantages compared with a pump or autoloader. It can be built with different chokes. It is more compact. Compared with an over-and-under or any single-barreled gun, its sighting plane is wider. These are objective differences rather than aesthetic ones.

Field doubles may have chokes of different sorts, depending on the type of shooting to be done. Chokes may be either improved cylinder and modified, or modified and full. When hunting upland game, the first shot is taken usually at closer range, the second at longer range; the shooter uses the more open choke for the first shot, then follows it up with the tighter choke. Conversely, when shooting driven game, the shooter often fires the more tightly choked barrel as the birds come into range, then uses the second, more open barrel as they are overhead or nearly so. This tactic is used by experienced dove hunters and, sometimes, by wildfowlers in appropriate situations.

A double is more compact than a pump or autoloader, either of which has a long receiver to feed in the next cartridge; a double is thus some 3 inches (8 cm) shorter. This enhances its balance, putting the greatest weight between the shooter's hands and making the gun more responsive, especially when handled by an experienced shooter.

The wide plane of the double is thought by some shooters to stand out far better in thick cover against a brushy, dark background than the narrower plane of the single barrel of a pump or an over-and-under.

By far the commonest action in side-by-sides is the box lock. With steady improvements in the steels used for actions, breakdowns, which were relatively frequent, have become rare. Since the box lock is less expensive to produce than the side lock, and does not weaken the stock of the gun as the side lock does, it has forged to the front in popularity. When ordering a fine side-by-side double, one should choose a gun that is suitable for a particular type of shooting. A duck hunter might want a fairly heavy, long-barreled, tightly choked gun, while a hunter who generally shoots upland birds might well prefer something different. A truly classic double might have barrels only 24 inches (61 cm) long; one might be bored a true cylinder, and the other an improved-cylinder bore. Such a gun can weigh less than 6 lb (2.8 kg).

There has recently been a trend toward heavier, blockier over-and-unders, pumps, and autoloaders, especially in North America, where heavier loads are being used more. These call for blockier actions and more solid stocking to absorb some of the recoil before it reaches the shooter's shoulder. At the same time, some shooters, particularly in 12-gauge, seem to be going back to lighter loads. In Europe, including the British Isles, 1-ounce and 1 1/16 ounce loads have long been popular; the 1-ounce load is beginning to attract many shooters in North America, for it is adequate for some types of game, notably in the uplands. In time, this might encourage the marketing of lighter shotguns of all types. At present, however, the top-grade side-by-side remains the ideal of hunters who prefer light loads.

Most American gunmakers ceased production of the side-by-side after World War II. The exceptions are Savage and Winchester. However, it is worth mentioning the now long-gone makes, as they have increased greatly in value over the past ten years or so. Leading the list is Parker, closely followed by L.C. Smith, Fox Sterlingworth, Lefever, Ithaca, and Baker.

The Over-and-under Double

Like the side-by-side, the over-and-under provides a choice of two chokes and is a shorter, better-balanced firearm than the pump or the autoloader. Its main weight rests between the hands, making it more responsive than a gun with a long receiver. Unlike the side-by-side, this type of double gun has a single sighting plane.

The over-and-under also differs from the side-by-side in how it recoils. The under barrel of the over-and-under is usually fired first, and its recoil tends to force the gun back into the shoulder, rather than up and into the cheek. In this way, the shooter is often able to get back on the target or to another target faster, since there is less muzzle jump.

The gun that made the over-and-under configuration so popular all over the world was the Browning Superposed. This extremely reliable gun was patented by John Browning in 1923 and was made first in Liège, Belgium; it has been in production ever since. The Grade 1, which was discontinued in 1976, was the model most produced; other models

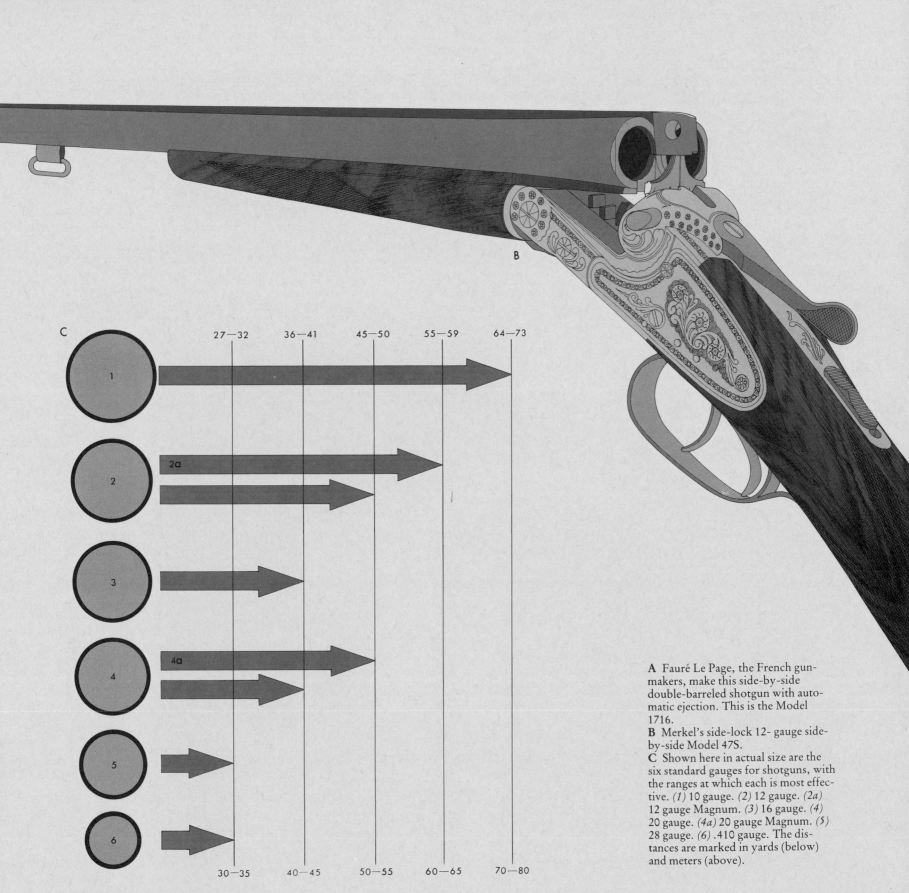

A Fauré Le Page, the French gun-makers, make this side-by-side double-barreled shotgun with automatic ejection. This is the Model 1716.

B Merkel's side-lock 12- gauge side-by-side Model 47S.

C Shown here in actual size are the six standard gauges for shotguns, with the ranges at which each is most effective. *(1)* 10 gauge. *(2)* 12 gauge. *(2a)* 12 gauge Magnum. *(3)* 16 gauge. *(4)* 20 gauge. *(4a)* 20 gauge Magnum. *(5)* 28 gauge. *(6)* .410 gauge. The distances are marked in yards (below) and meters (above).

27—32   36—41   45—50   55—59   64—73

30—35   40—45   50—55   60—65   70—80

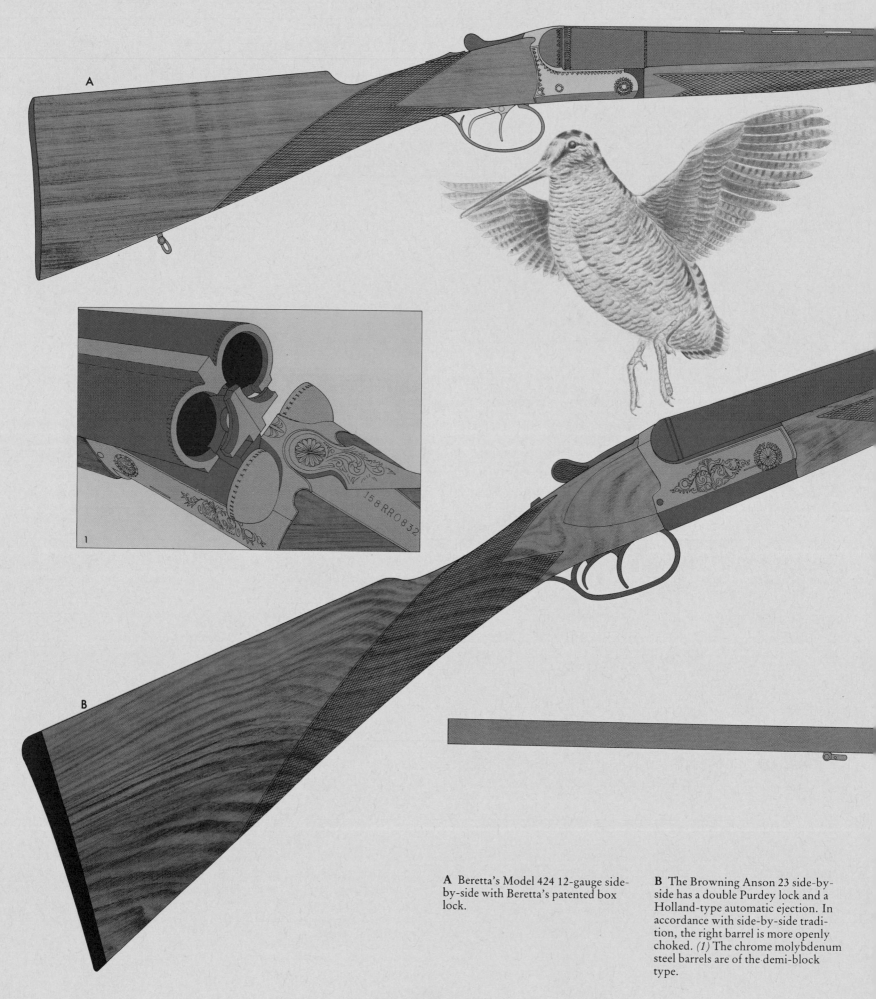

A Beretta's Model 424 12-gauge side-by-side with Beretta's patented box lock.

B The Browning Anson 23 side-by-side has a double Purdey lock and a Holland-type automatic ejection. In accordance with side-by-side tradition, the right barrel is more openly choked. *(1)* The chrome molybdenum steel barrels are of the demi-block type.

C The Savage Fox B-SE is the only American-made production side-by-side gun that comes in 12, 20, and .410 gauge.

D The Ithaca-SKB Model 100 side-by-side shotgun, 12 or 20 gauge.
E The Brno side-lock hammerless ZPE 47.

159

Some North American and Continental European side-by-side shotguns.
A The Winchester Model 21 is the only American-made custom-built shotgun.
B The Winchester Model 23 XTR is available in 12 and 20 gauge.
C Unlike British and American shotguns, this Suhler 127 double-barreled non-ejector gun is fitted for a sling. It is made in 12 and 16 gauge.

D The Bernardelli Premier Gamecock has the smooth lines of the straight grip.
E The Krieghoff 32 was made in 12 gauge only. It is a hammerless type, with a single, selective trigger, automatic ejectors, ventilated rib, top lock, and double bead sights. Illustrated is the Monte Carlo grade gun.

discontinued at the same time were the Pigeon, the Midas, and the Diana. The Superposed is still being produced, almost on a custom basis, in the current Presentation Series.

Side locks feature on only very few over-and-unders, the box lock being used on almost all such guns. Many Beretta models, however, have false side plates fitted to their box locks, so that the engraver can display his art; the Weatherby Regency has such side plates, too.

Many variations of box locks are used by different manufacturers. The Japanese-made Browning Citori has an "under" locking system, consisting of a lug on the monoblock that fits over a round surface (hinge) and into a matching hole cut into the bottom of the receiver. Two extension lugs at the very rear of the monoblock fit into two additional matching holes in the bottom of the receiver. Finally, a lug extends from the base of the action, engaging a lock on the rear of the monoblock. This locking system is extremely strong, but since the locks are all underneath the barrels, the hand on the fore-end is placed an additional half-inch (1 cm) below the line of the barrels, a characteristic that takes away something from the gun's natural pointing qualities.

Several locking systems are improvements on this in that they require

161

receivers of lesser depth, putting the hand on the fore-end into a closer relationship with the barrels. Among guns with such systems are the Remington Model 3200, and its forerunners, the Remington 32 and the Krieghoff 32. Their actions have trunnions or hinge pins on the forward part of the inside of the receiver, which match up with radii on the monoblock. Additionally, this action type has a hood or top lock which slides over the top barrel when closing. Finally, the 3200 has two matching surfaces, or locks, which fit closely together—the rear of the monoblock and the rear of the receiver.

The new Ruger Red Label shotgun employs the trunnions in conjunction with two heat-treated lugs which extend out from the back of the receiver upon final closing and match up with recesses in the back of the monoblock, but between rather than below the barrels.

The SKB over-and-unders have trunnions in conjunction with a variation of the Greener cross bolt, called the Kersten cross bolt. Two extensions built into the top rear of the monoblock fit into recesses in the top of the receiver. Upon final closing, two bolts, or lugs, protrude through these extensions to provide a most positive lock-up. A number of other locking systems are used in over-and-under guns, but the types described are basic and representative.

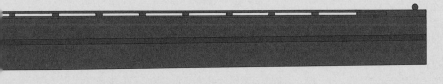

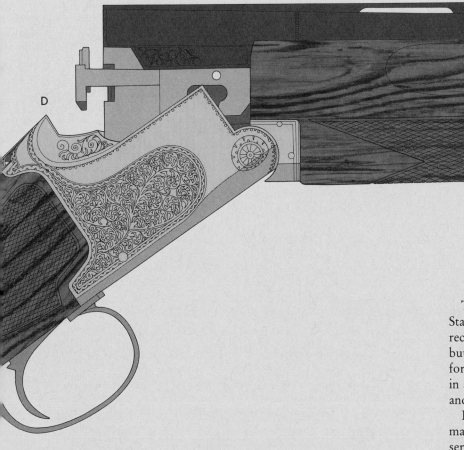

Over-and-under shotguns for hunting, and skeet and trap shooting.

A The Miroku Model 3700HS is a 12-gauge shotgun. The hunting version weighs 6½ lb (3 kg).

B The Remington 3200 Competition Trap 12-gauge.

C A cutaway view of the action of the Winchester Model 101 Field Magnum over-and-under. *(a)* The combined safety and barrel selector is a thumb-operated slide-button on the upper tang. *(b)* Selective automatic ejectors for ejection of the fired shell only. *(c)* Full-length side ribs prevent foliage and other matter from getting between the barrels when hunting in thick cover.

D The Winchester Pigeon Grade shotgun, which is made in 12, 20, 28, and .410 gauge.

Two over-and-under guns are currently being made in the United States: the Remington Model 3200 and the Ruger Red Label. Both are recent introductions. The 3200 has become a popular trap and skeet gun, but the field grades have been discontinued. It is rather a heavy gun, great for absorbing recoil, but it is not quick-handling and is difficult to carry in a ready position for long periods in the field. The Red Label is lighter and more responsive.

Perhaps the most important good-quality over-and-under guns are made in Japan. These include such game guns as the SKB 500 and 600 series, the Browning Citori Sporter series, the Nikko, the Winchester 101, the Weatherby Regency, and the Weatherby Olympian. All are excellent but still cannot match the quality of those made by Fabbri or FAMARS in Italy.

Italian makers are doing a fine job with medium-priced over-and-under guns, too. The Perazzis are among the most respected trap guns of all time; Beretta makes many models, some of them for the most discriminating shooters, and the same can be said of Franchi. German manufacturers make equally fine guns, such as the Krieghoff and the Merkel.

More over-and-under shotguns.
A The Nikko Golden Eagle 12-gauge can be used for hunting, and skeet and trap shooting.
B The Simson Bockhammerless 100 EJ 12-gauge ejector. This gun has twin triggers and is fitted with swivels for a sling.
C The Luigi Franchi 255 is a 12-gauge gun that weighs only 6 lb (2.8 kg). *(1)* The barrel selector and safety are combined. *(2)* The firing mechanism.
D The Beretta SO-4 is one of the most recent of a long line of Beretta guns.

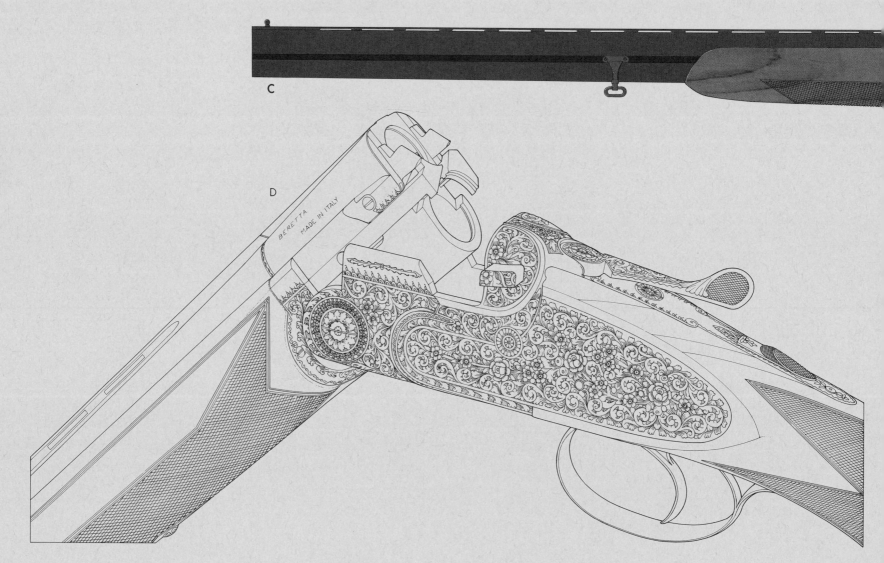

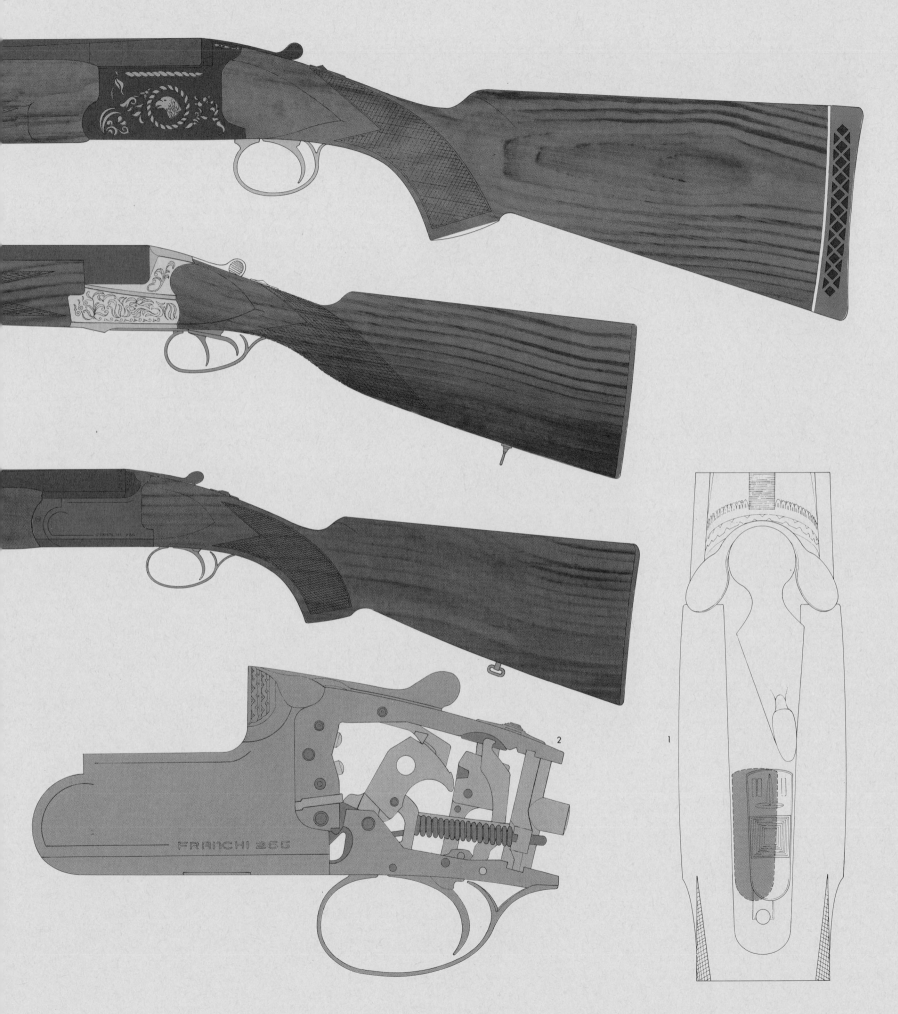

Chapter 2

European Arms

Tom Turpin

The type of gun most closely associated with hunting on the European continent is the combination rifle-shotgun, a weapon that was developed on the Continent and is the most commonly seen there today. There is, of course, an excellent reason for its continuing popularity, and that is the nature of the European drive hunt. Many such hunts do not limit the bag to either furred or feathered game, but include both. It is not uncommon, for example, for the participants in a drive hunt to get shots at hare, rabbit, partridge, pheasant, fox, wild boar, and—in some countries—even roe and red deer. In such a hunt, a combination gun is the ideal choice: it provides the hunter with a rifle for the furred game, excepting hares and rabbits, and a shotgun for the smaller game and the birds. Some years ago, combination guns were popular because the prevailing attitude was that a single gun, capable of taking any animal or bird that might occur on a hunt, was sufficient for a hunter. The gun fancier or collector who is interested in guns for their design or efficiency was then hardly known in Europe, but hunters who viewed firearms with aesthetic appreciation often had their combination guns engraved, carved, or embellished in some other way. Recently, however, it has become less uncommon to find a European hunter who owns several firearms.

Sporting firearms are made in most countries of Europe. Spain, Russia, East Germany, West Germany, Austria, France, Italy, Belgium, Czechoslovakia, Finland, Sweden, and Britain all export firearms for hunting. Production in some countries is rather limited or specialized; shotguns are produced primarily in Italy, Spain, and France, while both shotguns and rifles are made in Britain, Belgium, East Germany, West Germany, Austria, Czechoslovakia, and Russia. Combination guns are commonly produced in Austria and the two Germanies.

Combination guns are made in a variety of forms, varying from two to four barrels and, exceptionally, even five. The two most common are the over-and-under and the *Drilling*, which has three barrels. The usual *Drilling* arrangement has a rifle barrel beneath a side-by-side shotgun, while a much less common one has a shotgun barrel beneath a double rifle (*Doppelbüchsdrilling*). The major manufacturers of combination guns today are J.P. Sauer and Son, Krieghoff, and F.W. Heym, all of West Germany; Franz Sodia, and most members of the Ferlach Genossenschaft, in Austria; and Brno in Czechoslovakia. A few over-and-under guns, but not many, are made in Italy and Finland.

Although there are several technical variations in *Drilling* types, the guns most commonly produced are built on box-lock actions, with Greener cross bolt, Greener safety, and double underlugs. The selector for the rifle barrel is located where the safety would be on a double gun, and when it is pushed forward, a rear sight is raised on the rib and the front trigger is switched to fire the rifle; until this is done, the triggers fire the barrels of the shotgun. The hunter is thus assured of a means of rapidly changing from shotgun to rifle.

The other common type of combination gun is the over-and-under. German and Austrian guns usually have the rifle barrel beneath the

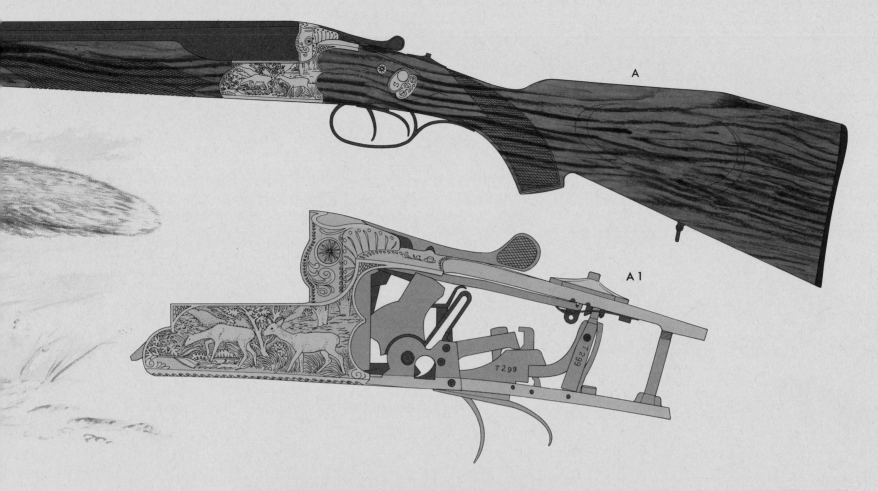

A The Carl Gustaf *Drilling* Standard: two side-by-side shotgun barrels over one of a range of rifle barrels. With 12-gauge, the range of calibers is from .222 Remington to 7×57. With 16-gauge, the range is 6.5×57 and 7×57. *(1)* The firing mechanism in close-up.

B The Merkel Model 32S is a *Drilling* that combines a side-by-side 12- or 16-gauge shotgun with a rifle of a caliber of between .222 and 7mm.

C The combinations favored by European hunters. *(1) Büchsflinte, (2)* rifle and shotgun, one above the other, *(3) Drilling, (4)* double rifle, *(5) Bockdrilling, (6)* single shotgun barrel under a double rifle, and *(7) Vierling.*

D A round-nose, soft-core expanding bullet and cartridge. *(a)* Primer. *(b)* Brass case. *(c)* Powder or propellant. *(d)* Thickening of jacket for added strength. *(e)* An expanding bullet after impact.

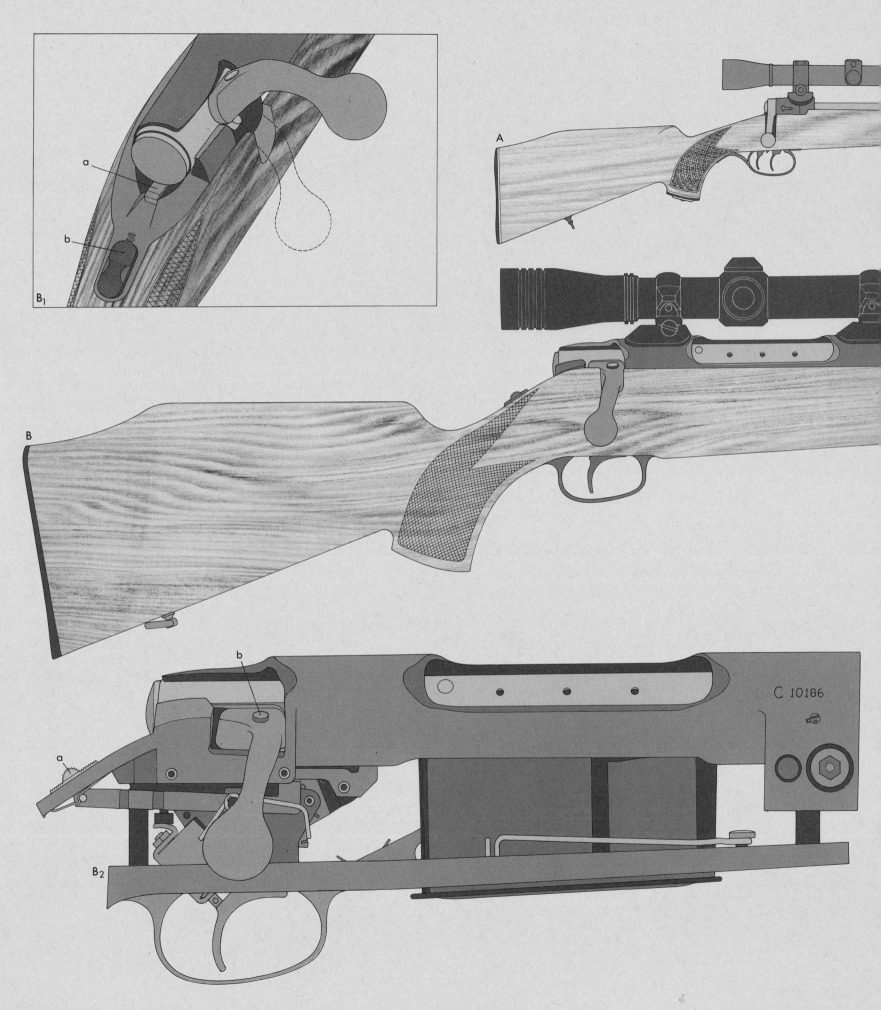

B₁

a
b

A

B

b

a

C 10186

B₂

168

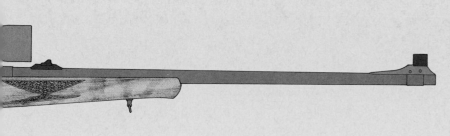

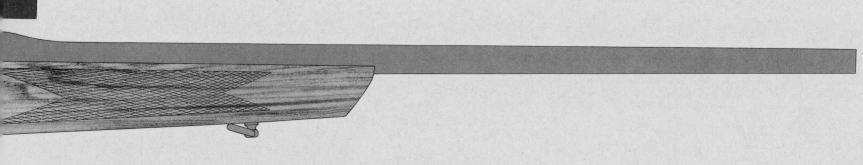

A The Anschütz Savage 7×57-caliber rifle fitted with a telescopic sight: a fine gun from the 1960s.
B The Carl Gustaf 3000 Standard is made with two mechanisms, one for 6.5×55, .30–06, and 9.3×62 calibers, the other—a shorter one—for .222 Remington and .308 Winchester.
(1) The bolt action on the Carl Gustaf 3000 Standard from the rear. A red point *(a)* is masked only when the safety *(b)* is on. *(2)* When the safety catch *(a)* is engaged, a button *(b)* on the bolt springs up. When the button is pressed in, the bolt can be opened to withdraw the shell in the chamber without releasing the safety.
C The Husqvarna 1979 Monte Carlo rifle, available in 6.5×55, .30–06, .308 Winchester, and 9.3×62 calibers.
(1) The engraving on the underside.
D The Sako Model 72, a modern Finnish bolt-action rifle.

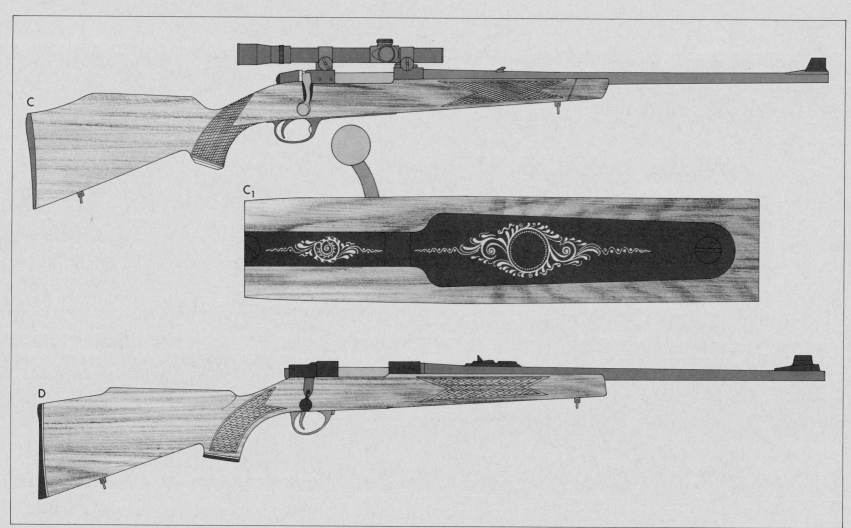

shotgun; on at least one Czechoslovakian model, and on some inexpensive guns made in the United States, the rifle barrel is the upper of the two. Some models feature a sliding barrel-selector button, others have two triggers. The latter arrangement, of course, gives the quickest choice between rifle and shotgun, being quicker even than the *Drilling*. It is sometimes a distinct disadvantage that the over-and-under contains one shot less than the *Drilling*.

Three further forms of combination guns are not produced in any significant quantities today. These are the Cape gun, or *Büchsflinte*, which is a rifle (usually the right barrel) side by side with a shotgun; the *Bockdrilling*, which is an over-and-under combination with a third barrel in the rib separating the other two barrels (the third barrel is normally chambered for a small, not too powerful cartridge, such as the .22 Hornet); and the most complicated of all, the *Vierling*, which combines no less than four barrels on one action. At a casual glance, a *Vierling* resembles a *Drilling*, but a closer inspection reveals the fourth barrel,

either in the heavy rib between the shotgun barrels and the rifle, or in the top rib. The fourth barrel is usually chambered for a small and relatively low-powered cartridge.

All the combination guns are somewhat more complicated than the standard double shotgun and are, consequently, rather more expensive. The over-and-under combination is less costly than the *Drilling*, for it has one barrel less and can be built on a strong over-and-under shotgun action. The over-and-under is often sold with two sets of barrels; the combination set and a set of shotgun barrels.

The *Drilling* is considerably more complicated, with a third lock for the rifle barrel and the barrel-selector system, in addition to its special action.

A telescope sight for the various types of combination gun is usually mounted on a claw mount, which presents several advantages. If properly mounted, it ensures that the scope, which can easily be detached from it, is always in exactly the same position. Once the scope has been

A The Merkel Model 220E double rifle has a caliber of 9.3×74.
B F.W. Heym have been making weapons since 1865. This is their repeating rifle Model SR 20L.
C The Ruger Model HR 38 de luxe.
D The HDF Standard rifle is made in 6.5×55, .30–06, .308 Winchester, and 9.3×62 calibers. It can put five shots into a circle of 1½ inches (3.5 cm) at 100 yards (90 m).
E The Krico Model 620L is available in .222 Remington and .308 Winchester calibers. It is unusual in that it is wooded throughout its length.

sighted-in, therefore, it may be taken off and replaced as often as this is necessary, without disturbing its aim or zero. The bases for the mount are not very noticeable and do not interfere with normal shotgun shooting. Claw mounts are expensive, however, for they require a great deal of hand work when being fitted.

For the shotgun fancier, Europe is a continent of double guns, both the side-by-side and the over-and-under models. There is also a large production of semiautomatic, or autoloading, guns, particularly in Italy and Belgium, but these are primarily for export. In some countries, autoloading guns are occasionally used for clay-target shooting, but it is relatively rare that anything but a double gun is seen in European hunting. A hunter who uses anything else might be regarded as a bit of an oddity.

The British best guns still enjoy a lofty reputation, but, in recent years, they have been challenged strongly by the Italian makes; there are many shooters today who say that the finest shotguns in the world are being made in Italy, and certainly, such firms as FAMARS, Fabbri, and Perazzi are turning out magnificent guns. But the debate will no doubt continue as to which is best.

Excellent shotguns are produced in Spain, too, for example by AYA, Victor Sarasqueta, Armas Garbi, and Ignacio Ugartechea, to name but a few. The great Belgian firm Fabrique Nationale has been making outstanding guns for years, and some French firms make limited numbers of excellent side-by-side shotguns. The German makers of combination guns, mentioned above, also make high-quality shotguns, primarily of the over-and-under type. Gebrüder Merkel, of Suhl in East Germany, has been recognized for years as a maker of top-quality shotguns. Austrian guns, particularly those from the Genossenschaft in Ferlach, are excellent, too, and so are those from the Czechoslovakian company Brno. Russian guns have also achieved a good reputation, and even the less expensive models are sturdily enough built to last the lifetimes of several careful hunters. The foregoing names should not be taken as an exhaustive list but as a representative sampling: a complete list would take too much space.

Rifles are made in Europe by a number of companies. The major producers are BSA (Britain), SAKO (Finland), Steyr (Austria), Mauser, Heym, and Sauer (West Germany), FN (Belgium), and Brno (Czechoslovakia). Some rifles are made in Yugoslavia, Spain, and Sweden.

The German rifle manufacturers are perhaps the most innovative, with Mauser taking the lead with a number of new technological developments. Their Model 66, introduced several years ago, has a multitude of new, efficient features, not the least interesting being interchangeable barrels. The recently introduced Model 77 also has many new features.

Voere, a smaller German company, has developed an excellent rifle which is an improvement on Paul Mauser's original design. This company is one of many that are not content simply to produce what are essentially copies of the venerable—but still excellent—Mauser design.

Among hunting accessories, not many are peculiar to Europe, but those that are have been developed to accommodate the style of hunting there: the use of high seats, for example, and the custom of hunting at dawn and dusk, for which special scopes and binoculars have been developed. Wild boar are hunted frequently at night, a fact that makes specialized optics all the more important. The 8×56 scope and binoculars were developed to provide maximum light-gathering qualities, as were the heavy, "picket fence" reticules so often seen on European scopes.

Many rifles and shotguns on the continent of Europe are equipped with slings, something that is seldom seen in North America. European hunters almost all carry hunting bags, made of strong leather, in which are carried ammunition, hunting knives, food, and other necessities. A game carrier is usually attached to the bag.

Hunting on the continent of Europe, and in the British Isles, is much

The European elk is the biggest game animal in Europe and is hunted in Sweden, Finland, Norway, and Russia. About 100,000 per year are shot in Sweden alone. Sturdy bolt-action rifles are a must when hunting these animals.

A The Walther Model A bolt-action rifle with double set trigger is available in a number of calibers. The European elk calibers are 6.5×57 and .270 Winchester.

B The Weatherby Mark V has a distinctive stock and a bolt action with nine locking lugs. The versions recommended for elk are the 7mm Magnum, the .340, and the .378. A .460 suitable for elephant is also available.

C The Tikka Deluxe bolt-action rifle is built in Finland in calibers that are suitable for elk: 6.5×55 and .308 Winchester.

more of a social event than it is in North America, and hunters in Europe are aware of aesthetic and social nuances, based on centuries of tradition, that continue to support a more complex, formal etiquette than is customary in other parts of the world. Dress, for example, is very formal compared with that normally worn in North America; it is predominantly green but can also be gray or brown. Hunters almost always wear ties. The hunting horn is used not only to control the hunt, but also to salute the animals killed in the course of it.

For many sportsmen, the formality of such traditions is extremely appealing, for it symbolizes the essential seriousness of the act of hunting, without detracting from its pleasures. Formality of dress, which may once have been an indication of aristocracy when game was exclusively the property of landowners, has come to stand for the aristocracy of the hunting spirit rather than a birthright. But, in fairness to the customs of others, it must also be said that formal dress of the sort worn in Europe would be impractical in many other parts of the world. The heat and humidity of Africa and Asia is hardly conducive to wearing a tie, while the hunting methods and extreme roughness of the terrain of North America would quickly shred a costly hunting jacket of the sort seen at continental European hunts.

Another European accessory that should be mentioned is the *Alpenstock*, sometimes called the *Bergstock*. It is a simple 6- to 8-ft (*c*. 2m) pole, usually of hazelwood and tipped with iron, which is used as a climbing and shooting aid when hunting in the high mountains, principally those of the Alps. The chamois guide would as soon go into the mountains, one might almost claim, without his shirt as without his *Alpenstock*.

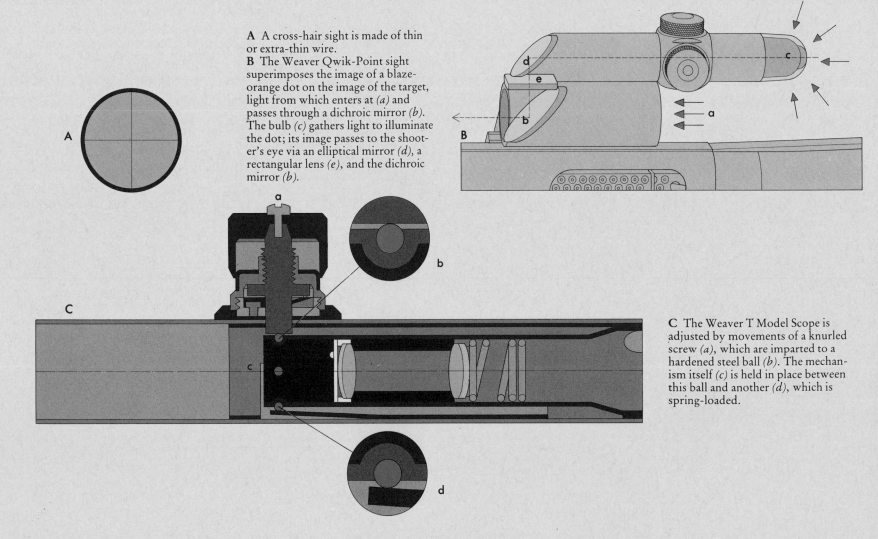

A A cross-hair sight is made of thin or extra-thin wire.

B The Weaver Qwik-Point sight superimposes the image of a blaze-orange dot on the image of the target, light from which enters at (*a*) and passes through a dichroic mirror (*b*). The bulb (*c*) gathers light to illuminate the dot; its image passes to the shooter's eye via an elliptical mirror (*d*), a rectangular lens (*e*), and the dichroic mirror (*b*).

C The Weaver T Model Scope is adjusted by movements of a knurled screw (*a*), which are imparted to a hardened steel ball (*b*). The mechanism itself (*c*) is held in place between this ball and another (*d*), which is spring-loaded.

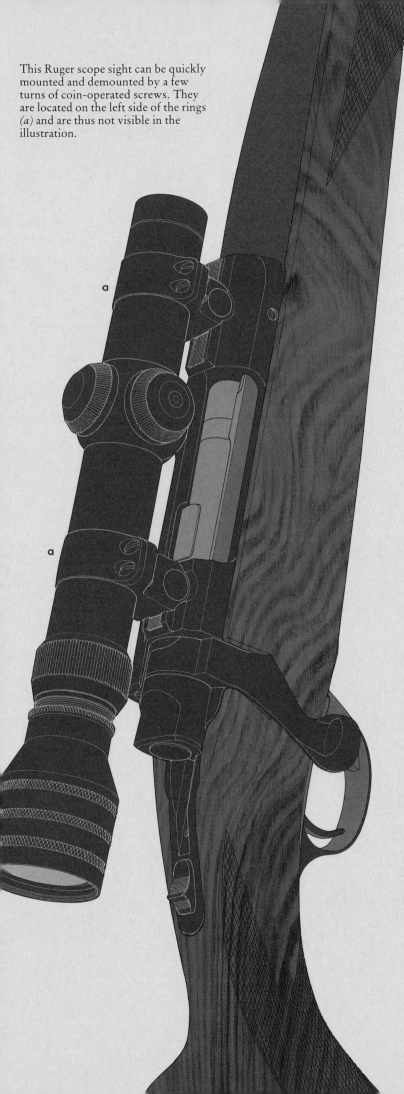

This Ruger scope sight can be quickly mounted and demounted by a few turns of coin-operated screws. They are located on the left side of the rings (*a*) and are thus not visible in the illustration.

Chapter 3

Rifles for American Hunting

Jim Carmichel

Bolt-action Rifles

The bolt-action rifle has recently come to dominate the North American hunting scene, especially among sportsmen who own, or intend to own, two or more centerfire rifles. One of the reasons is the modern emphasis on cartridge performance, most of all of Magnum cartridges. With the exception of the Browning BAR autoloader, the choice of a rifle firing a belted Magnum cartridge is limited to bolt-action guns.

Though most game in North America, as in all other parts of the world, is shot at ranges of under 100 yards (90 m), North American hunters like to be prepared for longer shots. This is most usual among hunters in the western states, where shots at pronghorn, elk, and mule deer may be at ranges as great as 300 yards (270 m) or more. This type of shot does not call for a high rate of fire, but it does require cartridges that deliver plenty of punch at long range, and a rifle capable of better-than-average accuracy. Thus, the appeal of bolt-action rifles is their combination of an excellent range of calibers and the inherent accuracy of the bolt mechanism. Added to that, some bolt-action rifles are extremely handsome and distinctive, and have a considerable appeal to today's shooters.

Though the basic bolt-action design has been updated and improved over the years, it has really not changed much since the days of Paul Mauser, who refined the turnbolt concept into a working reality a century ago. Its simplicity of design and operation, together with its high strength, makes it the safest and most reliable repeating action available.

Nothing quite matches the accuracy of a bolt-action gun. During the last hundred years, various falling-bolt, single-shot actions were considered the most accurate, but the bolt gun has ruled supreme for the past few decades. This is marked with current target rifles, both rimfire and centerfire, which are all based on bolt-action designs. The one exception, the British BSA rimfire match rifle, is notable just because it is the exception.

There are several reasons for this intrinsic accuracy. First among them is the inherent stiffness of the action. Any flexing or bending of a rifle action when it fires lessens accuracy, and the symmetrical locking arrangement of most bolt guns helps in resisting such flexing; so does the one-piece stock, which is (usually) rigidly attached to the action. The more modern bolt-actions are also capable of extremely fast lock times and have triggers that can be finely adjusted, two features which aid accuracy and performance.

Although the bolt-action is considered to be the slowest mechanism in operation of all repeating-rifle mechanisms, it can be fired at a surprisingly high rate. The American Match Course of Fire includes a 200-yard (183 m) phase which calls for ten shots to be aimed and fired within sixty seconds: the shooter begins in the standing position, must then get into the sitting position, fire five shots, reload the magazine, and fire five more shots. A good bolt-action rifle marksman can easily do this with seconds to spare and place all his shots into an area smaller than that of his hand.

Americans were introduced to the bolt-action rifle in a big way only during World War I, when hundreds of thousands of Doughboys were issued with 1903 Springfield rifles. Up until then, experiments with bolt designs had met with only limited success. In 1879, for example, Winchester began manufacturing the Hotchkiss bolt gun, and some 85,000 were made during the next twenty years. Remington made the Lee-designed bolt-action rifle from 1886 until 1906. A more successful rifle was the Krag-Jorgensen bolt gun, built under license by Springfield Armory and chambered for the 30/40 Krag round. This was the standard United States Service rifle from 1894 until 1904, the Army's first bolt-action rifle, and its standard arm during the Spanish-American War.

Since then, dozens of American-made and -designed bolt-action rifles have come and gone, and dozens of European models have been used by North American hunters. Most popular of the European makes have been the Sakos and various Mausers. At present, the most popular American centerfire bolt guns are the Remington M-700, Winchester M-70, Ruger M 77, and Savage M-110. Another popular bolt gun is the Weatherby Mark-V; this is the produce of an American company whose guns have been built in West Germany and are now being built in Japan. There are, of course, other bolt-action guns, too numerous to mention here, but the target-type centerfire guns should not be forgotten; smaller makers, such as Shilen and Wichita, produce guns that are among the most accurate in the world and are truly remarkable pieces of design.

The Winchester Model 52 rifle had been North America's most respected rimfire bolt-action gun when it was discontinued in 1979; for many years, it had been the leading target rifle in the United States and the one that had established a number of national records. The sportier version of the M 52 is considered to be the best of its type ever built in the United States, and collectors now pay several hundred dollars for a good specimen. At present, the German-made Anschütz Rimfire, another bolt design, is the overwhelming favorite among North American target shooters.

One of the goals of every American rifle-lover is to acquire one of the beautiful custom-made rifles built by one of the top American stockmakers. The demand exceeds the supply, prices are several hundred dollars at least, and, with very few exceptions, these superb rifles are all bolt-action guns.

Lever-action Rifles

The lever-action rifle, more than any other, has come to symbolize American hunting and the traditional American concept of arms design. This is so thanks to the tremendous publicity or image-making of popular literature, motion pictures, and television epics that consistently link the lever-action rifle with the "taming" of the American West.

It is fascinating to note that attempts to improve, refine, or streamline the basic nineteenth-century lever-action rifle have almost universally

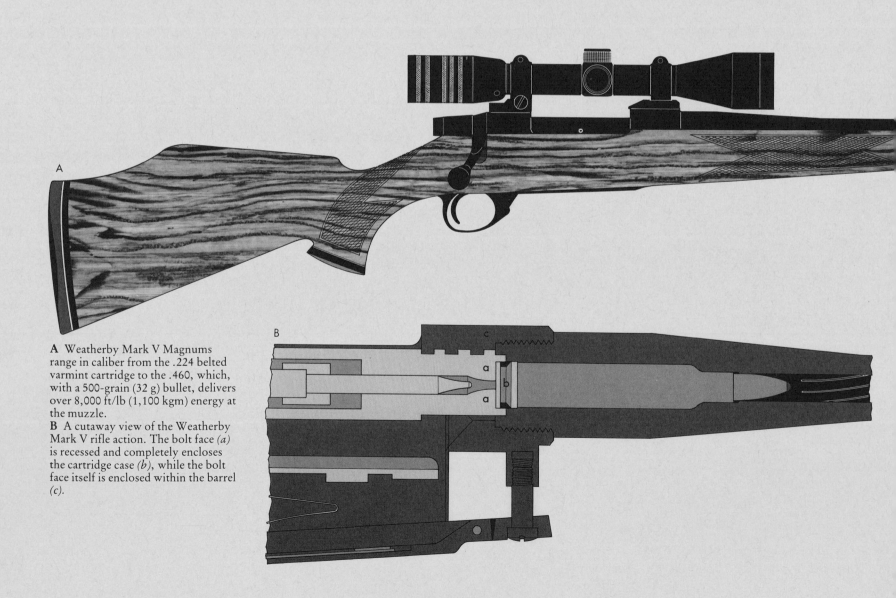

A Weatherby Mark V Magnums range in caliber from the .224 belted varmint cartridge to the .460, which, with a 500-grain (32 g) bullet, delivers over 8,000 ft/lb (1,100 kgm) energy at the muzzle.
B A cutaway view of the Weatherby Mark V rifle action. The bolt face (a) is recessed and completely encloses the cartridge case (b), while the bolt face itself is enclosed within the barrel (c).

failed. Examples of this are the modern-looking Winchester Model 88 centerfire (1955–1973) and Model 150 rimfire (1967–1973), Sako's Finn-wolfe (1963–1972) and Model 73 (1973–1975), Marlin's "Levermatic" rimfire Model 56 and Model 57, and centerfire Model 62 (1955–1965), and Remington's Model 76 (1962–1964). All were improved designs of the hammerless type, with short-throw mechanisms and greater strength and accuracy, but, despite their obvious improvements over lever-action designs dating from the nineteenth century, all were commercial failures within only a few years.

The most modern mechanical lever-action currently being produced, Browning's BLR, is carefully wrapped up in 1890s trappings to give it a distinctively "Western" flair. The only exception to the rule of Western appearance is the Savage Model 99, which, though dating back to 1899, has a hammerless profile. It has been constantly updated since its introduction; even so, Savage recently "reintroduced" the old Model 99A in an effort to lure shooters captivated by its "Gay 90s" configuration.

Historians of firearms seldom note that the lever-action was an early commercial disappointment, despite its place in American history. Oliver Winchester saw it as a military arm and promoted it as such in the war ministries of Europe, Asia, and South America. "Where," he asked, "is the military genius who will grasp the significance of this machine of war and thereby rule the capitals of the world?" The world's military genii remained skeptical and, except for sporadic orders for lever-action muskets, Winchester had to make do with a relatively small but steady civilian demand for his wares. Nevertheless, his Model 94 carbine has become the symbol of all lever-action guns and exemplifies them in discussions of their uses, virtues, and faults.

The lever-action gun in North America is most commonly classified as a "brush gun;" its use is in brushy or wooded areas where most shots are fired at less than 80 yards (75 m), and shots of over 100 yards (90 m) are an exception. For these conditions, a short, light, easily carried carbine capable of a relatively high rate of fire is needed.

Lever-action rifles have never been considered to be especially accurate, and certainly not when compared with bolt-action rifles and some types of single-shot rifle. This relative lack of accuracy is due to the two-piece stock design, the light barrel, and the comparatively non-rigid action (receiver) which flexes considerably on firing. Nor have lever-action rifles been chambered, until recently, for notably accurate cartridges.

Fine accuracy has, however, never been essential to the purposes of the lever-action rifle, although some models are capable of surprising accuracy. With selected ammunition, some guns can group five shots inside a circle of 2 inches (5 cm) diameter at 110 yards (100 m); even if this is an exception, virtually any modern lever-action rifle can group its shots within a circle of twice that diameter.

The first lever-action rifles were chambered for the early self-contained cartridges, which were also used in pistols. The Winchester Model 73 (1873–1919) fired .44/40 and similar pistol-type cartridges, which were barely adequate for deer and not adequate at all for bear, elk, and bison. Bigger, more powerful cartridges called for bigger, more massive rifles; a succession of lever-action rifles was designed for the .45/70 and larger cartridges. Winchester and Marlin made rifles to fire these bison-class cartridges, a development that culminated with the Winchester Model 1895 (1895–1931), which fired such high-powered cartridges as the .30/06 and the giant .405 Winchester round, which had a muzzle energy of 3,220 ft/lbs (444 kgm).

Lever-action guns might have been designed for bigger and bigger cartridges but for the advent of the bolt-action rifle; the surviving lever-action rifles are the light, fast-handling carbines used for hunting deer and black bear. An exception is the lever-action rifles made by Marlin,

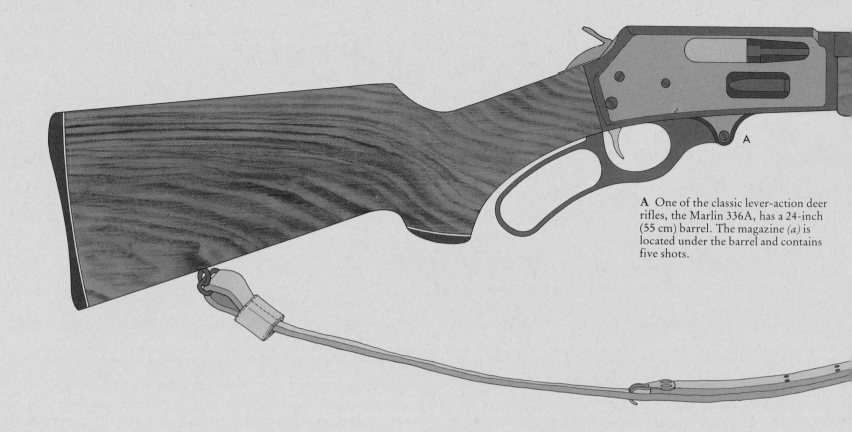

A One of the classic lever-action deer rifles, the Marlin 336A, has a 24-inch (55 cm) barrel. The magazine *(a)* is located under the barrel and contains five shots.

the .45/70 and the .444, which take Marlin cartridges made to a nineteenth-century pattern; these cartridges do not expand the practical use of the lever-action gun, and the combination appeals almost entirely to shooters who have a sentimental attachment to such old-fashioned styles.

The leading feature of lever-action rifles has been said to be their speed of action, but, in practice, this is seldom realized: to maintain a high rate of fire, the butt must remain against the shoulder and the sights be kept steadily on the target while the lever is operated and the trigger pulled. The typical hunter, however, is more likely than not to remove the rifle from his shoulder while he deliberately operates the mechanism between shots; this gives an operational speed about the same as that of a bolt-action.

The external hammer of most lever-actions has long been considered an important safety feature, but, in practice, this is not quite what it seems. To lower the hammer to the "safe" position, the trigger must be pulled; occasionally, the hammer slips from under the thumb and fires the rifle. To obviate this, Mossberg has recently introduced a modification to the Model 479 lever-action rifle; this takes the form of a manually operated cross bolt which blocks the hammer even if it falls by accident.

Lever-action rifles are usually sighted by means of open "V-sights" fitted in the factory; up until recently, this sighting arrangement could be refined by an adjustable "peep" sight fitted to the receiver or tang. While such peep (or aperture) sights are still manufactured by a few sight makers and are available for all current makes of lever-action rifle, today's buyer is most likely to choose a telescopic sight. However, this can lead to problems.

The popular Winchester 94 ejects its fired cases out of the top of the receiver, on which there is no solid place to mount a scope sight. Even if a scope sight can be mounted over the receiver, the ejected shells may strike it, fall back into the mechanism, and cause a stoppage. This problem is usually got round by attaching the scope mounting to the left of the receiver and positioning the scope off-center to the left, so that ejected cases do not strike it. Another solution, developed by the Leupold Optical Company, is to attach the scope to the barrel forward of the receiver; this calls for a scope with unusually long eye relief, such as Leupold's specially designed eye-relief scopes. They have 2× or 4× magnification and offer 10- to 24- inch (25 to 60 cm) eye relief. Some other lever-action models, for example those by Browning, Marlin, and Mossberg, feature side ejection and solid receiver tops, which permit conventional scope mountings.

The cartridge that is almost synonymous with the lever-action rifle is the .30/30 WCF and, indeed, the .30/30 caliber is one of the favorites for the lever-action rifles made by Winchester, Marlin, Mossberg, and Savage. While certainly adequate for deer and smaller bear, in terms of performance it is overshadowed by almost all other calibers for which lever-action rifles are currently chambered.

The Savage Model 99, for example, is currently available in .22/250 Remington, .250 Savage, .243 Winchester, .300 Savage, .308 Winchester, .358 Winchester, and .375 Winchester. The .22/250, a purely varmint cartridge, is not suitable for big game, but any one of the other cartridges is good for deer. The Browning BLR is available in .243, .308, and .358, all calibers of modern, high-intensity cartridges suitable for deer-sized game.

The Marlin rifles have not been adapted to high-intensity cartridges. They take medium-to-low pressure cartridges such as the .357 and the .44 Magnum pistol, the .30/30, the .35 Remington, and the .45/70. The Mossberg rifles are similar to the Marlin guns and take either the .30/30 or the .35 Remington.

It seems safe to say that lever-action centerfire rifles will remain popular for many years to come and that they will not vary very much from their present conventional configurations. The same can be said of

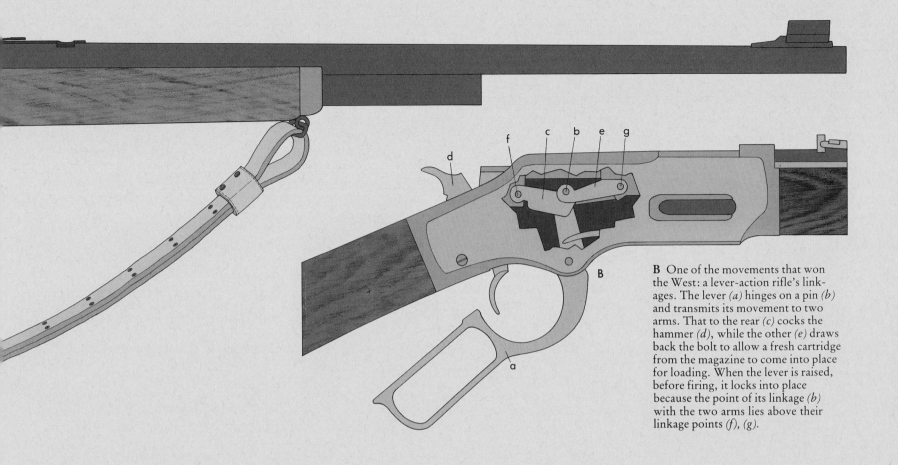

B One of the movements that won the West: a lever-action rifle's linkages. The lever *(a)* hinges on a pin *(b)* and transmits its movement to two arms. That to the rear *(c)* cocks the hammer *(d)*, while the other *(e)* draws back the bolt to allow a fresh cartridge from the magazine to come into place for loading. When the lever is raised, before firing, it locks into place because the point of its linkage *(b)* with the two arms lies above their linkage points *(f)*, *(g)*.

the lever-action rimfires in the .22 caliber; their appeal is based on their "Old West" styling, for their accuracy is about the same as most other rimfire rifles. In speed and ease of operation, they rank ahead of bolt-action rimfires. In one respect, they may be slightly superior to most other American rimfire hunting rifles, and that is that they are of an unusually high quality. The rimfire, lever-action rifles by Browning, Marlin, and Winchester are all markedly better made than most other rimfires, and if they are among the most expensive rimfires made in the United States, this is partly because they are made of the best materials.

Pump and Autoloading Rifles

No less a manufacturer than Colt made a pump-action rifle way back in 1885: the "Lightning." It was not especially successful and was discontinued after the turn of the century, even though it was well made. While the pump action is very popular in North American shotguns, it has never been really favored for rifles. The appeal of the pump-action rifle is mainly to those hunters who use pump- (or slide-) action shotguns and have become accustomed to ejecting shells by pumping the forestock.

Current centerfire pump-action rifles are pretty well summed up by Remington's Model 760 Gamemaster (in .243, 6mm Remington, .270, .308, and .30/06 calibers) and Savage's Model 170 (in either the .30/30 or .35 Remington calibers). In skilled hands, the pump-action rifle is second only to the autoloader in operating speed.

After firing, the forestock is pulled fully to the rear by the forward hand, then moved forward again until the action locks into battery position. This back-and-forth motion extracts and ejects the fired case, cocks the firing mechanism, and feeds a fresh cartridge into the chamber. It is a smooth, natural movement and offers the advantage of allowing the shooter's hands to remain in their firing positions. The main disadvantage in operation is the small mechanical leverage exerted during the extraction phase: if spent cases tend to stick in the chamber, extraction

may become difficult and may even cause a temporary stoppage.

Accuracy of pump-action centerfire rifles is on a par with that of lever-action and autoloading rifles. There can be considerable variation of accuracy, however, among rifles of the same make, model, and caliber, and even if blanket condemnations of the accuracy of pump-action rifles are sometimes heard, they are not necessarily justified.

Pump-action rimfires are somewhat more popular than the larger bores. Models are made by Browning and Remington, while the Brazilian firm of Rossi currently produces a replica of the discontinued Winchester Model 62, which was in production from 1932 to 1959.

No development of pump-action rifles seems to have occurred recently, if one excepts that incorporated in Browning's BPR rimfire, a pump rifle made possible simply because it has so many parts in common with the similar Browning rimfire BAR-22 autoloader.

Autoloaders, or semiautomatics, in centerfire and rimfire forms, are much more popular in the United States than pump-action rifles. At this writing, half-a-dozen or so American-made or -designed sporting-type centerfire autoloaders are on the market, together with another dozen or more copies of military-type rifles that should be classed as "junk guns." Browning, Harrington & Richardson, Ruger, and Remington all have centerfire sporting rifles available in many calibers, ranging from the .223 Remington and the .44 Magnum, up to the .300 Winchester Magnum. Experimental autoloaders have been made in the .458 Winchester Magnum caliber.

The obvious advantage of an autoloading rifle is its speed and ease of fire. The shooter needs only to pull the trigger and the extraction, ejection, and feeding operations are performed automatically. It is wrong to call these guns automatics, for an automatic is, correctly speaking, a machine gun which continues to fire as long as the trigger is depressed. "Semiautomatic" is more correct. On an autoloader, the trigger must be pulled for each shot. In the United States, private ownership of full automatics, or machine guns, is prohibited except under special license, and nowhere in the United States or Canada are automatics permitted for sport hunting. Autoloaders, by contrast, may be legally used for hunting, subject to the restrictions in force in some states, which limit magazine capacity to only a few rounds.

The objection to autoloaders that is most often heard is their alleged tendency to jam. The usual cause of stoppages is hand-loaded ammunition that has been improperly prepared, but apart from this, autoloaders are surprisingly trouble-free and reliable.

The mechanisms in current production are either the gas-operated or the straight-blowback. The latter is extremely simple: the rearward thrust of the fired cartridge pushes the bolt backward and thereby begins the new cycle of operation. The combination of simplicity and ease of manufacture has made this mechanism the logical choice for rimfire rifles, but it does not adapt well to use with higher-powered cartridges, which require an increasingly heavy breechblock to balance the rearward thrust. At one time, Winchester, for example, made centerfire sporting autoloaders that had simple blowback mechanisms—the Models 07 and 10—but they weighed up to 8½ lb (4 kg) with their massive breechblocks; they fired relatively low-energy rounds, the .351 and the .401 Winchester.

With rifles firing high-intensity cartridges, a more practical method is to use some of the gases from the fired cartridge to actuate the mechanism, the same system as that used for semiautomatic shotguns. This system is used, for instance, in the Browning BAR Sporter, the Remington 742, and the Ruger Mini-14.

Remington once built some autoloading rifles using the Browning long-recoil system, but they have long since been discontinued; this type of action is complicated to make and less efficient than the gas system, and it will probably not be used again for rifles.

Though the accuracy of autoloading rifles is often belittled, there is no reason to expect them to be less accurate than pump-action or lever-action guns, or, for that matter, many bolt-action rifles. Highly refined National Match versions of two United States Service autoloading rifles, the M-1 Garand and the M-14, are capable of astonishingly fine accuracy, sometimes grouping ten shots inside a 3-inch (7.5 cm) circle at 200 yards (190 m). However, many autoloaders suffer from hard, creepy trigger pulls and thoughtless stock designs, and these faults make for a lack of accuracy that has nothing to do with the actual firing mechanism.

Though autoloading big-game rifles are most common in the northeast of the United States, where close-range fast-firing is more desirable than long-range precision, they are widely used all over North America for every type of big game, while the rimfire versions are popular among those who shoot small game such as squirrels and rabbits.

A The Browning BAR 22 is a semi-automatic, and its magazine holds fifteen LR (Long Rifle) .22 shells. (1) A detail of the trigger (a) and safety (b) on the Browning BAR 22. The safety button has a vivid red color.
B The Remington "Nylon 66" Black Diamond has its stock and fore-end made of structural nylon. One of its advantages is its low weight: overall, the gun weighs only 4 lb (1.8 kg).
C The Harrington & Richardson Model 865 is a .22-caliber bolt-action gun. It has a detachable magazine holding five LR shells.

Chapter 4

Handguns

Jim Carmichel

A The Smith & Wesson Model No. 19 .357 Combat Magnum is shown here with a 4-inch (10 cm) barrel; other barrel sizes available are 2½ inches (6 cm) and 6 inches (15 cm). The revolver is fitted with an S & W Micrometer Click sight, adjustable for windage and elevation.

B Smith & Wesson's Model 29 .44 Magnum is a six-shot revolver. Depending on its barrel length, it weighs from 43 oz (1.2 kg) to 51 oz (1.4 kg).

Handguns—pistols or revolvers—are used extensively for hunting only in North America and, for the most, only in the United States. Most governments severely restrict the possession, ownership, and use of handguns, and that of the United States is no exception. There are federal and state restrictions affecting handguns (and rifled weapons in general), while some administrative units within states impose further, local restrictions. Some restrictions are in the interests of general safety, while others limit the use of small-caliber handguns to shooting only small game and vermin; others again prohibit the use of handguns with poor sights or very short barrels. Despite all these discouragements, a large and increasing number of North American sportsmen hunt with handguns wherever it is legal.

During the 1970s, the use of handguns to hunt small and large game in North America increased significantly. The reasons for this have been the growing availability of more powerfully calibered guns, improved ammunition loaded with hunting-type bullets, the development of scopes and mounts, and an emphasis on handgun hunting in a number of sporting journals.

The handguns that are used include revolvers and semiautomatics (or autoloading pistols, which are often mistakenly called automatics although they are not capable of fully automatic fire). Both single- and double-action revolvers are used. The hammer of a single-action must be cocked manually after every shot, while a double-action revolver is cocked and fired by the trigger pull alone, a mechanical action that gives so long and heavy a trigger pull that the gun wavers, spoiling the aim. For hunting purposes, such a gun is almost always cocked manually before firing. With a good double-action gun, this gives a light, very short trigger pull, a fast lock time, and good accuracy.

There are autoloading pistols with single and double actions, but the single-action models outnumber the others. With an "auto," single-action means that only the first shot requires the gun to be cocked manually, for, upon firing, the mechanism automatically extracts and ejects the empty cartridge, feeds in a new one from the magazine to the chamber, and cocks and locks the action for the next shot.

It would be presumptuous to say that one type of handgun is superior to the others for hunting: all are popular in North America, and each has advantages and disadvantages. Choice is guided by individual preferences and experience as well as by the type of hunting most often done with the gun in question.

While the types of handgun so far described are the most common, there has been an enormous revival in the popularity of single-shot pistols. In large measure, this has been due to improvements in cartridges and in telescopic sights, specifically those with long eye relief (which enables the hunter to hold his pistol in the normal manner, without bringing it too close to his face). The most accurate, comfortable, and safe firing method is the straight-armed, two-handed hold; it is all the more accurate when the shooter's hands or forearms—never the gun itself—are resting on or against a solid support.

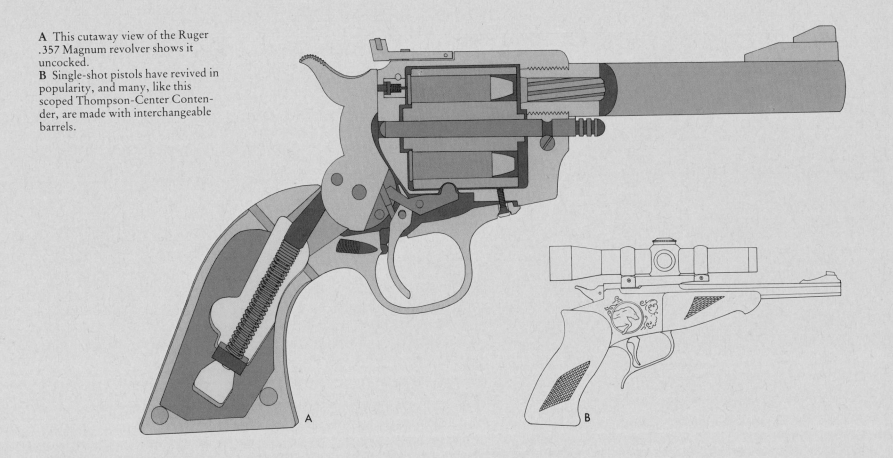

Fitting a scope sight to a handgun will, if the gun is chambered for an appropriate cartridge, significantly increase the range at which it is possible to hit game. For long-range hunting in open terrain, fast repeat shots are—or should be—unnecessary, if the first shot is carefully aimed and a number of factors, apart from the shooter's skill, are assumed: the gun's mechanical accuracy, the accuracy of the sighting equipment, and the proper velocity, trajectory, and energy of the bullet. Because the single-shot pistol has been chambered for a wide variety of relatively long-range cartridges, it has acquired in recent years a significant place, together with the repeating handgun, in North American hunting usage.

Every species of North American four-footed game has been hunted with handguns. The writer has used them for small game such as rabbits, squirrels, and raccoons, and for big game, too: wild boar, deer, bear, elk, and moose. Some of these animals were killed with a handgun because they appeared at close range and could more easily be shot with a pistol than with a rifle. Most of the larger species were shot with a .44 Magnum Ruger Blackhawk revolver and one, a wild boar, with a .41 Magnum revolver. A variety of guns were used with deer: a .357 Magnum revolver, a .30 Herrett single-shot, and even the .45 ACP auto. The last-named is not often used for hunting. In fact, no single caliber can be said to be representative of North American handgun hunting of big game. The available choice is too wide.

For hunting whitetail deer, the .357 Magnum is very popular, and deservedly so. Most hunters who are out after bigger game use one of the .44 Magnum revolvers, usually a Smith & Wesson Model 29 double-action, or a Ruger Blackhawk single-action. A smaller number use the powerful but scarce .44 AMP Automag semiautomatic pistol, or the Thompson-Center Contender single-shot break-action pistol. The latter is available in rifle calibers such as .30/30 WCF and .35 Remington, in addition to the traditional handgun calibers.

There are several relatively inexpensive .22 rimfire autoloading pistols and revolvers which serve quite well for hunting small game such as

squirrels and rabbits, but most serious shooters prefer a top-quality revolver such as the Smith & Wesson K-22 or one of the top-quality target-type autoloaders which, in addition to good accuracy, have adjustable sights and a crisp trigger.

One category of hunting in the United States is called "varmint" hunting because the animals that are shot were at one time classified as vermin. Although none of them is a candidate for a listing of the world's major game species, hunting them affords very popular sport in parts of the United States. Woodchucks, prairie dogs, and coyotes are the most hunted, although several additional species are, or have been, classified in the varmint group. When a hunter speaks of varmint rifles or pistols, he means arms designed for precise, long-range shooting, mostly at woodchucks or prairie dogs, but sometimes at coyotes and, on snow-blanketed open fields, red foxes.

Some varmint hunters use the same Magnum revolvers or rifles that they use for hunting big game, and it is typical that such hunters consider varmint hunting an enjoyable way to practice their marksmanship in preparation for hunting big game. There are, however, many devoted varmint hunters who use specialized arms for long-range shooting at these small animals, and they regard such hunting as a challenging sport in itself. A typical rifle for this sport is chambered for high-velocity .22 centerfire cartridges and is heavy-barreled and cumbersome; it may be equipped with very high-powered scopes. Some varmint rifles look rather like a cross between what is usually called a sporter and a target rifle. Stranger still in appearance are some of the handguns designed especially for varmint hunting; they are chambered for special varmint cartridges.

The best and most accurate of these is the Remington XP-100 which is, in effect, a short-barreled bolt-action rifle set in a plastic pistol stock. It fires the .221 Remington cartridge, a short, bottlenecked .22 centerfire cartridge best described as a shortened version of the .222 Remington rifle cartridge, as the rim and head diameters are identical. Fired from the

10½-inch (27 cm) barrel of the XP-100, the .221 has a muzzle velocity with a 50-grain (3.25 g) bullet of 2,650 feet (800 m) per second. This combination of pistol and cartridge provides an accuracy good even by rifle standards. Fired from a bench rest with a high-magnification (10×) scope and well-developed handloads, the XP-100 is capable of 110-yard (100 m) five-shot groups which measure less than one inch (2.5 cm) between the most widely-spaced shots. This standard of accuracy, combined with the relatively high velocity and flat trajectory, makes it not only possible to hit woodchucks or other similarly small animals or targets at 110 yards (100 m), but also increases chances of success to probability.

A shooter using a more traditional handgun with open sights needs a high degree of skill—and luck—to hit so small an animal as a woodchuck at even 100 yards (90 m). Even so, shooting at such targets with a handgun, especially one of the powerful Magnum revolvers, possesses a charm of its own and attracts many shooters.

Until quite recently, target shooting with handguns in the United States fell into one of three major categories, none of which has any truly close connection with hunting: bull's-eye shooting according to the rules and procedures of the National Rifle Association; Police Combat Tournament shooting or that of the Practical Police Course; and the shooting done at the World Shooting Championships, the Olympic Games, and other major international competitions which are governed by the rules of the International Shooting Union, or the Union Internationale de Tir (UIT).

A fourth, still quite new, category has interesting similarities to hunting and has quickly become enormously popular. This is known as metallic silhouette, or metallic game silhouette, shooting; it originated in Mexico and quickly spread to the United States. Since 1975, it has attracted legions of shooters who were previously uninterested in target competition. At first, it included only offhand rifle shooting at ranges of 200, 300, 385, and 500 meters (220, 330, 420, and 550 yards) at full-size steel profiles of chickens, pigs, turkeys, and sheep, respectively. The rules are simple: five shots are fired in 2½ minutes, and a point is scored by knocking a silhouette off its stand. This is harder to do than might be thought, for the silhouettes are heavy, and the bullet must strike the right part of the target with enough energy to topple it. A hit just anywhere will not do.

This form of competition proved so popular that it was quickly adopted by pistol shooters, who retained the targets but lessened the distances to 50, 100, 150, and 200 meters (55, 110, 165, and 220 yards). A variety of equipment and shooting positions may be used, depending on the particular match. Both single-shot and repeating pistols have been chambered for the cartridges used for this sort of shooting.

The first competitors using pistols immediately found that those available, and the ammunition, were neither accurate nor powerful enough to topple the heavy steel targets. As a result, more handgun research and development has taken place in the past five years than in the previous fifty. It is likely that, in the near future, some of the results will be applied to arms and ammunition for hunting. In addition, since silhouette shooting resembles live-game shooting, it has encouraged thousands of American sportsmen to hunt big game with handguns for the first time.

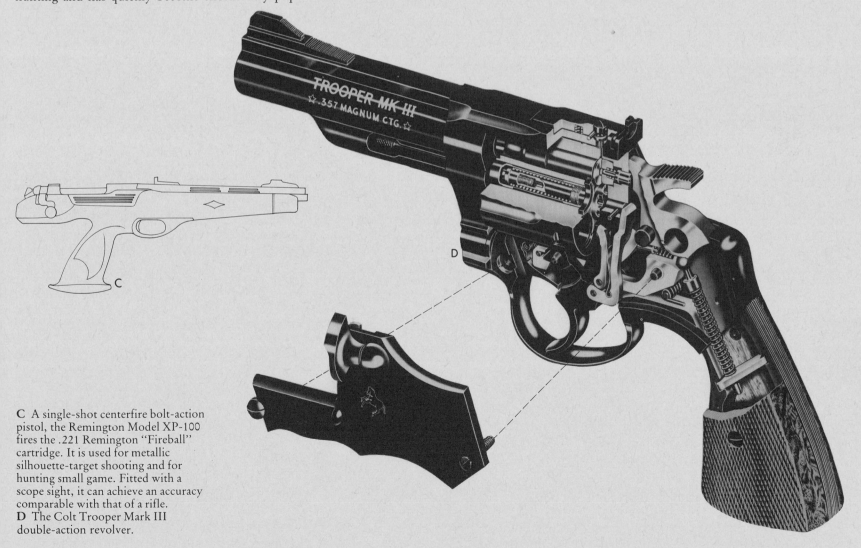

C A single-shot centerfire bolt-action pistol, the Remington Model XP-100 fires the .221 Remington "Fireball" cartridge. It is used for metallic silhouette-target shooting and for hunting small game. Fitted with a scope sight, it can achieve an accuracy comparable with that of a rifle.
D The Colt Trooper Mark III double-action revolver.

Chapter 5

Arms for Hunting in Africa and Asia

Robert Elman

Before undertaking a first safari in Africa or Asia, European and North American sportsmen tend to buy whole arsenals of new arms. This is wasteful for two reasons: a single rifle is fine for several kinds of game, and some of the arms commonly used in Europe and North America are appropriate for much of the game in Africa and Asia. Over and above this, one shoots best with a familiar rifle—a trusty old weapon that has taken game before and in which the shooter has confidence. In the following part, on hunting methods, there are suggestions for adequate calibers for African and Asian game and, valuable as these certainly are, they should not be taken as an encouragement to buy new weapons, if the shooter already has something suitable.

During the past decade or so, some unusual arms have been brought to Africa and Asia, expecially the former. Semiautomatic rifles have been used quite a bit, although their use is illegal in some countries, and even pump- and lever-action rifles have been seen. For that matter, a number of hunters brought their muzzle-loaders, which have been enjoying a great revival in North America because of the challenge, nostalgia, and romance of their use. In skilled hands, such a gun may be adequate for non-dangerous game.

But the rule, to which the foregoing examples are exceptions, is that modern bolt-action rifles are best for Africa and Asia. Some governments have restricted the use of certain types of arms and inadequate cartridges, but there will be no trouble about using a bolt-action of adequate power; there is no more versatile firearm for use in Africa or Asia.

Many professional hunters—that is, hunters who are outfitters and guides—treasure their traditional big-bore rifles with folding-leaf sights. Like the double shotgun, these classic rifles for Africa and Asia were perfected in Britain for the primary purpose of stopping big, dangerous game at short range. Though many have a series of three or more folding-leaf sights, these rifles have the "pointability" of a shotgun and can be aimed very fast; most of them are chambered for extremely large, powerful cartridges. They are sometimes called back-up guns, to be used by a professional hunter in the emergency caused by a client having fired unsuccessfully at some consequently enraged or wounded animal.

Cartridges for these doubles are not very accurate at long range, and their recoil in most instances is terrific. Although they can be lifesavers in particular circumstances and in the appropriate hands, they cannot be recommended to an average sportsman who has not practiced with big-bores. One must become accustomed to such a rifle, learn to handle it quickly and effectively, and become used to its recoil before it can be used effectively. Once it can be so used, the double rifle is a formidable weapon that has long since earned its reputation, although, at one time, doubles were even larger than they are now. Writing in the late nineteenth century, W.W. Greener noted that a double 8-bore of his manufacture, loaded with a spherical ball and backed with 10 drams (605 grains, or 39 g) of black powder, had put 8 shots into a rectangular target measuring about 1½ by 2½ inches (4 by 6 cm) at 50 yards (45 m)—impressive accuracy for such a cannon! He added that "the late Mr. A.

Henry, of Saigon, with a Greener double 8-bore rifle weighing only 13 lb., charge 10 drams, and spherical ball," had placed 147 out of 163 shots inside a 12-inch (30 cm) circle at 110 yards (100 m).

In 1906, Henry Sharp's book *Modern Sporting Gunnery* listed black-powder double rifles as large as 4-bore and the more modern Nitro Express models as small as .256 (a caliber more appropriate to gazelle than to elephant) but ranging up to .600. For the largest African game, Sharp recommended the .600 or .577. He noted that, in a test of accuracy, the .577 had placed ten shots (five from each barrel) into a 3¼-inch (8 cm) space from a distance of 100 yards (90 m). Loads were 750-grain (48 g) nickel-plated bullets propelled by the then modern charge of 100 grains (6.5 g) of cordite.

When the .577 had been introduced in the early 1880s, it was actually considered small, but it was an African favorite for many years and is still occasionally seen. Arthur H. Neumann, who has been called the most daring of all the ivory hunters, usually relied on a .577 double-barreled Gibbs rifle for elephant and rhino. "I always was an advocate of small bores," he explained. But many hunters preferred the .600 Nitro Express, introduced about 1910 and used in the very famous Jeffery double elephant rifles. For many years, it was the world's most powerful game cartridge: it fired a 900-grain (58 g) bullet with a muzzle velocity as high as 1,950 feet (600 m) per second and an energy as great as 7,600 foot-pounds (1,050 kgm). Since then, of course, many more modern chamberings have been popular, ranging from the .375 to quite a few in the .450 or .500 class. The most renowned of the latter-day elephant hunters, D.W.M. "Karamojo" Bell, has helped to popularize relatively small-bore bolt-actions, and the fact is that today's even more efficient bolt-action rifles are capable of handling any game in Africa or Asia.

In his book *African Hunter*, the well-known scientist and sportsman James Mellon recommends the following calibers for big African game such as elephant, rhino, buffalo, and hippo: .375 Holland & Holland Magnum, .378 Weatherby Magnum, .458 Winchester Magnum, and .460 Weatherby Magnum. (American and British calibers are most often recommended for African game.) He notes that the older British cartridges— .416, .450, .465, .470, .475, .500, .577, and .600—are also fine, although it has become difficult to find either rifles or ammunition in these calibers; very few double rifles, for example, are now being made.

For lion and eland, Mellon recommends cartridges ranging from the .378 Weatherby and the .375 Holland & Holland down to the .300 Magnums, versions of which are made by Holland & Holland, Weatherby, and Winchester. For zebra and the larger antelopes, he recommends the same cartridges plus the .30–06, the .308 Norma Magnum, the 7.62mm NATO (.308 Winchester), and the 7mm Remington and Weatherby Magnums. Other powerful European and American 7mm cartridges are also adequate for such game.

For gazelle and the smaller antelopes up to about 250 lb (100 kg), Mellon lists cartridges ranging from the .300 Magnums, the .30–06, and the 7.62mm down to the 6mm group. He classifies really small game as

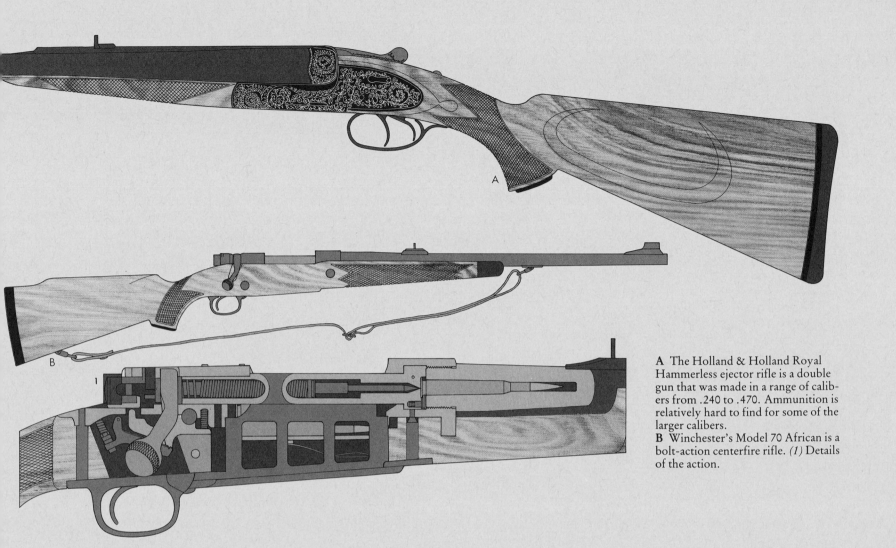

A The Holland & Holland Royal Hammerless ejector rifle is a double gun that was made in a range of calibers from .240 to .470. Ammunition is relatively hard to find for some of the larger calibers.
B Winchester's Model 70 African is a bolt-action centerfire rifle. *(1)* Details of the action.

including rabbit, birds, and dik-dik, all species weighing not more than 15 lb (6 kg), for any of which the smallest of the aforementioned cartridges is enough; so are, in the present writer's opinion, the .22 centerfire high-velocity cartridges known in North America as varmint loads. However, Mellon recommends rimfires—the .22 Magnum rimfire or the .22 Long Rifle cartridge. A great many sportsmen from many parts of the world own rifles chambered for one of these rimfires or for the slightly more powerful 5mm cartridge.

Asian game can be classified in pretty much the same way as the African, with the Asian wild cattle being comparable to the African buffalo and other large African game, while the antelopes are equivalent, too. The tiger can be compared to the lion, Asian deer to European and African deer, and Asian boar, goats, and sheep to those of Europe and North America.

Game birds, both upland species and waterfowl, are most often bagged with a shotgun, as in Europe and the Americas. While there are perhaps relatively few renowned as "major" game species, there is a variety that seems infinite to some visitors, who, after all, come to Africa and Asia for the most part to shoot big-game trophies. Many of the birds are fairly

large—guineafowl, some francolins, and some waterfowl, for example—and shots are taken at rather short to quite long ranges; not more than one shotgun is needed, but its bore must be adequate for whatever presents itself, and that means a 12-bore.

In recent years, North American sportsmen have demonstrated the versatility of repeating shotguns equipped with variable-choke devices, which can be almost instantly changed from tight to open choke and vice versa, but, although much can be said for such devices, the conventional double-barreled shotgun remains an excellent choice for either Africa or Asia; it is versatile, and malfunctions are less likely than with the complex mechanisms of some repeaters. Whether the shotgun is an over-and-under or a side-by-side is a matter of personal preference, but the important thing is that it has two barrels, not necessarily of the same bore constriction. It may, indeed, have interchangeable sets of barrels, so as to provide at least two combinations of choke. A shotgun of which the barrels provide one tight bore and one rather open bore can offer enough of a choice to match the birds and conditions that present themselves at any time and, in Africa or Asia, one can hardly be better equipped for wingshooting.

Chapter 6

Maintenance, Sighting-in, and Ammunition

Wilf E. Pyle

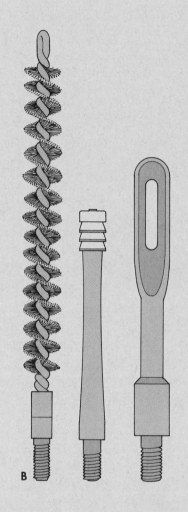

The committed hunter will not be satisfied with just taking his shotgun or rifle out on the day of a hunt and putting it back afterwards. He will spend much of his leisure time doing the many chores related to being a hunter, and these form part of the lore of hunting. Weapon care, sighting-in, and reloading your own ammunition are just some of these chores, but they are among the most worthwhile.

Cleaning, Care, and Storage of Guns

Years ago, it was essential for a shooter to clean his gun rigorously after every few shots, because corrosive primer compounds and soft barrel steels rendered barrel life very short unless guns were cleaned without delay after use. Humidity combined rapidly with powder and primer residues to cause rust, which soon spelled the end for many a fine bore. The use of black powder in many of the old cartridges was often blamed for the severe damage, but it was not until smokeless powder began to be used that it was found that the primer compound, in fact, was responsible for much of the trouble.

Propellants and noncorrosive primers of modern cartridges are far less destructive for, unlike the old black powder, they leave a protective coating in the bore, so that it does not require scrubbing after each shooting session. If a firearm is to be stored for any length of time, on the other hand, it should first be cleaned and protected.

A good cleaning kit must contain a well-fitting cleaning rod; it can be made of aluminum, steel, brass, wood, plastic-coated steel, or twisted wire. Many rods comprise two or more segments that can be joined together in one way or another, but one-piece rods are best. Most rods are provided with a screw-on tip, which allows the shooter to choose the type he should use; there are three basic types—slotted, button, or jagged—and each works well in normal cleaning procedures.

The next important item in the cleaning kit is a good supply of patches made of flannel or cotton, and, while they can be made at home from old clothes, it is probably wisest to buy ready-made patches; the shooter is assured then that they will be of the correct size for the caliber and will be less likely to stick in the bore.

A good brand of powder solvent and a supply of oil are also needed, together with a tube of gun grease, to be used if the rifle is to be stored for any length of time. Many kits include a fine wire brush.

Cleaning procedures are simple: after making sure that the gun is unloaded, remove the bolt, or open the action completely, as may be appropriate. Place a patch on the tip of the rod, push it into the breech, and move it back and forth a few times while keeping the muzzle pointed downward; this is to avoid causing the powder residues to drop into the action. This method works well with a bolt-action rifle, or a pump-, lever-, or autoloader gun. It also works well with most shotguns. It is unwise to disassemble other types of rifle just for a simple cleaning. In such cases, it is better to clean the weapon from the muzzle; this calls for some caution, for the rod can damage the muzzle, and so it should be guided carefully into the muzzle between protective fingers. An alterna-

A A pull-through works well on rifles that cannot take a cleaning rod from the breech. Drop the weighted end through the bore and place the cleaning patch in the breech. *(1)* A quick tug and the patch is pulled through. *(2)* A dirty patch.

B A brush and two kinds of tips commonly available in cleaning kits.
C Cleaning the face of the bolt is necessary, as this area picks up a surprising amount of primer compound, grease, dirt, and even brass shavings. Use a toothbrush for this.

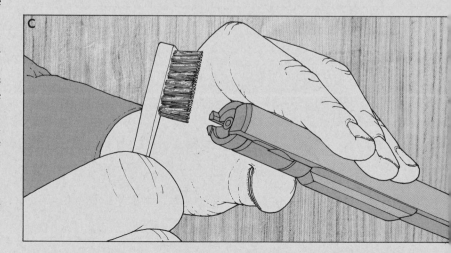

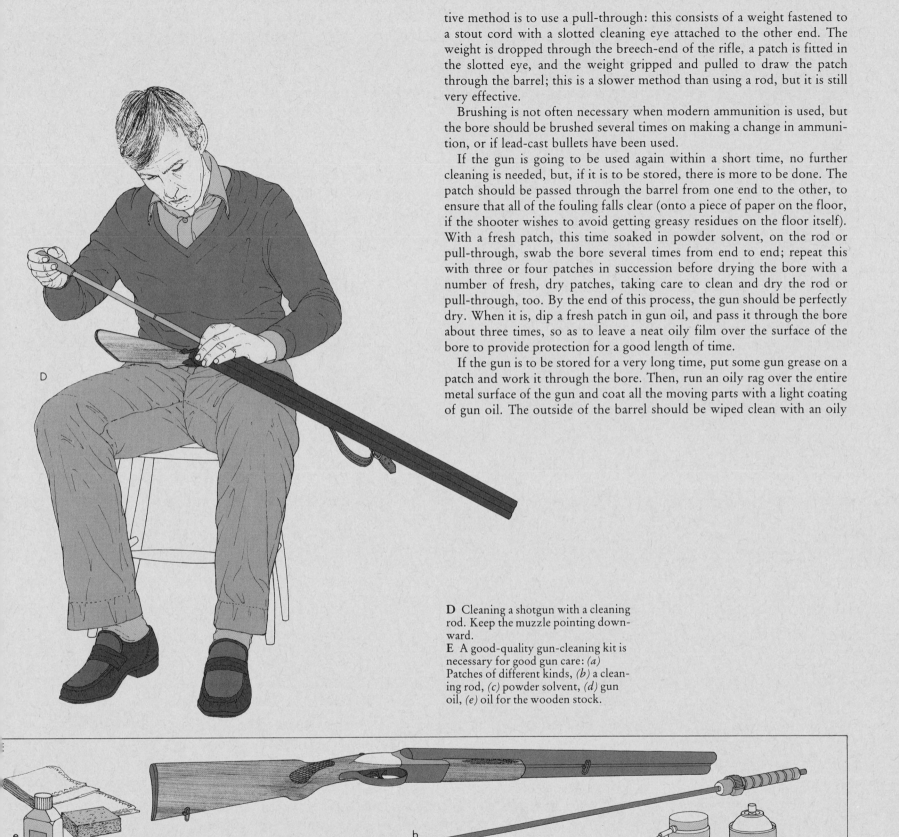

tive method is to use a pull-through: this consists of a weight fastened to a stout cord with a slotted cleaning eye attached to the other end. The weight is dropped through the breech-end of the rifle, a patch is fitted in the slotted eye, and the weight gripped and pulled to draw the patch through the barrel; this is a slower method than using a rod, but it is still very effective.

Brushing is not often necessary when modern ammunition is used, but the bore should be brushed several times on making a change in ammunition, or if lead-cast bullets have been used.

If the gun is going to be used again within a short time, no further cleaning is needed, but, if it is to be stored, there is more to be done. The patch should be passed through the barrel from one end to the other, to ensure that all of the fouling falls clear (onto a piece of paper on the floor, if the shooter wishes to avoid getting greasy residues on the floor itself). With a fresh patch, this time soaked in powder solvent, on the rod or pull-through, swab the bore several times from end to end; repeat this with three or four patches in succession before drying the bore with a number of fresh, dry patches, taking care to clean and dry the rod or pull-through, too. By the end of this process, the gun should be perfectly dry. When it is, dip a fresh patch in gun oil, and pass it through the bore about three times, so as to leave a neat oily film over the surface of the bore to provide protection for a good length of time.

If the gun is to be stored for a very long time, put some gun grease on a patch and work it through the bore. Then, run an oily rag over the entire metal surface of the gun and coat all the moving parts with a light coating of gun oil. The outside of the barrel should be wiped clean with an oily

D Cleaning a shotgun with a cleaning rod. Keep the muzzle pointing downward.
E A good-quality gun-cleaning kit is necessary for good gun care: *(a)* Patches of different kinds, *(b)* a cleaning rod, *(c)* powder solvent, *(d)* gun oil, *(e)* oil for the wooden stock.

187

rag; fingerprints should be wiped off without delay, for they are often harbingers of rust. The bolt of a bolt-action gun should be lightly oiled and the face cleaned with a small brush; a toothbrush is ideal.

When the gun is to be used again, it is vital to remove the grease from the bore and the working parts: a bulged barrel can be caused by firing a shot when there is an appreciable amount of grease in the bore. An oily bore will not shoot accurately on the first shot, while an oily chamber can cause a marked rise in chamber pressure upon firing, followed by blown primers or extraction problems or worse—a blown action.

Remember to store a gun muzzle-down if it is to be kept in store for a considerable period: this will prevent oil and grease from making their way into the action. Another caution is to use oil sparingly, for too much in the mainspring will impede the firing pin and cause unreliable firing; if in doubt, wash the bolt in gasoline.

Some shooters claim that they never clean their guns—and those guns show the consequences. Again, there are those who clean their pet guns so often that they do more damage to the bore than a year's shooting might do. The modern hunter must realize that many of the old ways can now be forgotten, even if good gun care, while not so crucial as in the past, is still important in maintaining a serviceable arm over a lifetime of use.

Sighting-in Rifles

Firearms and their related accessories are probably better made today than they have ever been, but, if a rifle is poorly sighted, the shooter who uses it will certainly miss shots.

Most hunting rifles come from the factory with some form of iron sights, and many hunters wrongly believe these sights to be correctly sighted-in for their purposes. The rifle may leave the factory capable of firing minute-of-angle groups, but its actual performance in the hands of the hunter depends on his or her physical build and how well the rifle fits it, and on the hunter's own style of shooting. Factory sighting does not meet the individual's needs of carefully tailored sighting-in.

There are three basic types of sights available: factory-installed front and rear sights, often called sporting sights; receiver, or peep, sights; and scope sights, which are the commonest type today.

The so-called sporting sights may come in many different styles and configurations, but, generally, they consist of a V or square-notched rear sight and a fixed-post front sight. Sometimes, the rear sight can be adjusted for windage, but, most often, it cannot. There is almost always an adjustment for elevation, often comprising a notched slide elevator or a sight with a screw holding the arrangement. Often, target-style or varmint rifles do not come equipped with these sights.

The second sort, the receiver or peep sight, in which the rear sight is some form of hole or aperture, is at present not as popular as it once was. When properly mounted and adjusted, such sights are very rugged and dependable; they are nearly always adjustable for windage and elevation, while older styles were adjustable only for height. Most modern receiver sights are graduated in half-minutes of angle ($\frac{1}{2}$ inch/1 cm at 100 yards/90 m); some front sights are adjustable, too.

The rifle scope common today is a tough, accurate, and reliable optical instrument, but it requires careful sighting-in. This is now very easy, for adjustments on most modern scopes are internal; they are made by means of elevation and windage screws placed on top of and to the right of the scope, respectively. The screws can be turned with a screwdriver or the edge of a coin; an arrow indicates movement up or to the left (or right), respectively, for elevation or windage. Many scopes are set in increments of one minute of angle, and lesser divisions are scribed between the full minutes: a minute of angle means, in practice, 1 inch (2.5 cm) at 100 yards (90 m), and proportionate differences at greater or lesser ranges.

Having acquired the sight you want, it is possible to sight-in the rifle,

provided you have access to a target range or to some location that may be used for firing. For deer hunting, which may be taken as a norm, the rifle needs to be sighted so as to fire a group that prints 3 inches (7.5 cm) high at 100 yards (90 m); this allows for shots of up to 275 yards (250 m) without further adjustment, for the vitals of a deer form a target about 18 inches (45 cm) square, and a shot that is 3 inches high at 100 yards will still be within this target area at the greater distance. You will need ammunition of the same brand and bullet weight as you intend to use when hunting—the performances of different brands differ sometimes significantly—and a supply of targets; these can be either purchased sighting-in targets, which are usually marked off in squares of about an inch, or home-made—a 2-inch (5 cm) circle inscribed on a piece of paper will do.

If you do not have access to a target range, any fairly level piece of ground will do, if it has a good back stop; make sure that it is safe and legal to shoot there, getting the permission of the landowner if necessary. Take a rest along with you: a small table or a mat that can be folded over, or the hood of a vehicle, suitably padded, will all provide ample support.

Illustrated here are the steps you should take when sighting-in a rifle. A typical .30-caliber rifle so sighted should give most hunters the capactiy of shooting out to about 275 yards (250 m) without having to hold over the target.

When carried out with the right equipment and an understanding of what needs to be done, most sighting-in jobs are easy. The shooter who is to use the rifle in the field should do the actual sighting-in. Never believe that a rifle straight from the factory and put directly into the hunting field will deliver accurate shots.

The Basics of Reloading

The reloading of rifle and shotgun cartridges is not only a fascinating hobby but also one that can save the hunter between half and two-thirds of the price of factory-made ammunition. The wide assortment of components available allows the hunter to prepare ammunition for a particular gun or purpose without any loss of quality, for the bullets, primers, and powder sold for this purpose are subject to rigorous quality control. Furthermore, a variety of loads gives greater versatility to a rifle, shotgun, or handgun.

The most expensive part of the cartridge is the brass case, which is often thrown away, although cases can be used several times, the eventual number depending on the design of the particular case and the kind of load it is used to fire. The first step in reloading is to inspect the case, which must be cleaned and then checked for cracks. These often occur in the neck and the lower part known as the head; any cracked cases should be discarded. So should any with a ring or bulge, for such cartridges can develop head separation, which can be very dangerous for the shooter. Once the cases are selected, there follow five basic steps.

1. Depriming, or the removal of the spent primer.
2. Resizing, or returning the used case to its original size.
3. Repriming, which is inserting a new primer.
4. Charging the case with powder.
5. Seating the new bullet.

There is a variety of loading tools on sale from a number of manufacturers. Apart from the actual reloading tool, which is often called a reloading press, one needs a set of reloading dies for the caliber in question, a shell loader, a powder scale, and any of the many available reloading manuals. Many of these outline the necessary steps and describe the common problems. New editions come out from time to time, and the hunter who does his own reloading should keep himself up-to-date by buying them.

From this source one can obtain information about the many manufacturers of shell holders, the interchangeability of different makes, the

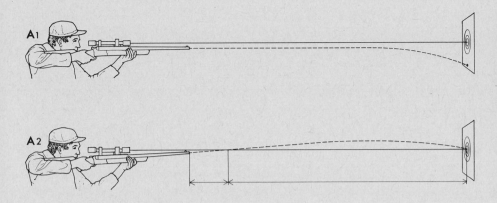

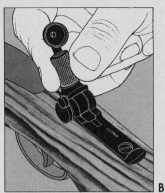

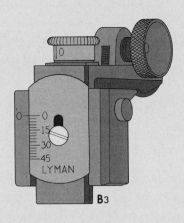

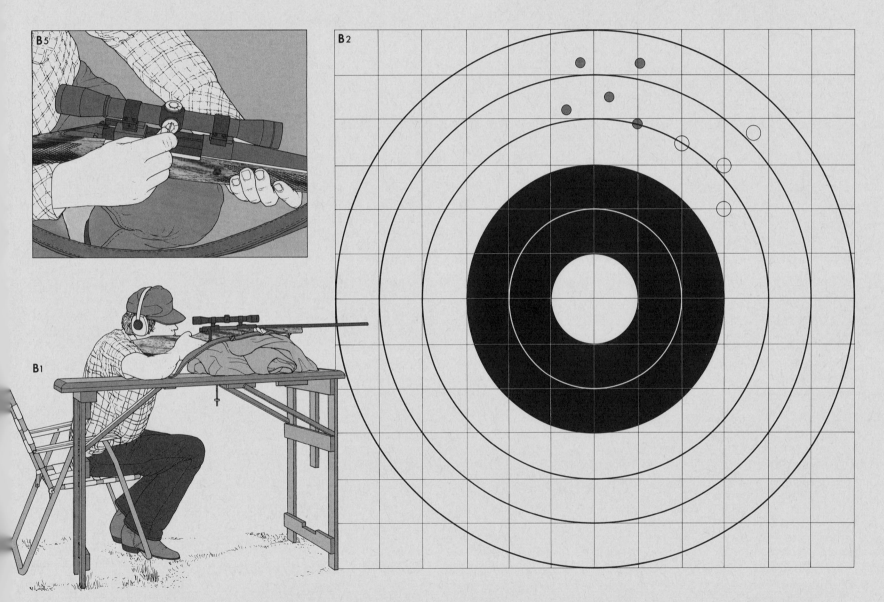

A *(1)* In the rifle that is not sighted-in, the line of sight and the line of bore are parallel, and the force of gravity will make the bullet fall low. *(2)* The trajectory of a bullet from a properly sighted-in rifle will cross the line of sight twice, once a short distance from the muzzle and once at the point of impact.

B To sight in a rifle, fire a group of shots at a target at 25 yards (23 m) with the forepart of the rifle resting on a padded support, such as this table *(1)*. Commercially available targets *(2)* that are marked off in square inches can be used. Locate the center of the group on your target and measure its distance above or below and to the left or right of the bull's-eye. Work out how many minutes of angle these distances represent. Adjust the calibration on the sights accordingly. When adjusting the rear sight, remember to move it in the direction in which you want the group to be moved. *(3)* A micrometer-adjustable peep sight with quarter-minute adjustments for elevation and windage. *(4)* The old-style peep sight is adjustable only for elevation. When you have made the necessary adjustments, fire another group, and if everything has gone well, the group will print out at the point of aim. With the close-range alignment now accomplished, fire a group at a range of 100 yards (90 m). The center of this group should be about 3 inches (7.5 cm) above the bull's-eye. *(5)* The modern telescopic sight can be adjusted easily with a coin. The elevation adjustment is usually on the top, and the windage adjustment on the right side.

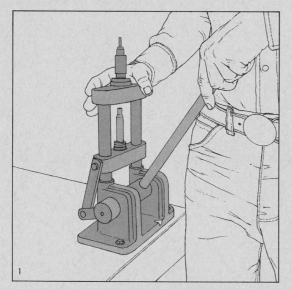
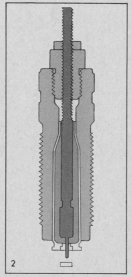
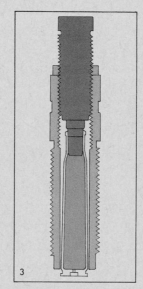
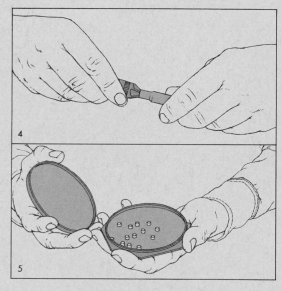

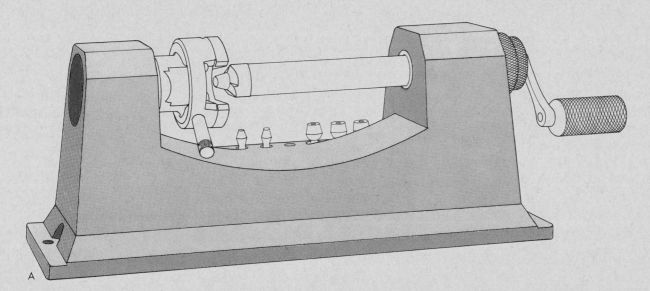

Reloading a rifle bullet. (1) The cartridge case in the reloading press, moving upward to engage with the appropriate die part. (2) A decapping rod. (3) An expanding plug. (4) Deburring and chamfering by hand. (5) Sorting primers. Try to handle them as little as possible. (6) Charging a case with powder from a powder measure. (7) Seating the bullet in the cartridge. (8) A cross-section showing the bullet in the bullet-seating screw. A Lyman's Universal Trimmer for trimming and chamfering cases. B Other necessary tools: (1) a weighing scale; (2) a deburring tool; (3) a powder funnel.

beginning and maximum loads for different cartridges, and new powders and bullets. Maximum loads should never be exceeded, while increases in loads should be made gradually, by not more than a grain or two of powder at a time.

Once the cases have been selected, they should be lubricated before running them through the full-length sizing die. Some reloaders dislike getting lubricant on the inside of the case, but if the lubricant is powdered graphite, there is not likely to be enough of it to damage the powder charge. Oil or lubricant that comes into contact with the primer can cause trouble, too, by breaking down the primer compound and rendering it inert or severely weakening it.

Depriming, full-length resizing, and expanding the mouth of the case to the correct size are all performed with a single stroke of the modern reloading press. The decapping is done by a shaft that runs through the center of the die to push out the fired primer by means of a pin. Screwed onto the shaft, or incorporated with it, is an expander ball or button that passes through the neck of the cartridge; as it passes, it leaves the neck with the correct diameter to accept a bullet of the correct caliber. The inside of the cartridge neck needs to be lubricated to facilitate this step.

When home-cast lead bullets are used, the expander button will not open the neck of the cartridge sufficiently, so it will be necessary either to use a larger size of expander, or to open the neck by hand with a pair of needle-nose pliers.

There has been much argument over the merits of full-length as against neck-sizing, which means resizing only the neck area of the case, a method that worked well enough until case shapes changed to the bottle-neck form, and chamber pressures increased. Full-length sizing is now recommended, because the actions of many autoloaders, lever-, and pump-action guns will not close properly unless cartridges have been full-length sized. The argument will continue among reloaders, but it is clear that neck-sizing will work if the cases are to be fired from the same gun.

The reloaded cartridge must fit what is called the head space: the distance from the face of the bolt, when closed, to the point in the chamber at which the cartridge is stopped from going any further into the chamber. The rim of rimmed cases stops them, while rimless cases are stopped by the shoulder resting against the chamber wall. Safety and accuracy depend upon correct head space; knowing what it means and how it relates to different cartridges is vital for successful reloading. The sizing die must, therefore, be set in the loading tool in accordance with the instructions for the particular set of dies in use, for incorrect placing of the die can give the wrong head space.

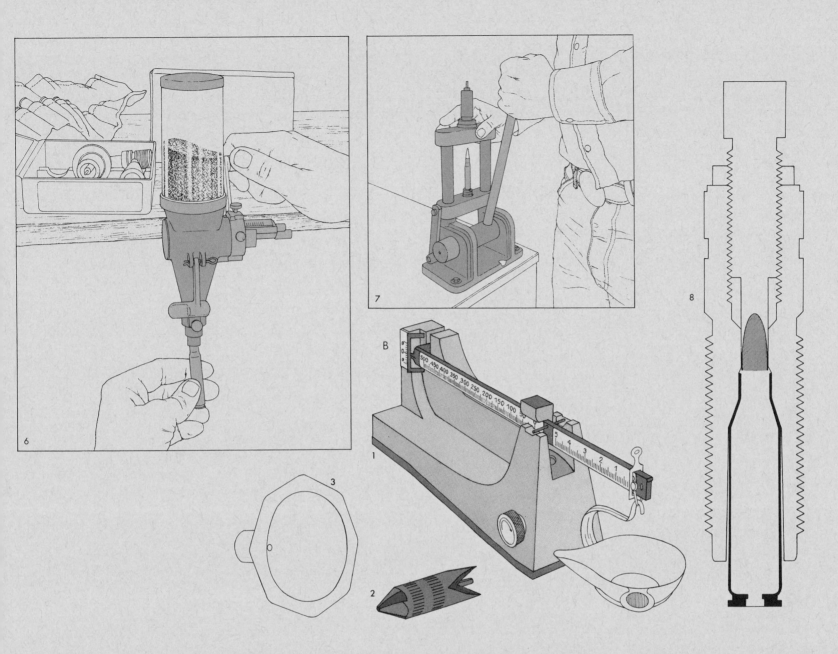

Priming the resized case is the next step, a simple operation, but still one requiring precautions. The primer must be placed anvil-side up on the priming punch or arm; most reloading presses are designed so that priming can be done when the case is extracted from the sizing die. Before the new primer can be neatly fitted in the priming pocket, all the old priming mixture must be scraped away or removed; a deburring tool can be used for this.

A primer is set in place with a gentle, steady push on the press handle. The primer must be seated firmly against the bottom of the pocket, and failure to achieve this could result in a hang-fire, since the force of the firing pin would be softened by the forward movement of the incorrectly seated primer. A caution: never seat a primer into a case that has been charged with powder. Once a case has been fitted with a primer, however, it may be charged with powder, and selecting a powder charge that meets the hunter's needs is what reloading is all about. As there are many powders, it is essential to consult a reloading manual. This will give a beginning load and, to begin with, this is what is best used.

The charge values for powders are expressed in grains, a standard unit of measurement for powder and bullets, and all reloading scales are marked in grains. There are 7,000 grains in 1 lb (16 oz); in metric, 1 grain is .065 gram. A pound (450 g) smokeless powder will load more cartridges than most hunters shoot in a year. Just which powder to use can be difficult to decide, for there are several types, and brands can be confusing; the best course is to read several manuals, see which powders are recommended for your needs, and experiment with loads and powder brands until you get the accuracy you can accept.

Once a load has been determined, weigh it out on a reloading scale and set the powder measure. Some writers recommend that each charge be weighed, but the excellent modern powder measures make this unnecessary. The scale is needed to set the powder measure and to check the charge periodically after that. Using the measure is, above all else, a matter of working systematically and consistently. Some powders, such as ball powder, pass through the measure more readily than other, more conventional powders; this will influence the accuracy of the charge given, and it is, therefore, wise to check every fifth charge on the scales.

The final stage is the seating and crimping of the bullet. Once again, set the die in accordance with the instructions. A couple of factors determine the seating depth; the rule of thumb for jacketed bullets is to seat the bullet to the bottom of the case neck, and this works well for most bullets. Another factor is the total length of the case and bullet: if the bullet is seated too far out, the cartridge will not work through the magazine of some clip-model rifles. Crimping is largely unnecessary, unless lead bullets are being used or a tubular magazine is on the rifle; jacketed bullets generally grip the neck sufficiently well for no crimp to be required. An exception may be when particularly hot loads are used in heavy Magnum cartridges. Bullets generally used in tubular magazines come with a factory-prepared crimping groove. Once seating has been completed, the cartridge is ready for a final inspection; wipe any grease or lubricant from the case.

Loading shot shells follows the same general procedure; there are six steps.

1. Deprime and size.
2. Reprime.
3. Place the powder charge.
4. Insert and seat the wad on the powder charge.
5. Drop the shot charge.
6. Crimp.

The plastic one-piece shot-protector wads have greatly simplified reloading and, in many instances, have enabled the powder charge to be reduced, as a consequence of the improved sealing of the plastic components. As with rifle-cartridge reloading, it is wise to choose a shell brand that is common in your area; the same applies to all the components. The combination of components is very important in shellshot reloading, and therefore, use only those that are recommended for the particular load you want.

Loading tools for shotgun shells are usually designed for an output of a large volume; many fine models exist. Although many older tools are still to be found, they were designed for paper cases using wads of card and felt, and are usually not effective in reloading modern plastic compounds.

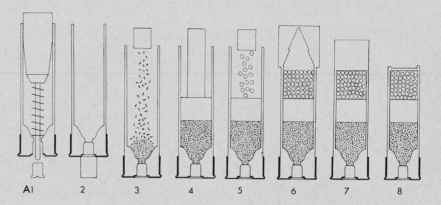

A1 2 3 4 5 6 7 8

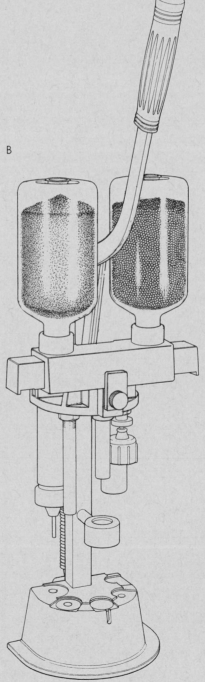

B

A Procedures for reloading can vary slightly, depending, for example, on the stage at which the cartridge is resized, and how crimping is carried out. In the illustration, sizing is the final operation. *(1)* Decapping; *(2)* priming; *(3)* charging with powder; *(4)* seating the wad; *(5)* charging with shot; *(6)* crimp starting; as some cases require different numbers of creases in the crimp, make sure you have the right head for the cases you are reloading; *(7)* crimping; and *(8)* sizing.
B This Pacific 105 Shellshot Reloader has five stations: resize and deprime; prime; load powder, seat wad, and load shot; start crimp; and finish crimp.

V Hunting Methods

Chapter 1

Hunting in Europe and North America

Shooting humanely means shooting to kill, and a bullet that hits a deer's central nervous system, the heart, or the lungs will kill. The target area is small (10×12 inches; 25×30 cm) and centered (1) above the foreleg or (2) between the forelegs. When shooting from the rear (3), a shot to the back of the head breaks the neck; one to the pelvis cripples the animal. (Below) A typical permanent high seat, well situated at the edge of a glade.

Red Deer in Europe

The red deer is native to Europe and western Asia, and has been successfully introduced into Argentina and New Zealand, in both of which countries there are no native species for it to compete with. In North America, however, where its introduction on a small scale has been, perhaps, regrettable, it competes for food and habitat with whitetail, mule deer, and wapiti. Except for in Scotland and some moorland areas of England, such as Dartmoor in the West Country, red deer inhabit wooded or forested areas, which call for hunting methods rather different from the bare-ground stalking practiced in the deer "forests" of Scotland.

On the Continent, where the red deer become larger the further east they are found, the sportsman ambushes the stags from a well-placed high seat, stalks them through the thick forests, or, during the mating season, lures them by imitating their calls.

In a high seat, the hunter may be unable to avoid his scent being carried on the wind to a stag, which will flee at the first such sign of man. In addition, movements made while on the high seat are easily detected by a red deer stag and will cause him to vanish; roe deer, by contrast, are less sensitive to such movement. Still, if the seat is placed with care in an area of the forest known to contain red deer stags, the method can be quite productive. High seats are also used for other deer than the red.

Stalking is a widely used method, but, to be successful, it requires that the hunter is able to move quite noiselessly through the forest without giving his scent to the beast. This calls for woodcraft of a high order, in addition to a thorough understanding of where in the forest the deer are most likely to be found.

Luring stags in the mating season is a matter of calling to them in challenge, in the manner of another stag—and red deer stags roar like lions. The hunter or his guide issues a "challenge" and, if they are fortunate, a stag will reply; an experienced ear can distinguish the higher tone of a young stag from the deeper one of an older, more mature stag. Challenge and response alternate until the stag has been lured into a position where he can be seen, evaluated, and, if a good trophy, shot. This method is, however, used only from about mid-September until mid-October, just before and during the beginning of the mating season. The reason is that the flesh of stags is unfit for human consumption once the animals begin breeding. [TT]

Roe Deer and Fallow Deer

Roe deer and fallow deer are two European species, the latter having its origins in Asia Minor and Mesopotamia. While both species are hunted, the fallow deer has been semi-domesticated, especially in parks, and its instincts have become blunted. It presents nothing like the challenge of the roe deer, and although the methods described here can be applied when hunting either species, it is the elusive, wary roe deer that tests the skills of even the most experienced hunter.

A number of different methods can be used when hunting roe deer: stalking or still-hunting; ambush from a high seat; calling or luring,

perhaps in combination with either of the two preceding methods; tracking in snow; driving with hounds or following with a dog.

The most demanding method is stalking; if the hunter makes only a slight mistake—a careless noise or movement—he will probably be detected and lose his chance of a shot. Even a small area affords good stalking, for the deer are strongly territorial and will not forsake their territory unless they have been much disturbed, for example, by human or canine intruders, during or outside the hunting season. A hunter who wants to stalk in an unfamiliar area can still follow the descriptions of someone who knows it well, rather than follow a guide, unless local requirements make the use of a guide obligatory. In any event, the hunter will need binoculars (and a telescopic sight) and should choose his clothes to match the colors of the season. Although rainy, blowy weather may be uncomfortable for the hunter, the resulting noise and movement of vegetation will help him approach the deer. Apart from the usual need to approach them from downwind, it helps to have the sun at one's back. A very early morning start is well worthwhile, for roe deer are then likely to be out feeding before seeking shelter for the day.

A high seat some 10 feet (3 m) or more above the ground will not only give the hunter a good field of view but will also be more likely to keep his scent off the ground and, therefore, away from the deer. Of course, any high seat affords an excellent way to observe birds and animals, so that the disadvantage of not being able to move through the hunting area is not that serious. Waiting in a primitive seat may be uncomfortable, but a seat can be a very elaborate structure, roofed and even equipped with a heater. The hunter or his guide will be able to keep a watch on the deer in the immediate neighborhood and determine if the animals in sight include any that should be shot. The question of shooting to cull is discussed below.

A good point about high seats of all sorts is that the trajectory of the bullet is most likely to end in the earth close to the shot animal. As a roe deer is relatively light, its body is often not enough to stop a bullet. For the owner of the hunting area, however, permanent high seats pose the problem of their use by poachers, and, for this reason, some are portable.

Roe deer bucks in rut can be called or lured quite easily, although the young bucks respond much more readily and obviously than the older ones. The sound that attracts them is made by blowing through the aperture formed by pressing the thumbs together, knuckles toward the face, with a blade of grass held between them: the noise to produce is a very faint mewing, the call of a doe trying to attract a buck. This is heard in summer, roe deer having an exceptionally early rut and, through the operation of the biological phenomenon known as delayed implantation, does enjoy the benefits of a summer's feeding before their reproductive cycle starts in earnest.

Where seasonal restrictions permit, roe deer can be tracked in snow by a hunter who takes advantage of their manner of moving off slowly when only slightly disturbed. They will usually stop and try to get a sight of the source of disturbance, a moment when a hunter who has managed to come up close to his quarry can get in a shot.

Dogs can be used to aid the hunter, but the sort of dog that does not frighten the deer away is essential. Some—dachshunds, for example—can exhibit traits that make the deer almost curious to find out what sort of beast is following them. An advantage of this method of hunting is that, as the scent of roe deer is very strong, the hunter does not need to make a start very early in the morning but should give the weaker scents of hares and foxes a chance to dissipate first.

The more usual form of drive, with beaters with or without dogs, works well with roe deer but, as with deer drives in North America, the deer should not be driven so fast that they present no chance of a reasonable shot. Roe deer are reluctant to leave their territory, however, and a drive without dogs may miss some deer, for they can hide themselves very capably. Even a concentrated line of beaters may not be enough to prevent a roe deer breaking back to its territory, while too much or too frequently repeated disturbance may cause roe deer to seek another territory altogether.

Roe deer are small and are best shot with light rifles, such as the .222 Remington, the .22–250, or the .243 Winchester. They present a small target area, too, not much more than the extent of a single hand, and situated just above and a little to the rear of the foreleg's joint with the body. Unless absolutely still, roe deer present a difficult if not impossible target; if a buck is moving only very slowly, a very slight intentional noise from the hunter may cause him to stop for a moment, which is when a shot should be taken. Shotguns are hardly suitable, except at very close range, and not always even then: the practice of driving deer toward hunters with shotguns was discontinued in Britain as recently as in the 1950s, when the method's brutality became obvious.

A consideration when hunting either roe or fallow deer is to cull the population rather than to shoot the most attractive trophy. Bucks that are past their prime, injured, or sick, or that are healthy and uninjured but undistinguished and likely to remain so, will all be shot. It would be a signal honor for a hunter to be allowed to shoot a buck in its prime: a fallow buck of about ten years of age, with fully developed palmations in his antlers, which would weigh about 5.5 lb (2.5 kg), or a roe of about six years, whose antlers look less impressive than those of a prime fallow buck but represent success in a finer test of hunting ability. [TT]

European Hunting Ceremony

Hunting in central Europe is more than a sport, it is practically a way of life. The would-be hunter cannot simply buy a hunting licence, as a hunter does in North America, for example; he must attend an approved course to learn not only hunting methods and law, but also the characteristics of the various game animals and birds, dog and hound care and training, shooting customs and traditions, and many other facets of the hunting life. In Sweden, elk-hunters are required to pass an annual test of their marksmanship. All this is evidence that hunting is something for which one must be capable and well informed.

The formalities required by law are matched, in some parts of Europe, by those exacted by custom. In this respect, central Europe is undivided, and a long tradition of how a day's shooting should be conducted continues unbroken. Naturally enough, these customs are most in evidence on occasions when many people participate and much game has fallen to their guns. As the light begins to fade, all the game shot during the day is arranged according to the rank each species enjoys. The numbers of each species can often be seen, almost at a glance, for every tenth bird or beast may be placed so as to show this—a tail is extended, for example. The whole display is sometimes framed with lines of fir branches. Huntsmen or gamekeepers who, during the day, have communicated with one another and the hunters by means of hunting horns, sound a tribute to each species of animal. The last hunt of the season may be marked by the firing of a salute by the assembled hunters.

A lighthearted moment comes when the hunting king is crowned, an honor accorded to the person who has shot most game during the day. Those who have been seen to have offended hunting custom and tradition are singled out for "punishment" before the whole party moves off, usually to meet in the evening for a hunting dinner. [TT]

Deer Stalking in Scotland

The antlers of red deer stags make magnificent trophies. With good feeding, stags from low ground in Europe can exceed the fourteen or, exceptionally, sixteen points that would be the limit for Scottish beasts, which live at high altitudes on the treeless hills and glens that are, nevertheless, called deer forests. Here, the deer are found together with grouse, ptarmigan, sheep, and other fauna, on ground subject to weather that, even in late summer and early fall, when the stags are stalked, can change from bright, warm sunshine to almost freezing mist in an hour or less.

Although roe, fallow, and sitka deer exist in Scotland, when "my heart's in the Highlands, a'chasing the deer," it was the red deer, *Cervus elaphus*, that the poet had in mind. This is the majestic, even self-satisfied animal painted by Landseer as "The Monarch of the Glen" and celebrated in many lesser-known works of art.

Deer stalking, in Scotland at least, is the term given to the sport of getting to within shooting range—80 yards (75 m)—of a red deer stag, and shooting it without its being aware of the presence of the sportsman and his accompanying stalker, who have approached it over open country for perhaps five hours or more. The stalker selects the approach routes and tactics; this may require the sportsman to walk knee-deep in the icy water of a burn for half an hour at a time, with his back bent double so as to keep out of sight of the deer or, perhaps, only of a single sheep that could alert the deer to the presence of intruders; to climb and descend a succession of hills; or to lie motionless in a stream or bog, while the deer, startled by a covey of grouse disturbed by the sportsman and the stalker, stare in the direction of the two men for ten or fifteen minutes continuously. The penalty of an unsuccessful shot that only wounds a stag at the end of such a stalk is not merely to see the animal vanish over the nearest hill. Deer stalking etiquette requires that the animal be followed and killed by the hunter, regardless of the time this takes.

Despite of, or perhaps because of, these difficulties, deer stalking in Scotland is in increasing demand, and many British devotees can no longer afford to compete against the many rich visitors from Europe, the Middle East, and North America. The costs of maintaining deer stalking are very high, and they are offset in part by the sale of venison. Although the British public have never acquired a general taste for it, there has been an increasing demand from the Continent, notably from Germany, and almost all carcasses find their way overseas, where the meat sells at high prices. The sportsman who shoots the stag is not thereby entitled to any more of it than the head, and, unless he has been stalking for about a week, in which case he may well be presented with a haunch, he will have to buy what he wants.

The legal season for shooting red deer in Scotland opens on 1 July and closes on 20 October; the season for hinds opens the next day, 21 October, and closes on 15 February. Different seasons are the rule in England and Wales (and there are different seasons, too, for other sorts of deer). In practice, very little stalking of stags is done in July and early August, when the beasts are still on the highest tops and consequently very difficult to find; also, their antlers are still in velvet then. Stalking proper begins at about the time of the opening of the grouse season (mid-August) and increases in popularity as the fall progresses, with the shortage of high-altitude grazing bringing the herds down to lower and more accessible ground. Hind shooting goes on throughout the legal season, often taking place in all but the most extreme of winter weather. This type of hunt is definitely not for the beginner, nor for the unfit, and invitations to stalk for the hinds are often extended only to hunters who have already shown themselves to be keen, agreeable, and expert stalkers of the stags.

Hind shooting is liable to take place in weather that varies between the miserable and the impossible, and there is no point in staying out longer than is necessary to complete the cull; half a dozen or more beasts may well be killed in a day's outing. When stalking stags, by contrast, it is very rare to take two in a day, unless there is absolutely no difficulty in getting both off the hill by night.

The laird and his stalker should have a good idea of how well stocked

Deer stalking in Scotland is a trial of a hunter's skill, patience, and endurance, and of the stalker's knowledge of the terrain and the animals on it. Even before the season opens, the stalker will have been out spying the herds (1) and the stags, still in velvet in July (2), that will be his quarry. The day's hunting starts early, with the approach march. Two or three hours' walking over the hills is often necessary before the stalker can begin to spy for herds and good stags; even at a half a mile's distance, he can tell if a stag is a good one. As the wind is blowing straight down to the herd, a long detour is necessary. This is the most demanding part of the stalk, as hunter and stalker must keep out of sight, sound, and smell of the ever-vigilant herd. The stalker, who is familiar with both the terrain and the herds on it, will, if need be, lead his "gentleman" over the rockiest ground and through the coldest water, in order to get him within range of a fine

stag. Often, a further detour is necessary if some sheep are in their way. When they have got to within 120 yards (110 m) of the herd, the stalker takes the rifle out of the case, loads it, and hands it to the hunter, signaling him to advance the last few yards on his own. *(3)* The hunter crawls forward until he is about 80 yards (75 m) from the stag, waits until he has a clear shot, and fires. "Reload!," the stalker orders, in case a second shot is necessary. At the sound of a shot, the pony-ghillie, who has been waiting in the far distance, comes up and helps with the gralloching (disemboweling) of the stag. *(4)* The carcass is loaded onto the pony for the long trek back.

the hill will be during the coming winter and early spring by reference to the calving successes of the previous spring, actual counts of deer during the summer and fall, and the number of stags shot during the season. This knowledge is the basis for their cull. First to be taken must be the barren—"yeld"—hinds, or those showing signs of not having calved that year; very old hinds are also likely to have given up calving and should be taken if recognized. A proportion of hinds will have natural injuries, causing limps and other ailments, and they should be shot; their calves are unlikely to thrive and should be taken, too. Occasionally, there will be a beast wounded by a careless sportsman (always, of course, from an adjoining forest), and that, too, should be added to the cull.

In many forests, no one applies to shoot hinds, and the job is left to the stalkers. For sportsmen who have the guts to go out in snow and gales, and, perhaps, lack the cash to pay for high-season stalking, a few evenings at hotel bars and a goodish outlay on drams of whisky might easily bring an invitation from a friendly stalker to join him for a day. But he will first have to be convinced that his prospective companion is an accurate shot with a rifle, and fit, into the bargain.

The rifle will be .240 bore or larger (anything smaller is illegal for red deer in Britain), and while a crack shot can consistently put a bullet into a 6-inch (15 cm) target at 200 yards (183 m) on the rifle range, the circumstances of shooting stags, to say nothing of hinds, are not those of the rifle range. When stalking stags, it is customary for the stalker to ask his gentleman to "test the rifle" before beginning the stalk. This may well be by shooting at a white-painted target, a sheet of tin, or a rock, visible 100 yards (90 m) away. The stalker will keenly inspect the results of one or two test shots and decide for himself what will be a safe range when a stag is to be killed. Many stalkers will not allow their gentlemen to take a shot at more than 80 yards (75 m), at least not until the individual has proved his skill and sang-froid at shorter shots. Running deer are never shot at. Wounding a deer is the worst thing a sportsman can do; he will certainly have to trail it for the rest of the day, and he will, perhaps, be obliged to devote the following day to finding and dispatching it.

Ammunition should be such as to give a more or less flat trajectory for a couple of hundred yards (or meters); performance over that range is of academic interest, for shots should never be fired at more than that distance from the target. Judging distances is often hard for those unused to the soft, changing, and uncertain light of the high hills. Many shots have to be taken downhill, and they are often missed. If the stag is below the gun at an angle of 45°, calculate the horizontal distance, and set the sights on that. At 80 yards (75 m) horizontal, the deer's eye is visible; at 150 yards (140 m), the ear is just visible; and at 200 yards (185 m), the ear is invisible. These indications do not apply, of course, to guns with telescopic sights, which are now widely used in deer stalking, having formerly been scorned by traditional stalkers. Most visitors would be given the option of shooting with one if, as is often so, the visitor does not have his own rifle with him, but borrows one from the estate. It should be noted, for visitors to the United Kingdom, that extremely strict regulations govern the ownership and possession of firearms—rifled weapons as distinct from shotguns—and it is not always possible to be granted a firearms certificate.

Dressing for deer stalking, as for grouse shooting, is not a matter of fashion but of camouflage. Heavy tweed is best, not only for its visual qualities, but because it generates no noise when moving against itself. Knickerbockers are preferable to trousers and should be worn with whatever leather shoes or laced boots will be the most comfortable, wet or dry.

A visitor to Scotland may recall, or hear references to, the feat known as doing a Macnab. This got its name from a novel called *John Macnab*, published by the Scottish writer John Buchan in 1925. In its essentials, the story concerns the poaching of deer and salmon from a private estate, after the owner has been given notice that "John Macnab" is going to attempt this feat. He does and succeeds. The name now applies to the considerable sporting—and organizational—achievement of killing, in the course of one day, a salmon, a stag, and a grouse. The day to choose will probably be in late September, when all three seasons coincide. It is more or less essential to try for the salmon before breakfast, shortly after dawn, when light, wind, and temperature all provide tremendous stimuli for the fish. With the fish landed, a rapid move to the stalking ground must be made, where a stalker must be on hand. It can happen that, with both salmon and stag killed, rain descends with such force and persistence as to make the grouse quite unapproachable. In the writer's experience, success was achieved when the sharp-eyed stalker spotted grouse feeding on stooks of oats in a stubble field, where they could be stalked, like deer. [JMG]

North American Deer and Antelope

North America, and particularly the United States, is rich in a wide variety of deer, which occur throughout the continent, and in the state of Hawaii. Deer afford an abundance of hunting, in which many different methods—some familiar from the Old World, others learned from one or other of the North American Indian tribes—are used to follow, drive, or attract the animals. They range in size from the 100 to 125 lb (45 to 55 kg) pronghorn, which can run at over 60 mph (100 km/h), to bull moose, which can weigh up to 1,800 lb (800 kg).

Probably the most challenging, elusive, and wary of North American big-game animals are whitetail deer. They are primarily nocturnal feeders, normally moving toward their bedding areas at daybreak; some go directly, others browse on the way. In hilly or mountainous areas, feeding grounds are often in the valleys, where wet soil supports good browse, or on hardwood flats at the foot of slopes. Once the hunter has located the feeding grounds and identified the routes the deer take to reach and leave them, he should watch quietly from dawn to about 8 or 9 o'clock in the morning; deer follow a routine, but, if disturbed, they are inclined to wander, and to feed more by day than at other times.

In wilderness areas, where little hunting takes place, the hunter must be prepared to hunt the deer in their resting areas, where they have bedded down for the day. High ground under a ridge line, preferably along the margin of a thicket, and in the sun, is a likely area to find them; by contrast, deer bedded down in thick swamp are difficult to locate if the hunter is alone and confined to narrow, winding game trails. Still-hunting—walking very slowly on ridges or game trails, stopping every few steps—is a good technique. Look and listen continuously. Move upwind, for deer have good noses. Keep both eyes open for signs of deer. The bucks leave marks called rubs and scrapes. In late summer and early fall, the bucks rub the velvet off their antlers, using—and frequently destroying—saplings in doing so, for they rub off the bark as they rub the velvet from their horns; trees are marked from about 12 to 36 inches (30 to 90 cm) off the ground. Later, throughout the rut, which may fall anytime between mid-October and early January, depending on the latitude, the bucks continue to rub and polish their antlers on tree trunks, saplings, and accessible branches. It may not always be possible to see if a rub is fresh or not, but scrapes—bare patches of ground, pawed out by a buck's front hooves—containing fresh prints are a sure sign that bucks are in the area. The scrapes mark out their mating territory.

Two hunters stalking together more than double their separate chances of taking a deer. One hunter should move along the side of the hill, just below the crest, taking care not to break cover; the other should precede him by some 50 to 100 yards (45 to 90 m), but some way down the hill on a parallel course. Deer started from a resting place but not so badly alarmed as to flee headlong downhill, often try to move uphill and around the cause of disturbance before doubling back around it. The

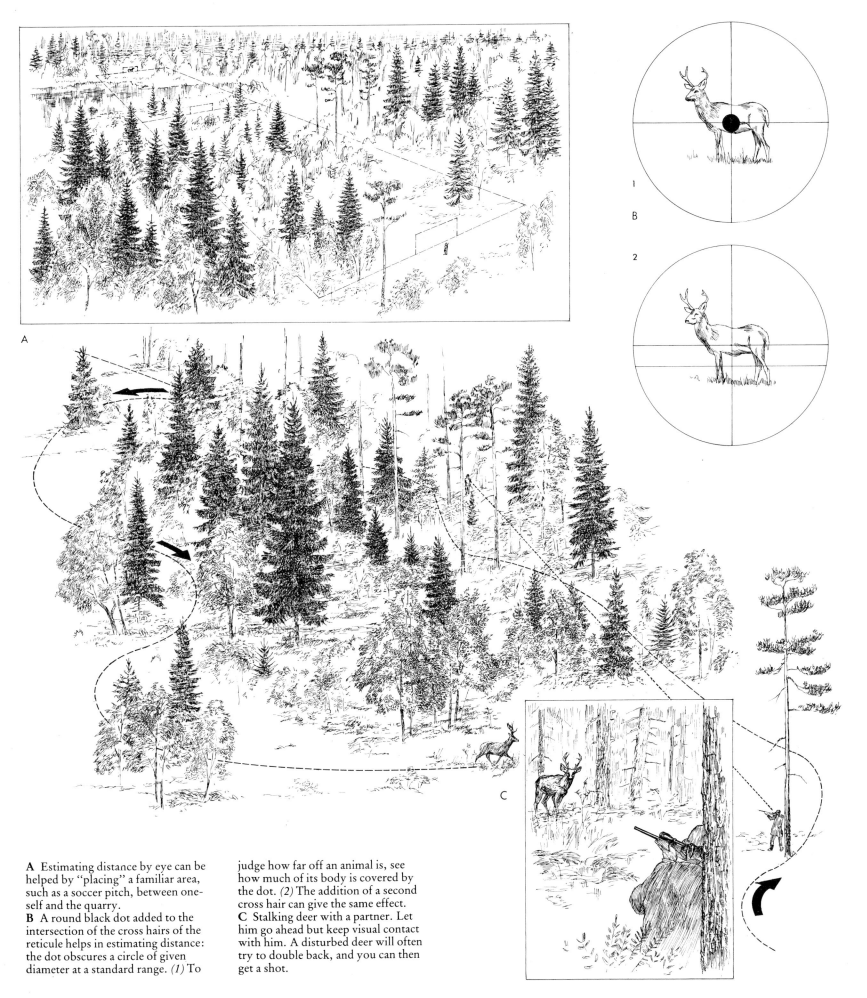

A Estimating distance by eye can be helped by "placing" a familiar area, such as a soccer pitch, between oneself and the quarry.
B A round black dot added to the intersection of the cross hairs of the reticule helps in estimating distance: the dot obscures a circle of given diameter at a standard range. *(1)* To judge how far off an animal is, see how much of its body is covered by the dot. *(2)* The addition of a second cross hair can give the same effect.
C Stalking deer with a partner. Let him go ahead but keep visual contact with him. A disturbed deer will often try to double back, and you can then get a shot.

upper of the two hunters will have a good chance of getting in a shot, even if his companion will not; for obvious reasons, each should have an exact knowledge of where the other is.

Something of an elaboration on this is the use of the high seat or tree stand, a method much used in Europe and popular also for whitetail in parts of Texas. Some high seats are very much more than mere rough platforms in trees; those in Europe may even be equipped with heaters. High seats keep the scent of the hunter well off the ground; they also place him above the usual level of observation of deer, with the exception of red deer. A further advantage of a high seat is that the trajectory of shots fired from it is generally downward, so that bullets that miss their targets are most likely to expend their energy in the earth.

Deer are also hunted by means of drives. A simple drive involves no more than a single gun and two or three drivers; an elaborate one, with many guns and drivers, properly requires almost military precision. The more drivers, the better the results, if care is taken to work the deer slowly and quietly, so that they break cover at hardly more than a slow walk. Does and yearlings usually show themselves first; the bucks hang back, sometimes trying to sneak past a stand. This sort of driving is much used in Europe for shooting wild boar.

One of the advantages of a drive is that the participants need not know the country intimately; they need a reasonable sense of direction, and a guide who knows the terrain well enough to ensure that areas are driven that actually contain deer. Short drives, of perhaps not more than about half a mile, or one kilometer, are more effective than longer ones.

Two or three hunters who are used to hunting together sometimes organize a still-hunt over country they all know well. Agreeing in advance to converge simultaneously on a given point, each of the hunters should be able to get a number of chances of shots at animals moving away from the disturbance.

In the southern United States and in Ontario in Canada, hounds are used to drive whitetail deer past hunters on stands; this is the only effective way to hunt them in thick swamps and forest. When shot at, the animals are nearly always moving at close range (30 to 40 paces); for this reason, shotguns loaded with buckshot are used in the United States; in Ontario, however, most hunters use rifles.

A particular method of luring whitetail bucks has been successfully developed in the southwestern United States, especially in Texas. It involves the use of a pair of whitetail deer antlers, which the hunter clashes together to simulate the noise made by two bucks fighting over a doe, so as to lure another buck to the scene. This method can be practiced with any chance of success only in the rut. The hunter should conceal himself well, usually on the edge of a thicket; some hunters mask their own scent in the odor of skunk glands, which can be purchased or prepared at home.

Whitetail deer have been introduced into Czechoslovakia and Finland. In the first of these countries, they are not too abundant but provide limited hunting; the usual method is to take up stands along game trails. In Finland, they are doing very well and have become second in number only to the moose (or European elk); the most popular, indeed virtually the only, method of hunting them is the drive, which is conducted very much as in the eastern United States.

A diminutive form of the whitetail, called Coues deer, occurs primarily in the southwest of the United States and just over the border in Mexico, in the state of Sonora. Another relatively small deer of the American west is the blacktail, a small subspecies of mule deer.

In the mule-deer country of the West, the mountains and hills have broken patches of pine, fir, and aspen, usually growing on the shadier sides of draws (shallow ravines); the patches of trees are interspersed with low grass, sagebrush, and isolated clumps of head-high chaparral and chokeberry bushes, which can be as extensive as a city block.

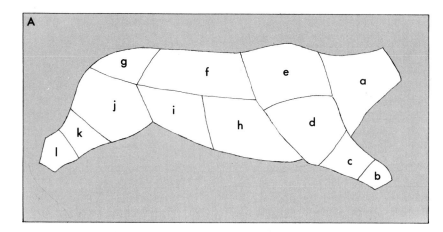

A Cuts for butchering. *(a)* Neck gives ground meat. *(b)* Knee: good only for your dog. *(c)* Shank: stews or ground meat. *(d)* Knuckle: roast. *(e)* Shoulder: roast or steaks. *(f)* Loin: chops or steaks. *(g)* Rump: roasts. *(h)* Ribs: roasts or stew. *(i)* Flank: steaks or stew. *(j)* Round: steaks. *(k)* Shank: stew. *(l)* Hock: throw it away or give it to your dog.

B, C Two ways to move a carcass. The first employs a hitch around the muzzle once the line has been secured to the horns. The other requires a stout canvas sheet secured to a pole. The animal is placed on the sheet, and its head or antlers are secured to the pole.

D Once in camp, the deer should be gutted and hung up to cool. The carcass should be held open— thin sticks can be cut to size—to speed up the cooling.

E When field-dressing a deer, some hunters remove the metatarsal glands *(a)*; others simply take care not to touch them. The first essential cut is between the genitals *(b)* and the base of the rib cage *(c)*: the cutting edge of the knife is held upward, so as to

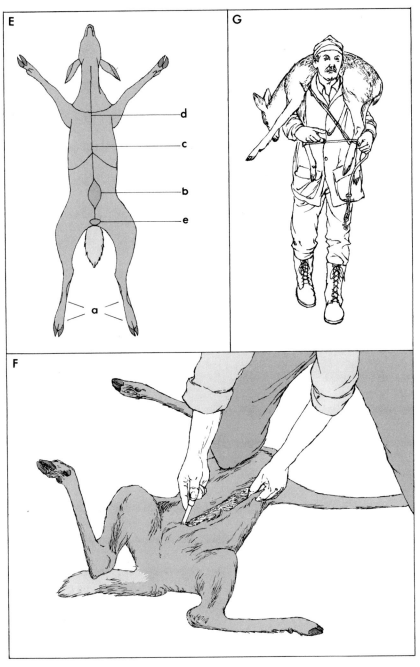

avoid puncturing the intestines. Once this cut is made, the intestines and stomach begin to bulge out. They can be gently removed, being attached to the walls of the stomach cavity only by delicate tissue which can easily be severed with a knife. It is not necessary to open the rib cage (although it can be done with a light ax).
The windpipe and the esophagus can be reached and severed as close to the animal's head as possible (d). Then all the viscera can easily be removed together. The genitals (b) and anus (e) are then detached by a series of rela-

tively deep cuts around them, care being necessary lest the bladder or anal canal be punctured.
F The latter part of gutting is done straddling the carcass, facing away from the animal's head.
G Relatively light deer can be carried on the hunter's shoulders. "Flag" the animal's horns, lest some unobservant hunter take a shot at the head.
H Even a relatively big and heavy animal can be hoisted up with a light block-and-tackle.

Just after daybreak, and in the evening when the hills begin to cool off, mule deer can be seen respectively going to and leaving cover. A hunter with binoculars can observe a wide area and can try either to stalk or intercept a deer, or mark where it has bedded down, and go there later, with the wind in his favor, to try to jump it. Particularly the old, wise bucks frequently bed down just below ridges of hillsides and canyons, whence they can keep watch for their traditional enemies—wolves and coyotes—which, like inexperienced hunters, approach from the valleys. An experienced hunter uses the high ground.

A single hunter or, better, a pair of hunters, should slowly and carefully work into every clump of cover, out of which a disturbed muley will usually try to escape uphill. A variation is for the hunters to stalk around each clump, and for the man uphill to throw stones into the cover; the deer will often try to get away downhill.

In some parts of the West, there are forests, and driving methods can be used there. Small wooded valleys and brushy canyons can be effectively driven by only three or four hunters. In larger expanses of woods, still-hunting, such as is used for whitetail, is a good method. Blacktail deer, being a forest form of the mule deer, can be hunted in this way. In the rain forests of the Pacific coast, which are usually too thick to permit clear shots, the hunter should remain near openings, such as meadows, fire-clearings, logged-over areas, and logging and access roads; these generally contain shrubs and small trees, and blacktail deer emerge to browse there early in the morning and late in the afternoon. Taking a stand by a game trail is effective, too.

Hounds may be legally used to drive deer in some western states, but not all; the methods are similar to those used in the southern states. The hunters take up their positions on forest roads, ridges, or game trails.

Pronghorn are very numerous in the western part of North America and can be stalked, once they have been observed, for example, through binoculars from a high ridge. They are not only very wary but very fleet of foot, too, being capable over short distances of speeds in the order of 60 mph (100 km/h). For these reasons, shots are usually taken at long range; rifles must be very accurately adjusted and equipped with a 4× or even 6× telescopic sight.

A good rifle for deer in the forests of eastern North America should be light and handy for quick shooting. The caliber is unimportant, but the larger calibers—.30 and up—are better when shooting through brush.

A good rifle for mule deer should be relatively flat-shooting, for shots can be long compared with those for whitetail deer. Any caliber from .243 to .30 is a good bet. Many hunters like the flat-shooting .25–06 and the .270. The 7×64 would be an excellent choice; so would the new 7mm Remington express.

Pronghorns are generally shot at long range, and a high-velocity cartridge with a flat trajectory is needed. Anything from .243 or 6mm to a .300 Magnum is a good choice. Calibers such as the .25–06, .270, and 7mm Remington are probably best. [JK]

Elk, Moose, and Caribou

Three more outstanding game animals in North America are the American elk, or wapiti; the moose, which is known as the elk in Scandinavia; and the caribou, which is also familiar as the reindeer. The elk and the moose are lovers of undisturbed country; the caribou is a sub-arctic species, occuring at high latitudes all round the northern hemisphere, where it roams the treeless or almost treeless tundra.

Hunting caribou is not technically difficult. Especially in remote areas, where hunting rarely takes place, the animals tend to be inquisitive and may even approach a hunter. The best method of spotting them is to use binoculars from the crest of a hill or ridge. In Newfoundland, hunters out after woodland caribou walk through the forest and glass the flat expanses of muskeg barrens. The forest animals are generally more wary

Hunting mule deer in the southwestern part of the United States. On typical terrain of the sort depicted, a simple drive can be organized by two or three hunters. One of the hunters moves slowly down a canyon. At the end, the other two have taken stands. If there are deer there, they will move toward the hunters. The young deer and does usually come first, while the stag hangs back cautiously. It is important that the driver goes slowly, so that the deer are moving at not more than walking pace. Sometimes, the driver can get a shot at the stag, especially if it tries to double back.

than those living on more open ground. The method of getting within range of any sort of caribou is a stalk, using available cover, and working upwind toward the animal.

Any moderately powered rifle, from .270 up to .300, preferably with a scope sight of moderate power, is suitable for caribou. The woodland animals weigh up to 400 lb (180 kg), those of the arctic tundra less than half this, but caribou flesh is probably the best venison of all in North America. It is superior to that of the elk, but the hunting provided by elk more than compensates for that.

Elk are animals of the deep wilderness and readily move away from disturbing noise; when hunting elk, therefore, it is important to keep noise to a minimum. Despite their fondness for quiet, however, bull elk in rut emit loud, unmistakable bugling or high-pitched trumpeting calls, almost a cross between a squeal and a deep whistle; they start on a low note and go up by overtones through four steps, before descending the scale again. The volume increases with the pitch; the crescendo is a deafening screech. Bulls challenge each other by this means, much as red deer stags do by roaring; individual animals are attracted to the source of the noise, especially if it comes from some point downhill. These habits have given rise to the hunting art of elk calling.

The hunter calls either to locate bulls, from their responses to his imitation of their calls, or to attract them. In the first case, he positions himself on a ridge in a likely area, whence he can hope actually to see the answering animals, once he has a line on them. The best time is early on a frosty morning. Calling to attract bulls is best done from some relatively low-lying position, ideally at the edge of a small meadow or by an opening in trees, where the hunter can sit comfortably with his rifle ready, yet be reasonably well hidden. Then, he utters a call and waits for replies. It is important not to call too frequently, but to maintain a tempo—with the answering animal or animals—that keeps up the excitement. Some bulls, however, will approach quite silently, and the hunter must therefore have his eyes about him, for one may appear without warning.

Elk calls can be bought in many sporting-goods stores or can be made by the hunter; a ½-inch (1 cm) conduit pipe or bamboo of the same dimension is good. A piece about 12 inches (30 cm) is the right length. The call is really just a big whistle. Bamboo gives a more mellow note than metal or plastic, but elk are attracted by calls from instruments of any material.

Elk provide challenging hunting for those whose woodcraft enables them to move silently in heavy forest. Once an elk has been spotted through binoculars, the hunter must keep his scent away from the animal, for elk are keen-nosed as well as sharp-eared. When spooked, an elk clears out at once, unlike a whitetail deer, which may try to sneak round a hunter before returning to where it was.

As a bull elk is a big, tough animal, the hunter needs a rifle of at least .270 or 7mm caliber, but the more powerful .30 calibers, such as the .30–06 or the various .300 Magnums, are probably even better.

Moose are even bigger than elk and, as they have different habits, hunting them requires slightly different methods. In North America, especially in the remote regions, a moose that evades a hunter is very likely to get away. As moose are good swimmers, they can cross lakes and streams which the hunters cannot. Moose are stalked in North America, but they are even more wary than whitetail, and noises or scents that make them nervous cause them to move off at once. In the West, where their terrain is more open than in the East, they can be spotted at a distance and approached, perhaps at first on horseback, then in a stalk. In winter, when they are very much slowed down by deep snow, they can be hunted by those who can use snowshoes; even if moose tracks cannot be found, the noises made as moose break down saplings while feeding— the noises sound like pistol shots—indicate where the moose are, and an

In the early part of the rutting season, a wapiti bull can give away its position by the noise it makes when rubbing off the last of the velvet or when staging mock battles with saplings or bushes. The guide lures it into the open by issuing a challenging call with his wapiti whistle, cupping his palm over the end of the whistle to control volume and tone. The bull often reacts aggressively to the call and comes out into the open, looking for a fight. When the animal is within range, the hunter, who has been examining it through binoculars to establish if it is worth taking, can take a shot at it.

Bugling wapiti is an art that goes back to the early American Indians. A hunter should train at bugling before trying it out, as it must not be done too often or too low; this can scare the wapiti off. Normally, it is best to leave the bugling to the guide.

A typical drive for moose (European elk) in Sweden, where over 100,000 moose must be shot annually. The shooters are positioned at numbered stands. Before the hunt, the arc of fire for each stand is marked and cleared of hindering vegetation. When moose are disturbed, they make for swamps or heavily wooded cover, and they normally move downwind, to keep track of where their pursuers are. The drivers, positioned between 50 and

100 yards (45 and 90 m) apart, move the animals along slowly, for if the moose become scared, they can move at such a pace that there will be no chance of a killing shot. Here, the hunter on stand 12 has a clear shot at the cow (the team will have been allotted a certain quota of stags, cows, and calves). (Below) Wounded moose are tracked down by specially bred and trained hounds.

(Top right) Getting the carcass out of the woods is no easy job, and the team of drivers and hunters have often to lend a hand at getting the animal to where it can be butchered. Horse- or tractor-drawn sleds are sometimes used, too.

approach upwind is often successful. With these exceptions, the method that is most effective is the oldest. North American Indians long ago learned how to call moose, and the art is still very much alive today.

Two types of call are used, one to imitate a bull in rut, the other, a cow in heat. Many sportsmen have learned these from Cree and Ojibway Indians. While most guides still use birch bark and spruce-root thongs to make their calling megaphones, equally effective ones can be made from stiff paper. A prosaic way to learn to make the right noises is to buy and imitate a record or tape; these are sold in sporting-goods stores.

The functions of the two calls, in the field, are to challenge a bull (the bull call) or to entice him (the cow call). The latter works, naturally enough, only for a bull in rut without a cow; the former may induce any bull, even one with a cow, to set off to challenge the supposed intruder. After calling only a few times and only relatively softly—novices often call too frequently and too loudly—the hunter listens some ten or fifteen minutes before calling again. If a moose answers, a soft call is a much more effective response than a loud one. A wrong note at any time can ruin the effect. A moose will not approach even the most seductively calling hunter from downwind. Sometimes, moose content themselves with answering without moving out of cover, or begin to move and then stop or turn aside.

Many hunters believe that calling works only in the eastern parts of North America, but this is unjustified, for it works well with western moose, too. Even if there are some openings in the woods of eastern Canada—for example, in Ontario, Quebec, and northern Manitoba, there are cutovers, old forest-burns, and marshes—the country is generally too thick for stalking, and so calling is very much in favor. In the western part of Canada, the country is open enough to permit still-hunting or stalking, and guides seldom call moose. [JK]

European Elk in Scandinavia

Elk shooting in Scandinavia is carried out in the fall. In Sweden, a complicated system of licensing ensures that seasonal differences between the north and the south of the country are not overlooked, and that the rights of landowners and of the owners of hunting rights are balanced against the national policy of preserving the ecosystem of the elk. The season in both Norway and Sweden provides, in effect, a national cull. The numbers of animals—bulls, cows, and calves—that may be shot in each administrative area are calculated; hunters who exceed their permitted totals land in trouble.

In both countries, the visiting hunter is not exempt from a requirement that each hunter must demonstrate his or her abilities with a rifle suitable for the game to be hunted. The formalities are not great, and an experienced shot will have no trouble in passing this test.

The different methods of hunting relate to the size of the area being hunted: in areas that are relatively small, dogs are kept on the leash. In larger areas, the dogs are slipped. Whoever possesses a good elk dog is able to pick and choose his hunting, for finding and tracking elk with a single dog is the classic method of hunting in Sweden, and a good dog and his owner will always be welcome. Sometimes, two or more dogs are used in very much the same manner. A dog is virtually essential in tracking a wounded elk.

The method used in a large area is to slip the dog and let it range back and forth in front of the hunter or hunters until it picks up a scent. A well-trained dog will often sniff the wind from some high point, such as a rocky outcrop, whence it may also catch sight of its quarry. Some dogs are uncanny in their ability to detect the sounds made by an elk. A dog must be able to keep silent when it picks up the scent of an elk. If the quarry gets frightened or startled, it will run off, and the hunter, if not his dog, will have trouble keeping up. But a good dog can bring an elk to bay and, when this happens, the sound and tone of its barking informs the hunter of what is happening and where. A shot might be taken at up to 100 yards (90 m).

Some hunting is done without dogs, in the manner of North American still-hunting (stalking). This requires sound woodcraft and is a method that is effective at dawn and dusk. Sometimes, high seats are used, and care must be taken to make them inconspicuous.

Driving elk is popular and much practiced, especially in southern Sweden, where extensive areas can be driven. When shooting stands are determined in advance, it is prudent to cut vegetation that may obscure the hunter's sight in directions giving onto likely target areas, and to mark the arcs of fire that are forbidden, as a grouse shooter might do on first entering his butt before a drive begins.

Two problematical matters in Sweden, particularly for hunters in smaller areas, are wounded animals that cross boundaries into other, neighboring hunting areas, and the shooting of more animals than have been permitted by license. The second of these often troublesome events can be guarded against by the use of an unambiguous system of signaling between hunters, sometimes by means of multiple shots; walkie-talkie radios are perhaps more reliable. National regulations require hunters to track down and despatch any wounded animal. For this reason, prudent hunters cease shooting some time before sunset, the legal close of the day, for tracking can take a very long time. This is one reason why responsible hunters shoot only when confident of being able to kill the animal.

When an elk is hit in the central nervous system, it falls at once. A heart shot will drop it within ten or fifteen seconds and so will a lung shot, but this margin of time may be quite enough for the animal to vanish from the sight of the hunter and pose problems of tracking. A shot in some other relatively vital area—the liver, for example—may well kill the animal after some minutes, when it has sought and found shelter; if not immediately pursued, this is where instinct will take it. The problem for the hunter, and his companions if he is not alone, is to find it. Over and above the legal requirement to do so, the excellent meat the animal provides spoils unless it can be taken care of without delay; this is an urgent matter in warmish weather.

A wounded animal should be given time to find shelter because, once it has begun to rest, the effects of shock progressively weaken it, making it less and less able to get up and get away. An hour's delay is enough. The time must be spent examining the terrain where the animal was hit; the hunter must be able to ascertain what kind of wound it has and where it went afterwards. If the wound is only light, a trail may have been left on tree trunks, bushes, or on the ground. A tracking dog is of very great help, but it must be so well-trained that it will follow only the scent of the wounded beast, and not that of any other elk it may encounter. It should be kept leashed, lest it find the carcass of the shot beast, give no audible sign of its find, and then go on to look for something of greater interest.

Elk hunters in Sweden generally use medium-caliber rifles—6.5×55, for example—in part because it is customary to do a lot of practice shooting before the season begins, and ammunition of this caliber is relatively inexpensive. Hunters in North America might regard such a rifle as on the lighter side; most knowledgeable hunters would not recommend the .270, for example, except for a shooter who had problems with recoil. The 7mm Magnum, with a heavily constructed bullet of 175 grains (11 g), is a better bet than the old faithful .270. The .308 Magnum or, if the hunter can handle them, one of the .338s or .350 Magnums would be an excellent tool for elk hunting. Such rifles weigh about 10 lb (4.5 kg), or about twenty-five percent more than a .270, but they provide the power to get the job done. [RE]

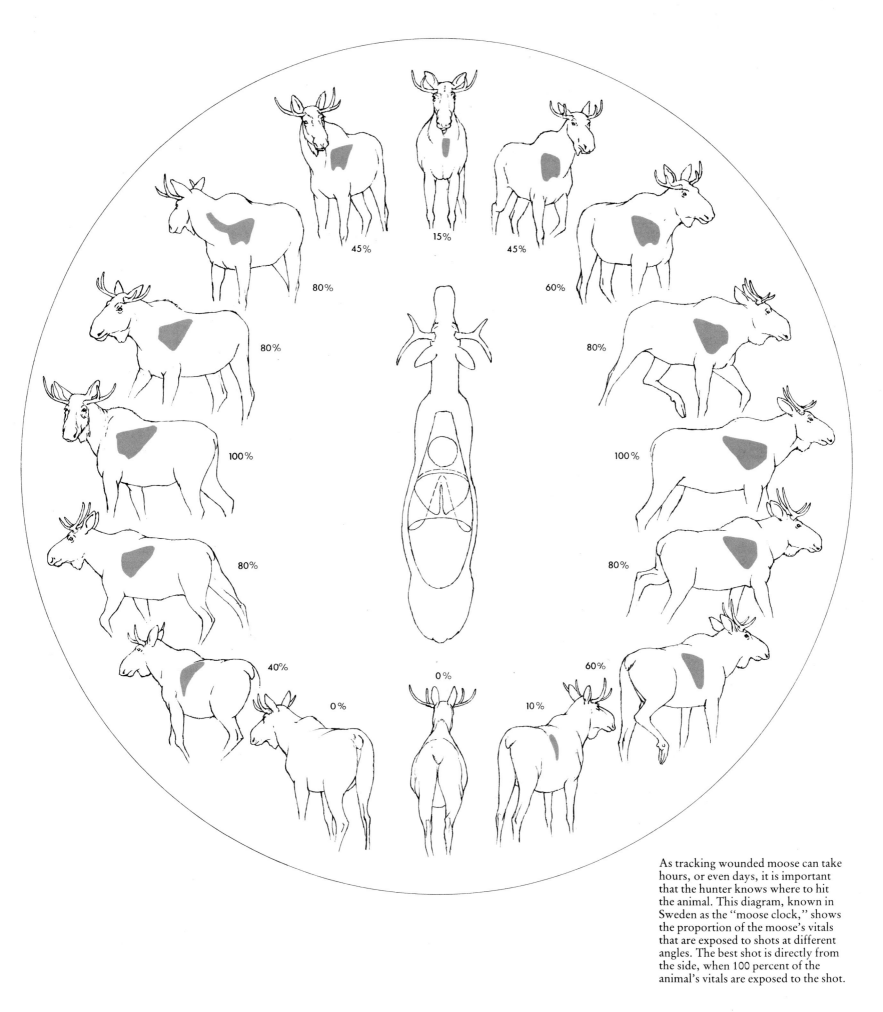

45%
15%
45%
80%
60%
80%
80%
100%
100%
80%
80%
40%
60%
0%
0%
10%

As tracking wounded moose can take hours, or even days, it is important that the hunter knows where to hit the animal. This diagram, known in Sweden as the "moose clock," shows the proportion of the moose's vitals that are exposed to shots at different angles. The best shot is directly from the side, when 100 percent of the animal's vitals are exposed to the shot.

Wild Sheep and Goats

The high mountain ranges of Europe and western North America afford hunting that is as demanding and, physically, perhaps even more rigorous than deer stalking in Scotland. The quarry are the wild sheep and goats of North America, the chamois, which is a relative of the mountain goat of British Columbia, southern Alaska, and the Yukon, and the rare mouflon, or wild sheep, that has been introduced from its native Corsica and Sardinia to the mainland of Europe, and thence to the Hawaiian island of Lanai.

The method of approaching to within range of any of these animals is the stalk, although some hunters use a four-wheel-drive vehicle for scouting, or as an aid in stalking; this is, however, unusual and, in some parts of the world, actually illegal. In North America, it is usual to get into the mountains on foot, with the necessary gear carried on pack horses (see Part VI: Hunting Allies). But whatever the means employed to get to the mountains, the hunter needs to be in good physical shape and prepared for a great deal of climbing and walking.

One of the best tactics is to climb to a high vantage point and to glass the surrounding country with binoculars. However, the animals often blend in well with their backgrounds. Brown bighorn sheep, gray Stone sheep, and, in winter, white Dall sheep may not be easy to spot; both chamois and mouflon are dark brown to black. A contrasting background, such as green vegetation, will help, but when the animals are set off against rocks or a stony terrain, particularly if irregularly shadowed, the hunter will need sharp eyes to locate his quarry. It is always possible to begin by glassing from below, before undertaking a climb, but all these animals are keen-sighted; the natural enemies of Dall and Stone sheep—wolves and cougar—usually approach from below, and the animals are sensitive to movement below them. Mouflon are particularly wary, but can be distracted from noticing a hunter and his guide if they inconspicuosly leave a vehicle that is then driven off in full view. Chamois are sometimes just as wary, especially in areas where small populations have been subjected to heavy hunting. Where little hunting occurs, such as in the more inaccessible heights, chamois seem not to associate the sight of man with danger.

Once an animal is in sight, the hunter must decide, from a careful scrutiny through binoculars and telescopic sight, if it is a good trophy and, if it is, how he can approach within range of it. His approach route may require mountaineering techniques (with his rifle slung on his back to leave both hands free for climbing), and a scrupulous attention to the avoidance of noises likely to alarm the animal; mistakes can be fatal to the progress of the stalk, to say nothing of the life and limb of the hunter. It can happen that the animal is so placed as to be inaccessible to the hunter, or likely to fall and be lost or broken up when shot; in some parts of the world, it may be possible to induce the animal to move in a helpful direction, for example, by firing a shot so that the bullet strikes a rock to one side of the animal and so causes it to move to the other.

A rifle for sheep hunting should be chambered for a cartridge that drives a bullet at moderately high velocity to achieve a flat trajectory. Such calibers as .25–06, .270, 7mm, .30–06, and any of the Magnums, are good bets. Goats are harder to kill than sheep and nothing under .270 or 7mm is recommended. Rifles for either sheep or goats should be fitted with a scope sight of moderate power.

Excellent American calibers of rifle for the chamois are the .243, .257, .270, and .25–706; for the mouflon, the .270, .308, 7.62mm NATO, and .30–06 are adequate calibers. Fine European calibers for either animal are the 6.5×57, 7×57, 7×64, and 7×65; the 8×57 is satisfactory for the mouflon. Relatively long shots are sometimes called for, because it is not always possible to get as close as might be desirable, particularly to chamois, before taking the shot. [JK, TT]

The mouflon is the only European wild sheep. It is a wanderer by nature, and this and its extreme wariness make it a difficult and challenging animal to hunt. Perhaps the best method is to use a vehicle for scouting and as an aid in stalking. This method of hunting is illegal in some parts of the world but is often used in Europe for taking mouflon. Like many other animals, mouflon have little or no fear of a horse-drawn wagon but will immediately take to flight if they sense a human being. When the mouflon herd is spotted, the hunter and his guide determine if there is a shootable ram among them. If so, they sneak out of the vehicle, which is then driven away, keeping the attention of the animals. The hunter then gets into a shooting position and tries for the ram. The best ram is known as an A-class ram and is at least six years old. Its horns must be at least 24 inches (60 cm) and form a three-quarter curl.

Stalking is the only method for hunting chamois. Like most other high-mountain game, the chamois is spotted normally from below with the aid of a spotting scope or binoculars. Once a shootable ram has been found, the hunter has to find his way to a shooting position above the animal without being seen. The biggest challenge is often provided by the moun-tain, rather than by the game itself. (Inset) A common shooting fault in the mountains is to aim too high when shooting at a target below you. Within an actual range of about 300 yards (275 m), you need to allow only for the horizontal distance between you and your target.

Bears

In North America, the ranges of the Dall and Stone sheep, and the mountain goat, overlap that of the black bear and, in the Northwest, that of the grizzly. For these bears, the .270 rifle is at the lighter end of the scale; for grizzlies, the .30–06, the 7mm Magnum, the various .300s, the 8mm Remington, and the .338 and .350 Remington are all good; the .358 Norma and the .375 Holland & Holland are even better, provided that the hunter can shoot them accurately, for they afford greater bullet diameter and heavier bullets; still, placing the shot is more important than its size.

Rifles and cartridges for black bears include the old .30–30, which is adequate in the hands of a good rifle shot. Others may prefer more modern cartridges, such as the .270, the .308, and the .30–06, particularly in the West, where ranges can be quite long. In the eastern woods, cartridges such as the .35 Remington and the .358 Winchester are excellent.

Both grizzlies and black bears may be observed by hunters glassing for sheep, goats, moose, or caribou. In the fall, grizzlies may be seen in meadows and on mountain slopes, or near streams, along which numbers of the bears gather to fish for salmon; lesser concentrations of grizzlies gather in berry patches in late summer and fall. Among their other vegetable foods are many different kinds of leaves, sprouts, twigs, roots, and tubers. Grizzlies eat carrion and animals they kill themselves; these include marmots and ground squirrels. On emerging in spring from their winter dormancy, grizzlies feed almost exclusively on green grass shoots and other vegetation.

Black bears love wild berries, fruits, honey (and bees), nuts, and a wide range of other, largely vegetable, foods. They catch and eat fish, too (but not on the same scale as grizzlies), and feed on carrion, such as the carcasses of winter-killed animals. In spring, black bears feed to a very large extent on fresh vegetable growth; later, toward the end of summer and in the fall, they may be expected to be seen on the blueberry barrens of the Midwest and in abandoned orchards anywhere in their range.

Once a bear has been seen and identified as a trophy animal, it must be stalked to within good rifle range. Bears have very keen noses and ears, even if their sight is relatively poor; it is essential for the hunter to work upwind toward the bear as quietly as possible. Open mountain country is ideal for this method; stalking in forests and forest meadows requires more patience. It is literally vital to get as close as possible to the bear, especially to a grizzly, to reduce the chances of merely wounding him; wounded bears have mauled or even killed many guides and hunters.

Both sorts of bear may be shot over bait in those parts of North America where this method is not illegal: baiting for grizzlies with meat or fish is illegal, but natural baits—winter-killed moose, elk, or caribou, or such animals drowned by breaking through river or lake ice—may be used. The trick is to find such carcasses, and to watch them, hoping to see the bear. Offal from animals shot by the hunter may also be used. Baiting for black bear is legal in eastern Canada, in some Rocky Mountains states, and in some northern Great Lakes states, but some hunters might consider the method unsporting, even if legal.

Most of the black bears taken over bait are shot at dusk. The bait is hung in a burlap bag or a metal pail on a tree, just a little too high for a bear to reach it comfortably; the tree should be one just on the edge of thick cover, for old boars—male bears—seldom cross open spaces during the day but will do so at night. The bait should be replenished daily if need be: pork fat or meat scraps are good; rotten meat may attract bears, but they seem to prefer to eat fresh meat; fish is not so good. Scent baits—vanilla extract, aniseed, or peppermint oils, for example—may be used if not illegal.

Hunting over bait requires enough persistence and patience to wait quietly for several hours a day, day after day, hoping to see a bear; a bear will itself watch a bait for half an hour or more before coming to it, frequently circling round, testing the wind, and will not approach more closely if its suspicions are aroused. However well placed the hunter may have been at first, a change in the wind, or movements by the bear, can put him upwind of the bait or the bear, rather than downwind, which is where he wants to be while he is keeping watch. A black bear against a background of dark woods can be difficult to see at twilight, and a scope sight will give the hunter a better chance of placing a killing shot.

The most exciting and sporting method of hunting black bears is with hounds, a tradition developed primarily in the hill country of the southern United States, where the hound tradition is still strong. There are now fine packs of bear hounds, some private, and some available for the clients of commercial outfitters, in many parts of the United States.

The classic method is simple: the hounds are taken to good bear country, and, when they find a fresh trail, they are let loose to chase the bear. The hunters follow. When the bear is brought to bay—usually against a fallen tree, in thick brush, or by an upturned stump or a rocky outcrop—he stands his ground and fights off the hounds, frequently mauling or killing some of them, until the hunters close in, from upwind, to take a shot. This is the method used in Finland and Russia. Winter hunting of bears in their dens is still practiced in Russia but is illegal in many areas of North America.

In the old days, all this was done on foot, over forest trails or even directly through the forests in bear country. This has given way to the use of a pick-up truck, driven on logging or forest access roads, sometimes with the keen-nosed strike hound riding on the hood and baying when it scents a bear. Another hound or two may be used to test the trail and, if it is fresh enough, the pack is released from the back of the truck, where they have been confined. Following the pack on foot, carrying a rifle, is not a sport for unfit hunters.

A modification of this method is used in areas where there are many roads through likely country. Hunters take up their positions at stands in a forest that is believed to contain bears; the stands are always placed at the ridgetops or ravines overgrown with brush, which bears would probably cross. Two or three hunters walk with the hounds and, if they put up a bear, their fellows who are waiting may get a chance for a fast shot at the moving bear.

Most black bears, however, are not shot in front of hounds but incidently, so to say: a bear disturbed by hunters may amble into sight of a perhaps surprised deer hunter waiting on a stand with a rifle loaded just for deer.

Polar bears, having been hunted to excess from aircraft off the coast of Alaska, are subject to the United States Marine Mammals Protection Act, which makes illegal in the United States the hunting of, or importation of trophies from, polar bears (and other marine animals). Very restricted hunting, with the help of the Eskimo of northern Canada and their sled dogs, is still available to sportsmen prepared to undergo the rigors and dangers of hunting polar bears on foot on the ice. Because of the restrictions in the United States, this is of greater interest to Canadian and European hunters. [JK]

Wild Boar

Another "international" game animal occuring in North America is the wild boar. The hound chase is the most exciting way to hunt boar and is similar to bear hunting with hounds. Hunters are posted at points where boar may cross ahead of the hounds; the hounds are used to find and follow a fresh track. Like bears, wild boar can be brought to bay by hounds, but a pursuit can last for several days. In Florida, hounds are used to bring hybrids—razorbacks, as they are called—to bay so that one hunter or more may actually catch the animal, which is then taken off to be penned and fattened before being slaughtered.

(Above) In Europe, wild boar are tracked and driven in winter, when there is snow. Tracks *(a)* are noted leading into an area surrounded by country roads. As no tracks emerge, the animals must be in there. Drivers *(b)* enter the area. Hunters *(c)* take up stands at intervals of about 100 yards (90 m) and the boar are shot as they emerge. The hunter must never shoot into the area being driven or before the boar has cleared the line of hunters.

(Above) Boar can very quickly destroy a field of vegetables, so they are not the most popular animals with farmers. When boar are feeding in cultivated areas, they are hunted by night from portable high seats. Here, a seat has been erected in a field of sugar beet.

(Left) Boar hounds are used to hunt in the United States. A typical situation is illustrated diagrammatically here. The hounds are released where the road crosses a stream (a), which flows through a valley covered with brush and trees. The hounds track upstream, and hunters (b) wait at the foot of the ridges enclosing the valley or where streams meet (c).

Still-hunting, however, has become the most common way of hunting wild boar in many areas. The animals are most active at dawn and dusk, when they feed out in the open. As when hunting deer, the hunter must walk slowly, working upwind, for wild boar have a very keen sense of smell and sharp hearing. He must stop frequently to look and listen. He must concentrate his efforts in areas where there are plenty of signs of wild boar, such as tracks and droppings, fresh mud wallows, and rootings in the earth for roots and tubers. It is a good idea to look for such indications before starting the actual hunt; waterholes and other places where the boar drink are rewarding places to look.

Two typically European methods of hunting boar are driving and using a high seat. The latter method is often employed at night, using a portable seat that can be moved to fields where wild boar have been observed. Further equipment, in addition to a rifle, includes binoculars suitable for night use—usually the heavy but effective 8×56—and a telescopic sight with good light-gathering qualities. Again, the 8×56 with a coarse reticule is most desirable, if not actually essential.

Driving is often employed in winter after snowfall, for it is then relatively easy to track boar to specific areas so as to drive them out. Because wild boar are nomadic, one must be certain that there are boar in an area before driving it. The success of a drive depends on having beaters who know their business and can be relied upon to beat through thickets where boar may be lying. The hunters, too, must understand the rules: for instance, never to shoot into the area being driven but to wait until a boar has run through the line of hunters before shooting.

Drives can take different forms. In the more elaborate, each hunter takes up his place by a numbered stand and stays there until the drive is over; especially in Germany, where hunting methods are highly developed, the hunter will need to be familiar with the system of signaling by hunting-horn when a hunt is to begin and end, when shots may be taken, and when they may not. Walkie-talkie radios may be used instead but lack the panache of the horn.

A circle drive, as its name suggests, entails encircling an area with a ring of hunters alternating with beaters at distances apart of perhaps 20 to 50 yards (or meters), depending upon the type of country being driven. The circle may have a diameter of up to 1 mile (1.6 km). In major hunts, with between seventy-five and a hundred hunters, each must clearly understand when shooting is permitted into the circle, and when not. In this form of drive, the hunter must be prepared for all sorts of game, both four-footed and feathered. In its final stages, only the beaters converge on the center of the circle. The hunters remain at some prearranged distance, and shots are taken only when animals have passed through the line of guns.

Wild boar are heavyset, muscular animals but do not require an exceptionally heavy rifle. The .270, the .30–06, and the .308 are all adequate; European cartridges include the 7×57, 7×65, 8×57, and any of the 9.3mm loadings. Some European hunters prefer a *Drilling*—a three-barreled gun, usually with side-by-side shotgun barrels over a rifle barrel—loaded with two shotgun slugs for close-range shots, and a rifle bullet for one at longer range. At short ranges, the shotgun slug is most effective for boar.

Wild boar are also hunted in Asia and Africa (where other sorts of wild pig are to be found), while the collared peccary, known as the javelina, occurs southward from the southwestern United States through Central America, and southward again into much of South America. [TT]

Collared Peccary (Javelina)

Javelina can be hunted by one or more of the methods used for wild boar. The wise hunter, intending to hunt over a particular area, will go out before the season begins and look for fresh signs such as tracks and droppings, or for a waterhole used by these little desert pigs. When hunting, he can wait by the waterhole, if he is patient, but still-hunting is perhaps more appealing and more productive. The hunter must move slowly along the edges of brush patches or scrub forests and surprise the pigs in the open. They congregate in herds, and one or two animals are always on the alert; getting close to a herd is not easy. Planning his stalk carefully, the hunter works upwind toward it, avoiding dry, noisy brush and undergrowth. Sometimes, one disturbs an entire herd in thick cover and suddenly the animals appear on all sides, racing away in different directions.

Javelinas can be hunted with dogs. Unlike wild boar proper, javelinas have no great endurance and are soon brought to bay by well-trained dogs. But javelinas have sharp tusks, and dogs can be injured. Hunting with dogs is not legal in all parts of the United States, however. Rifles for javelinas are of calibers suitable for wild boar; some American hunters have taken to using bows-and-arrows, others again use large-bore handguns, but both should be used only by hunters who are proficient in handling them. [JK]

Chapter 2

Fowling: Upland and Water

Capercaillie

This great grouse holds a position of lofty esteem in the eyes of hunters in central Europe, where it ranks high as a trophy. It is hunted during the spring, when advantage may be taken of its preoccupation with its mating display to approach it. In Scandinavia, however, it may not be shot during the spring, and other methods must be employed to get close enough to shoot it. The capercaillie occurs quite frequently in Scotland but does not excite the same interest as it does on the Continent.

During the mating season in April and May, the hunter must be up early, long before sunrise, if he is to stalk it successfully. Well before the season has begun, hunting guides have ranged the forests and mountains in the areas where capercaillie live. The birds use certain trees year after year for their mating displays and, if one bird is shot, another will take over its tree. About an hour-and-a-half before sunrise, the cock begins his morning serenade, a repeated four-verse call. Although it is normally a very wary bird, with excellent senses of sight and hearing, the capercaillie is vulnerable during the fourth verse of its song. This is a hissing, during which it is to all appearances deaf. The hunter listens for the start of the call: a snapping sound. This is followed by a warbling and then a popping. The hunter can move only when the hissing begins. It lasts for no more than a few seconds, time enough for three or four careful steps. The hunter then "freezes." The bird begins his song again, and the hunter moves again. While he waits, he plans his next move.

Even under the most favorable conditions and with the most well-planned stalk, it may not be possible to get within shotgun range. For this reason, the most suitable gun will be a *Drilling* or some other combination of rifle and shotgun. If a shotgun is used, it should be a 12-bore and loaded with heavy shot, for capercaillie have thick feathers that take a lot of piercing.

On warm, dry days, when the birds have already flown down and begun feeding on the ground, they can be hunted with the help of a pointing dog. If a covey is found, the hen birds are likely to fly up first, cackling as they do so, but the cocks may run before lifting. The dog needs to be a good and fearless retriever, for if a cock is only winged, it is large enough to present quite a challenge.

In the fall and winter, the hunter must use other methods. The birds inhabit woods, where they perch in trees and fly down to feed in stubble fields or on the edges of the woods. Dogs are used in Sweden and Finland; they are trained to find the birds in the woods and to scare them up into the trees; the dog barks and draws the bird's attention from the hunter, who must work himself into position downwind of the bird and take whatever chance offers itself. As when stalking in spring, distances may be so long that only a rifle is suitable. Later, when the ground is frozen, the birds can be stalked and shot. A light-caliber rifle with a telescopic sight is necessary, as the range may be as much as 150 yards (135 m). The birds can be driven, too, if the members of a small party of hunters take turns to drive and shoot. A good retrieving dog is essential. [TT, JMG]

Grouse Shooting in Scotland

The red grouse (*Lagopus lagopus scoticus*) is indigenous only to Britain. It is found largely in Scotland, especially on the drier east side; in Wales; in Derbyshire; occasionally in Devon; and extensively in Lancashire and Yorkshire, which probably provides the cream of the shooting. It has been introduced into the Ardennes in Belgium.

The red grouse does not seem able to survive without a partial diet of young heather shoots, and good moor management includes burning old heather so that the young growth can come up. Such "muirburn" is governed by ancient laws and customs; it is performed in late winter, on a ten- to fifteen-year cycle.

The terrain for grouse is wild, high, and often damp. Grouse share the land with sheep and cattle, and with red deer, blue hare, rabbit, fox, wild cat, and other game birds such as black grouse, ptarmigan, and snipe, but the grouse are the most numerous birds on an average stretch of country. Attempts to rear grouse artificially have always failed. Keepering is concentrated on good heather management and on a ruthless war on vermin, notably stoats, weasels, and foxes.

Grouse are found in coveys of a pair of old birds plus anything up to a dozen young. Late in the season, the coveys amalgamate into packs that can contain a hundred or more birds. Numbers of grouse are said to have increased tremendously since the introduction of driving, which was made possible by the invention of the breechloader and cartridges in the nineteenth century. When grouse are driven toward the butts, the old birds fly in front and get killed off, to the benefit of the younger stock, who are thus rid of quarrelsome and barren oldies.

Grouse shooting is very much of a social sport, with anything between 3 and 100 persons involved at a time. In Scotland and Yorkshire, huge parties assemble in country houses for "the Glorious Twelfth"—12 August, which (unless the day is a Sunday) is when the legal season opens. It closes on 10 December, but little shooting goes on after the end of October. Both sexes of grouse are shot, for it is virtually impossible to distinguish between them on the wing.

There are three principal methods of shooting grouse. Walking up is a gentle and undemanding form of sport normally practiced at the beginning of the season, when the grouse have not yet become afraid of man and will allow the Guns (as the shooters are called) to get within range before getting up. Shooting over dogs is a refined form, now increasing in popularity after some decades of neglect. It gives the additional pleasure of seeing well-trained dogs indicating the whereabouts of the game. Pointers and setters are used, as against labradors and spaniels when walking up.

The best-known method is, perhaps, driving. The Guns stand in wait in butts made of stone or peat or a mixture of the two, while a line of beaters drives great stretches of moorland toward them. There may be half-a-dozen or more drives in a day, and very large bags of grouse may be obtained, the record being 1,464½ brace by eight Guns in Lancashire in 1915. (As with partridges, grouse bags are counted by the brace, while pheasant and most other game go singly; snipe are counted by the couple.) There are no legal bag limits for game in Britain, but a prudent landowner and his gamekeepers would never allow dangerously large bags, lest the following season's population be diminished. This has always been a sporting consideration, but recent increases in the costs of estate management have forced most lairds to regard their shooting as a business. They now let their grouse shooting either to a season-long syndicate or by the week or even by the day to parties of overseas sportsmen. The demand is now for driven grouse, and on a big commercial moor, the gentlemanly few days of walking up are now sacrificed to the start of driving on the Twelfth—a practice simply Not Done before World War II.

The logistics of grouse driving make the same demands on the owner

Grouse shooting—at the butts. The grouse come in fast and low, and the Gun and his loader have their hands full, shooting, loading, and marking the fall of the birds. When he reached his allotted butt, the Gun took careful stock of the surrounding terrain, noting the positions of the other butts and marking a 45° safety angle covering the area within which he will shoot. Some Guns, knowing the tricks of light, especially in the Scottish highlands, pace out 50 yards (45 m) in front of the butt and mark the distance with a stone.

as taking a company of soldiers into battle, even to the extent that bad organization can lead to fatal casualties. The object in driving is to put the greatest possible number of fast-flying grouse over the waiting Guns as many times as possible during the day's sport. On a typical day, there would be eight Guns, and, on a very prolific moor, each would use two guns and be accompanied by a loader. There would be five or six drives, each lasting about an hour. The bag could be around 150 brace, and a Gun would expect to get through 150 cartridges or more. There would be half-a-dozen gamekeepers, and twenty or more beaters.

Before the first drive, the host produces a leather case the size of a playing card, from which protrude a number of ivory or plastic slips. Each Gun draws one and memorizes the number now visible, for it is the number of the first butt he will occupy. Butts are numbered from lowest to highest up the hill or, on level ground, from the right. After each drive, each Gun adds two to his number to identify his next butt: thus, number 3 at the first drive takes butt number 5 at the next; if there are eight Guns, number 7 takes butt number 1 on the next drive, and so on.

Grouse driving, of all forms of shooting in Britain, is the most likely to produce accidents. Once the coveys start arriving, the action is extremely exciting, the light is often poor, the terrain is unfamiliar to most Guns,

In the western United States, sage grouse fly down in the evenings to water holes, ponds, and other expanses of water from the dry hills and mesas. Hunters hide themselves behind haystacks and shoot at the passing birds.

and it may be hard to remember that one or two butts are in a gully out of sight, and that number seven is only 80 yards (75 m) away through that slight haze. The biggest danger is when an inexperienced Gun follows a covey "through the line" and fires when his gun is pointing toward neighboring butts: it is possible for him to bag several fellow-sportsmen, loaders, and spectators with one unforgettable shot—after which he will be required to unload and make his way home. Even swinging through the line, without firing, is considered totally taboo, and the wise Gun raises his barrels almost to the vertical, greatly exaggerating the normal 45° safety rule to show that he is ultra careful, before bringing it down again to take a shot at the departing covey. Guns must avoid the temptation to shoot even at high birds that are directly over the line, since pellets can ricochet and alarm, even if they do not harm, neighboring Guns.

The most skilled Guns make most of their bag in front of the butts, a practice much praised by their host, since a hit in front is nearly always a kill, while a miss is a miss, and leaves no bird wounded. By contrast, hosts look unkindly on Guns who fire one shot in front and another—easier—shot behind at the birds going away, since many pellets find their way into the unarmored rearparts of the birds, making them barren or wounding them, so that they die much later when they do not drop immediately. An expert shot with two guns and a really good loader can drop five or even six birds from a big pack, especially if the birds are flying against a stiff wind.

Near the end of a drive, care must be taken by Guns to see that they mark the distance remaining between the butts and the approaching beaters, and begin to anticipate the flight of the grouse and the likely positions of the coveys at which shots can safely be taken. When the beaters reach the line, the drive is over. All guns should be unloaded and put into their leather or canvas slips to avoid a dog knocking into them, for example, and damaging them. During the pickup, it is better that a wounded bird should get up and escape than that Guns should take urgent and unsafe steps to bring it down while keepers, beaters, Guns, and spectators are scattered everywhere.

In grouse driving, it is accepted practice to count your bag, not to boast of it, but to make sure that all birds are picked up. It would be appropriate to say to a keeper: "I have six still to find." To tell him, "I shot eighteen but have found only twelve," might sound like bragging. It often happens that two neighboring Guns shoot simultaneously at the same bird, which drops dead. There is no quicker way to friendship than to award it to your neighbor. If the drive was very successful, be quick to congratulate host and head keeper on the way the birds were presented.

The bag from your butt is laid out and collected by keepers for transfer to pony or Landrover, and the host usually tells the Guns the total for the drive before moving on to the next. At the end of the day, each Gun is often given a printed card with the totals of the types of game—Grouse, Blackgame, Snipe, Hares, Rabbits, and Various—filled in as a memento of the day.

A moor of the minimum size to provide a day's grouse driving—say 3,000 acres (1,200 hectares)—will need 3 to 6 lines of butts. A large commercial shooting estate, of 200,000 acres (80,000 hectares) or more, may have as many as 100 lines, each consisting of eight or more butts. A great deal of the time of keepers and other estate staff during the close season is spent on building and maintaining butts, especially on moors that are grazed by cattle, which seem to have a natural inclination to destroy butts.

According to the foremost grouse expert in Scotland, Richard Waddington, the ideal butt should be square or rectangular, rather than the normal round shape; a Gun may thus be more likely to keep his sense of direction, by reference to the recognizable corners, during an exciting drive when considerations of safety may be hard to keep in mind. The entrance should be at the side, which enables the butt to be used from either direction. The minimum inside width should be 48 inches (120 cm) and the height from the floor to the top of the wall from 48 to 54 inches (120 to 135 cm); the top turves should be movable to accommodate extra tall or short Guns. Butts can be sunk, semi-sunk, or built entirely above ground. The first type wins for concealment, but such butts are expensive to construct and hard to drain—an hour spent by a Gun in a butt

with water over his shoes spoils the pleasures of even the greatest drive. Butts above ground are cheap to construct but are easily seen by grouse and very easily damaged or even destroyed by cattle. The best compromise is the semi-sunk butt.

The best butts have a rough wooden floor mounted on stakes, a plank seat, and a shelf for cartridges. Peat butts are made from turves 24 by 12 inches (60 by 30 cm) and are about 6 feet (180 cm) deep; all the turves except the two top layers should be laid heather side down. Stone butts are sometimes essential on steep hill faces where the ground is lacking in heather but is covered, instead, with rocks and scree. They last for a long time compared with peat butts; their rims must be covered with earth or peat, however, so as to afford a soft surface on which to rest guns without damage.

The siting of butts is an art in itself. Even on moors where grouse have been driven for 50 or 100 years, perfect butt positions sometimes have to be altered after a farmer has reseeded some old grass or has erected a haystore on the hill. New or altered butt positions should be tried out for a season with a makeshift wall of peat or planks until the success of the new position has been tested. Part of the skill in siting butts lies in the point of view adopted by the constructor: think only of the grouse, do not think of the Guns. The grouse wish to make for a warm and secure resting place, such as a dry, well-heathered hillside. The butts should be sited so as to intercept their line of flight there, being best sited just below the skyline on the side from which the grouse are to be driven. It is apparently tempting to put butts along the bottom of a ravine or gully, but the result is often poor shooting, with the birds in sight and shot for only a second or two, and often so high as to be virtually out of range; this results in a lot of pricked birds with few killed. However, a line of butts across the V of a wide ravine can result in spectacular sport when the birds are driven downhill.

On many moors, particularly in the north of England, that lack the scenic hills of the Scottish highlands, the country is flat or bumpy, and different tactics are used. One highly prolific moor has only one line of butts, in which the Guns face alternately one way and the other, the birds being driven back and forth by two teams of beaters, who receive signals to start by means of a Very pistol.

In planning a day's driving, a good rule is to start with the best drive first, preferably downwind, and arrange to repeat it again as the last drive of the day. In theory, at least, a moor can be worked so as to accumulate the stock from all over the ground as the day goes on, with an increasing number of birds going over the Guns at each drive. It will be apparent, however, that at least one drive on such a day must be taken against the wind, the direction in which grouse are most reluctant to fly. If such a drive can be kept short, there is more of a chance that the birds will not turn back over the beaters' heads and be lost to the Guns. In working out the tactics, it should be borne in mind that grouse at the beginning of the season are unwilling to remain in the air for more than a minute, and not more than a minute and a half at the end of the season.

Beating is not a mechanical business, and Richard Waddington is emphatic that a drive cannot be successful unless the beaters act intelligently; for this reason, he chooses university students as beaters. One beater in a line may, for instance, round a bluff and find himself putting up covey after covey which escapes sideways, there being no other beater in sight. It is best, then, if he furls his flag and sits down until the line on either side has advanced, so as to help to push the grouse forward—where they are wanted. The flag is part of the normal equipment of each beater—a white one, some 2 feet (60 cm) or more across. The line of beaters, which may be nearly 1 mile (1.6 km) in some cases, should be controlled by the head keeper, who stations himself near the middle. On some moors, he is armed with red and green flags for signaling to the flanks; the extreme flanks should be manned by experienced keepers or others who can swiftly remedy mistakes by altering the rate of advance.

Flankers are really specialist beaters whose job is to funnel the birds along the required lines, and agile and intelligent flanking can do more to perfect a drive than any one other factor. When a line of beaters nearly 1 mile (1.6 km) long is trying to drive coveys of grouse toward a line of Guns only some 400 yards (360 m) long, many grouse are likely to pass on either side of the line of Guns, usually on the downwind end of the

223

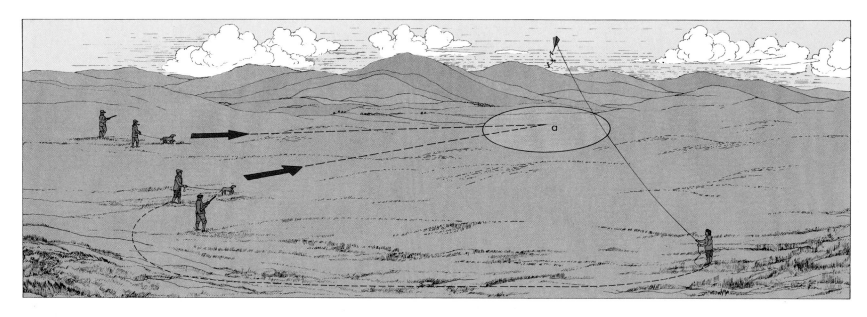

When walking up, you form part of a line of anything from three to twelve Guns, with a Gun on each end and a spectator or gamekeeper between each pair of Guns. In warm weather near the start of the season, when the grouse are sitting tight, the people in the line may be only 10 yards (9 m) or so apart—and still be able to walk by a sitting covey crouching invisible in the heather. Later in the season, if walking up is done at all, the birds move out if the people are 50 yards (45 m) apart, and this can give a very long line. Whoever is in charge—host or gamekeeper—should be in the middle of the line and be able to communicate with the flanks either by shouting or whistling, or passing messages. Since grouse favor the face of a hill as a resting spot, the walking line customarily follows the contours of a slope, with the lowest Gun taking his mark from a burn (stream). Since the dogs used are for retrieving only, it is seldom that Guns get advance warning that a covey is about to get up, which may happen just under foot or at medium range. When the Guns are close together, three of them often get a chance to shoot at one covey.

When a bird or birds are shot, the line stops walking without further instructions and waits until the keepers and their dogs have accounted for all the bag. A straight line is essential for the safety of all present, and a host is within his rights to tell a Gun very firmly if he is constantly pushing too far forward or lagging behind. Experienced grouse shots have learned to expect a very large safe angle of fire and are much upset if this is cut down. Bags from walking up are not large—five to ten brace a day per Gun would be perfectly satisfactory.

(Above) When shooting over dogs, the party follows the animals' noses, the dogs being held on very long lines by their handlers. If two dogs make a point at the same covey *(a)* but from different angles, an exact fix on the birds' location should enable the Guns to be entirely ready for their appearance. Shooting over dogs is most likely to be successful when the approach is made upwind, but, unless the wind shifts during the day, some part of the day's walking will be downwind. Late in the season, or after wet weather, when grouse tend to be easily scared and rise too far out for shooting, it is possible to keep them sitting until the Guns are within range by use of a kite. Given enough wind, one of the keepers moves to the windward of the covey the dogs have pointed, raising a small kite as he walks. While it is hovering over them, the birds are reluctant to fly until the Guns have approached to within a dozen paces or so. Shooting over dogs is for the connoisseur who savors the way in which his quarry is taken, and is less interested in the grand total, which is likely to be smaller than that achieved by walking up.

line. So one stations four to six men there, to lie in the heather, flags furled, with orders to show themselves suddenly with waving flags when a covey would otherwise go wide of the Guns. On occasions, it may be necessary to station flankers directly in front of the line of Guns, particularly when known combinations of wind and terrain have in the past allowed covey after covey to escape without being shot at. Here, the Guns must be particularly careful and alert, making sure that they know where each flanker is, and that they do not shoot in their direction. Flankers are most useful when working at the foot of slopes rather than on the tops of hillocks, where they often ineffectually station themselves, as grouse do not fly over, but rather round, hills.

Dress for grouse shooting is largely a matter of camouflage, and, in the opinion of most Guns, there is nothing to beat tweed. The special color known as heather mixture is a little too dark, and a lighter color is normally better. The kilt is often worn by those entitled to it, but it can have its awkward moments. The writer's grandfather and his two brothers once had to cross a stone dyke topped by barbed wire and, as they jumped down, a sudden gust of wind swirled up their tartans so that all three caught up behind. Since all three men were dressed, so to say, as Scots traditionally are, the keeper who was required to unhitch them was greeted by a strange sight. Those whose everyday business is on the hill—the gamekeepers—universally wear knickerbockers, and there is no more practical garment for the job. The best approach to the feet is to assume that they will get wet in any form of grouse shooting and to wear stout shoes with tackets (studs) in the soles. Walking through the abrasive stems of heather is extremely tough on shoes or boots, and toecaps soon wear through. Some kind of waterproof coat is essential: in the Scottish highlands, even the bluest sky can turn to mist or rain within an hour. A hat is essential, too, for a head, especially a bald one, can spoil the sport for the rest of the party.

Normal side-by-side 12-bore ejector shotguns are almost universally used. An automatic would certainly be frowned on and, in any case, would get far too hot during a hectic drive. Over-and-under guns are thought to take longer to reload because of the greater distance that must be traversed to load the lower barrel. Bores smaller than 12 are sometimes favored by those walking grouse, on the score of lightness, but for driving, it is hard to beat the killing power of the 12-bore. A leather or canvas full-length slip is a great advantage in avoiding damage to guns in Landrovers and other vehicles. For cartridges, modern thought suggests that 1 ounce (28 g) of shot will be perfectly satisfactory, particularly as today's crimp closure of cartridges is much more efficient than the former style of disk closure. Certainly, for anyone at a good day's driving and shooting 300 or more times, it will be far less fatiguing and headache-inducing to fire 1 ounce (28 g) than $1\frac{1}{8}$ ounce (32 g).

Other equipment includes, for walking up, a cartridge belt holding 20 or 25, although many traditional Scottish sportsmen still carry a dozen cartridges loose in each jacket pocket. A leather or canvas bag holding 100 is desirable, especially if someone else can be persuaded to carry it, for it weighs over 10 lb (4.5 kg) when full. A canvas game bag is necessary if you are shooting by yourself or on a small informal shoot lacking a keeper. For driving grouse, it is a good idea to carry a shooting stick, which aids the unfit up hills, when folded, and opens out to provide a rest for the legs when at the butts. Many Guns carry a plastic or paper chart marked in concentric circles, on which they can mark any prominent features around their butt, such as rocks or clumps of heather, and then pencil in the fall of their birds as they occur.

While grouse shooting has recently become a most expensive business if done on a full scale, there do exist a number of hotels in second- or third-class grouse country, whose guests can get permission to walk a moor with the chance of getting a brace or so by the end of the day. On an organized shoot, it would be a mistake to assume that the Gun may take home all the birds he shoots, for lairds nowadays rely on the sale of grouse to recoup part of the costs of running their moors, and a brace of birds per guest is the standard to take home; two brace would be extra generous.

The occasional sportsman may have the problem of tipping the keeper adequately but not over-adequately, and the best advice by far is to consult an experienced fellow-sportsman about the right amount, and whom to give it to. As with all such situations, of course, the most important thing is the warmth of your handshake and the thanks you give along with your money. [JMG]

Grouse in North America

Many North American hunters feel there is no finer shooting than for grouse in the woodlands. Fall is a special time for all hunters, but for hunters after forest grouse, it is extra-special. There are three North American species of forest grouse, the ruffed grouse, the blue grouse of the western forests, and the spruce grouse of the coniferous northern forests.

The ruffed grouse has acquired the disparaging name of "fool hen" in remote wilderness areas where it is little hunted and has no fear of man; offering little challenge, it is, when sitting, an easy target. Further south, by contrast, it has lost this innocence and flushes explosively with a thunderous whirring of wings. One needs lightning-fast reflexes to get off a shot before a ruffed grouse has vanished into the trees or disappeared in thick cover.

Ruffed grouse prefer edge cover near forest openings and young forests that are still in their early stages of growth. Plenty of saplings and brush are the keys to good habitat. The bird feeds on a variety of fruits, berries, grasses, and wild clover, which is primarily found in young forests and along the forest edges. Winter is the critical time for ruffed grouse, when their major foods are buds of white willow, catkins of hazel, and buds of male trembling aspen.

Pointing dogs are best for grouse, but a dog must have a keen nose so that it does not "bump" the birds—accidentally flush them. Some hunters use springer spaniels with good results.

The other species of North American grouse are those of the rolling prairies and open park-land forests. They are the sharptailed grouse, the sage grouse, and the prairie chicken.

The places to hunt sharptails are where grasslands are interspersed with trees and shrubs in semi-open country, with the best shooting occurring near clumps of poplar and brush that westerners call bluffs: hunters walk from bluff to bluff to try to find the birds. Sharptails also live in open woodlands, coniferous areas, large burns or cutovers, muskeg, and bogs; in consequence, they have a wide distribution. In agricultural areas, they visit fields of corn and other grains.

The sharptailed grouse holds very well for pointing dogs. It is a strong, fast flier, and, if it lived in such dense terrain as the ruffed grouse, not many would ever be shot.

The sage grouse is a large bird—cocks weigh as much as 8 lb (3.5 kg) and the hens rather less—of the sagebrush of the dry plains. It eats sagebrush, roosts and nests in sagebrush, and, in summer and winter, seeks shelter in the thickest stands of sagebrush; it also tastes of sagebrush!

As it is not a very fast flier, it does not provide particularly good shooting. But its plumage and size make it a rather spectacular game bird.

One hunts sage grouse usually by walking up or by pass-shooting. Walking up is generally the more popular, and hunters simply walk through the stands of sagebrush in the hope of finding and flushing the birds. Dogs are very useful—flushing dogs are better than pointers—for the birds tend to run ahead of the hunters. When pass shooting, one relies on the birds' habit of flying mornings and evenings to a stream or

pond to drink; having first identified the water, the hunter hides behind bales of hay, brushy fence rows, or even behind fence posts, and waits for the birds to fly in.

Prairie chickens are birds of the North American West but, when the prairies were plowed and turned over to wheat, the prairie chickens lost their habitat, and their numbers plummeted. They became extinct in Canada, although they exist in shootable numbers in several western and midwestern states. The season is the fall. Hunting prairie chickens is similar to hunting sharptails. Weedy draws and grasslands near grain fields are the best covers. Like other game birds, they hold well early in the season, when cover is still thick. The young "birds of the season" hold better than the older ones, but, as a general rule, prairie chickens flush wildly, especially as winter approaches and they gather into large packs comprising of several coveys. As they flush, they cackle, a sound they also emit when running through thick grass; hunters should listen for this.

Walking the birds up is the favorite but probably the least effective method of hunting them. A better way is to hide in a field where the birds congregate regularly to feed. Bales of hay or straw, brushy coppices, or tall grass provide good cover. The birds fly in from the surrounding countryside to feed at dawn or in the late afternoon.

A good gun for all these grouse is a light 12-gauge. For ruffed grouse, the gun should be open-choked; for prairie chickens, full-choked at the end of the season, with a modified choke earlier. No. 7½ shot is suitable, but for prairie grouse, perhaps No. 6 shot may be better for late-season shooting. [JK]

Wild Turkey

Wild turkeys have become shy and secretive birds. They were first hunted by American Indians with bows and arrows, and are now hunted by hunters of all sorts with guns. Many North American hunters claim that the shooting of a big, wise, tom turkey is much more difficult than shooting a whitetail buck.

Turkey hunting in spring is done by calling the toms, in imitation of a rival for the hens or in imitation of a hen trying to attract a mate. In the fall, calling is employed, but with a different purpose: the hunter, having found a flock of turkeys, causes them to scatter, then calls in the manner of a lonely turkey seeking to regain its flock.

The gun most commonly used for wild turkeys is a 12-gauge, full-choked shotgun, loaded with No. 4 or No. 2 shot. Some hunters prefer a rifle, such as the .22 rimfire Magnum or the .222 Remington, if the use of a rifle is legal; the ordinary .22 rimfire is inadequate for turkeys and is illegal. Rifles are used chiefly in western states, where cover is rather open and shots tend to be long. [JK]

North American Quail

The bobwhite quail is the most common and most widely distributed of the six species of quail that occur in North America. More bobwhites are shot each fall than all the other quail species together.

Bobwhites need weedy fencerows, ditches, and brushy corners of uncultivated land for all aspects of their life: feeding, hiding, roosting, loafing, cover, and, particularly, shelter in the hard winter months. Clean farming, however, is destructive of this growth and, where it is practiced, bobwhites (and pheasant) have suffered. Bobwhite quail can also be found in grassy pine woods, but not in mature hardwood forests.

They are gregarious birds and live in coveys. During the season, in the early fall, hunting is most productive in the middle of the morning and the afternoon, when the coveys are out feeding. Bobwhites feed after rain, too, and when they are moving about then, their scent is more easily picked up by pointers.

A fine, fast brace of setters or pointers dashing with style and verve through the fields in quest of a covey of bobwhites is one of the classic experiences of North American hunting. The birds hold well, but a covey will scatter when flushed and a hunter is successful when he marks the single birds well. Hunting bobwhites without a dog is a frustrating business; the quail merely run ahead of the hunter, who can expect to bag only few of them.

There is no dyed-in-the-wool bobwhite hunter who does not have at least one bird dog. English pointers and English setters are the most popular, but more and more hunters are turning to Brittany spaniels and the German pointing dogs; the wirehairs are popular in country where there are lots of spiny brambles. The German dogs are used more as "singles" dogs, to hunt the scattered quail once the covey has been flushed; they work closer to the hunter and, being relatively easy to control, can be directed toward the spots where the hunter has seen single quail land.

The mountain quail and the California quail are two western birds, and the best hunting for both species is in California and Oregon. They can be confused with one another only if the hunter does not note that their plumes are different: the mountain quail's is straight, the California quail's curves forward. Both species are gregarious, and both run to escape danger.

California quail are to be looked for in tall shrubbery, brush interspersed with open areas, and grassy or weedy rows; any farming area that is not clean-farmed is thus likely to contain California quail. They eat weed seeds, grain in stubble, and wild fruits and berries. When a covey has been flushed, the individual birds scatter and rely on their coloration for protection, holding tight until the "all-clear" signal has been given by the older birds in the covey. It is this habit that gives the hunter his best chance to bag California quail, but he will still need a keen-nosed dog to find the single birds; they stay put until almost stepped upon.

The mountain quail is the largest of the North American quail, and the cock bird can weigh $\frac{3}{4}$ lb (350 g). The preferred habitat is highly diversified, ranging from chaparral thickets to humid hillsides. When the birds live near farmland, they feed on waste grains, including corn, but weed seeds make up the bulk of their diet.

Hunting mountain quail requires much walking over steep hillsides, centered around dense roosting and loafing cover and feed such as mountain rye, timothy, and wild oats. Water is another requirement, and, generally speaking, mountain quail are not found far from water. The key strategy is to approach the birds from higher up the hill, for they otherwise try to escape by running uphill, and if this direction of escape is closed, they will flush.

Scaled quail, sometimes also called blue quail, are birds of arid, brushy areas; thick stands of chaparral and mesquite with open spots are good hunting grounds for them. But such brush cover as scrub oak, greasewood, broomweed, and desert hackberry are all good habitat for scaled quail. Weed seeds are their principal item of diet, but, in farming areas, the birds feed also on corn and other grain. They need water, too, and any cover close to water holes or cattle-watering ponds is a good bet for them. Scaled quail do not hold well for dogs and prefer to run rather than fly. As they run at better than 15 mph (25 km/h), it is not so unsporting as it might sound to say that a fair number are shot on the ground, where they present a challenge similar to that of a running cottontail rabbit.

Gambel's quail are bird of the desert and live in drier habitat than other quail. They are capable of obtaining from their feed the water they need, but they prefer a daily drink if obtainable, and will even fly to a water hole or cattle-watering pond. Patches of hackberry are good ground for Gambel's quail. Grains are eaten in farming areas, but the birds eat a variety of seeds and wild fruits, including mesquite beans.

Gambel's quail are difficult to hunt because they prefer running to

flying; they do not hold well for dogs on point. Single birds hold better than coveys, but in the desert, where cover is sparse, coveys will not hold at all. The only technique that seems to work is literally to run at a covey, or have a dog do so, and then to concentrate on the single birds. Needless to say, this is a method suitable only for the fit; hunters who practice it wear light boots so as to be able to run a little faster. Apart from the strains of running, the desert country menaces the hunter and his dog with the risks of heat prostration, cactus spines, burrs, rattlesnakes, and so on.

Harlequin quail are birds of the dry grasslands and the best places to hunt them are grassy ridges and weedy fields; in very dry country, they are found near water holes. Harlequin quail nearly always prefer to sit rather than to run or fly, and, although this makes for good sport with a pointing dog, which will find birds that a hunter would otherwise walk past, they sometimes continue to sit even when a hunter is in plain view. For this reason, they have acquired the colloquial name of "fool quail."

A shotgun for quail should be light in weight and short-barreled. For bobwhite quail, the gun should be open-choked, with No. 8 shot. For the other quail, a modified or full-choked gun is the better choice, together with No. 7½ shot or perhaps No. 6. [JK]

Doves and Pigeons in North America

Of all the game birds in North America, none is harder to hit with a shotgun than the doves and pigeons. Their swift erratic flight makes mourning doves, the whitewing doves of the Southwest, and the band-tailed pigeons of the Pacific coast extremely elusive targets.

Bandtailed pigeons are normally hunted by pass-shooting when the birds are flying between roosting and feeding areas, or during migration. Hunters take stands on ridges or on high passes between hills, and gun the birds as they fly by. The higher ridge tops are generally best, because the birds are more likely to be within shotgun range there. Shooting is fast and extremely difficult. Bandtails fly faster than teal, and, if there is any wind, they slip and spin in the air currents with the agility of snipe. If a hunter has experience of shooting high-flying duck, or partridge or snipe driven as in Europe, he will probably shoot more pigeon than the average upland hunter.

A shotgun for bandtails should be full-choked but must be light and fast-swinging. Experienced bandtailed shooters advise leading the bird about twice as far as you would figure—and then doubling that.

The most popular method of hunting mourning doves is to take a stand behind cover on the edge of a recently harvested grain field where doves are known to be feeding. (It is sometimes said that mourning doves are hunted by telephone, for hunters find out in this way where the birds are feeding.) Dull-colored clothes are sensible, and gunners should be placed strategically so as to prevent the birds from resting or from slipping in and out of the field without presenting chances for a shot. In drier areas, water holes are a big attraction for mourning doves, which seem to choose one hole and water there in large numbers. The best hunting time is late in the afternoon, but hunters should never take a stand too near the water lest the birds be frightened off and abandon the hole altogether. Further, doves cupping their wings to land present unsporting targets. It is wise not to shoot near the same water hole for more than a day at a time; every fourth day is best.

Mourning doves can be hunted by jump-shooting. Hunters simply walk through fields where doves are feeding and shoot at those that get up within range; they are wary and seldom let hunters get very close. A retrieving dog is very useful, as downed doves can be hard to find, particularly in corn fields and lush soya-bean fields where the plants cover the ground.

Whitewinged doves of the Southwest are hunted in much the same way as mourning doves, but as whitewings live in drier terrain, shooting near

In northern Scandinavia, ptarmigan are hunted in winter by hunters on skis, who may also have the chance of taking capercaillie and hare. As the temperatures during the day can remain below -20°F (-30°C), the gun mechanism—and the day's supply of food and drink—can freeze solid. During the winter, the ptarmigan gather in largish numbers and are completely white except for a black band at the eye and at the tail. The hunter must be extremely fit to ski the distances necessary and should be familiar with weather conditions in the hills. Needless to say, he should never venture out alone. White clothing and a white-taped light rifle are usual, although if the hunter is extremely skillful, he can get within shotgun range.

water holes is practiced perhaps more than field shooting. In some places, it is possible to go pass-shooting.

Dove guns should have either full or modified chokes, because ranges tend to be long. Generally speaking, a 12-gauge gun is best, but smaller gauges can be used. The best shot sizes are No. 8 or No. 7½. [JK]

Pheasant

Pheasants have declined in number in North America since the mid-1950s. Many areas have only a marginal ability to sustain pheasants, and the onset of "clean farming," chemicals, and fall cultivation made matters worse. Mowing machines, for example, cut alfalfa but destroy pheasants' nests, and the harsh truth is that the pheasant population has fallen to the level that can survive in the face of these discouragements.

The British style of rough shooting is the way in which pheasants are usually hunted in North America. Typical places for hunting are weedy fields, overgrown ditches, fencerows, and small ravines. Corn fields are good if overgrown with weeds. In the late season, pheasants hide in the thickest cover imaginable—the edges of marshes and wetlands and even small woodlots.

What makes the pheasant such a fine game bird, apart from its qualities on the table, is its ability to hide: it can run, skulk, and take advantage of every bit of cover, and flies only when it has been compelled to do so. Without a good dog that can flush pheasants into the air, hunting them is a frustrating business. Springer spaniels are best, but they should also be good retrievers, for a winged pheasant will run off and be almost impossible for a hunter to trace on his own.

Pheasants are driven in the corn fields of the Midwest of the United States, somewhat in the same way as they are driven in Europe. A line of shooters walks through a corn field toward a line of blockers at the other end. The pheasants run ahead of the shooters and begin to flush as they near the end of the corn. The blockers tend to get most of the shooting, but the drivers do get some; when they reverse their roles in the next field, the balance is restored. In Europe, and in Britain, the shooters have the birds driven by beaters, and they themselves wait in a line, either in the open, at "pegs," or strung out along a clearing in woods, for example. In Britain, most pheasants are shot in organized drives, and a day's pheasant driving on a big estate is as much a social occasion as a sporting. The ladies, for example, will often stroll around and stand with the Guns during the drives; the shoot often involves a lunch for a couple of dozen gentry, and as many as forty or more beaters and keepers will be used to drive the birds over the waiting Guns.

Contrary to the opinion of uninformed laymen, the driven pheasant probably presents the most difficult target in all shooting, especially if the bird is still climbing, or turning right or left, when in range of the Gun. Very big bags—sometimes thousands of pheasants in a day—are achieved on the larger estates, where stock is bred specially for shooting and put out into the woods in spring and early summer.

In Britain, both cocks and hens are shot during drives, although by custom the last shoots, which are normally in January, are "cocks" only, since an excess of cocks during the breeding season merely makes trouble among the wild breeding stock. [JK, JMG]

Partridge

The gray partridge (*Perdix perdix*) of the European farmlands and the chukar partridge (*Alectoris chukar*) of the arid hills of the Middle East have both been successfully introduced into North America. Both offer fine shooting in areas where few other game birds can prosper. The gray partridge is commonly called the Hungarian partridge—or Hun—in North America, because the birds were first imported from the plains of Hungary.

In North America, the gray partridge is hunted almost exclusively over pointing dogs. It holds extremely well but, when it runs, it is trickier than the pheasant, even if slower, and only the keenest-nosed dog can follow a covey after it has twisted and circled around. The places to hunt gray partridge are grain stubbles, weedy fencerows, and fields near grain stubbles. Unfortunately, modern agricultural practices have not been kind to partridges, and the birds are less abundant than they once were. When cover is sparse, the birds flush far out, and shots may therefore be long.

Like pheasants, partridges fly unwillingly: when undisturbed, they have been estimated to fly voluntarily for no more than one or two minutes a day. They fly fast, however, and present a challenging target for the hunter.

The chukar partridge, which is slightly larger than the grey, prefers the rugged habitat of the deep-sided valleys and canyons of the eastern slopes of the Rocky Mountains, from southern British Columbia to Arizona. These areas are characterized by rocky debris at the foot of mountain slopes; vegetable growth is sparse, with cheat grass, sagebrush, juniper, or greasewood predominating. The birds move to slightly lower elevations in late fall, sometimes even to the farmlands on the valley floors.

In good cover, chukar partridge hold well for a pointing dog, but good cover is rare. Usually, they try to evade hunters by running first uphill and then flying downhill if need be; frequently, one can see a whole covey running away far ahead and out of range. Hunters who approach the birds from above, however, frequently get within shooting range before they flush and fly away downhill. They fly fast and are difficult to bag as a result.

The partridge (*Perdix perdix*) and the French, or red-legged, partridge (*Alectoris rufa*) are both hunted in Britain (the latter only in the south of the country). The normal method is walking in line across grain stubbles, and through fields of root crops such as potatoes and turnips. If coveys from grass and stubble can be maneuvered into roots, the coveys are often split up, the birds rise in ones and twos, and many can be shot.

The best partridge shooting occurs when there are enough birds for driving. The birds present a very fast and testing target, and a right-and-left of driven partridge will be remembered for a long time by the average shot. [JK, JMG]

Woodcock and Snipe

The North American woodcock is smaller than its European cousin but, apart from this difference, the birds resemble each other closely.

The woodcock's specialized habitat of moist woodlands dictates where it should be hunted, and it is quite easy to see if a particular woodlot has woodcock in it. When probing for worms, woodcock make small "drill holes"; their droppings are conspicuous, being white splotches about the size of a small coin. The birds are migratory, however, and can be present one day and gone the next; cold weather in fall causes them to move further south and weather forecasts of colder weather to the north arouse enthusiasm in woodcock hunters. Woodcock migrate more in north-south valleys than in those running in other directions. Light, sandy, or loam soils make for easier probing than heavy clays. These are two factors to be borne in mind when scouting for new coverts.

The woodcock has a nearly perfect dead-leaf coloration, and the birds can crouch down and often escape detection. A hunter without a dog should walk slowly, stopping every few steps, hoping to make the birds nervous. Woodcock flush wildly in windy weather, when natural noises mask the sounds of an approaching intruder. Woodcock hunting is most enjoyable and productive when using a good pointing or flushing dog. Either a springer or cocker spaniel is good for flushing—the latter acquired its name from its skill with woodcock. Some dogs, however, refuse to retrieve woodcock, perhaps because the small feathers loosen easily in the mouth or perhaps because the bird's taste or scent is unlike

that of other upland birds. But even a dog that will not fetch woodcock is valuable if it can find those that fall in tangled cover.

In Britain, if suitably moist ground is being driven, woodcock are occasionally shot during grouse drives, and less rarely during pheasant drives. Woodcock occur, too, in wooded country, where their twisting erratic flight can require quick evading action on the part of those not actually shooting. The story is told of a British gamekeeper who was celebrating his hundredth birthday. When asked to what he attributed his healthy old age, he replied, "I always threw myself on my face whenever I heard a shout of 'woodcock'."

Snipe should be looked for in moist meadows, mudflats, and on the edges of bogs and marshes: they are birds of open wetlands. The best way to hunt snipe is to walk through this sort of terrain with a flushing or pointing dog; one that retrieves is almost essential, for snipe that fall in or beyond pools of water are hard if not impossible to recover without wading. Like woodcock, snipe that are known to be present one day may have vanished by the next: a tidal flat with dozens of snipe on it may be empty within hours.

Snipe are fast on the wing and, when flushed, fly off with a characteristic zigzag flight that straightens out after a few seconds. A hunter who keeps his head and does not shoot at once is more likely to hit this elusive bird. To say silently, "Snipe-on-toast," before shooting has been held to induce the right delay...

A good woodcock or snipe gun should be light and open-bored, although a double bore, with one barrel of a tighter choke than the other, is even better because some of the shots can be long. The best shot size is No. 9, but No. 8 or even No. 7½ can be used. [JK, JMG]

Wildfowling

Wildfowling is the art of shooting water birds—above all, ducks and geese. Many methods are used; some of these originated long before the use of guns for hunting. Several thousand years ago, North American Indians lured ducks within range by laying out decoys and, probably, by using calls. These methods are used all over the world today.

Dabbling ducks can be stalked where there are enough ponds to make it worthwhile for a hunter on foot. Using whatever cover is available, the hunter gets as close as he can to the water before flushing the ducks into flight. Sometimes, it is possible to hear them quacking on a pond or marsh, so the hunter should be able to distinguish between the sounds made by the various species. Another stalking method is to use a canoe or a small rowing boat on a stream or smallish waterway; ducks are often not particularly disturbed by them as they float downstream.

Tolling for ducks is apparently practiced only in Nova Scotia, where the Nova Scotia retriever, a rusty-colored, fox-like animal, was developed for the sport. Ducks are inquisitive, if not distracted or alarmed, and they swim closer to investigate if they see a dog running up and down the shore, ignoring them and having a carefree time. This effect can be attained if the hunter hides himself and throws a ball or stick along the shoreline for the dog to retrieve. Once the birds are within range, they can be flushed and shot at. Tolling originated in Europe, when dogs were used to lure ducks into huge trap nets.

Bay, or diving, ducks include such sea ducks as eider and scoter, as well as scaup, canvasback, redhead, ringneck, and goldeneye. They generally are to be hunted on extensive lakes and estuaries. When taking off, they head into the wind and patter along the surface until airborne; their wings are smaller and less powerful than those of dabbling ducks, which take off with a spring from the surface.

The late fall is the peak season for shooting diving ducks, when bone-chilling winds sweep down from the north and the ducks fly south with the wind. Hardy and fast-flying, they always seem to come in with severe storms, as if they enjoyed them. The semi-darkness of the hours around daybreak, waves breaking on a lee shore, lots of ice-encrusted decoys—this is all part of the sport, which is a specialized, open-water business, requiring many decoys; sets of sixty are the minimum and twice that number is better, for diving ducks fly in large skeins. Once an area is found where ducks are seen or are known to feed, the decoys must be set out. This is done so that they float with plenty of open water between them and the hide, or blind, so that the ducks have room to land. The well-built blind will conceal the hunter(s) as completely as possible. It should be built and positioned before the ducks are due to arrive. This is important, because, if some ducks—such as scaup and redhead—will lure easily to decoys, others will not. Canvasbacks, for instance, are not easy to lure.

From the concealment of his hide, the hunter should watch the ducks as they approach. If they intend to land on the water, they will start trailing their feet while still some distance away. If their feet remain tucked up, the ducks will only "buzz" the decoys, picking up speed as they fly over; in such a case, it is important to give them plenty of lead, or forward allowance, to compensate for this. Different species approach in different ways, however.

Redhead come eagerly to large rafts of decoys, if hunting pressure has not been excessive; occasionally, they drop from great heights, plummeting down zigzag, but more often, they make several reconnoitering passes, descending gradually, and the hunter must be patient and not alert them too soon. Greater scaup seldom fly very high, but they sometimes frustrate a hunter by alighting on the far side of a decoy spread, just out of range; when they settle like this, they can be lured closer by an imitation of their call—a sort of mellow, feline purr—or by fluttering a cap or handkerchief above the blind or camouflaged boat. Greater scaup are intensely inquisitive of movement that is other than human. Lesser scaup, however, are not like this but are wary and suspicious.

Scoters are not wary and will be lured to just about any kind of decoy,

if they have not been intensely hunted. Wooden blocks are frequently used as decoys and, years ago, cork floats from fishing nets were used. Some hunters use silhouette decoys nailed in a row on a long board. If the hunter merely sits still in his boat, he need not otherwise disguise his presence—the birds sometimes even circle and drop in behind him, if he is in a boat.

A good place to hunt scoters is in a bay with a headland striking out to sea. If there are two or more hunters, they should moor their boats about 100 yards (90 m) apart, and each should set out his own decoys. Scoters are fast-flying birds that usually keep low, almost skimming the water and rising only to clear obstacles. They can be lured to one set of decoys and, when fired on, will fly to the next. Almost any kind of dully painted, stable boat can be used: experienced hunters often use old skiffs or dories. If two hunters share a boat, they should sit back-to-back and thus keep the whole compass covered. Even if one is shooting from the shore, it is necessary to have a boat to retrieve fallen birds.

Hunting for geese and ducks over fields of stubble after the grain has been harvested is a favorite North American method. The majority of geese shot in North America are bagged in this way, and so are many ducks; mallard, pintail, and widgeon all love grain. So do white-fronted and Canada geese, and they will feed on it in preference to anything else. The state of Maryland has fine goose shooting nowadays, for this reason; geese seem even to have altered their migration habits to take advantage of the grain production there.

Hunting Canada geese over stubble can be exasperating; the technique is the same as for ducks, but geese require greater care. Once a hunter knows where the birds are feeding, he must set up his decoys and dig his pit well ahead of the arrival of the flight, even the night before. For duck, it may be enough to use a low blind built of straw and weeds in a fencerow or at the edge of a shelter belt, but geese are too wise to land near fences or shelter belts. When digging a pit in which to conceal oneself from geese, it is necessary to remove all the freshly-dug earth

A hunter plants lesser snow goose decoys in a field where the geese like to feed. The lesser snow goose is an inland grazing bird, the greater preferring coastal feeding. Lessers come to much less sophisticated decoys, too—white rags or pieces of paper are just as effective. The hunter either shoots from a blind or he lies on his back, covered with a white sheet and, as the geese come in, he sits up and fires.

When preparing to shoot over decoys on water, set them out so as to resemble a raft of ducks, perhaps together with a few geese. Spread them out in a "fish hook" pattern (or in the form of a C, J, or V), for the incoming birds will tend to land in the space enclosed by your decoys. For this reason, the decoys farthest from your blind must not be more than about 50 yards (45 m) away: this should bring the ducks into easy range. When choosing or making decoys, remember that the hens of many duck species look rather alike—generally a dull brownish—and that, at the beginning of the season, the male birds are still in their eclipse plumage, which they will gradually molt later on. Over-sized decoys are good when you want to attract birds from a height. Your blind should be camouflaged with vegetation that is natural to the area in which you are hunting, and clothing should be as drab as possible. Keep your head low until ready to shoot.

from the vicinity of the pit, lest the geese see it and shy away. When they have been heavily gunned, they become extremely wary, avoid any flocks on the ground, refuse to decoy, and seldom feed in the same field on two consecutive days.

For a morning shoot, the hunter must be concealed in his hide well before the first hint of dawn. As the day begins to break, seemingly endless skeins of mallard fly out from the sloughs and marshes, and, occasionally, small flocks of other ducks—pintails, baldpates, or gadwalls—can be seen. When a flight begins to circle over his decoys, the hunter must wait patiently until the birds are within range and must restrain his dog from retrieving at once, for the flights can continue for some time. Only when they have ceased, or the hunter has shot his legal maximum for the day—perhaps five or six ducks—may his dog start to pick up and retrieve the birds. The last thing to do before leaving is to fill in the pit, unless the hunter has paid to use one provided by the landowner; some maintain permanent pits or blinds in or by hedgerows.

Goose decoys should imitate a flock of geese feeding: some of the decoys must have feeding heads, some resting heads, and a few upright, alert heads—but only a few: too many will send a message of unrest and caution to the birds to be decoyed. Once a flight of geese is in sight over the horizon, the hunter should begin calling but should stay concealed and, unless he is an expert caller, should fall silent as soon as the birds come close or start to head for the decoys; a false note can warn them off. Estimating their range is difficult, for they are larger and fly faster than inexperienced hunters realize; give them plenty of lead for this reason.

Hunting brant geese in North America is generally done over water in areas where these geese are known to feed. Scouting the shorelines for brant or stands of eelgrass, the plant they love to eat, is the best way to start. Brant decoys are almost always used, but the birds can be shot from passes, such as rocky points jutting out to sea.

Pass-shooting for geese in general is often chancy in clear weather, because the birds fly high until they come down into the fields, but, in foul or foggy weather, they do stay low and offer chances for shooting.

233

Geese generally spend the nights on big lakes or on rivers, and this is where one should look for them before finding a pass.

Pass-shooting is the hardest form of wildfowling; the birds are usually flying much faster than they would be when setting in to decoys, and ranges are considerably longer—60 or even 70 yards (55 to 65 m). It is a simple, uncluttered form of the sport, however, for no decoys are used. The hunter relies on his knowledge of the birds and the area; he selects a pass on a flyway which the birds can be expected to use, depending on the weather, between their feeding and roosting areas. A good pass can be a creek or a narrow neck of land or water between two marshes; the shortest routes between marshes and lakes and grain fields can give good positions. On the sea coast, reefs, breakers, or points of land can all be good passes if, once again, the wind is right and the birds are flying to feed in particular fields inland.

Other wildfowlers can pose immediate and other problems: an individual may have concealed himself in suitable cover sometime before dawn, only to find that he is too close to some other hunter for their separate comfort and sport. Even if this does not happen, a general increase in the level of shooting will cause ducks to change their flyways or to fly high; they may even fly to their feeding grounds long before dawn, which, in North America, is the earliest that shooting may be legally enjoyed. In some European countries, however, it is not illegal to shoot ducks and geese at night by moonlight. A good retrieving dog is a must for pass-shooting, if many ducks are not to be lost.

Pass-shooting requires a full-choked gun and heavy loads, and it is when the Magnums come into their own and enable the hunter to hit and kill wildfowl at the long ranges demanded.

Sculling is another method and is really a specialized form of stalking, but one that uses a small, extremely low-profiled scull boat in which the hunter lies down. He or a companion propels the boat with a single oar over the stern or a pair of small paddles held in the hands over the side of the boat. The art is to bring the boat into range of a raft of wildfowl, and,

as the boats are generally flat-bottomed and have a very low freeboard, it is a skillful business to man them if there is anything of a wind; even small waves can break over the gunwales. Punt-gunning is a variation of the sport pursued in the British Isles, mostly on the coast of East Anglia. It relies on an immense gun mounted over the bows of the punt—a bore of over an inch (2.5 cm) and a barrel length of some 60 inches (150 cm) giving a weight of 30 lb (14 kg); not merely the gun, but the entire boat, must be aimed at the birds. This sort of hunting is the preserve of a small, dedicated minority of wildfowlers. The shot is taken as the raft of wildfowl starts rising, so that wings will be clear of the more vulnerable flanks of the birds. As many birds are wounded by the one big bang of the punt gun, the gunner has to have a conventional shotgun with him to deal with those that are not killed outright.

Wildfowling in Britain is, apart from the punt-gunning already mentioned, usually a matter of solitary or nearly solitary expeditions on "saltings" and other maritime areas, walking through marshes and similar expanses of land between the low and high tide marks, to wait for morning or evening flights of ducks and geese.

Inland shooting in Perthshire, Scotland, is celebrated, for the area is exceptionally rich in geese. When resident between migrations, graylag and pink-footed geese spend the day feeding on grass and stubble and, at night, fly short distances to open water on various lochs, of which Carsebreck, Auchterarder, is probably the most famous. The water is privately owned and is shot only three or four times during the season. Invited guests are stationed in hides around the loch and on islands, and the bag of geese can reach several dozen in an evening. No decoys are used.

In areas like the Solway Firth, wildfowling almost brings the tourist industry a second season. Hotels organize shoots for their guests—for example, dawn expeditions to fields where geese are known to be feeding in large numbers. Guns hide behind stone walls and other natural cover, and silhouette decoys are used. [JK, JMG]

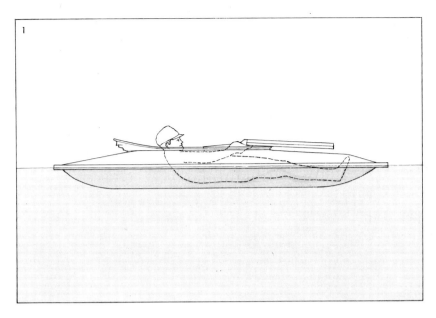

A sort of short, broad, shallow canoe, the layout boat enables a wildfowler to remain unobtrusively at water level far out from the shore. *(1)* The form of the boat is a little reminiscent of a punt-gunner's craft. Other means of hunting wildfowl include blinds built over water *(2)* or in reeds *(3)*. If well covered with local vegetation and allowed to weather, such a blind soon becomes accepted by waterfowl as part of the landscape.

Small game can be hunted in many ways. The biggest bags are usually shot during drives, a method common in Europe and rich in social tradition. Anything from twenty to a hundred beaters and hunters may be involved, and some of the game that may be expected includes (1) pheasant, (2) woodcock, (3) partridge, (4) fox, and (5) hare. The beaters with their dogs, often with a few shooters in the line, walk through the fields or cover toward the shooters, who must take care to aim well clear of those approaching. In the final stages of the drive, shooting is permitted only when game has passed through or over the line of shooters.

Chapter 3
Hunting Small Game

Rabbits and Hares

Methods of hunting rabbits and hares in North America are not elaborate, and the sport is one that can be enjoyed without lengthy journeys or expensive equipment. Rabbit hunting reaches its best when the hunter uses beagles or bassets to start the animals. The best rabbit hounds are relatively slow; too fast a pursuit will drive rabbits underground. If this does not happen, they run in large, irregular circles, as they try to return to their home ground, and the hunters must estimate which vantage point will give them the best chances of a shot.

If the hunter is without a dog, he must walk slowly through the sort of cover likely to hold rabbits, stopping every few steps to look around; this sort of overhanging threat makes rabbits nervous enough to break cover and bolt from where they have been crouching down almost invisibly. The wise hunter goes into every bit of thick cover—brush piles, for example, and clumps of thick grass—kicking as he goes. In the northern United States, cold winter weather forces rabbits to take shelter in woodchuck burrows and other holes, but the first warm days will bring them out. Rabbits can be stalked after a snowfall by a hunter who has the patience to walk very slowly, looking carefully and meticulously into thick cover to locate rabbits at rest; most frequently the hunter catches sight of a rabbit's eyes.

A good cottontail gun is an open-choked shotgun, from 20- to 12-gauge, loaded with No. 6 to No. 7½ shot. It should be light and fast-swinging. For swamp rabbits, many hunters prefer a bigger shot size: No. 5 or even No. 4. A .22 rimfire rifle is suitable when stalking in snow.

Swamp rabbits are best hunted with dogs. In the thick cover of wetlands, for example in south-central Tennessee, where swamp rabbits are plentiful, chases can last up to an hour or more. The rabbits run helter-skelter through the undergrowth but, when they come close to a hunter, they seem to know this, and then they sneak through the cover in an effort to keep out of sight.

Several species of hares are common in North America: the arctic hare of the northernmost tundra, the snowshoe hare of the northern forests, the three species of jackrabbits of the western prairies and the sagebrush deserts, and the European hare, which, after introduction into several areas of eastern North America, is still to be found there. Jackrabbits are regarded as pests in some states and may be shot as such; in others, they are protected by seasonal restrictions. When jackrabbits become numerous, drives are sometimes organized by hunters and ranchers: a group of hunters simply walks in a line, with gaps of about 100 yards (90 m) between each man, and the hares are shot at as they are started; a good choice for this sort of shooting is a full-choked shotgun loaded with No. 4 shot.

A couple of hunters can jump jackrabbits by walking slowly through areas where the animals lie up during the day, but the best time to hunt them is in the morning or evening, which is when they are most active. Once jackrabbits start running, they are difficult targets; they have been clocked at 40 mph (65 km/h), and whoever can consistently hit such a

Raccoon hunting with coonhounds is finest on a warm night in fall. The raccoon often patrols back roads looking for carrion left by automobiles, and hunters very often start their hounds along such roads.

When the hounds have put up a raccoon he will run for it, but inevitably, the chase ends with the raccoon up a tree. When the hounds bark "treed," the hunters recognize this from the change in voice and rush to the scene, for a raccoon will not always stay treed for long. Most hunters wear headlamps—"miner's lamps"—to leave both hands free. A .22 rimfire or a pistol is sufficient for this close-range shooting.

238

target will have little trouble with deer and antelope. The sportiest gun for this type of hunting is a light "varmint" rifle, such as a .222, with a scope of moderate power.

A few individuals in the West still practice the old and exciting sport of coursing hare with hounds. The animals traditionally used are greyhounds or whippets. The sport is common in the British Isles and is conducted in open country where hares are plentiful. Strictly regulated, the sport lays at least as much emphasis on the style of the pursuit as the kill—and kills are the exception, for most hares escape. After some forty-five seconds of chase, the hare, which is given a start of some 80 yards (75 m), starts gaining on the greyhounds, for its stamina is greater than theirs. Salukis, which are sometimes coursed in Britain and North America, cannot match greyhounds in pace, but have greater stamina.

In the Canadian province of Ontario, European hares are also hunted in drives, usually with five or six hunters. Some like to use hounds—foxhounds, black-and-tans, blueticks, or very large beagles. The European hare runs in a much larger circle than the cottontail and may cover 3 or 4 miles (5 to 8 km) before returning to its territory. Some hunters use full-choked shotguns with No. 4 or No. 2 shot; others prefer .22 rimfire Magnum or centerfire varmint cartridges in a .222 rifle.

Snowshoe hares can be hunted with hounds but, when this is done in deep snow, the hounds need to have long legs; larger beagles or hounds of some other large breed are best. Unless pursued by hounds, the snowshoe hare is apt to sense no great danger from a hunter and will not run at top speed; this is especially so in the remote wilderness areas. A .22 rifle is a good weapon for such hunting, but a handgun can be used, too. When hunting snowshoe hares in thick cover, such as young forests in logged-over areas or in old burns, ranges are likely to be short, and the best gun would be a 12-gauge, although 16- or even 20-gauge guns are sometimes used.

The arctic hare is rarely hunted for sport because few sportsmen venture so far north. These hares increase in population to an extraordinary extent every ten years or so—as lemmings do—and become an important source of food for Eskimos and northern Indians who, at one time, made blankets and clothing from hare skins.

Hares are shot as pests, not for sport, in Britain. The shooting does not take place in the season, and there are no social overtones. For many who work on the land, hare shooting is the only time in the year when they shoot in company (and legally!), and, for this reason, the hare shoot is considered a particularly dangerous business. Estate gamekeepers are often in charge. The hares do not move very fast, and shooting is easy, made slightly less so by the hunter's having to carry maybe 30 to 40 lb (14 to 19 kg) of dead hares in a gamebag while walking over the fields or moors. The hare is not eaten by the majority of the population other than the sophisticated classes. Many country people are inhibited by the remnants of old superstition—ill-luck and so on—from eating hare.

To farmers, the rabbit is a highly destructive and expensive pest, in extreme cases devouring a tenth of the crop. To sportsmen in Britain, it is a welcome addition to the bag of a day's mixed or rough shooting, although it is seldom the entire or even the principal quarry of a day's sport. The sole sport in England and parts of Europe in which rabbits are the only quarry is ferreting, a sport for a small team—ideally, two Guns, a gamekeeper to handle the ferrets, and an extra keeper who can be delegated for the job of digging out or otherwise apprehending a lost ferret.

The ferret is a mustelid, a relative of stoats, weasels, polecats, martens, and badgers. It is the right shape for going down rabbit burrows—long and thin—perhaps 12 by 2 inches (30 by 5 cm). Many are off-white, with evil-looking red eyes. Others, more nearly related to the polecat, are gray or gray-brown, and slightly larger. The ferret's instinct is to explore below ground and to attack anything it finds there. Its menacing approach makes all but the boldest of rabbits immediately bolt from the burrow into the open air—where Guns and nets await them.

On a typical ferreting day, the Guns quietly station themselves so as to have a downhill and commanding view of the burrows, and the handler inserts a ferret into a likely hole. Five minutes later, the bleary white face of the ferret emerges at the same hole, and the ferret is taken to another possible entrance. The loud thump from the burrow is a rabbit stamping its hind legs in alarm. For a while, there is no more action but, without warning, a rabbit bursts from a hole, executes a quick right turn, and re-enters the burrow. Experienced Guns know not to shoot, for a wounded rabbit in the burrow is certain to be found by the ferret, who will then lie up for hours and probably have to be dug out.

The greatest drawback to ferreting is the delay caused by ferrets that lay up underground. Keepers have developed many ways of inducing them to come out—short of digging: gutting a rabbit and placing the entrails at the windward hole of the burrow; calling; imitating rabbit noises; even firing a gun down the burrow. To prevent the ferret from eating the quarry, it is often muzzled, or it can be withdrawn if a long line is attached to it by a shoulder harness. The latest development is an electronic bleeper which at least tells the owner exactly where to start digging.

Ferreting is a sport of the unexpected. In a classic instance, a sportsman seeking to entice a ferret out of a hole had his head at its entrance when a rabbit, having decided that guns were a lesser evil than the ferret, bolted with such force as to break the nose of the face blocking its exit. At the hospital, the patient was asked by a kindly nurse how the accident had happened. "I was kicked by a rabbit," he replied.

There is no pleasanter form of gun sport, however, when all goes well, and one has the satisfaction of ridding the farmer of vermin while providing someone with quite cheap food—and of excellent quality, too, if well cooked. Two Guns, with two keepers to handle the ferrets, can expect to have a day of fifty couple of rabbits on good ground.

Unlike hares, which benefit from several days of hanging entire, rabbits should be cleaned as soon as possible after shooting or being netted. In any case, before transfer to the gamebag, a rabbit should be held by the head while the hind quarters are squeezed in such a way as to expel any urine in the body; this is otherwise capable of souring the flesh. [JK, JMG]

Raccoon

The portly, low-slung, bushy-tailed, black-masked raccoon is not very glamorous game but is popular quarry in many parts of the United States and southern Canada.

Raccoons take a substantial amount of aquatic prey, but they are omnivorous; a chicken house or cornfield may attract more raccoons than a stream, but all the same, a good place to start a hound pack is near water. The presence of tracks, droppings, and obvious damage around poultry enclosures would make a start worthwhile there, too.

As raccoons are nocturnal animals, the best time to hunt them is at night. Hunters equip themselves with headlamps. Where raccoons are not an agricultural problem, a hunter may tree one just for the pleasure of watching his dogs at work and listening to their barking; if he does not want the meat or pelt, he hauls his dogs off and lets the raccoon go about its business. Some old raccoons become accustomed to this and seem to enjoy leading hounds on a chase through the woods. If the hunter wants to shoot the raccoon, an open-sighted .22 rimfire rifle or pistol is the best weapon and most often used, as a treed raccoon presents an easy short-range target. Shotguns put too many holes in a handsome pelt.

The dogs may be any of the coon-hunting breeds described in Part VI. Several dogs are better than one; the hunter can tell from their voices when their quarry is treed. Dogs that give tongue readily are better than

240

In some parts of Sweden, fox are shot at night over bait. This is mainly done in winter and at full moon, when the moon and the snow make for excellent visibility. Shotguns are used, very often equipped with telescopic sights with good light-gathering qualities. The bait—carrion of any kind will do—should be well weighted down with stones to prevent the fox from taking it away. It should be placed within easy shotgun range of a farm's outhouse or even of the farmhouse itself. A light on the outside of the building can be a help, if visibility is poor. A string from the bait to a muffled bell beside the waiting hunter will warn him when the fox has come to the bait.

silent ones, for one dog's barking will attract the others and, together, they have a better chance of keeping the raccoon treed.

In recent years, it has become popular to use a predator call, which emits a squeal as of a rabbit that is injured or, in some models, the cry of a small bird or rodent in distress. The hunter, usually wearing camouflage, remains hidden and lures the raccoon to him. Where hunting at night is not legal, success is greatest just after dawn and before dusk. Where hunting may take place at night, and calls and lights are legal, success is greatest. A headlamp with a red lens disturbs wildlife less than one casting a bright white beam. In addition to raccoons, a predator call lures foxes and, in some regions, coyotes and bobcats, and part of the enjoyment of this form of hunting is the knowledge that one must be prepared for the unexpected. In some regions, phonographic calls are legal for raccoons, but a mouth-operated call is more sporting and, with practice, can be just as effective.

Raccoons are very active in late fall, when they are feeding voraciously to put on winter fat: hunting is best then. It is good, too, in February, when the males are wandering about in search of mates. Some states permit hunting in late summer and, while this is a good time, many of the coons that are treed or lured will be young and small. [RE]

Foxes

There are several methods of hunting the foxes of North America—the red fox and the gray fox. There is the formal foxhunt, in which the hunters, dressed in scarlet and mounted, ride to hounds. This is very similar to foxhunting in the British Isles, where foxes are highly valued for the sport they afford; except as pests in suburban areas, where they cannot be hunted with hounds, foxes are not shot in Britain.

Another form of hunting in North America is practiced by farmers and country people, without formality, and mostly at night. The purpose of the hunt is to enjoy the "hound music," while the owners of the hounds sit around a fire and listen to the baying. Owners can identify their hounds' voices and so can tell when the hounds have lost the track, when they recover it again, and when the fox is going flat out. This type of chase is mostly practiced in the South, where there is a deep appreciation of hounds and hound music. Occasionally, the hounds may be followed by automobile.

Foxes can be hunted, after a snowfall, with only two or three hounds. Beginning in the early morning, the hunters start by looking for fresh tracks. The hounds are released, and the hunters try to intercept the fox so as to get a shot at it. Foxes run in irregular circles within their own territory, but shooting at them is not simple; they are too intelligent, sharp-nosed, and keen-eyed to let themselves be bagged easily. Some hunters prefer rifles, such as a .222, while others use a full-choked 12-gauge shotgun and No. 4 or No. 2 shot.

Other methods include walking through good fox country in winter, tracking the animals, while hoping to get a shot with a rifle. In clear weather, an even better method is to glass snow-covered hillsides for foxes sleeping in the sun. Particularly at dawn or dusk, gray foxes can be attracted with a varmint call that imitates the squeal of an injured rabbit. Gray foxes are not as clever as red foxes, which are not attracted in this way.

Occasionally, three or four hunters may conduct a small drive, when they know where a fox is likely to have bedded down for the day and where he will run when flushed. One or two of the hunters take up positions along fence lines or wooded ridges, where foxes are likely to cross, and the others drive or track the fox. It is, by the way, fairly easy to distinguish between the tracks of a gray and a red fox: the former has much larger toe pads, and the latter has so much hair between the toe pads that the prints of individual pads are sometimes almost obliterated. [JK]

Squirrels

Only the larger species of squirrel—the gray, the fox, and the tassle-eared—are considered as game animals. One of the finest ways to hunt them is to go into good squirrel woods at dawn. As soon as the sun rises, squirrels come out to feed, and the hunter must then keep quite still, with his eyes and ears open. On a still morning when squirrels are feeding, an experienced hunter can identify the sound of fragments and cuttings of nuts and acorns being dropped on dry leaves on the ground. Where a beginner will see a squirrel only when it is completely visible, the experienced hunter will spot a squirrel when all that is visible round the stem or branch of a tree is the squirrel's ear, paw, or tail, or when an odd silhouette on a bough indicates that a squirrel is lying outstretched there. This is sport for a good shot with a rifle: an accurate .22 rimfire with a low- or variable-powered scope is the best choice. Ranges can be up to 100 yards (90 m).

Another good technique is to walk very slowly through squirrel woods, listening and looking. A pair of hunters will fare better than one on his own, for squirrels dodge round the backs of trees, thus evading a single intruder. Once squirrels start moving through the trees and branches, a hunter needs a tight-choke shotgun; No. 6 shot is best.

Squirrels can be hunted late in the afternoon, too, and calm, warm, windless days are best. They are active after rain, especially if it is followed by sunshine. In cold or rainy weather, they do not come out.

The nuts and mast that squirrels feed on grow on trees that thrive in river valleys; for this reason, drifting downstream on small streams or rivers in a canoe is not only a pleasant way to hunt the animals, but also an effective one, being almost noiseless. Shooting from a moving boat may increase the demands on marksmanship, however. It is worthwhile, though, for the canoe-borne hunter to go ashore in promising territory and scour the woods; the rewards may include wildfowl and woodcock, to say nothing of pigeons or doves. Some hunters even take fishing equipment with them on such trips.

Squirrels can be called, if the hunter can get himself into a good squirrel wood without being noticed by the animals. Once he is concealed, he can begin calling; if he has been seen, he should wait for some ten minutes, and, during this time, the squirrels are likely to forget about him. A makeshift call can be produced by tapping a coin on the buttstock of the gun or rifle, or by clicking two stones together, but neither of these ways produces as good a call as that from a bellows device. Most manufactured calls are of this type and effectively reproduce the rapid "chucking" of a squirrel. Two long series of chucks are followed by several shorter sequences and, after a pause of about a minute, the whole call is repeated. The hunter then waits and listens for squirrels to appear or answer. If nothing happens within five minutes, he tries again, and keeps on for perhaps a quarter of an hour. If no squirrels show up then, he moves to another part of the woods. [JK]

Chapter 4
Hunting in Africa, Asia, and South America

African Lion

Lions can be hunted in a variety of ways: by baiting, by tracking in desert country, and by locating them from the sounds of their roaring. Baiting is the best bet, if it is legal.

The method of baiting is to hang the carcass of a zebra, buffalo, or wildebeest from a tree, well off the ground so that small carnivores cannot reach it, and then to wait in a blind some 60 yards (55 m) away, beginning two or three hours before sunrise. To be assured of a clear lane of fire, it may be necessary to cut grass and brush between the blind and the bait tree. Once a lion appears and there is light enough to shoot, one watches the lion until it is in a position that offers a good target.

Tracking, a very sporting method, can be done only in desert or very sandy terrain, unless a lion obligingly keeps to the bed of a dry watercourse. Expert trackers can follow spoor left in dew, but even they can see nothing once the sun has burned off the dew. When tracking, the chances of surprising a lion at close quarters are very good. On seeing the hunter, it either runs or charges. The hunter has only a few moments to decide if the lion is a good trophy; a clean killing shot is always desirable and sometimes essential.

In reasonably open plains, woodland, or savanna, a hunter out at night may hear a lion roaring, one of the greatest sounds in Africa. A very deep roar would indicate a big chesty lion. The hunter sets out on foot in the direction of the roaring, correcting his approach from successive roars; with luck, the lion will roar once more just before dawn, when the hunter has a 50–50 chance of finding him, provided the country is open enough.

On occasion, the hunter may see a pride of lions when he is cruising in the hunting car. He then leaves it unobtrusively and, as the lions watch it drive away, gets into position for a shot.

The ideal shot for a lion is on the shoulder about a quarter of the way up the body; this breaks at least one shoulder and pierces the heart. Other shots are more difficult: a brain shot between the eyes from the front, or at the base of the ear from the side. A frontal brain shot, however, is the only means of stopping a charging lion, which can move at about 60 mph (100 km/h); the hunter has almost no time at all to shoot.

In most African countries, the minimum caliber for hunting lions or any dangerous game is .375; the hunter is advised to use this or something heavier, with soft-nosed bullets. The Francophone countries of Africa permit 9.3×62mm or 9.3×64mm. [BH]

Leopard

Leopards are shot over bait. To attract a leopard, one ties the bait firmly to a sturdy, comfortable branch of a decent-sized tree in thick cover. The bait need not be large: a small antelope or baboon is the right size. The blind must be in thick bush, as close as possible to the bait, which should be silhouetted against the sky, for you shoot in poor light at dawn or dusk. While a distance of 30 yards (27 m) is about average, many leopards have been shot from as little as half that distance.

Killing shots for four of the big game of Africa: *(1)* brain shot, *(2)* heart shot, *(3)* shoulder shot, *(4)* neck shot. The frontal brain shot, the only remedy when one of these massive animals charges the hunter, must take account of the angle at which the oncoming beast holds its head. The buffalo's forehead armor is especially difficult to pierce.

243

The Cape buffalo is a difficult and dangerous animal to hunt. The dawn ambush is one of the most effective methods. Buffalo usually remain in cover during the heat of the day and move to watering places in the late afternoon or early evening. They drink and feed at night, returning at dawn to cover.

(Inset) The hunter, having established where the herd spends its nights and having picked out a suitable bull, makes his final approach on foot and in darkness. He positions himself where he will intercept the dawn movement of the animals. A range of 40 yards (35 m) is considered the maximum.

A shoulder shot, as with a lion, kills the animal outright. A wounded leopard is more dangerous than a wounded lion; even if a fallen animal is apparently dead, it may be merely stunned, and a second shot is only prudent. A wounded leopard takes cover and waits for his attacker; tracking requires a very cool head indeed, the help of a superb tracker, a 12-bore loaded with buckshot, and a fair measure of luck to survive and come home with a trophy.

Sometimes, you can surprise a leopard when you are out hunting during the late evening or early morning. It is a good rule never to shoot at a range of over about 80 yards (75 m), even under ideal conditions. Your rifle should be a .375 or larger, fitted with a scope sight.

It is sometimes possible, when out at night in the bush, to hear a leopard grunting as it approaches a kill (or a bait); the sound is similar to a throaty buck-saw, a sort of sawing cough, and, when you have heard it once, it is unmistakable thereafter. [BH]

African Elephant

The great fascination of hunting elephant in Africa has been the need literally to hunt the animals, usually by the now almost lost art of tracking, which is the only sure way to catch up with an elephant. As elephants cover great distances, a hunter has always had to be prepared to cover them too, most of all during the rains, when elephants scatter far and wide, and travel further than they do in the dry season.

To be worth following, an elephant's track must be both fresh and big—at least 20 inches (50 cm) wide. A smooth footprint indicates an older animal. Inspection of dung is a valuable source of information: if the dung is still not much attacked by dung beetles and other insects, it is fresh; the dung of older elephants contains undigested vegetable matter. Where an elephant rests, marks on the ground or on fallen logs and nearby trees may indicate the size of the tusks.

The hunter approaches the elephant from downwind, and, once close to the animal, it may be possible to hear the sounds it makes as it feeds: internal rumblings, sighs, and flapping of ears, which may be the only sound audible if the animal is resting. A herd at rest takes up positions like the spokes of a wheel; each animal faces outward.

An ideal range at which to shoot is 30 yards (25 m), or closer if possible. If the animal is in profile, the brain is about 3 inches (7.5 cm) in front of the ear on a line running to the eye. An accurate brain shot drops an elephant at once. A heart shot from the side is aimed about one-third of the way up the chest half behind the shoulder; an elephant so shot does not fall at once but goes at least 30 yards (25 m) before collapsing.

Elephants' tusks now seldom weigh more than 60 lb (27 kg), whereas weights three times as great were known about the beginning of the twentieth century. When the animal was hunted, rifles of a caliber of not less than .375 or .400 were used with solid bullets. Normally, the rifles were double-barreled or equipped with magazines.

Nowadays, the elephant is a threatened species, competing for its food with many other species in the national parks of Africa and constantly threatened by the farming needs of the growing population. Poaching is also creating great problems for the elephant and for those who want this magnificent animal to survive. [BH]

Rhinoceros

The white rhino is hunted only in South Africa, where the species is preserved on private property under strictly controlled conditions. The animals are located either by spotting or from a safari car; tracking is not required.

Black rhino are generally tracked, however, insofar as they are still legal game; tracks less than 8 inches (20 cm) wide are unlikely to indicate a trophy-sized animal. The first sign of a nearby, resting rhino is the raucous squawking of the oxpecker birds that exist symbiotically with rhino; their cries of alarm arouse the rhino, which either runs away or charges blindly toward the sounds or smell of the hunter. The animal dashes at full speed through whatever thick cover stands between it and the hunter, who will have to shoot at close range, perhaps 20 yards (18 m). The point of aim is the sloping forehead above the eyes and on one side or the other of the horn.

On a standing animal, a heart shot is aimed about a third of the way up the shoulder, and while this does not drop the rhino at once, it will at least not get very far. Rhino are, of course, thick-skinned: over the neck and shoulders, the skin is as thick as 2 inches (5 cm); elsewhere, it is more than an inch (3 cm). No caliber of rifle less than .375 should be used; bullets should be solid. [BH]

Cape Buffalo

Most hunters regard the buffalo as the most dangerous of all African game, as it has excellent sight, hearing, and sense of smell, as well as being immensely strong, alert, and cunning. These attributes make buffalo hunting exciting and unpredictable.

A hunter looking for a good bull scans a herd of several hundred animals or tracks a solitary bull or a group of perhaps only three or four bulls that have retired from the herd. In plains or savanna country, a hunter first spots a herd at a distance and then stalks it on foot. In forests, he must scout along trails or glades at dawn. Escarpments or hillsides provide vantage points from where he can glass the surrounding country. In miombo forests, which occur throughout much of the buffalo's range, the hunter may be able to track a single animal or a herd. He has to get very close—between 10 and 40 yards (10 and 35 m)—to the bull he wants to shoot. Anything much over 40 yards is too risky. Approaching from downwind is necessary to get within range. Each herd has several animals on watch the whole time, and if one of them is alerted, the chances of a trophy vanish. The odds of finding a trophy animal are greater in a herd of bulls than in a mating herd. A bull whose horns protrude more than 2 inches (5 cm) beyond his ears will qualify as a trophy.

Once the hunter has selected his bull and got within range, he settles down for a shot. The best shot is a heart shot, about one-third of the way up the chest, in line with the leg. Even if he is hit with a perfect shot, the animal will not drop at once but will jump slightly or rush off at full speed, moving the whole herd, and falling dead within about 40 yards (35 m). If a shot pierces the chest cavity, but neither strikes the heart nor breaks a shoulder, the buffalo goes a considerable distance and several shots may be needed to finish him off. A shot to the spine, at the point where neck and body meet, drops the animal at once but does not kill it outright, so that a second shot, to the heart, is needed. The frontal brain shot is the most difficult and should be attempted by a novice only to stop a charge, for nothing else will. When a buffalo is feeding, the point of aim for a brain shot is between the eyes at the edge of the boss of the horns. In the typical stance of enquiry, when the animal is looking down his nose, the target is just at the top of the nose. When a buffalo charges, he starts with his head up and ends with it right down (the victim's initial injuries are nearly always to the legs and thighs).

The dawn ambush is another method of hunting buffalo. During the early hours of the morning, the hunter must position himself near a trail that the herd will use to a nearby water hole. Great care must be taken to stay downwind of the herd at all times.

Following a wounded buffalo is difficult and dangerous. If he stays with the alerted herd, shots at ranges of up to 150 yards (135 m) might be necessary. If the animal is on its own, it makes its way through some of the thickest bush on hand and stops there, only to charge out suddenly and at short range. There will then be only a split second to get off a shot.

The right weapon and bullet are essential for buffalo hunting. Nothing under .375 is adequate. The .458 is excellent; so are the heavy doubles, from .450 up through .470, .500–.465. The bullet must be solid. Although a soft-nosed bullet would do for a body shot, it would be almost certainly useless in stopping a charge. [BH]

Asian Wild Boar

There are wild boar over much of Asia. They live in widely different sorts of terrain: snowy, open forests in Siberia; arid locations, such as those in India; and in tropical forests and jungles. The wild boar of India are almost hairless and are smaller and darker than the boar of Siberia or those of the tropical jungles. Wild boar that inhabit regions where rattan palms grow—mainly in the East Indies—are among the few animals that will attack man without provocation; they become bad-tempered from the thorns picked up while rooting under the rattans.

Shooting a trophy-class wild boar, especially in the deep forests, is usually a matter of following a spoor, which is often to be found along streams or in other rooting spots. When the marks of the fore hooves exceed a width of 2 inches (5 cm), the animal can be of interest; this size of hoof indicates a weight of about 250 lb (110 kg), and every additional $\frac{1}{4}$ inch (6 mm) indicates about an additional 100 lb (45 kg) in weight.

Tracking can involve many hours of difficult slogging through the bush in mountainous terrain. Great caution and alertness are always needed around grazing places and when tracking into dense underbrush and thick grasses, in which boar may have bedded down. With good luck, a hunter may see a boar early in the morning when it is still rooting and grazing; this would be his only chance of finding a boar preoccupied and possibly unaware of a human presence.

Wild boar of all regions have the peculiar habit of making beds of branches, twigs, grasses, leaves, and general debris. In mountainous regions, piles of this sort are usually formed on ridgetops; in open areas, they may be found under trees. When still fresh, leaves and grasses may be obvious and evidently out of place but, after some time, they may be difficult to detect. The boar beds down under all this vegetation and, when disturbed, erupts spectacularly, usually to head away downhill. It is prudent, therefore, for a hunter to approach a known bedding area from the top of the hill or slope.

Less permanent bedding places used by boar do not have this covering. The animals blend well into natural cover. Even when a boar is sleeping, its senses are still alert.

A boar's tracks zigzag about when they approach its bedding place and, on observing this, the hunter must move very carefully. A charging boar is very fast and agile, and it is only wise to select a 10- or 12-gauge double or repeating shotgun, loaded with heavy buckshot, when tracking wild boar. They are most formidable animals. [GY]

Tiger

Tiger were once hunted for pleasure by Asian potentates and their guests, who were borne through the jungles on the backs of elephants. Later, the great Jim Corbett won lasting credit for altering the sportsman's approach to the hunting of the big cats of Asia, so that the balance was made more even between the hunter and his quarry. Baiting, waiting in the vicinity of a kill, and tracking all became methods used by the visiting hunter; sometimes, local skills in imitating the squealing sounds of some small animal in distress were used to lure a tiger out of cover. Hunting was always dangerous, and the risks entailed in coping with wounded tigers were very real. It is now illegal to hunt tigers. However, if the conservation efforts that have been made since the mid-1970s prove successful, tiger hunting may be allowed again one day, as numbers will need to be kept within the limits set by supplies of wild game and an increasing human population. [GY]

Blackbuck and Nilgai

These two species are hunted in India, often in the same areas of open grasslands, on the fringes of the Gir and Sal forests; nilgai occur in cultivated areas, where they are agricultural pests. When near cultivation, both species are often extremely shy and wary. Stalking them is difficult, and great precaution must be exercised when shooting in such densely inhabited areas.

On open plains, both species either keep a distance from an approaching hunter or simply move out of sight. Driving may endanger beaters. The best bet is to circle round the animals, slowly getting closer until within range. Distances are hard to estimate in the absence of trees. The heated air distorts visibility, too, and shots at more than about 300 yards (270 m) should not be taken.

Less sporting but perhaps more effective methods are used by local hunters, who wait at or near watering-places. If suitable cover exists, a visiting hunter can employ such methods, arranging for the animals to be driven back from the water to the cover. Blackbuck in motion are hard to hit, for they move with a fast, bouncing gait and take great leaps when they want to go still faster. [GY]

Southern Asian Bears

In the tropics and deep forests, tracking is the basic method for hunting bears, especially when the rains have left the ground soft. The hunter should be accompanied by a guide; as they follow the tracks, the hunter should watch ahead and to the sides of the trail all the time. This is particularly vital when the tracks suddenly change direction, for this may mean that the bear has started looking for a place to bed down, or has become aware of being followed. In the latter case, it will be waiting in ambush. If it attacks, it will be silently and at great speed. All three Asian species of bear are dangerous, but the Tibetan black bear is by far the worst. Perhaps the best thing in dense jungle is to leave bears alone, unless the hunt is for a bear that must be shot because of its attacks on local people.

In drier regions and open mountain terrain, tracking is difficult, but bears may easily be spotted some distance away because visibility is relatively good. A hunter must aim carefully at a bear that is uphill of him, for, unless he kills it outright, it may tumble and roll downhill, only to halt itself on reaching him. The Tibetan black bear is frequently only wounded because of its peculiar anatomy and its habit of contorting itself into flatly-spread stances. More often, however, the animal will be only wounded because the hunter has shot in nervous haste; the hunter who goes after bear must be able to shoot well and calmly. [GY]

Asian Sheep and Goats

Hunting in the Asian mountains demands that the hunter is in very good physical shape and equipped for cool to cold mountain conditions. Rifles need to have scope sights and be low-caliber: the .270 Winchester or an equivalent is good. The .300 Magnums are excellent for sheep and goats. Rifles are zeroed at 250 yards (230 m) or used with matching loads that are at zero at 200 and 300 yards (180 and 270 m): the average ranges to be expected fall within these limits, although ranges may be longer in the Altai and Pamir regions.

The base hunting camp is established within an hour or two of the area inhabited by sheep or goats; this is usually below 10,000 feet (3,000 m) but at the beginning of the "thin air" zone; a hunter may need time to get used to this. The camp should be small and quiet, for mountain game can often be spotted without leaving the camp; many ibex, tahr, and markhor have been taken soon after a tent flap is opened in the morning.

Most animals of the high mountains, and especially sheep, have very keen eyesight and can spot an approaching man at a great distance. The hunter should, therefore, have taken up a good vantage point before dawn, so that he may rest, if need be, and glass at first light. Drab clothes blend in with the terrain. As few movements as possible lessen the risk of scaring the animals into immobility, which makes them all the harder to see. The hunter must be downwind of the animals; his scent would spook them at once. If they take themselves off, they are not likely to be seen again by the hunter. A quiet initial watch, constant alertness, and calm, unhurried walks pay dividends.

Before taking a shot, it is important to consider if the animal would fall into an inaccessible crevice, or suffer damage in falling, if it were hit. An animal can sometimes be induced to move to a "safer" place by a shout or a shot, provided it cannot see the source of the noise. This is an important tactic in the Himalayas and other similar regions. [GY]

Asian Deer

Asian deer are animals of deep forests and jungle, and the hunter must be prepared for jungle and forest conditions. He must expect to get wet, but his footware should repel both water and leeches; his personal equipment must include one or two canteens of drinking water. Furthermore, he must bear in mind that most shots are taken at relatively close range (under 100 yards) and that bullet deflection is a problem, most of all when bamboo is abundant. High-velocity cartridges are generally less effective than heavier, slower loads, or even shotgun slugs or buckshot. A telescope sight can hang up on jungle vines, while its lenses may fog up in the damp; the more streamlined a rifle is, the better.

European and North American concepts of fair chase may not be understood in many parts of Asia where, after all, the inhabitants hunt for meat and may not appreciate a hunter's regard for a trophy. A visiting sportsman needs to make sure that his guide understands his desire for sporting methods.

Tribal hunters themselves in some highland regions often employ very sporting tracking and stalking methods for deer. These demand stamina, patience, and skill. All Asian deer can be hunted by "pussy-footing" in search of the animals when they are feeding very early in the morning or late in the evening. During the rest of the day, the hunter should concentrate on selected tracks or walk slowly through areas known to contain bedded deer. Except for chital and barasingha, Asian deer bed deep in bamboo thickets and other dense forest growth; it takes much skill to surprise a bedded animal or to get close enough for a clear shot before it has run away.

Most deer commonly bed just off the ridgelines or on the slopes. The hunter keeps to the higher ground, somewhat behind his tracker, who moves noisily somewhat lower down the strip of hillside. They keep within earshot of one another, and the hunter knows where the tracker is. On wider slopes, an experienced tracker usually shows the hunter where to wait, while he "kicks up" the deer noisily from a direction that will move them toward the hunter. Such deer seldom move slowly, so the hunter must be ready to shoot at them on the run.

In some areas, the local people use whistles and calls to decoy the deer; such methods may be the only way for a hunter to see a deer in daylight. [GY]

Big Game Hunting in South America

South America has often been called the world's last frontier, yet, despite an abundance of relatively small creatures, it holds only a few species of big game, of which several have been introduced from Europe. The largest native creatures are the jaguar, the puma, the tapirs, and the Andean bear, which lives on the western side of the Andes. The big cats are now protected in one way or another, and no longer really the quarry of sporting hunters. Literally innumerable species of small animals, birds, insects, and fish, some of which have hardly been classified scientifically, inhabit the tropical rain forests, most of which are too thick for hunting.

The animals of major interest to the sporting hunter include those already mentioned and the European red deer, which has been introduced into Argentina. The world's largest rodent, the capybara, is a jungle species that is good to eat but not a very challenging target for a hunter. Central and South America are well known for their wildfowling and upland-bird shooting (notably doves).

It is not easy to go hunting in South America, even if one lives there. The forbidding jungle, transport difficulties, official attitudes that do not always tend toward an active encouragement of sport hunting: these prompt the caution that a hunter must not expect merely to arrive in the continent and go hunting. Arrangements must be made in advance.

Almost every South American country has a national hunting club through which the prospective hunter can get in touch with game agencies, organizers of hunting tours, guides, suppliers of equipment, and so on. This is the way to find out about hunting seasons, game limits, firearms, and other regulations, including those affecting species threatened with extinction. [LC]

Red Deer in Argentina

Argentina has fantastically good red-deer hunting. It is the only country in South America where there is a huntable population, and the chances of shooting a world-record rack are good. The deer are hunted on large ranches, many of which exceed 70,000 acres (29,000 hectares), called *estancias*; gamekeepers in full-time employment manage the herds of deer so as to breed the best possible trophy animals. Old and inferior animals are culled, and hunting is one of the means used to achieve this.

There are many ranches near Bariloche, a regional tourist center about 1,100 miles (1,800 km) from Buenos Aires. The town is dominated by the nearby Andes, which soar up to heights of 12,000 feet (3,500 m) to the west of the town. Hunters can call on the services of well-established guides who can ensure enjoyable and successful hunting.

Some of the ranches are private estates, to which the visitor could expect only to be invited. Others, however, are commercial ranches with ready access for hunters. A fee is paid for each animal shot, and a bonus may be charged for an exceptional trophy; this method of charging will be familiar to those who have enjoyed traditional continental European hunting.

Each hunter is provided with a guide; both of them must expect to do a lot of walking while searching the mountain meadows and alpine slopes. It is the guide's job to help spot the deer, before he and the hunter stalk it until they get within range. The hunter needs stout boots, warm clothes, and well-trained legs. [LC]

Hunting in the Jungle

Some hunters may be interested in adding tapir and capybara to the list of their trophies, but it must be doubtful if most hunters would travel a great distance to shoot only these rather innocuous jungle animals. But for a hunter who is already there, why not?

Tapir and capybara both provide good eating. The Indian villagers hunt them for this reason, and the visiting hunter, therefore, cannot reckon on finding either sort of animal near a village. In addition, tapir and capybara are shy: a tapir scurries back into cover at the first sign of danger, and capybara, being good swimmers, dive into the water, or run away into the jungle, when approached. Shooting from a small boat on a stream or river is perhaps the best method for capybara but, even so, shots are usually taken at relatively long ranges.

Tapir can be hunted with dogs, if a pack can be assembled, but tapir are elusive and can rush through thick undergrowth that is impenetrable for men and dogs, before vanishing from sight in the jungle or when they reach water or a swamp. [LC]

Bird Shooting in South America

Tinamous are the premier upland game birds of Central and South America. Various species are plentiful on the grasslands, where the hunting method is to get out in the open and walk. Pointing dogs are used in some areas, but, in the sandy areas of the pampas, the dogs get sand burrs between their toes and become incapacitated before long.

A species of tinamous occurs in the mountains of Ecuador, typical elevations being 10,000 to 12,000 feet (3,000 to 4,000 m).

Tinamous behave rather like pheasant, flushing with a furious beating of wings, then fly on, gliding from time to time on stiffly outstretched wings. The birds are found in coveys, but coveys do not flush together as do coveys of bobwhite quail, for example; tinamous rise one at a time, which can give good sport when a covey provides a succession of ten, twelve, or even more birds. [NS]

Wildfowling in South America

One of the world's greatest concentrations of teal is to be found in the huge marshes at the mouth of the Magdalena River in Columbia, on the Caribbean coast. Bluewing teal begin to arrive there in mid-October; some stay as late as mid-April. These marshes teem with birds and teal outnumber any other species in some parts of the delta. Hunters shoot over a dozen or so rubber decoys; they use dugout canoes or other suitable small boats, both to traverse the marshes and as a shooting platform. On some occasions, hunters need only conceal themselves in the rushes.

The Magellan goose provides hunting in the southern part of the continent. The birds fly north from Tierra del Fuego in April. In the Argentinean state of Chubut, local farmers welcome hunters, for the geese are very numerous and crop the grass intended for the farmers' sheep and cows. Hunters take up positions on the edges of swamps, lakes, or rivers, where the birds seek refuge at night. If there is no wind, newspapers can function as makeshift decoys in the pastures. Hunters conceal themselves as best they can, usually by wearing drab-colored clothes and standing still, for example by a large fence post. The geese often swing right into gunning range and even land among the decoys. The ashy-headed goose is less numerous than the Magellan, but it occurs together with it, sometimes even flying in formation with it. [NS]

VI Hunting
Allies

Chapter 1

The Hunting Dog

Nick Sisley

Dogs are important, and sometimes crucial, in both big- and small-game hunting, and they always have been. The hunting breeds are now separated into four basic categories, depending on what help the dog gives the hunter: retrieving, pointing, flushing, and chasing. While any hunting dog should be able to retrieve game, some species are specialists at doing this. The following selection of hunting dogs is not, of course, comprehensive, but nevertheless, it covers the important types used.

RETRIEVING DOGS

The three most important breeds are the labrador, the Chesapeake Bay retriever, and the golden retriever. The labrador is the most popular. Although technically spaniels, the American water spaniel and the Irish water spaniel are also retrieving dogs. All these breeds were developed for retrieving waterfowl, but the labrador and the golden retriever have, in recent decades, proved capable of flushing and retrieving game such as pheasant, grouse, woodcock, pigeon, rabbit, and others.

Labrador Retriever

The labrador is an ideal, all-round hunting dog and a perfect specialist for waterfowl retrieving. Hardy and tough, with a level of understanding rarely equaled by other breeds, a labrador can learn from a professional trainer, or from someone with less experience, although an amateur will take much longer to achieve the same results.

The most common color for a labrador is black, but they are also yellow and chocolate colored. They have a most friendly disposition, are particularly good around children, and are always ready to please the person who feeds them. Powerfully built, they usually weigh between 55 and 75 lb (25 to 34 kg). They have a relatively short but thick coat that keeps off the cold, and, as it is somewhat oily, it keeps the animal's skin dry even when it is swimming.

Labradors have an excellent record in field trials. The dogs were first imported in the nineteenth century to Britain from Newfoundland, having been brought there by Portuguese fishermen who had used them to retrieve fish and items of tackle (buoys, floats, net blocks, etc.) that were washed overboard during cod fishing. The name "labrador" has no connection with the Canadian territory that now bears that name but did not do so then. The word is simply the Portuguese for "worker" (i.e., working dog). The labrador's popularization in Britain is a subject on which there are conflicting versions, as the breed was already developed when imported into the country. The pioneers of labradors in Britain were, and still are, the Radclyffe family in Dorset.

Golden Retriever

This breed combines outstanding physical appearance with many qualities that make it a favorite among both waterfowlers and upland-game enthusiasts. While they are less hardy than labradors and Chesapeake

Bay retrievers when fetching late-season waterfowl, golden retrievers are excellent for upland hunting. They take naturally to quartering and ranging fields, swales, and woods within easy gun range of their masters, and can flush and retrieve what is shot.

Generally weighing about 60 to 75 lb (27 to 34 kg), and standing over 20 inches (51 cm) at the withers, golden retrievers have longer hair than labradors. While their color is always golden, there can be a wide variation within this hue.

They are very affectionate animals and respond well to training that uses repetition, coaxing, and affection. Harsh methods are likely to produce a "cowed" retriever, but the breed's very ready affection can be almost a fault. The golden retriever is very popular with bench-show enthusiasts but, as yet, this has not had a detrimental effect on the breed.

It is generally accepted that the breed originated in 1865 in England, when a yellow dog named Nous was mated with a bitch of the now-extinct Tweed water-spaniel breed. Later, in the 1870s and 1880s, breeders introduced bloodhound and Irish setter blood into the breed, which was officially recognized by dog registries in England in 1910, in Canada in 1927, and in the United States in 1932.

Chesapeake Bay Retriever

About the same size as the other retrievers, the Chesapeake Bay has a unique coat: very thick, extremely oily, short with a slight curl, and with a woolly undercoat. No other breed's coat is so impervious to water. Its skin hangs loose on its body. Chesapeakes are brown, ranging from a dark shade to one that resembles dead grass. Unlike the friendly golden retriever, which usually wags its tail at an intruder, and the labrador, which usually barks, the Chesapeake will chase him off.

Not especially popular with field trialers, the Chesapeake is nonetheless highly favored by dedicated waterfowlers for, when called on to retrieve a bird from water half covered with thin ice, the dog plunges in when other breeds would be standing by shivering. However, the Chesapeake is not so good a dog on the uplands.

It is said that the breed had its beginnings when a dog and bitch swam ashore from a shipwreck off the Maryland coast in 1807. These two—Canton and Sailor—were, apparently, outstanding retrievers. The breed was developed through the latter part of the nineteenth century and was recognized by the American Kennel Club in 1933.

American Water Spaniel

This breed is smaller than the other retrievers, with a weight of between 25 and 40 lb (11 to 18 kg) and with a height of about 16 inches (41 cm) at the shoulder. Its color is a solid liver—dark, reddish brown—or chocolate, and its coat is compact and curly. Its tail is short and slender. It is easy to train, being biddable, easy to please, and also easy to care for (because it is relatively small). Its coat tends to pick up burrs and "stick-tights."

The American water spaniel was developed in the upper midwestern

A German shorthaired pointer puts
up a cock ring-necked pheasant and
the hunter steadies himself for a shot.

(Opposite) **GOLDEN RETRIEVER.**
The properly trained dog will sit still as the hunter shoots and will move only when given the order to fetch the downed birds.
(Below) **LABRADOR.** This fine retriever has just fetched a mallard drake.

United States for use in small boats and canoes when hunting the lakes and marshes of the region. It is still much admired there, but less so elsewhere, although it deserves to be more popular with waterfowlers than it is. This is partly explained, perhaps, by the fact that the breed does not conform to the standards of beauty of the labrador and the golden retriever.

The breed is reputed to have descended from the old English water spaniels, with admixtures of Irish water spaniels and curly-coated retrievers, until the present breed took form. It was recognized by the American Kennel Club in 1940.

Irish Water Spaniel

This is a curly-coated breed that was developed in Ireland and first became popular in Britain and continental Europe before becoming widely accepted in North America because it could withstand tough, wintry conditions well. The breed generally weighs between 45 and 60 lb (20 and 29 kg) and has a solid liver color—dark reddish brown. The breed's popularity has fallen off, perhaps because shooting of waterfowl is now no longer unrestricted, and other breeds are better suited to a variety of uses.

As with many sporting breeds, the early history of this one is not definitely known but is believed to have started when Irish setters were crossed with French poodles.

Curly-coated and Flat-coated Retrievers

These breeds are similar in build—55 to 70 lb (25 to 32 kg)—and in coloring, being either black or liver, but they differ in temperament. The flat-coated tends to be a somewhat easy-going dog that is very biddable in marshes and uplands, and will flush and retrieve small game. It does well for a hunter who wants a close-working dog that seldom moves far from the gun.

Until the labrador "explosion" in the first decade of the twentieth century, the flat-coated retriever had been the dominant British gun-dog breed for thirty years. It supplanted the curly-coat in the 1880s after twenty years of curly dominance since the introduction of breechloading guns made driven game shooting possible, and thereby created the need for specialist retrievers. In muzzleloading days, all shooting was "rough," and pointers, setters, and spaniels did the retrieving, along with their other functions.

The curly-coated tends to be more spirited, and can flush and retrieve effectively. Only in New Zealand, however, have its qualities been fully recognized, for it is appreciated there as a superb water dog and is also popular among upland hunters. But both breeds deserve a higher standing than that which they are accorded.

POINTING DOGS

These breeds get their name from the way they respond to the immediate presence of the game they have located: they hold themselves rigid, pointing with their entire bodies towards the place where the game is concealed, waiting for a sign of command to flush it. Some point with a markedly upright stance, others in a lower crouching position. In order to find the game in the first place, pointers are trained to range systematically within gunshot, exploring each piece of cover in which birds or other game can be lying hidden.

They are invaluable in hunting game such as partridge, pheasant, woodcock, snipe, and quail, and any other game that characteristically does not fly up or run as soon as it detects danger.

They are naturally adept at finding wounded game that has gone to cover and at retrieving it. Like a retriever, a pointer will be considered "hard-mouthed" if it cannot carry an egg in its mouth without breaking it.

English Pointer

While the origins of this breed are both mixed and debated, it is generally regarded as the classic pointer, a rather aristocratic English dog, aloof where the setter, for example, is demonstratively affectionate. It is a short-haired breed, and generally white with markings or spots of liver, black, lemon, or yellow. It is trimly built and weighs between about 45 to 58 lb (20 to 26 kg).

One of the English pointer's most obvious characteristics is eagerness to hunt—occasionally to a fault. This can make a dog difficult to handle, as he is determined to find game, no matter where, and may range too far from the gun. However, a good trainer can curb this tendency to range too far. A well-trained dog is very staunch on point, steady to wing and shot, and almost tender in his manner of bringing to hand small birds such as quail. Occasionally, pointers are "hard-mouthed," but with training most of them can be excellent retrievers.

Very popular in the British Isles, the pointer is even more popular in North America. It is a favorite, for example, for ruffed-grouse shooting in the midwestern and northeastern United States, and it is used by pheasant hunters in many regions. Quail hunters in the southern states favor pointers when shooting in the immense grain fields, where the dogs will cast along the field edges while the hunters wait patiently in the center; when the pointer has picked up a scent, it will point until the hunters can move up and command the dog to flush the birds.

Some authorities hold that the breed originated in Spain at about the beginning of the seventeenth century, but dogs resembling pointers are to be seen in paintings from France from about the same period. The most generally accepted opinion is that the pointer evolved from a mixture of foxhound, greyhound, and bloodhound, crossed with the setting spaniels. As with much else characteristically British, the pointer developed its significant form in the middle and later nineteenth century, when the pioneering breeders—Thomas Statter, Sir Vincent Corbet, and J. Armstrong—contributed also to the development of the English, Irish, and Gordon setters.

When the world's first field trial was held, in England in the 1860s, pointers were not permitted to compete with setters, which were considered far superior, a position they held for a number of years, with the English setter holding first place. Eventually, the pointer came to the forefront and has maintained this position ever since.

In recent years, however, continental European breeds such as the German short-haired pointer and the Brittany spaniel have become relatively popular.

English Setter

A field-bred English setter stands about 21 to 26 inches (53 to 66 cm) high at the withers and weighs about 43 to 53 lb (19 to 24 kg). It is thus a little smaller than the pointer. The breed is basically white (making for a dog that can easily be seen in cover), with some ticking or spotting in one other color—black, blue, tan, lemon or orange, or liver. Some present-day breeders strive for dogs that are solid or nearly solid white. A setter with ticking but no real spotting is known as a belton, with a qualification to indicate coloring: most often blue belton. "Blue" here means a gray with a bluish sheen. The hair is fairly long, and the tail is beautifully "feathered."

A setter usually points in the manner of a pointer, that is to say, in the upright position of pointing head, uplifted front foot, and backward-pointing tail, but it will sometimes exhibit a trace of the crouching stance for which the breed's ancestors were noted some four centuries ago. John Caius, writing *Of Englishe Dogges* in 1570, remarked that when they detected scent strong enough to indicate that game was very close, they stopped and crouched—belly close to the ground—whereupon the huntsmen hurled nets over the concealed game. Setters possess a very strong inborn desire to hunt, and so are eager and hard-working, responding well to encouragement and repetition in training, and not to stern discipline. They point patiently and retrieve excellently.

Just when setters were first distinguished from other breeds is hard, if not impossible, to say with certainty, but it seems that they evolved from land spaniels, at least as early as the last quarter of the fourteenth century. Gaston de Foix, in *Le Livre de la Chasse*, from 1387, wrote of both land spaniels (springing, or flushing, spaniels of a sort used in falconry) and a type of setting spaniel. Later, some suggest, there were contributions to the breed from Spanish pointers, large water spaniels, and from springers.

Irish Setter

Even if this breed did not come from Ireland, its strikingly red coat and impulsive temperament would suggest its origins. It is slightly larger than the English setter but in recent years, bench-show tendencies have caused the breed to degenerate into a show type with little or no tractability, a complete lack of hunting sense, and an overall foolishness. A few breeders have counteracted this by breeding only from field-quality setters, and by infusing English setter blood from time to time in an effort to increase the animal's hunting instincts.

While there has been a revival of interest in the British Isles, a greater one has taken place in the United States, where the breed is registered with the American Field Dog Stud Book as "Red Setter," rather than Irish. It is popular, too, in many parts of continental Europe.

Gordon Setter

This is a black and tan setter of which only a few strains are being bred for the field at present, for their dark coloration has been a handicap in the field, while they—like the Irish setters—have become a victim of bench-show enthusiasm over superficial good looks. They might benefit from an infusion of English setter blood, for the typical Gordon setter tends now to be close-working and somewhat sluggish, if thorough, but can be trained to point well and to retrieve.

The breed derives from the southern English county of Sussex, where the Dukes of Richmond, whose family name is Gordon, are substantial landowners, and—once again in the nineteenth century—were responsible for the development, but not the inception, of this breed, for there is no question but that black and tan setters were trained and bred before then.

German Shorthaired Pointer

Weighing from about 50 to 70 lb (23 to 32 kg), the German shorthaired pointer is larger than the English pointer and raw-boned in comparison, although the breed is still developing fast, having become popular after World War II. Their tails are usually docked. Color is generally liver with some white ticking, although in many countries the breed has a great deal of white. This is claimed by some to be a result of unpublicized crosses with English pointers, made with the purpose of increasing the German dog's speed and willingness to range from the gun. Others consider it to be the result of selective breeding for color as well as good conformation and breeding.

However, the breed must still be considered a medium-ranging one, tractable and industrious, but without the pointing instinct of the English pointer or setter. In the hands of a good trainer, however, the German dog can develop this instinct well and become a staunch pointer.

The breed is an all-round one, a quality deriving from the general nature of its traditional work on the continent of Europe, where it has been used not only for birds but also for tracking and cornering boar, for bringing down deer if necessary, and even for killing cats and foxes on preserved ground. As a result, it is often too hard-mouthed to make a good retriever, but it can, as noted, be improved by good training.

Like most other breeds of hunting dog, this one has an ancestry that is undoubtedly ancient but equally undoubtedly obscure. Crosses between Spanish pointers and bloodhounds or Saint Hubert hounds, and later—in the nineteenth century—with English setters, produced a breed to which foxhounds and possibly setters had also contributed before a recognizable German shorthaired pointer emerged at the beginning of the twentieth century.

German Wirehaired Pointer (Drahthaar)

The longer of these two names for the same dog describes it the better, for its very coarse coat is wiry to the touch, and its face is whiskery. It is roughly the size of a large English setter, standing about 24 inches (61 cm) at the shoulder. Its color is predominantly liver, or liver with white ticking or small spots. Occasional examples are roan, an unusual color, but not unacceptable. The Drahthaar takes readily to waterfowl retrieving, but as it does not have the heavy coat of the labrador, golden, or Chesapeake Bay retriever, it is not recommended for retrieving in water in extremely cold weather. Its wiry hair does tend to dry quickly, however.

Most dogs of this breed are medium-ranging but tend to hunt out a little further than the average shorthair. They have excellent noses, are tough and resilient, and are eager to a fault to please their trainers or handlers, even to the point of becoming so attached that they forget what they are being trained to do; but this seldom happens in the field. They tend to be aloof with strangers.

The breed was developed in Germany by crosses between the griffon, the German shorthaired pointer, and the Pudelpointer.

Wirehaired Pointing Griffon

This breed is a solider version of the German wirehaired pointer, a slow-paced methodical worker for which grouse and woodcock are natural quarry; almost all other pointing dogs will beat him to coveys of quail and to pheasants. Its coat, while stiff and protective, has a much softer feel to it than those of other wirehaired dogs, and it is most commonly steel-gray or whitish-gray splotched with chestnut. Its tail is docked to about 6 inches (15 cm).

Griffons are easily handled, and are versatile, capable of pointing game, of trailing in the manner of a hound, and of retrieving from water. They are good in thick cover, where their coats protect them from briars.

The breed originated in Holland.

Brittany Spaniel

At 30 to 40 lb (14 to 18 kg), the Brittany spaniel is the smallest of the pointing dogs, but the only surviving pointing spaniel. It is extremely popular in France, Belgium, and Italy and has been increasing in popularity in the United States, but it does not have an established position in Britain, perhaps because of its French origins.

The typical Brittany has rather long legs on a compact body, giving it a slightly gangling appearance. Its coloration is normally white with orange, liver, or roan ticking or spots. The breed is usually soft in temperament, and it is best trained with coaxing and repetition. While they make fine family dogs, many remain aloof to affection, as do many dogs of pointing breeds.

They excel as retrievers and, with training, can learn to range out from the gun a little further than a medium distance. On game they can be trained to be very staunch, although they usually lack the intensity of point of typical pointers and English setters. They have become espe-

(Above) **ENGLISH SETTER**.
(Right) **GORDON SETTER**.
(Opposite) **GERMAN SHORT-HAIRED POINTER**.

cially popular with American hunters of ruffed (American) grouse and woodcock in the midwestern and northeastern United States and lower Canada. Brittany spaniels can make the switch to other game, such as snipe and waterfowl, but most make it less smoothly than the German shorthaired pointer, for example.

Vizsla

This is a Hungarian pointing dog—its name means "alert" or "responsive" in Hungarian—and about the size of a large pointer. It has a docked tail, weighs 50 to 60 lb (23 to 27 kg), is slim, and has a solid rusty-gold-colored coat. Its coat is short, making the breed unsuitable for work in thick cover, briars, or brambles but, with this exception, it is good at close work and at retrieving in the uplands. Vizslas seldom have the versatility to work marshes and other wetlands.

A few breeders have introduced some German wirehaired pointer or griffon blood into the breed, to remedy the thinness of its coat, while an enterprising kennel in the United States has taken to calling the breed the uplander, intending its dogs to be used for grouse and woodcock hunting.

Dogs strongly resembling modern vizslas were used by tenth-century

Magyar falconers, and the developing breed was used by the Hungarian aristocracy in hunting on the plains, but in modern times, the breed has spread all over the bird-game hunting world.

Weimaraner

This breed is a large one: a big male can weigh almost 85 lb (38 kg) while standing no more than about 26 inches (66 cm) at the shoulder. The dogs have short, rather sparse hair, a tail that is usually docked, and blue-gray or pale amber eyes. The color of their coats is silver with mauve or taupe (gray with a brownish or other tinge) undertones when the light strikes it at a certain angle.

Like the vizsla, the Weimaraner is a dog for the uplands, where the breed works close, but without the tireless energy and eagerness of some pointing breeds: The Weimaraner's short hair renders it unsuitable for cold climates or frigid wet work.

The breed was developed in the mid-nineteenth century in Germany at Weimar, with the intention of producing an all-round performer in the hunting field and, although it has its loyal supporters, it is not among the most popular of breeds.

Two German wirehaired pointers on point and back. The dog in the foreground has located and pointed the birds, and the dog in the background is honoring the find by "backing."

FLUSHING DOGS (Spaniels)

These dogs work close to the hunter—once a falconer or hawker, now a shooter—quickly quartering the cover and finding a scent. As they do this, their tails wag faster and faster, thus signaling to the hunter that the appearance of game is imminent. When the scent becomes very strong, or when they see the quarry, they run in and bolt or flush it.

In England and on the continent of Europe, sportsmen expect a properly bred and trained spaniel to hunt furred and feathered game equally adroitly and eagerly. In North America, many prefer a spaniel to concentrate only on birds, evidently fearing that a bird dog that also bolts rabbits will lose his skill at putting up birds. This would be true of a pointing dog, for furred game behaves differently from feathered game when a dog approaches and points, and a pointer thus learns to specialize on the one or the other. But a flushing dog is not harmed by running a variety of game, and the hunter who restricts his spaniel to birds is denying his dog and himself an enjoyable and rewarding day's shooting. It is unfortunate that many American spaniel owners fail to understand this.

The word "spaniel" derives from the latinate name for Spain—Hispania—for dogs of a spaniel type were common there in the early medieval period, and spaniels of one kind or another evidently existed almost 2,000 years ago. By the mid-seventeenth century, several breeds were classified as either land or water spaniels, depending on their major talents, but since then, water spaniels have largely been replaced by the dogs classified as retrievers. The larger land spaniels are generally quite skillful at retrieving ducks. The most popular breed—the English springer spaniel—is accustomed, at many field trials, to display skill in making land and water retrieves, and to find, and flush or bolt, both winged and furred game.

While a number of other breeds have been equally impressive as the English springer, and are mentioned briefly here, only the English springer is described in detail. Chief among the other spaniels is the cocker, originally developed to flush woodcock. It is so handsome and small, and has so warm a personality that it become a great favorite of bench-shows and house-pet breeders. They bred it for the wrong qualities, lengthened its coat, weakened it, made it smaller, nervous and timid, and in the process lost its stamina, keen nose, and hunting desire, and so all but ruined it as a field dog. This was especially true in the United States.

Today, many people classify the English cocker spaniel as distinct from other cockers, and especially from the American bench-show type. It is more robust, if small by comparison with other bird dogs, and a fairly skillful and vigorous hunter. A few sportsmen still use it to hunt woodcock and even pheasant. It is good for hunting squirrels, too. It has not regained its former popularity, however, and good field strains are few.

Other spaniels of limited renown include the Clumber, the Sussex, and the Welsh springer spaniels. Even now, a Welsh springer that comes from field stock can be a good hunting dog, and it may be described as a slightly blocky, more stolid version of the English springer, so the hunter who wants a flushing dog is likely to choose the latter.

English Springer Spaniel

There are two distinct types of English springer spaniel: show and field. While they are registered as the same breed, they do not look alike, but it

is the field springer that has been, and is, the very best of the flushing spaniels from the hunter's point of view, and a hunter who wants a dog of this great breed must be careful to obtain one (or more) from field stock.

The field-bred springer is small as bird dogs go, is stockily built, standing typically less than 20 inches (50 cm) at the shoulder and weighing about 40 lb (18 kg) on average. Some are notably smaller. Those much larger are probably of show stock and should be avoided. The most common colors are white and liver, or white and black, with some ticking being typical, although not essential. The hair should be smooth to the touch, of a length similar to that of an English setter. There is some feathering at the back of the legs, and at the bottom of the docked tail. The ears are comparatively short, hanging not below the line of the jaw.

Perhaps the springer's most important quality is that it can be effective in the field with limited training. Merely being in "bird" country is usually enough for a dog to show he knows the fundamentals. Dogs of field-trial quality are another matter and must be trained with as much work and thoroughness as any other breed.

Springers tend to range naturally within gunshot and to quarter the territory effectively. They are also excellent retrievers, sometimes taking to it without training. Though their coat is relatively thin and does not permit water work in extremely cold conditions, they are excellent water dogs during moderate weather. A hunter who wants a dog for waterfowl should select one with a preponderance of black or liver, and a minimum of white, so that the dog will be less easily visible to wary ducks and geese. On the other hand, a whiter dog is easier for the hunter to see and keep track of in upland country.

Springers train readily, responding well to encouragement, and will cower before a strong verbal rebuke and seem confused if struck or treated harshly. They are perhaps the most affectionate and playful of all hunting dogs, and so make good family pets. In the field, the springer is the ideal pheasant dog and can also serve well on rabbits and hares, woodcock, snipe, partridge, and other game. While several breeds are known as utility dogs, this one is probably the most versatile all-purpose performer.

The breed was first accorded official classification in England in 1902. Springing spaniels had been known before then, as early as the sixteenth century, but there was no recorded attempt at developing a single uniform breed until much later. The Boughey family, of Aqualate, Shropshire, began carefully breeding dogs in 1812, and so established the first pure line of English springers.

The breed has been a very important one to shooters in the British Isles for many years. One of the most famous and successful breeding programs ever undertaken by a sportsman has been devoted to springers. Talbot Radcliffe, an English breeder, never sells a bitch, but his springer dogs have been exported and have established an international reputation for themselves, and for Talbot Radcliffe.

Many breeders in North America have also been extremely successful with springers, but it was not always so. Pointers and setters were much more popular at the turn of the century, for the most abundant game was the bobwhite quail and, in the Midwest, prairie chickens and sharp-tailed grouse; these were best coursed over the prairie and flushed by a pointer. It was the introduction of the ring-tailed pheasant, which prefers to sneak off or run from a point, that drew attention to the springer's skill at running in and flushing birds within range of their masters.

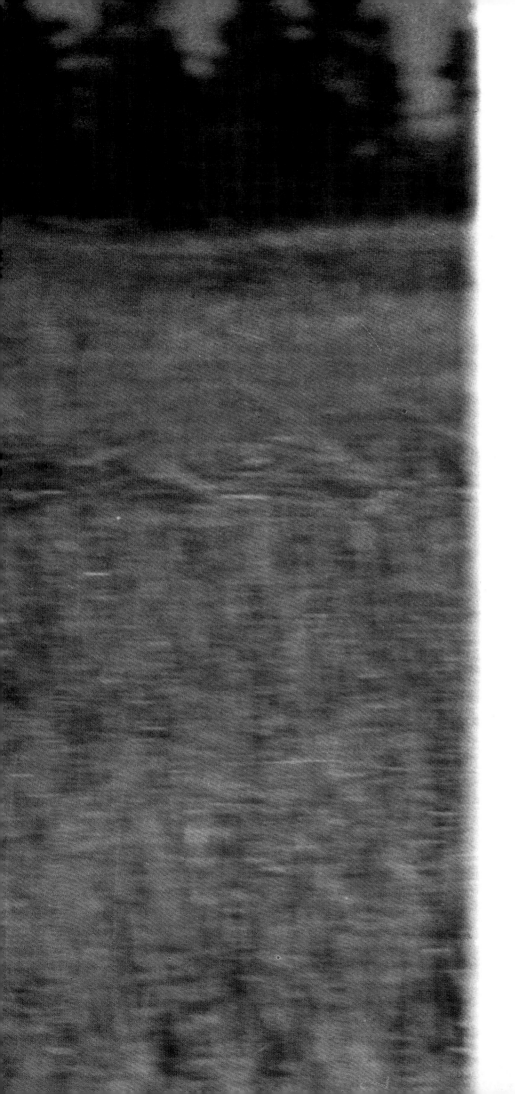

HOUNDS

Hounds are for the pursuit of game by scent, and while some are bred for speed—English foxhounds, for example—others run with endurance rather than great speed—beagles, for example, that are followed on foot in pursuit of hares. Most, however, follow the scent from the ground rather than from the air, as bird dogs do, and almost all give tongue when in pursuit: English foxhounds, Swedish elk-hunting *spetshund*, and American coon hounds are each of them unmistakable to their followers.

A great many breeds of hound still exist, although they are no longer used for hunting. The Afghan is perhaps the most ancient of them, and the bloodhound the best known (from detective fiction). Greyhounds and whippets, which hunt by sight, are still used extensively in Britain for coursing hare, while otterhounds—grey or grizzle rough-coated hounds—are now going to survive as show dogs, if at all, for otter-hunting is now illegal in Britain. Dachshunds are still occasionally used to bolt game rather than to pursue it. Other hounds include the Rhodesian ridgeback, the Irish wolfhound, the borzoi, the Scottish deerhound, the saluki, and the basenji, a hound that rarely barks.

Beagle

Beagles are the most popular hounds, both as pets and for hunting. For a hunting hound, the dog is not big, standing 13 to 15 inches (33 to 38 cm) at the shoulder. The typical coloration is a mixture of black, white, and tan. Beagles are short-coated, with long ears. Various explanations of the origin of the name sum them up: some consider "beagle" to derive from the Gaelic "beg," meaning small, others that it comes from the Old French "beegeule," meaning a noisy person, and the two together well describe a pack of beagles throwing tongue, as the expression is, on the scent of a hare, when they sound merry and musical, falling silent only when they lose the scent.

They work best in two or three couples or more, but single beagles will do well when hunting cottontail rabbits, snowshoe hares, or squirrels in North America. They will also flush pheasants, but they are fundamentally pack hounds, originating in Britain, where many organized packs of beagles exist, from the south of the country to the north.

Basset

Apart from the beagle, the basset is the only small hound of great importance to modern hunters. It is a short-legged, heavy-boned, large-bodied hound, standing about 12 to 15 inches (30 to 38 cm) at the shoulder, and most commonly has a color combination of black, white, and tan. Its ears are long and floppy, and its face, with its heavy flews, is solemn-looking.

Bassets are hare specialists and although slow—much slower than beagles—are keener-scented than any other pack hound and are exceedingly thorough, so that even if the hare outpaces them, it cannot hope to throw them off its track. A basset working alone will track a rabbit or squirrel and will flush a pheasant—but at its own deliberate pace. Bassets have deep, resonant voices.

The breed is of French origin, and is believed to have come about as the result of crossing the old French bloodhound with the small hounds of the Abbots of St. Hubert, a monastic order in Belgium several centuries ago. (St. Hubert is the patron of the hunt.) The breed developed in France, Belgium, and Russia, and in Britain in the late nineteenth century. The modern North American field strains have been bred from English and Russian stock and are somewhat trimmer than those of Britain.

English Foxhound

English foxhounds evolved into roughly their present form between two and three centuries ago, and have since then been bred for speed and stamina, largely within individual packs. In the 1920s and 1930s, Welsh foxhound blood was introduced into some English packs, to give an infusion of hardiness and scenting powers. A number of English packs, however, display marked individual characteristics, the hounds of the Belvoir Hunt, for example, being tan, a coloration noticeable in packs into which Belvoir hounds have been bred. In general, foxhounds are black, white, and tan, and stand about 21 to 25 inches (53 to 64 cm) at the shoulder. They are smooth-coated, have dropping ears, and carry their tails erect; their feet are hard-sinewed, making it possible to hunt twice a week in the season, and sometimes even more.

Their function is well known: to search an area where a fox is known or thought to be, and to force him into the open while, at the same time, communicating what they have found by "throwing their tongues"—a medley of sounds that the huntsman and experienced followers can interpret. Thereafter, the hounds pursue the fox across country, still "speaking to the fox" as they go, and they may cover 8 to 10 miles (13 to 16 km) in an hour.

American Foxhound

The history of the American foxhound can be traced to 1650, when the first European hounds were brought over. During the next couple of centuries, a good many more imported hounds—mostly English foxhounds not much different from those seen today—continued to be added to American stock. At the same time, there was considerable development of local strains throughout rural America. Families or geographic areas developed their own strains, and in many instances these dogs were used to pursue animals other than, or in addition to, the red and gray foxes. The most important additional game has included the raccoon, bobcat, bear, boar, cougar, and coyote.

Some authorities claim that no breed can match the American foxhound in the qualities needed for successfully trailing both the fox and other assorted game. Such a hound must have exceptional scenting ability, speed, stamina, a good voice, intelligence, a strong homing ability, proficiency at negotiating difficult terrain and ground cover, aggressiveness, and an eagerness to run the quarry either alone or with a pack. Some of the hunters who use hounds are careful to cast their animals only after a single species of game, and a dog of this type must be thoroughly trainable, so that he will not be distracted by the wrong quarry. Yet American foxhounds (and other American breeds) also have the inherent instincts that will permit them to be trained for hunting a variety of game.

Like the English foxhound, the American is usually tricolored—white, black, and tan—but orange, lemon, and other shades are often seen. The coat is short and dense, the average shoulder height 24 inches (61 cm), the average weight 50 to 60 lb (23 to 27 kg).

Of the many strains of American foxhounds, three have become most famous: the Walker, the Trigg, and the July. The Walker hound has now been developed into a separate, registered breed, while the other two are still registered as American foxhounds.

Walker Hound

The Walker hound is named for John Walker, a Virginia settler who moved to Kentucky and, primarily together with a fellow foxhunter, George Washington Maupin, bred this now distinct breed. Those hounds that showed ability to tree raccoons were bred further for this sport, and Walker hounds are now well known to raccoon hunters.

Both types of Walker are the same size, having an average shoulder height of about 24 inches (61 cm) and a weight of 50 to 70 lb (23 to 32 kg). Most are tricolored in black, white, and tan, and variations occur and are permissible for registration.

The breed was enhanced by a famous foxhound from Tennessee—Tennessee Lead—and has also English foxhound blood, in addition to infusions from the finest dogs of various strains from the surrounding region.

Today's Walkers are wide-ranging, relentless hunters with great speed, endurance, and homing instinct. One of their abilities, which contributes to their speed, is to take scent both from the air and from the ground.

American Coon Hound (Utility Hound)

This is a general name for a number of breeds of large hound that are mainly, but not exclusively, used to hunt raccoons. Packs of these hounds are also used to hunt foxes, as well as bear, boar, cougar, and bobcat (American lynx). In some regions, a hunter or guide may refer to his pack not as coon hounds but as bear hounds, boar hounds, or cat hounds, depending on their specialty. And depending on the region, the hunter, the available game, and the dogs themselves, they may be used to trail only one kind of game, or more—perhaps, for example, both bear and bobcat, or bear and boar.

In some regions, hound owners are unusually permissive with regard to cross-breeding, especially if the hounds are not registered. The owners are far more interested in trailing and treeing performance than in breed coloration or conformation. Such a pragmatic approach would not commend itself to the owner of a good English pointer bitch, if he were offered the services of an equally good Brittany spaniel.

The packs used for larger, dangerous game, such as bear or boar, must be fearless and tough, capable of keeping their quarry at bay by circling it and by repeatedly attacking and retreating. Naturally enough, hounds are sometimes injured or killed in this way. A cougar may be reluctant to come down from a tree or a ledge where it may have been cornered, but when it does, it will leap down and run, often killing any dog that stands in its way. A prudent hunter will, on such occasions, tie up his hounds before shooting a treed cougar.

The most important coon hounds are the black and tan, the bluetick, the English, the redbone, and the Plott. All are about the same size as the American foxhound, although the black and tan can be slightly larger, and the Plott slightly smaller.

The black and tan is black with tan markings on the legs and face, and often has a white blaze on the chest. Its ears are long and floppy, and it weighs 60 to 75 lb (27 to 34 kg). It is relatively slow, shows great determination, and can withstand the cold well. Black and tans take the scent from the ground and, with their fine deep, resonant booming voices, show evidence of their bloodhound ancestry. They are the oldest of the coon-hound breeds.

The bluetick has a bluish tinge over the whole body but is generally whitish and is tipped with tan points. It is less trim and racy-looking than the Walker but makes an excellent big-game hound, learning characteristically to run a trail well at a very early age.

The English hound is sometimes—helpfully—known as the redtick, being reddish where the bluetick is blue. Not such a showy hunter as some of the other coon hounds, this one is unswervingly steady and has a good record of finding a trail and treeing its quarry.

The redbone is similar in size to the bluetick and redtick, and to the American foxhound, if a little heavier. A typical color is a rusty red all over, and white spots are permissible on the toes and chest; although records are not complete, the breed is thought to owe its color to Irish hounds, perhaps setters, in the last quarter of the nineteenth century. It trails well, is skillful with raccoons, and makes an excellent bear hound, too. A good bear pack will combine redbones and Plotts.

Plotts are attributed to one Jonathan Plott, an emigrant from Germany to the Smoky Mountains of North Carolina in the mid-seventeenth century. The hounds he brought with him proved to be exceptionally good at hunting the black bear, which abounded in their new homeland, and their fame spread throughout the late eighteenth and nineteenth centuries, and then dwindled, perhaps because the Plott family was not interested in commercial exploitation of the breed, preferring to breed the hounds for themselves and their acquaintances. In the twentieth century, after the wild boar had been introduced into the Smoky Mountains, Plott hounds again became famous. Like their German ancestors, they are exceptionally fine boar hounds and are now used to hunt both boar and bear, as well as other game. Good Plott hounds are found throughout North America, and many have been bought by hunters in Europe.

The breed's shoulder height varies from about 21 to 25 inches (53 to 61 cm) and its weight from 45 to 60 lb (20 to 27 kg). The dog is stocky, very muscular, and has very strong jaws. It is brindled, that is, streaked with black and brown, over most of the body. There is usually a dark or black saddle, and there may be white points on the feet, chest, or both. A lighter shade appears in the occasional litter. This paler hue is said to be the result of the only out-cross that ever occurred—the breeding of a Plott many years ago with an outstanding bear hound from Georgia.

(Left) **COON HOUND.**
(Below) **ENGLISH FOXHOUND.**
(Opposite) **BEAR HOUND.**

Chapter 2

Training Hunting Dogs

David Michael Duffey

As mentioned in the previous chapter, there are four categories of hunting dog: hounds, pointers, flushers (mainly spaniels), and retrievers. Very often, the latter three categories have overlapping assignments. For example, spaniels are expected to retrieve, some retrievers are asked to hunt in front of the gun to flush game, and most hunters want their pointers to fetch dead birds as well as to point live game. Some basic training procedures are, therefore, shared by all breeds of these categories. Training curbs and controls a gun dog's natural instincts in order to provide the gun with sporting shots and to ensure the recovery of game that is hit.

A properly trained gun dog should be started early on the basic procedures. When coupled with experience, this introductory training will teach the dog to satisfy all but the most demanding sportsman, who may wish to further his dog's development as a hunter by using the techniques that the professional trainers have perfected.

To a great degree, well-bred hunting dogs "train" themselves, perfecting their natural talents and the skills they have been taught, while actually hunting. This is especially true of hounds.

Hounds

Hounds used for tracking in North America work differently to those that track in Europe. In Britain, tracking hounds work in packs and are used in the classic hunt, that is, hunting from horseback with a pack of hounds and no weapons of any kind. In Scandinavia, the hound is used, singly or in pairs, for tracking European elk. Hounds are also used to drive rabbits and hares toward the guns. In Britain, however, this is considered pest destruction, not sport, although it constitutes a popular sport on the Continent.

Training a hound to hunt properly requires very little in the way of formal instruction. A good trail or tree hound must be naturally sagacious and independent, and it learns chiefly by doing. (The hound that trees its quarry is largely an American phenomenon, although one does find Scandinavian hounds treeing capercaillies, for instance.) Any decent hound will have hunting bred into him, and he is best trained by being hunted as often as possible on whatever game he is expected to run—rabbit, fox, raccoon, wildcat, bear, and so on. It is largely a matter of encouraging him to do what comes naturally.

An old and almost certain method of "starting" a hound is to run him as a pup with good, older, and experienced hounds that are "straight" on a particular game species, that is, they ignore all other scents except those of the species they are trained to trail (a straight foxhound trails nothing but foxes, a straight elkhound trails nothing but elk, and so on).

A pup in training needs a good example to follow, so pick an honest hound (or hounds, if the pup is to be trained to run in a pack) that knows his business and does it with undeviating concentration. A dishonest hound that runs off game will set an example that a pup will almost inevitably follow.

Sometimes, a pup will become discouraged at not being able to keep pace with the older hounds. The following is a method to give him confidence and is one often used with bassets and beagles.

Take the pup into the field at a very early age, at first simply to be out in the open having fun with his master. Between the ages of six and twelve months, he will begin to show an interest in rooting around in the undergrowth, first sniffing at rabbit tracks, and then following them. Finally, he will automatically begin to look for rabbit scents when you let him loose in a likely piece of land. When he does this, use an older dog to start a rabbit for him. Then, rather than just toss the pup into the chase, station yourself with the pup at a spot where the rabbit is likely to circle. The pup will show interest in the baying of the running hound, and when he catches sight of the rabbit, he should be released and his instinct should be allowed to take over. Do not distract him by shouting or urging; he will sight-chase by instinct, and when the rabbit disappears, he will put down his nose to trail for a short distance. Let him do this several times, and when he shows keenness, allow him to join the older dog for short chases.

The next step is to take him out on his own in likely rabbit country and help him to make his own strikes (so that he does not become dependent on experienced dogs) by flushing rabbits from their forms or from undergrowth, so that the pup can see them take off. If he does not see a flushed rabbit, call him over to the scent line, point it out, and encourage him to follow it. In a short time, he should be able to run straight scent lines quite easily. When he comes to his first check (the point at which a rabbit changes direction or makes some maneuver to confuse the dog), allow him to try to work it out for himself. If he is nonplussed or swings too wide off the check, point out the line to him and encourage him to follow it (see pages 272–273). This procedure can also be used to introduce a dog to hunting if no other dogs are available to help him out.

Tree hounds is a designation given to those dogs that chase a quarry, such as raccoon, until it trees. They then stay and bay on the tree until the hunter gets there. Here again, frequent hunting with an honest hound or hounds is the best basic training. Few tree-hound pups will learn to hunt on their own, but when an eight- to twelve-month-old is turned loose with an old dog that cannot run so fast any more, the aged dog will show the pup what is expected of him, and at a pace that allows the pup to absorb what is happening and, in time, to take over the initiative himself. The alternative is simply to let the pup find his own way as part of a pack—and hope for the best. When trail hounds are run in packs, as in American Southern-style night-time chases, this may be the only way.

However, hunters who have the snow to aid them in their day-time hunts and who often use only one or two dogs at a time can introduce a young dog to hunting by finding him a fresh fox-track in the snow early in the morning. Keeping the pup on leash, this cold trail should be followed to where the fox has bedded. Here, the scent should be almost overpowering, and the scent line leaving the bed, being freshest, is known as "hot." The young hound should be encouraged to follow this scent line.

There is no such thing as instant success when it comes to developing an honest hound. Different hounds will learn at different paces. In the training of all hounds, little can be expected if they are not taken to the woods at every opportunity and given the chance to develop the instinct they have inherited from their forebears.

Retrieving

Because they must work closely with hunters and respond to commands, bird dogs, whether pointers, flushers, or retrievers, require more training both in and out of the hunting field than do hounds. The first skill to be taught is retrieving, for retrieving is the cornerstone of a gun dog's education.

Once a sportsman has taught a dog to retrieve, he can quickly develop a perhaps imperfect (by trial standards) but very practical hunting dog. In some countries, hunters demand dogs that behave in a highly correct and formal way, and this usually requires a professional trainer. The following training methods will enable the hunter to get himself a good working dog in the field.

Not only is retrieving a must in the make-up of a complete hunting dog, but it is one of the first things a hunter should teach his dog in order to establish whether the pup has the necessary instincts and "biddability" to be worth further training, and to discover whether the hunter himself has the diligence and the rapport with the pup that are necessary to train him successfully.

How the pup responds to retrieving lessons and how training channels inbred instincts into producing the proper responses will provide a prognosis of the success that both hunter and dog can share in the field.

There are two ways to teach reliable retrieving: the force method and the fun method. Both have their advocates. Force training to retrieve is repetitive, rather distasteful work; it is extremely effective but best left to professionals who can carry to completion the mechanical procedures that ensure success. The fun method, "play training," is also repetitive but is hardly laboriously formal in its early stages. It should reward amateur trainers with at least ninety percent success.

Play training starts at an extremely early age. The best time to bring a prospective gun dog home is between the ages of seven and twelve weeks, and that is when training should begin.

No training ground or special equipment is needed for the first steps, just a room where you and the pup can be alone, and an old glove, a knotted sock, or a handkerchief. An old leather glove that will not catch on the pup's sharp teeth is best. First, wave the glove around in front of the pup to get his interest; then, skid it a bit along the floor, and the pup will chase it and pick it up. Do this several times a day, gradually increasing the distance, and even tossing the glove through the air.

For the purpose of this explanation, let us call the pup Pat. When he picks up the glove, call his name and squat down, coaxing him to you and saying, "Here, Pat. Fetch!" Keep repeating until he comes to you, making his first "retrieve." In a short while, you can drop the "Here"

A hunter and his dog like and trust one another. Good results in training, hunting, and field trials depend on such a relationship. It may take time to build it up while training a pup, but it has its rewards later.

(which you probably established as a command when you first started calling the pup to you) and just say, "Pat, fetch!" when you toss the glove. Position yourself between the pup's "home" (his sleeping box) and the place where he will pick up the glove. His instinct will be to carry the glove to a safe place, just as his ancestors had taken food back to their dens. If you are positioned to intercept, you will instill the habit of coming to you with whatever he has retrieved.

Praise the pup when he brings the glove to you. Steer him in close to you with your hand. Then firmly but gently remove the glove from his mouth, telling him, "Drop!" He may not want to let go. Do not play or engage in a tug-of-war. Hold the glove in one hand, slide the thumb of your other hand into his mouth, pressing his lower lip against his teeth and squeezing just enough so that he will open his mouth in protest, releasing the glove. Make a fuss over him and repeat the game no more than half-a-dozen times that session. Do not bore him.

You have now established that your pup has the instinct to pick up and carry, something every gun dog must possess. This instinct is probably much stronger in a spaniel or a retriever, although pointers also have it and should begin to pick up and carry when they are properly encouraged.

Within a couple of weeks of regular sessions, your pup will be looking forward to playing this game of catch-and-carry. Some pups are not content to bring the glove immediately; they tease, try to go round you, and avoid you. They are, after all, only pups. Be patient and coax such a pup to you. If you squat or kneel down, putting yourself more on his level, he will be more sure of himself. As he approaches, twist your upper body away from him, so that he is approaching you from the side or from behind. As he gets older, you may even have to turn and walk away from him in order to get him to bring it to you. Pups, and even grown dogs, do not like to be stared at and are reluctant to come to you head-on, preferring to approach at least obliquely. But they do like to be followed and chased, so if you move toward him, or make a quick move, he may run away or even spit out the glove.

At about six months of age (depending on his breed), your pup should be big enough to handle a retrieving dummy. This is usually a canvas boat fender. Earlier on, you may have used some bird wings as alternatives to the glove. Now, tape some wings onto the retrieving dummy; this will accustom the pup to picking up feathers and to the scent of game.

If the pup is too small to take along during the hunting season, bring home small birds intact and tease him with them, tossing them for him to fetch.

By the age of six months, if the pup is not picking up and carrying what is thrown to him and at least making it some of the way back to you, you may have to resort to force training. Let a professional trainer do this. You may also consider replacing the pup with another, more biddable dog. A pup that will not pick up and carry, and refuses to bring objects to his owner for praise, will cause other problems in training. Early retrieving is an important indication of willingness to cooperate and of eagerness to please. These characteristics are as important as a good nose and stamina.

From about six months on, the pup should be chasing and retrieving the dummies as far as you can throw them, and he should be enjoying every minute of it. By this time, you have probably thrown them into deep grass or some other kind of cover where, although he has seen the dummy land, he has to use his nose to locate it. Often, trainers impregnate a dummy with a commercially available game scent, if they have not attached feathers to the dummy.

Your pup is now ready to be introduced to game and gunfire. The entire idea of play-training him to retrieve is to instill good habits in him at an early age, so that when he is ready to go into the field (at eight to

268

A Use the leash to teach the pup to heel. A short, sharp tug will show him his correct position when walking with you. Always accompany the tug with a command word, such as, "Heel!"

B When exercising with your pup, drill him to obey your commands. Here, we show the "lie still" sign being used.

C When the dog can heel, get him going on a long leash. Teach him to walk so that he does not entangle the leash round a tree trunk or suchlike.

D A pup will learn to come when called if he becomes used to getting food when he responds.

E It is important that a young dog spends a lot of time in the field with his master. This will accustom him to the various scents and to the feel of the outdoors.

Training a pup to retrieve in water. *(1)* Toss the dummy into shallow water, so that the pup can wade in *(2)* and retrieve *(3)* without having to swim. Praise him and throw it in a little bit deeper, so that he has to swim to reach it. If he shows fear, wade into the water and move around with him, supporting him if necessary *(4)*. Keep throwing the dummy farther and farther in until he has learned to dive in *(5)* and swim as long as necessary in order to retrieve *(6)*.

eighteen months of age), he will be ready to absorb the more serious and formal training that he will encounter there.

Regardless of his abilities or the amount of training that he has had, the gunshy dog is worthless to the hunter. The naturally gunshy dog occurs so rarely that we can describe gunshyness as a man-made fault. It is usually caused in an emotionally stable dog by indiscriminate shooting (or by some unpleasant experience the dog has had with, say, firecrackers). The proper introduction to the sound of gunfire eliminates the risk of gunshyness, as the dog will come to associate the sound with something enjoyable. One well-tried method is to discharge a cap or a .22-blank pistol some distance from a hungry pup when he dives into his food. In his excitement at the food, he will pay little attention to the firing. Work closer to him as he eats, and he will come to ignore the noise completely or merely associate it with something pleasant. Another method is to shoot over an eager pup while he is busily engaged in chasing game that he has smelled and flushed. Again, he will not pay any attention to the sound and will associate it with the excitement of hunting.

Once a pup has learned to retrieve, the hunter should introduce gunfire as part of the fun of fetching, so that the pup will associate what he likes to do with the sound of shooting. Four or five months of age is a good time for the pup to be introduced to gunfire in the field. The following method is recommended.

In an open field where cover is not too high and the pup is rustling around about 25 yards (*c.* 20 m) from you, fire a blank shot, aiming away from the pup. When he looks up, startled by the sound, toss whatever it is he likes to fetch, so that he can see it fly and fall. He should go and fetch it to you. Praise him and then toss the object and let him fetch it again. Some time later, when he is again off on his own, repeat the shot-toss-and-retrieve procedure. Then, quit for the day. Subsequently, do this several times each day, making sure that the retrieves are easy.

Repeated lessons in this manner will accustom the pup to gunfire, get him looking for something to retrieve whenever he hears a shot, give him retrieving practice, and prepare him for the time when his first bird is shot over him.

Introducing Flushing Dogs to Game

The ideal way to show a young dog what hunting is all about is to take him on walks in good game cover and to allow his natural instincts free rein. Encourage him to find game and to flush and chase it. Once this love of starting game birds is imbued in the pup, the training that brings him under control and makes him a manageable and useful hunter will not adversely affect either his desire to start birds or his hunting style.

A more contrived way to introduce your spaniel or retriever to game does not even require a real bird. You can use the wing-wrapped dummies of the type that the pup is by now used to fetching. "Plant"

several dummies in cover when the pup is not looking at you. Toss them some distance from where you have walked, so that he does not get into the habit of trailing your foot scent to the dummies. Be sure that you remember where you have planted them, so that you can "steer" the pup to them, when necessary. He has to learn to rely on your judgment. If you direct and encourage him properly, he will pick up the basic hand signals and will develop a close-working, quartering pattern at the same time.

When the dummies are down, start the pup about 25 yards (*c.* 20 m) from the first one, working him into the wind. Depending on his mood and temperament, let him scamper or nose about in front of you, as you gradually work toward the dummy. No one has yet solved the vagaries of scent, so be patient, even when he gets very close to the dummy but fails to smell it. Later on, you can push him at a brisk hunting pace, so that he learns not to dawdle, but take your time now.

When he winds the dummy, he will go and pounce on it, picking it up and returning it to you when you tell him, "Fetch!" After all, this is a familiar object that he has been fetching for months. Now praise him. If he is confused because he has not seen it thrown, he may not pick it up. In that event, put your toe under the dummy and flip it up into the air. He should then chase and grab it. Turn, trot away from him, and tell him, "Fetch!"—and he will come after you with the dummy. If he does not, pick it up and excite him by waving it in front of him and then toss it, telling him to fetch it. He will make the retrieve and, eventually, grasp the idea that any birdy thing that he stumbles on in the field should be caught and fetched.

When you have trained him to go out, locate, and fetch the dummy, you can substitute it with live or freshly killed birds. Do not just drop a dead bird in cover, because, until the pup knows that he is supposed to retrieve dead birds, he may refuse to pick it up. Once he has been shot over, plant live, unfettered birds (pigeons or pen-reared game birds) and let him flush them. Then shoot them and have him retrieve.

Some pups, due either to their age or temperament, need to be introduced with care to their first birds, dead or alive, and they must be encouraged, should they show hesitation. Some pups balk at warm birds. Some ignore cold, long-dead ones and, occasionally, are intimidated by a live bird's movements and flapping wings.

One method to help a timid pup surmount his fear is to use a clipped-wing pigeon cast out on a lawn. The pup that is otherwise reluctant to take live feathers in his mouth will often find this exciting and will run down and grab the bird. A very reluctant pup that will not grab a bird on land will often swim after and catch one that is cast a bit out from the shore of a still pond.

However, most well-bred pups are eager to capture their first bird, particularly if the transition from dummy to real bird has been made over a dummy with wings taped to it. If your pup is not, and if the exciting,

coaxing methods mentioned do not eventually overcome this problem, then discard him.

Mention of swimming brings up the point that all spaniels and retrievers are expected to retrieve from water as well as on land, as are some of the pointing breeds. Teaching pups to take to water and to swim is not very difficult. Some bold pups just plunge in directly and swim by instinct. Wade into shallow water in warm weather with more timid pups, and they will soon get plenty of confidence and start swimming.

Another way to acquaint your pup with water is to toss the dummy into puddles or shallow ponds. He will wade out and pick it up just as he did on land. Get him going gradually deeper until he has to swim a few strokes to get to the dummy. Increase the length of the retrieves until he can swim as far as you can throw the dummy.

As a finale to his water training, shoot some pigeons or pen-reared game birds over water and let him fetch them. If he does this without problem, you can be sure that, when you shoot a duck or when an upland bird drops into a water-filled ditch or across a stream, your dog will know what he has to do and will recover the downed game.

Training a Pointer

There is considerable disagreement among hunters about some of the more technical aspects of pointer performance; there is also some minor quibbling about the basics. However, it is generally agreed that hunting dogs that are expected to point, rather than flush, game should diligently seek game birds at distances beyond gun range, should point the birds, remain staunch (also called "stanch") on point (at least until the hunter gets close enough to get off a shot, and preferably until the birds have been flushed by the hunter), and, after the shot, should pick up or "point dead" any bird knocked down.

Pointing breeds cannot be started in as artificial a manner as flushing dogs, although they can be taught to retrieve with training dummies and dead birds. However, the use of flying birds is essential to a pointer's education. If wild game birds are not available, pigeons or pen-reared birds will do.

If you hunt often in good game country and are willing to treat a dog's first hunting season primarily as training time, then you may be able to develop a useful pointer without having to resort to too many formal and mechanical training methods.

The instinct to point should be as strong in the well-bred pointing pup as the pick-up-and-carry instinct in the well-bred flushing pup. A pup should not have to be taught to point, but he must learn that, once in the pointing posture, he must hold it until the birds are flushed or he is ordered on. If the hunter shoots only those birds that he himself has flushed and consistently refuses to shoot birds his dog has flushed by jumping in and putting them to flight, the dog will learn that, when he points, he must hold that point until the hunter comes up to flush the

birds. If the hunter can get a young dog into plenty of birds and consistently show him that he is to point and not to flush, the pup will soon learn to remain staunch on point, without having to go through a staunching program, which involves restraint with a check cord (a length of rope attached to the dog's collar and jerked to make him remain on point when he shows signs of breaking).

"Shoot only when the dog does right," is a good rule to follow at all times, even with a dog that has been taught staunchness with the aid of a check rope.

"Whoa!" is the most important command a pointer must learn to obey. An effective means of teaching a pup that "Whoa!" means "stop, cease all motion, and stand right there" involves food. At feeding time, set the dog's food in front of him, say "Whoa!", and restrain him with your hands. When you say, "Okay!" or "All right!" or whatever release command you prefer, pat the pup's head and allow him to eat. A variation of this is to use morsels of food when you are out in the yard exercising and playing with the pup. This gentle restraint in play training can begin as early as twelve weeks of age.

An alternative method of teaching a pointer pup what "Whoa!" means is to use the check cord during his yard training, when you teach him to retrieve. Once he is excited about fetching a thrown dummy, put the cord on his collar and prevent him from chasing the dummy when you command, "Whoa!" Once he settles down and stands relatively quiet, release him, wave your arms in the direction you have thrown the dummy, and tell him, "Fetch!"

It is important that the pup knows what "Whoa!" means before he goes out in the field, because if you have to use the check cord to discipline him to stand staunch, you will be using it because he disobeyed your "Whoa!", a learned command, and not because he went for the birds. A pup should never get the idea that the birds are the cause of the unpleasant interruption of his chase. If he does, he may well become a "blinker," a dog that deliberately avoids game or backs off from it once he has found it.

The first time you take your pup out hunting, you will discover how well he can adapt what he has learned in training to the realities of the field. When he establishes a point, order him to stand staunch with a "Whoa!" and move in to flush and shoot the bird. If he obeys and stays until you have put the bird up, shoot it and order him to fetch it. You may never have to resort to the check cord. However, if he breaks and chases the bird, do not shoot. Wait until he comes back; then, stand him on the spot where he established the point, restrain him with your hands, and stroke and praise him before releasing him. From then on, use the check cord. The next time he points, stand on the end of the cord while you lay down your gun. Then, take the cord and move up to him, encouraging him to stand by saying, "Whoa!" If he does stand, praise him. Have a shooting companion move in, flush the bird, and shoot it.

Release the dog and let him fetch it. Give him a lot of praise when he does.

However, if he breaks, as you have anticipated, hold onto the check cord and, when he reaches the other end, pull him back sharply, shouting, "Whoa!" It will not take too many sharp snaps or backward tippings to convince him that you mean what you say when you say, "Whoa!" When he shows willingness to remain staunch on point, run him without the cord. If he defies you again, bring back the cord immediately.

A consistent use of reward (stroking, praise, and shooting birds for him when he does it right) and punishment (use of the check cord, and not shooting when he does it wrong) will produce, after a few days of hunting, a staunch-pointing dog. The check-cord procedure can also be used to train your dog to the niceties of "backing" (honoring the find of another dog by stopping when the dog is seen on point) and "steadiness to wing and shot" (remaining stationary when flushed birds are flying and being shot at, and moving out to retrieve only on command).

Patterns and Control

When you first take out your spaniel or retriever pup, you can stroll casually about and let him amble around on his own. However, by the time the pup is four or five months old, you should avoid aimless wandering about. Instead, set a zigzag course as you would when hunting. Check out likely looking cover, encouraging the pup to poke into it and investigate it. When he finds birds, or dummies that you have planted there, he will come to trust your judgment, and he will also start hunting on his own.

As the pup starts doing this, call his name or blow a couple of blasts on a whistle when you change direction. When he looks at you, wave in the new direction and urge him to cross in front of you, so that he works out in front and to the sides of the direction in which you are heading.

If his vim and vigor prompt him to hunt out beyond gun range, turn him with a whistle or a voice command, or call him in to you and make him walk heel for a minute or two. Then, cast him off again and proceed in the zigzag hunting pattern. In time, he will realize that he can hunt with abandon as long as he stays within the set limitations, but that if he persists in kiting off, he will be punished by being made to walk heel, when he could be out investigating all those interesting scents.

A pointing dog can also be taught to work in a close quartering pattern within or at the extreme edge of gun range. The dock-tailed breeds, such as the Brittany spaniel and the German shorthair, are particularly good at learning this, and they specialize in working close to the gun in dense cover.

However, the proper hunting style for a pointer involves casting out well beyond gun range and making loops to the front and sides of the hunter, rather than casting out in a controlled, almost windshield-wiper pattern. Casting out beyond range allows a dog to hunt more independently. However, he must always be near enough to hear whistles and shouts from the hunter, who may want him to change direction or to check out some piece of likely cover.

A When training a young hound to pick up a scent, you will often have to find a line, either real or artificial, for him and point it out, urging him to follow it.
B Weather, ground conditions, and the length of time game spends in a place dictate how strong the scent will be. (1) A weak scent is left by a hare running on stony ground. (2) A stronger scent is left if it runs on grass. (3) The strongest scent would be left if it sat on the grass for a time.

C Teaching the hound perseverance. If, on one of his first hunting days, the hound flushes a hare and follows but loses it on a stony road, make him search along either side of the road, forward and back, encouraging him to seek the scent. Hare often use the "stony-road trick" to lose pursuers, but if the hound perseveres, he will find where the hare swung back on to soft ground again. (Inset) If the hare is finally shot, reward the hound by letting him nose the body properly, to show him the results of a good chase.

C

When you have your pointer pup out in the field, swinging along in front of you, and you want him to change direction, pick a time when he seems to be about to make a direction change of his own or is about to make a break in his cast—that is, a time when he is not concentrating and is amenable to a "suggestion" from you. Alert him with a couple of whistle blasts or shout an appropriate command like "Come round!" or "Get over!" Then, angle off the course you have been walking and wave your arm in the new direction. If you have been out often with your pup, the chances are good that he will swing over as you wish.

If he fails to respond, keep at it. Eventually, he will get the idea, particularly if you guide him in this way to productive bird cover or to where you have planted some birds. When he is hunting as he should, leave him alone and follow along. Too much shouting or whistling will be ignored or will make him totally dependent on you.

To ensure that a dog of any breed will hunt for you, will keep track of you while you are in the field, and will be responsive to your voice, whistle, or hand signals, it is important that you are friends with the dog and that you have been taking him out into the field from a very early age.

Start when the pup is about two months old. Frequent walks in natural cover from the time he can toddle will not just accustom him to the hunting field, it will also help him to connect his handler with these enjoyable outings. It is good practice to hide on him occasionally, so that he must find you. His apprehension at being left alone in the world will make him keep an eye on you. This hide-and-seek game, played once or twice on every outing, instills in him the habit of paying heed to your whereabouts and of quickly seeking you when contact is lost.

Two Important Rules

Success in training a hunting dog will be more certain if two important rules are kept in mind.

1. There is no way actually to teach a dog to hunt. A dog must be a natural hunter to be worth training. If he lacks the instinct, the desire, the nose, the brain, or the stamina, the best training in the world will not make him a hunter. Very good dogs more or less teach themselves. They are born knowing how to find birds. However, they are of no use to the hunter unless the qualities they are born with can be controlled in such a way that game is produced for the gun and, once shot, is recovered.

2. Dogs that respond immediately to training techniques are extremely rare. There is no such thing as the instant hunting dog. Dogs learn chiefly by repetition, by doing something over and over in drills in which good behavior is rewarded and bad behavior punished. No dog will be trained in any one phase of his work in just a single session. Even those that catch on quickly will require repetition to ensure that the desired response will always be forthcoming. Slow developers will certainly try the patience of the trainer, but, eventually, they will respond to persistently applied training techniques.

There are several things a gun dog must learn to do, however, that are not directly connected to retrieving or pointing and which must be taught mechanically and by rote. These are the proper responses to the commands, "Sit!", "Stay!", "Heel!", "Kennel!", and a few basic hand and whistle signals.

Sit and Stay

Teaching a pointing dog to sit and stay is optional training and may be eschewed by those who fear that it will complicate training or interfere with style. "Whoa!" is the pointing-dog equivalent of ensuring that the dog will stay put, but in a standing position.

For retrievers and spaniels, the procedure is the following. The trainer places his left hand flush against the juncture of the pup's neck and chest, preventing him from moving ahead. The pup's hips are then straddled by the right thumb and forefinger, and when the command "Sit!" is given, squeeze them and push down. This forces the pup into a sitting position. Repeat this half-a-dozen times per session, praising him each time he "obeys." First, he will resist a little before sitting; then, he will sit on command only. Once he has learned this, give the command, blow one sharp blast on a whistle, raising an arm above your head. Soon, he will respond to any of the three signals—voice, whistle, or arm—that mean "sit" to him.

To teach him to hold the sitting position until you give him permission to move, hold him for a few seconds and then slowly back off, keeping your arm upraised and cautioning him to continue to sit by saying, "Siiit!" or "Staaay!" Should he move before you say, "All right!" or "Okay!", reposition him and go through the same procedure. Gradually, he will hold longer, until you can leave him and he will not move until you tell him to.

This can be taught to a pup as young as two or three months, or you can drill it into a mature dog of any age.

Heel

Teaching a pup to walk quietly at your side (to "heel") can be done when he is six months of age. In preparation for this training, the pup should have got used to having a collar and to walking on a loose lead.

Use a slip chain collar with attached leash. When the pup surges ahead, jerk his head back and say, "Heel!" When he lags behind, jerk him forward. Pull him to you when he strays to the side. Precede each jerk with a command, "Heel!" He must learn that his position is alongside your leg. When bringing him into that position, do it with a sharp tug on the collar. Do not apply sustained pressure. When the pup walks alongside you for a few paces, praise him. Stop and order him to sit. Praise him and fuss over him. Start walking again and order him to heel. When he has heeled passably for half a minute or so, unsnap the leash, give him the release command, and allow him to cavort and play.

When he has got his confidence back, snap the leash on and heel him some more. In every five- or ten-minute session, you should take plenty of breaks. The pup will learn that, if he responds to the heel command, he can walk comfortably at your side.

When he is heeling correctly on leash, unobtrusively snap off the leash and, as he continues to heel correctly off the leash, praise him. If he breaks or lags, command him sharply to heel. If he does not, remind him what you mean by using the leash again and sharply jerking the collar.

Kennel

This is the command normally given to a dog to tell him to get in to something, be it his kennel, a car, a boat, a travel crate, or whatever. Of course, you do not have to use "Kennel!"—some people say, "Get in!" or "Load up!"

Every time you want your pup to enter something, hold him with one hand, point to the entrance with the other, snap out, "Kennel!", and scruff-of-the-neck and seat-of-the-pants him into it. Soon, when you point and say, "Kennel!", he will run or jump into virtually anything you indicate.

Hand and Whistle Signals

The hand and whistle signals that a hunting dog needs to know for practical work in the field are few and can be easily taught. Training dogs for the various signals used in field trials is a more difficult and time-consuming job.

An upraised arm and a single whistle blast indicate to a dog that he should halt, sit, and await further orders.

A series of short blasts call the dog to the hunter. This may be used alone or in conjunction with "Here!" or "Come!"

While learning hunting patterns in the field, as previously described, the dog will have learned that a wave of the arm is a command to go to a spot you want hunted, or to change direction. To get a dog to hunt out the area of a fall to retrieve a bird that he has not marked, the following method is effective.

Hide a bird or a dummy in cover and bring the pup near to it, telling him, "Hunt them out!" , and making a hand gesture toward the cover. With repeated finding of game when he responds to this gesture and command, the dog will soon learn to hunt out any area you tell him to, producing game or recovering dead or winged birds that would otherwise be lost.

Chapter 3

The Mountain Horse

Erwin Bauer

In prehistoric Europe and Asia, man tamed wild horses and used them to pursue game and carry it, and he had done this long before the wheel was invented. By the twelfth century, Genghis Khan, an ardent hunter, was employing horses, asses, camels, buffaloes, and yaks for his hunting expeditions. To this day, yaks are used by some few Argali hunters in the mountains of Central Asia. Both bactrian and dromedary camels are probably still used for hunting—illegally in most instances—disappearing desert species in Africa and Asia; until recently, legal camel safaris were available for hunting in northern Kenya.

Until only a few years ago, elephants were commonly used in big-game hunting in India, Burma, and Nepal, and mahouts—those who trained and cared for the elephants—devoted almost their entire lives to their tasks. A well-trained elephant would not flinch from the charge of a rhino. Hunters rode in state in howdahs, while other elephants were used to drive the game. Tigers were among the most popular quarry, but many other animals were shot, including one-horned rhino and sambar deer. Such hunts could be extravagantly elaborate, with hundreds of elephants and thousands of servants taking part. Elephants are still employed for camera safaris in a few Asian national parks—Chitwan, Manas, and Kaziranga are examples—but the era of trophy hunting from elephant howdahs is a thing of the past.

In parts of Asia, horses and mules, and sometimes asses, are still used (though less extensively than formerly) to transport hunters and their guides' paraphernalia: equipment, supplies, and trophies. In the western parts of North America, the use of horses is thriving, even in remote areas which can be reached from the outside world only by pontoon-equipped "bush" planes. The mountain horses, as they are known, are of no particular breed but are selected for their ability to carry packs, to bear riders, and to negotiate mountainous terrain. Remarkably sure-footed for horses, they are surpassed in this respect only by mules, which are also often used together with mountain horses. Working together in "strings," these animals are made available to hunters by guides and outfitters who play the same role in North America as professional white hunters do in Africa.

Horses are also used in the deer forests of Scotland, but their use there is confined to carrying the shot deer back to a track which is negotiable by motor vehicle. As indicated above, however, it is in western North America that the use of the horse as a hunting ally is most highly developed. Horses—and mules—are used on high-altitude trails from Mexico northward through the United States and Canada to Alaska. Such trails as exist are often not wide enough for vehicles, and many of the streams can be crossed only by horses and mules. If the terrain is too steep for riding, the brush too thick, or the obstacles too numerous and difficult, the horses and mules can usually be led. Beyond these immediate considerations, the animals do not damage the environment as vehicles and roads would do.

A mountain horse in good condition can carry a rider or an evenly distributed load on a pack saddle for extraordinary distances, even on

(Above) The mountain horse is a short-necked, deep-girthed, large-barreled animal with well-defined withers and a low croup. The back and loins must be short, straight, and strong. The horse should have well-developed hindquarters, and the legs must be straight and strong.
(Below) (1) The Decker pack saddle was specially developed for mountain horses. (a) Back straps. (b) Hip pad. (c) Hip straps. (d) Breeching. (e) Soft leather binding. (f) Connecting straps. (g) Canvas-pad pocket. (h) Canvas-pad pack board. (i) Cinch. (j) Breast collar. (k) Breast-collar rigging. (l) Canvas pad. (m) Right bar. (n) Steel hoops.
(2) Canvas pannier. (3) Leather halter with leading chain.

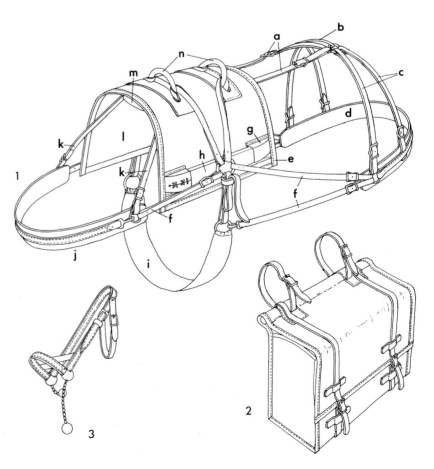

Leading heavily loaded pack horses. The rider keeps the lead rope in one hand, while the pack horses are tied to each other, head to tail. The landscape is typical of the high country of western North America.

A Details of a common pack saddle. *(a)* Bucks. *(b)* Rigging. *(c)* Breast collar. *(d)* Connecting straps. *(e)* Back straps. *(f)* Hip straps. *(g)* Breeching. *(h)* Latigos. *(i)* Cinches.

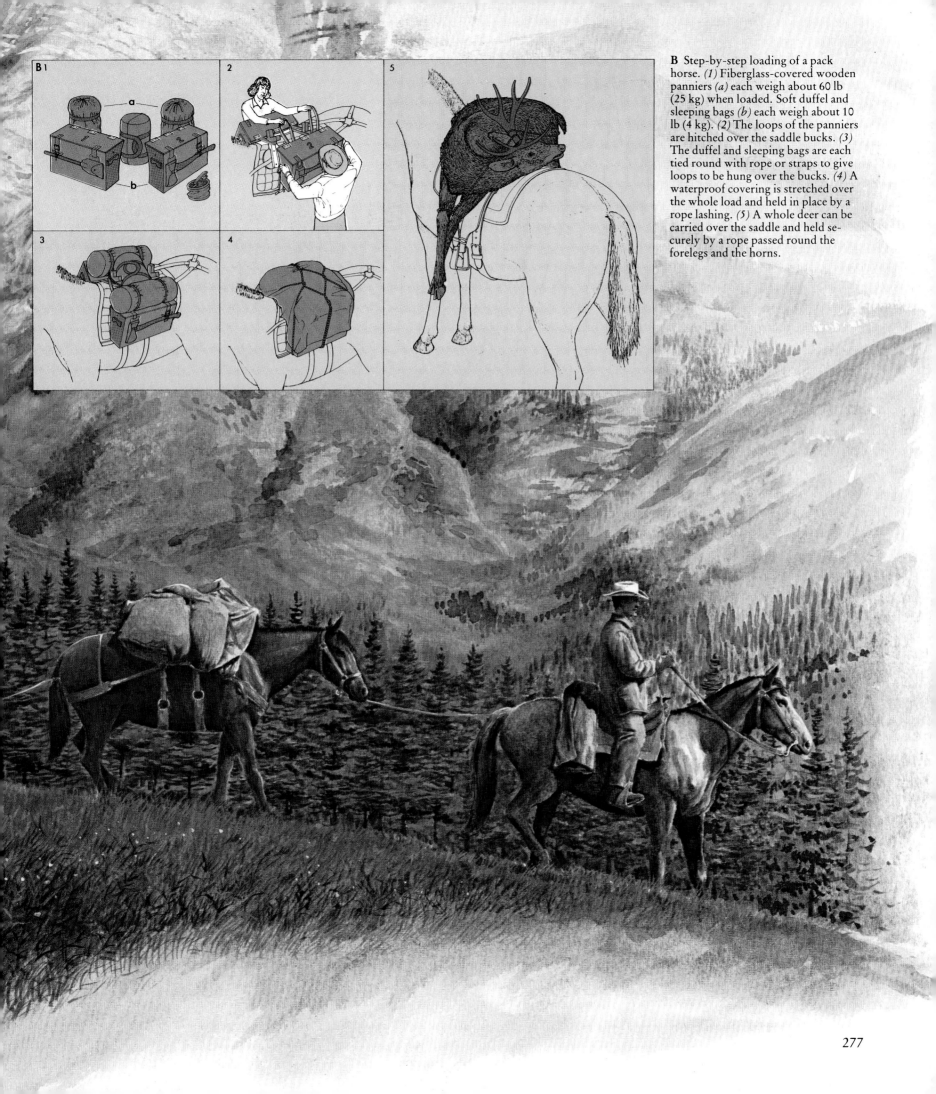

B Step-by-step loading of a pack horse. *(1)* Fiberglass-covered wooden panniers *(a)* each weigh about 60 lb (25 kg) when loaded. Soft duffel and sleeping bags *(b)* each weigh about 10 lb (4 kg). *(2)* The loops of the panniers are hitched over the saddle bucks. *(3)* The duffel and sleeping bags are each tied round with rope or straps to give loops to be hung over the bucks. *(4)* A waterproof covering is stretched over the whole load and held in place by a rope lashing. *(5)* A whole deer can be carried over the saddle and held securely by a rope passed round the forelegs and the horns.

B1

2

5

3

4

a

b

poor trails. While 30 miles (50 km) in a day can be achieved, 20 to 25 miles (30 to 40 km) is much closer to normal, and an inexperienced rider cannot spend longer in the saddle without torturing himself.

By normal horse-judging standards, most mountain horses are not very attractive, being hairy, squat, and even slovenly looking, yet their outfitter or rancher will have selected them by breeding or by trial and error. In this way a type of horse has developed that is unsurpassed for carrying hunters, equipment, food, game meat, and trophies in the mountains, but it bears no more than a superficial resemblance to injury-prone racing and trotting animals. In the same way, the ponies used by the nineteenth-century Plains Indians developed their ideal characteristics long after their ancestors had been introduced into North America by the Spaniards, but the Indians would not have worried about the animals' ancestry. Like the Indians, the outfitter is more interested in performance than bloodlines.

The mountain horse's physical characteristics are plain enough. A good fully-grown mountain horse weighs about 1,200 lb (544 kg), more than that when the hunting season opens and significantly less when it ends. The animal has a large "barrel" body with a deep chest and a short heavy neck, its withers should be well-defined, and its back and loins short, straight, and well-muscled, with no sagging. The hindquarters are powerful for climbing, and its feet are large in proportion to its size and weight, and are tough, too. Its legs are straight and strong. Altogether, it is a creature with strength and endurance, but it is neither speedy nor graceful.

The good mountain horse is incredibly tough and can survive not only the intense cold that usually occurs some time during every hunting season, but also the heat of summer. It can plow through snow or bogs, plod up slopes steep enough to defy many a man on foot, and swim rivers fully loaded. Whether carrying a man or 300 lb (136 kg) of supplies, it is extremely surefooted (although many outfitters feel that mules are even more so). Furthermore, the good mountain horse is adaptable and can carry either a man or a loaded pack, and do either with very little rest.

Some mountain horses can be sullen or balky at times and may have strange quirks that can disconcert riders who are not used to them. For example, a horse may form a strong attachment—what can best be called a friendship—for another horse in the string, and separating them can cause trouble. On the other hand, the horse may develop an equally strong dislike for another horse, and the wise owner will then keep them separated.

Many mountain horses have an uncanny ability to sense the presence of game. Their eyesight, hearing, and sense of smell are many times more acute than those of human beings. For this reason, good guides pay close attention to their horses' behavior. Although a horse may shy away from, or in rare instances even panic at, the faint scent of a bear or a cougar, it may not seem even to notice a mule deer, an elk, or a moose that is discernible on a distant slope. However, an experienced guide will detect from the horse's "body language"—its ear movements, for example, or the direction in which it is looking—that there is game out there. This kind of "radar" is invaluable to the guide.

Because a mountain horse will be handled by many hunters, some of whom may be unfamiliar with horses, it should be friendly and gentle, and not fearful or suspicious of people. A nervous horse is not suitable for a novice, whom it would make even more unsure, but can better be used to pack cargo. Some horses are better than others at picking a way through difficult ground, but whether this is a matter of intelligence is debatable. Professional hunters cannot afford to keep horses that are not sure-footed and easy-riding for "dudes"—client hunters—on rocky or uneven trails. But one thing is certain of even the most stupid horse: it cannot get lost, even in unfamiliar terrain, and all a hunter who thinks himself lost has to do is to stay mounted and give his horse its head, and it will invariably find its way back to camp or its home base.

Even the finest mountain horse must be trained and broken to saddle, and some horses take more readily than others to training. The first step is to teach the animal to lead on a halter rope, easily and willingly. Next is teaching it to stop when tied to a tree or post, or when its halter rope is dropped. It must get used to being hobbled—having its forelegs tied together to prevent it from wandering too far from camp while grazing. And, of course, it must get accustomed to a Western riding saddle and to the various types of pack saddle, loaded and unloaded.

For some horses, accepting a rider in the saddle is the most difficult part of training, and reaction to this can be violent; a few horses never become really at ease with a rider, but most do, and they become very realiable riding animals.

Most of the best mountain horses are owned either by full-time professional hunting outfitters (or guides) or by working ranchers who escort sportsmen during the hunting season. Some of the owners naturally are better than others, and some have better horses than others, just as an outfitter may have anything from a few horses—for small parties and custom trips—to a hundred or more. The ambitious outfitter will continually weed out poor animals and replace them by better, and will not hesitate to acquire mules when he can find good ones.

Much effort is needed to prepare horses for the open hunting season. They have first to be exposed to rifle fire, and other loud, sudden noises,

The mountain horse is tough.
Although not very graceful, it is sure
on its feet on all kinds of terrain, even
when crossing a wild torrent, as
shown here.
(Inset) *(1)* How to pack the front
quarters of a large deer. The dotted
line shows how the hind quarters
would be packed. *(2)* How to carry
deer (or caribou or moose) antlers.

so that they will not be startled when out hunting. But no horse, however well trained, can be expected to stand still when a hunter shoots from the saddle. Few horses are calm when exposed to the scent of bear, so they have to be trained to carry bear skins and other trophies without giving trouble.

Packing and rigging a horse may seem a simple task when an expert guide is doing it, but it is a difficult art, and fascinating to understand. Moreover, a hunter who learns to help will add to his own enjoyment, and will not only earn the respect and liking of his guide—a valuable asset in itself—but also will be able to cope in an emergency. While the hunter may have to learn to knot, lash, and hitch with nylon och other synthetic ropes, he will remember that the art of packing is very old: Hannibal and Marco Polo used pack animals to cross some of the highest mountain ranges in the world, and in North America, beaver hunters, explorers, cavalrymen, and even missionaries have had to pack all they needed on the backs of their horses.

Pack saddles are usually small sawbucks or saddle trees roughly shaped to fit the horse's blanketed back. The saddle is held in place by wide cinches—originally a Spanish term for a saddle-girth, usually of twisted horsehair—strapped tightly round the horse's stomach. A breast collar in front and a breaching in back help to keep the saddle from shifting backward or forward. A pannier, luggage box, or bag is hung on either side of the saddle and balanced. Gear is then put into the panniers, and also on top of them when they are filled, and the entire load is then covered with a waterproof mantey cloth.

The art of packing is to balance the load on either side of the horse, and then to secure it so firmly that it cannot shift on even the roughest, steepest trails. If the load is unbalanced, the horse will be, and the twisting caused by an uneven load will eventually injure the horse or at least make it balk. In North America, the best big-game hunting is to be had in the remotest and most rugged areas with often severe weather, so the packing must meet the demands this imposes.

The outward stage of a hunting trip is the least demanding, for the gear can be loaded carefully and adjusted before setting out, and a wise hunter will allow for an extra day of "packing-in" to get accustomed to the country, to his saddle horse, and to all the routines of using pack animals. The homeward stage can be more difficult, especially if the hunter has been successful and is bringing home trophies, meat, hides, and skins which are not just heavy and irregular in size, but nothing that any horse likes to have near it.

A typical, strong mountain horse can—when trained—carry a field-dressed deer, a black bear, a mountain sheep, or a goat, but two horses are needed to carry an elk, a caribou, or a moose; if a heavy moose bull is to be carried, three horses are better than two.

Just as the horses must be trained before the season, the wise hunter knows that he too must train to get into the good condition that the lofty altitudes and rough terrain demand. He will want to trim off excess fat, increase his stamina by climbing and jogging, and—if he intends to ride a mountain horse for 20 or 25 miles (30 to 40 km) a day in the mountains— he will do as much riding beforehand as possible, and perhaps remember the old sound piece of advice: "The best thing for the inside of a man is the outside of a horse."

VII Conservation

Chapter 1

Modern Trends in Game Management

Richard F. LaRocco

A Burning heather on the Scottish grouse moors is known as "muirburn" and is an important aspect of grouse management. The young shoots that grow out of the fertilizing ashes provide the grouse with its favorite food.
B In winter, when the snow is so deep that deer cannot reach the grass, felled saplings provide them with food.

Conservation is an overused word today. Politicians, environmentalists, oil-company executives, housewives, and even schoolchildren talk of conservation—of the world's forests, its energy resources, its farmlands, its wildlife. To the average person, however, conservation means nothing more than making a resource last longer by reducing consumption of it. Yet it signifies much more, particularly to the sport hunter.

Conservation is more than simply preservation. It is wise *management*. And in the case of wildlife resources, it is the management of a supply of riches that will never end if cared for properly. An oil well, once partially drained, never fills again. A copper mine, once relieved of a single ounce of its metal, is reduced permanently. But a healthy, properly managed game population can supply man with meat and recreation, hide or feathers, for generations—forever. Wildlife is a renewable resource—a replenishable resource. As such, it is one of man's most valuable possessions and one of his most priceless treasures.

In Britain and Europe, with a conservation record many times longer than any in Africa, Asia, or the New World, landowners and gamekeepers have long been motivated by purely practical considerations, and recently, they have been joined by scientists in protecting this self-replacing wealth by further improving the art of wildlife management. Its practitioners have various objectives. Sometimes, their only purpose is to promote a particular species, to increase its numbers. This is often the case with rare or endangered animals, which are encouraged to multiply to lessen the threat of extinction. Sometimes, wildlife is managed to provide recreation, not only for those who shoot, but also for those who observe, such as bird-watchers and wildlife photographers. Most game birds and mammals are managed with human recreation in mind. Game animals, of course, also provide meat and often income for governments, landowners, tour operators, hunting guides, lodge and hotel owners, and others. Frequently, much of the revenue generated by the recreational use of wildlife is used to support and promote the wildlife. Sometimes, the only objective of wildlife management is to control: when red deer invade farms in parts of Europe or when waterfowl by the thousand sweep into the southern Canadian grainfields, their numbers must be controlled or crops will be destroyed.

Wildlife management is nothing new. Egyptian nobles hunted for sport, and it is likely that they reserved certain game species and choice hunting areas for their own use. In Europe, royal forest preserves have existed for a least twelve centuries. Genghis Khan restricted the kill of certain animals in short supply. American Indians used fire to promote the growth of deer browse long before the white man set foot in the New World in the fifteenth century.

Modern conservation had its start round another fire—a campfire deep in the wilds of North America's Yellowstone Valley in 1870. Round its flames were gathered a group of Montana citizens, who had organized an expedition into the region after having heard rumors of the Yellowstone Valley's natural wonders. The sight of these features was even more

A

B

C Specially contructed bird-feeding shelters like this can help upland birds to survive a harsh winter, when the cold and the snow make it impossible for them to find food.
D Branches from deciduous trees, stuck in snow, provide winter fodder for small game, such as hare and rabbit.

inspiring and incredible than these men had thought possible. Though the explorers could have claimed the land under United States law and exploited it for their own profit, they decided that the Yellowstone region was too wondrous to be held in private hands. Talking round the campfire that September night, they decided to give the region to the people of the United States, giving birth to the idea of the world's first national park. Congress set aside Yellowstone National Park in 1872 as a "public park or pleasuring ground for the benefit and enjoyment of the people."

Soon, other parks were created: Yosemite and Sequoia in California, 1890; Mount Rainier in Washington, 1899; Crater Lake in Oregon, 1902; Wind Cave in South Dakota, 1903; Mesa Verde in Colorado, and Platt in the Territory of Oklahoma, 1906. The idea quickly spread to other nations. By 1920, there were sixteen parks in the United States, and parks were created in Argentina, Sweden, Switzerland, Canada, New Zealand, Australia, and Yugoslavia. The movement continued to spread until, by 1939, there were parks in Africa, Asia, Russia, and eastern Europe.

The existence of these preserves is credited with the saving of many wildlife species. Even today, game animals are trapped in national parks and moved to areas where the game has been extirpated. Many of the now-vigorous elk (wapiti) herds in the western United States, for instance, are descended from Yellowstone stock.

Governmental agencies were created or assigned to manage these new preserves, and many additional lands were set aside for wildlife. But wildlife management was still an embryonic science, and the agencies made many mistakes. Predators, long feared and hated for their occasional intrusions into human efforts, were destroyed by the thousand. This resulted in a tremendous increase of prey species, but because hunting was thought to contradict the purpose of a wildlife preserve in many cases, the animals were allowed to multiply. Yellowstone's elk became so numerous that, during the severe winter of 1919–20, more than 20,000 died. There were simply too many animals on the range. During the winter of 1961–62, trained park personnel killed more than 4,000 elk to bring the herd down to a level compatible with the range. Despite occasional grumblings from hunters, guides, and outfitters, park policy still does not allow hunting within Yellowstone's boundaries.

The elk controversy illustrates a basic tenet of conservation as we know it today. Nature operates in a balance as delicate as that of a fine Swiss watch. When man in all his ignorance pries it open and gropes about in its innards, discarding parts at will and damaging its fragile mechanisms, the whole machinery is thrown into disarray. Sometimes, it is so severely damaged that repair is impossible. But there is one major difference between a watch and an environment. Man can make a new watch; he can never replace a wrecked environment.

This lesson has been ignored in too many parts of the world. Even when it has once been learned, it may need to be re-learned when man, prompted by political motives, greed, or simple curiosity, decides to tinker with wildlife and its habitat.

A case in point is the introduction of animals into areas where they have never before been present. This has been going on during the past century at a feverish rate and has usually had tragic consequences. The few successful introductions, such as those of the ring-neck pheasant and the brown trout into North America, seem to receive more attention than the thick history book of out-and-out failures.

The carp, hailed as Europe's wonder fish by the United States government, has so successfully invaded the waters of North America that it has pushed aside valuable native game fish and destroyed much important waterfowl habitat. The proposed introduction into Britain and France of the coho salmon, for example, has caused anxieties about its effects.

The muskrat was introduced into Europe as a valuable fur-bearer, but in most European countries, these North American natives became

A

A In an essentially undisturbed condition, the coniferous forests of northern Scandinavia would, and did, support populations of such animals and birds as *(1)* moose and wolf, *(2)* marten, and *(3)* capercaillie. The forest itself *(4)* had little or no deciduous growth, and its trees grew, aged, fell, and rotted in a centuries-long rhythm *(5)*. The first impact of man was borne by the predators—most of them desired for their furs—and as their numbers fell, conditions grew more and more favorable for an increase in the non-predator population. At present, however, only the moose is thriving, as it is far more adaptable than the marten or the capercaillie, which need primeval-forest conditions before they can flourish.

284

C1

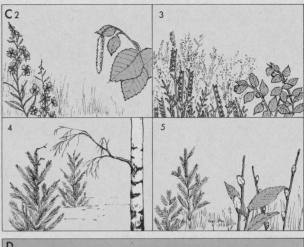

C2

D

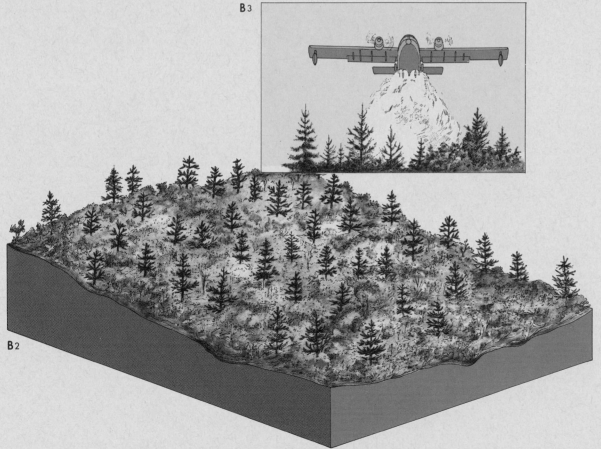

B3

B2

B The modern forestry industry's clear-cutting techniques remove all the trees in an area, and the land so cleared is replanted *(1)* with coniferous seedlings. After a few years, the young conifers are in danger of being crowded out by a rich growth *(2)* of deciduous vegetation—principally birch and aspen—which, together with certain young conifers, provides excellent food for moose. *(3)* Spraying with herbicide keeps the deciduous growth under control.

C *(1)* The moose thrives in the young pine plantations, where it eats the pine and deciduous plants. So great is the damage caused by moose to young pine in some areas that foresters are changing over to spruce, which the moose in those areas do not find so tasty. The moose's diet varies throughout the year: *(2)* in summer, it eats fireweed, willow herb, leaves, and grasses; *(3)* in fall, heather; *(4)* in winter, leaves, and shoots of pine and birch; *(5)* in spring, pine shoots and grasses.

D In the absence of the control once exercised by natural predators, the moose population in Sweden is culled annually by the carefully controlled shooting of a fixed number of bulls, cows, and calves. The numbers are based on census takings for each region.

A Finding out about an animal's habits, range, etc. is an important part of game management. Gathering information scientifically is made more easy by modern methods. *(1)* A wolverine is fitted with a collar bearing a radio transmitter. *(2)* The animal's whereabouts can now be plotted by means of a radio fix. *(3)* In winter, wolverines often run down and kill reindeer. *(4)* The wolverine's track. Although it cannot run fast, it has great stamina. *(5)* Its foot is relatively large and allows the animal to run on the surface of the snow, whereas the reindeer's hoof *(6)* plunges through the snow when it runs, and it soon becomes exhausted, falling prey to the wolverine.

anything but valuable: they tunneled into railroad and bridge embankments, dikes, and ditches, and the authorities spent a fortune on trying in vain to destroy these pests. Another introduction from North America, less than a century ago, was that of the gray squirrel; at home, it occupied its own ecological slot, but it developed into a major pest in Britain.

The red deer, though a valuable game animal in Europe, became a pest in New Zealand after several were released there; so much so, in fact, that the government offered free ammunition to anyone who undertook to shoot one.

Mongoose were brought to Jamaica to control rats that were destroying the sugar cane. They controlled them nicely at first, but soon turned their predatory skills onto domestic poultry, land crabs, reptiles, and amphibians.

Yet the animal-moving trend continues. Coho salmon have been found in a Canadian stream that empties into the Atlantic, apparent escapees from a Maine fish farm. Some biologists fear that the cohos, which are natives of the Pacific coast, will compete with and drive out Atlantic salmon, which have been on the downswing for years. New Mexico and Texas are going full steam ahead with introductions of exotic big game, including oryx and Barbary sheep from Africa. Hungarian gray partridge are being hailed as the answer to declining pheasant hunting in the American Midwest.

Wildlife agencies, to be sure, are more careful with their policies than they have been many times in the past. Over much of the world, conservation is being practiced with wisdom and moderation. Wildlife management has developed into a respected, and often exact, science.

The work of the Game Conservancy in Britain is a leading example of organized investigation of game problems and restorative techniques. The Conservancy's experience has been drawn on not only in Britain but throughout Europe, including the Eastern Bloc, and in the Middle East. Game managers work in several ways, often building, but usually repairing damage to, wildlife populations. One of the most important of

their functions is game research. Through it, biologists learn about the animals they want to manage and gain clues that aid them in making intelligent decisions. Such facts as reproductive potential, age and sex structure, food requirements, cover needs, and population trends are vital for the development of a smoothly working management plan. All these facts can indicate, for example, how much hunting can be sustained by a herd of gemsbok, the oryx of southern Africa, before its numbers fall drastically. A game manager needs a rough idea of what percentage of the animal population can be shot without ill effects on the herd as a whole. Then he develops a set of hunting regulations designed to allow an optimal harvest in order to persuade law-makers to set those regulations.

This is the point at which many perfectly good management plans are destroyed. Rule-making bodies often pay little attention to biological facts, preferring to regulate animal numbers for political or economic reasons. At times, law-makers decide that they are qualified to interpret biological findings and wildlife needs; so they set rules based upon their own false notions. This problem has been especially acute in North America.

Over the objections of wildlife biologists, several state legislatures in the United States have prohibited the hunting of female deer—a perfect example of how well-meaning law-makers can overrule politically powerless wildlife agencies. Habitat has been severely reduced during the past few centuries. Therefore, when doe killing is banned, the deer invariably multiply rapidly until the animals are too numerous for their range to support them in good health. Not only do deer starve, but the hungry animals damage their restricted range, sometimes so severely that dozens of years are needed for recovery.

In many parts of the world, agriculturists exert strong influence over game agencies, usually to demand more liberal game laws and, thus, fewer game animals to compete with livestock or to destroy crops. This is the case in much of Africa today and a major reason why elephant stocks

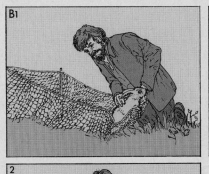

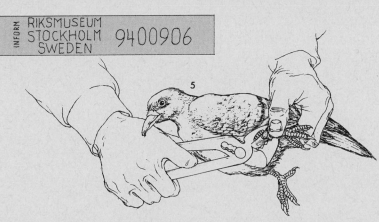

B *(1)* Hares are trapped in nets for marking. *(2)* This hare is being marked with paint on its leg. *(3)* This hare is tagged behind the ears. The tags will be invisible when the hare lays its ears back; predators will not be able to spot it too easily. *(4)* Birds are ringed on the leg with color-coded plastic rings. *(5)* Numbered rings are also used for marking birds. Hunters who shoot a tagged animal or bird should always mail the tags to whoever has carried out the marking.

are declining rapidly. The ponderous pachyderms are destroyed because their tree- and fence-crashing habits are incompatible with the needs of the ever-encroaching farms.

Properly used, however, hunting regulations can result in a maximum supply of game birds and mammals without allowing the resource to be degraded. Several species of ducks produce more juvenile males than juvenile females; yet the birds are seasonally monogamous—they mate with only one duck of the opposite sex. Thus, nature creates a surplus of male ducks—a surplus that can be harvested without resulting in a significant reduction of the next year's duck numbers. This is the underlying reason why hunters in certain areas are allowed to take more drakes than hens of particular species.

Preservation of key wildlife habitat is another game-management tool. How well man cares for and sets aside habitat today will determine to a large degree whether there will be sufficient wildlife to hunt in the future. Habitat preservation takes many forms: national parks, wildlife-management areas, wilderness-designated areas, government-financed leases of private lands, and private lands where development is prohibited by zoning laws. Some tracts of important wildlife land remain simply because they are unrewarding for cultivation or development. Builders frequently avoid flood plains and river bottoms, for instance. Farmers find their work too difficult on rocky, thin soils or on extremely steep slopes.

The tsetse fly, which carries the dreaded sleeping sickness in Africa, spreading it among livestock and humans, deserves credit for preserving many important game ranges. The tsetse has resisted control, and until recently, no vaccination against sleeping sickness existed. The invention of the new vaccine has worried some wildlife observers. If the tsetse is defeated, much game land will be opened to settlement, and some of the last remaining natural African wildlife areas will disappear.

Other important habitat seems secure. Some parts of the Rocky Mountains, for instance, particularly those drainages near population centers, are managed primarily as watersheds. To prevent soil erosion and loss of domestic water supplies, the government allows neither logging nor extensive livestock grazing.

Predator control is another management tool, but one that is not used as much today as it has been in the past. Only in the past few decades has the value of predators been accepted. Wolves, bears, wildcats, and other carnivores have been extirpated in much of the world, notably Europe and the eastern half of the United States. Now, efforts are under way to restore the predators—a plan that meets resistance from citizens who still regard wolves as nothing but cattle killers and bears as man killers. Such opposition notwithstanding, farsighted scientists in Europe are attempting to restock the European lynx into areas where it once existed. Mexico is working to raise the numbers of its native wolf, an endangered species. Just fifteen years ago, mountain lions and black bears were considered vermin in much of North America, but now they are classed as game animals practically everywhere they occur—except where numbers are too low to justify hunting.

Re-introduction of decimated wildlife, incidentally, is a relatively new, and extremely useful, tool of today's wildlife managers. It is used everywhere, from Asia to South America, but is most common in the United States, where the drug-dart was developed to immobilize animals. Biologists there are attempting to restore to former ranges several game mammals, including Rocky Mountain and desert bighorn sheep, pronghorn, and elk. Some mammals are moved to suitable habitat that, because of geographic barriers, never supported those species. Mountain goats have been introduced into the high mountains of Utah's Wasatch range and apparently are increasing. Moose were moved into Colorado in 1977, and reports are that the big deer are taking well to their new range.

Modern civilization is presenting wildlife biologists with new problems that demand solutions. In some parts of the world, road vehicles kill more game animals than hunters do. Conservationists have attacked this problem with enthusiasm but still have a long way to go. By charting road-kill reports, wildlife officers pinpoint trouble spots, and then erect

1

2

A

A In any ecosystem, the number of predators varies with the number of prey. If the latter diminishes, the former's rate of reproduction will decrease, until a balance exists. This is especially marked in areas where the predator's choice of prey is limited; for instance, in the treeless fells on the left of the landscape, the lemming *(1)* is one of the few sources of food available to the fox *(2)*. In a "lemming year," which occurs about every four years, these tiny rodents increase greatly in number. Shortly after, the number of fox cubs born rises sharply. If there is a shortage of lemmings, fewer fox cubs are born. On the lower ground, where the ecosystem consists of a greater number of elements, there are more prey species available, so the fox has a greater choice, and a more even supply of food, for instance field mice—a nest of young is shown *(3)*—rabbits, and ground-nesting birds; here, the variations in the number of cubs born annually is not so great as in the fells above the timberline.

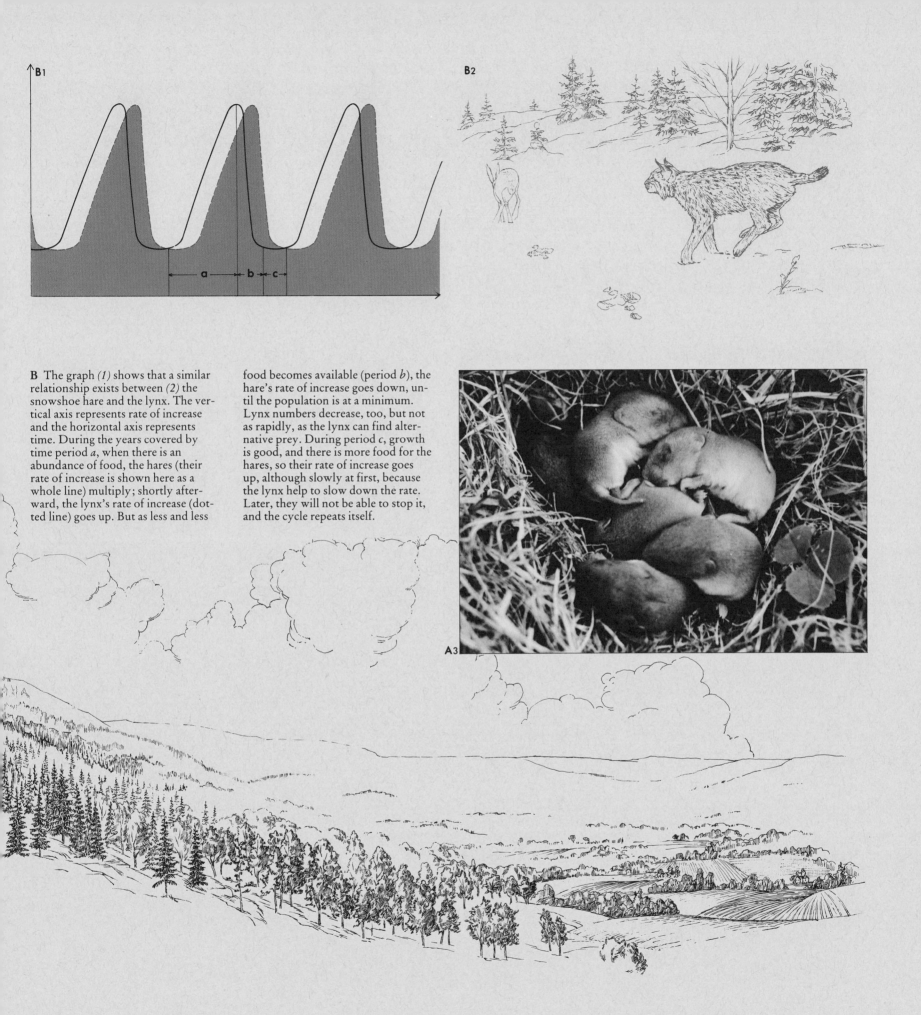

B1

B2

B The graph *(1)* shows that a similar relationship exists between *(2)* the snowshoe hare and the lynx. The vertical axis represents rate of increase and the horizontal axis represents time. During the years covered by time period *a*, when there is an abundance of food, the hares (their rate of increase is shown here as a whole line) multiply; shortly afterward, the lynx's rate of increase (dotted line) goes up. But as less and less food becomes available (period *b*), the hare's rate of increase goes down, until the population is at a minimum. Lynx numbers decrease, too, but not as rapidly, as the lynx can find alternative prey. During period *c*, growth is good, and there is more food for the hares, so their rate of increase goes up, although slowly at first, because the lynx help to slow down the rate. Later, they will not be able to stop it, and the cycle repeats itself.

A3

Every year, thousands of game animals are killed in road accidents, and the cost in human life and suffering is immeasurable. Many areas are now being fenced in, but when this is done, the game will not be able to pass freely from one area (which, perhaps, has become overcrowded) to another, so tunnels under the roads should be built.

signs warning motorists entering deer-crossing areas. In some instances, roadsides can be fenced to keep wildlife away from cars. But that is an expensive and frequently impractical solution. Fences also prevent game animals from migrating—a genuine threat to such creatures as pronghorns and caribou, which must roam over large areas to find sufficient food. Other attempts at reducing road kills have included reflective tape on roadside posts and large tunnels under the roads. The tape reflects the lights of oncoming automobiles, warning deer and other animals that danger is approaching. Tunnels have proved successful in some areas but have failed in others.

Feral dogs and cats are a problem around many populated areas, killing thousands of deer, pheasants, and other wildlife. Conservationists have fought this problem by encouraging laws that prohibit pet owners from allowing their pets to run loose and laws that promote birth control of pets. Most game departments encourage their employees—and often the public—to shoot feral dogs found chasing wildlife.

As game concentrates on the refuges man has set aside for it, the incidence of wildlife disease rises. This has forced wildlife scientists to learn to identify and fight these diseases. Unnatural concentrations of waterfowl frequently cause the birds to fall prey to such maladies as avian cholera and botulism. Though vaccines have been developed, inoculating large numbers of wild birds is out of the question. The solution is prevention, for once an epidemic strikes, thousands of birds can die within hours. To scatter large concentrations of birds, wildlife scientists have used aircraft, noise-making machines, and even hunters. The best method seems to be to eliminate one or more of the flocks' needs—primarily food or water. Often, the food that draws great numbers of waterfowl is man-produced—corn or other grain.

Some large ungulates can become infected with diseases borne by domestic animals. Brucellosis, for instance, can rush through and kill a herd of bison. Often, these large beasts can be trapped and vaccinated.

Other new immunizing techniques are also being tried. In parts of Europe, red foxes are the most common wild carriers of rabies. In an attempt to immunize the foxes, their most heavily used habitat areas are baited with pieces of chicken infused with an oral vaccine. If this experiment proves successful, the technique will surely be adopted in many regions. To reduce diseases among such animals as sheep, fodder laced with drugs is being used at some feeding stations. This is another experiment that seems promising.

But many types of wildlife cannot be given disease-preventing drugs, and so, many countries have passed laws strictly enforcing the examination and quarantining of imported domestic and wild animals.

Environmental pollution is a major conservation problem in modern countries. Though it probably affects game fish even more adversely and directly than game animals, its effects in many areas are extremely serious. Oil spills are bad and common enough, but the use of chemical cleaning agents along affected coastlines is probably no less harmful than the oil itself. One immediate effect of an oil spill is that a waterfowl's feathers, when soaked in oil, lose their insulation ability, and the bird dies unless it is rescued and cleaned. Pesticides and chemical defoliants, less visible but more threatening than oil, have directly killed thousands of birds and small mammals in some countries. The flora and fauna of Vietnam and Cambodia suffered immensely, not only from soldiers' guns, mines, and bombs, but from the defoliants used there to destroy enemy-hiding cover. Pesticides and other pollutants usually affect game animals indirectly. The young of most birds require the high protein found in insects, but areas heavily attacked with insecticides have few insects.

A major trend in game management today is toward intensive habitat manipulation. Ecologists have proved that most game animals prefer ecotones, which are edges between two distinctly different habitats—a forest and a meadow, for example. Ecotones often can be created by the use of fire, bulldozers, irrigation, seeding, or other methods. Such work is expensive and time-consuming but is often valuable, particularly when an increase in small game is the objective. Many of the most important wildlife refuges in the United States are controlled by systems of dikes and dams. By regulating the level of water, a refuge manager can create conditions suitable for the species he wants to increase. Certain kinds of ducks, for example, build their nests over two to three feet (1 m) of water. If the water is allowed to build to that level, those kinds of ducks generally raise their young successfully. Another use of regulating the water level is to control fish. When undesirable fish such as carp spawn in shallows, the water can be lowered to reduce the numbers after the eggs are scattered.

Fire control has only recently come into its own as a tool of wildlife managers, even though it was used by American Indians and has always been an important part of grouse management in Scotland. Many game animals, including most species of deer and upland game birds, are best suited to areas recovering from recent fires.

Fire prevention benefits the forest creatures but results in less habitat for animals that need brush, grass, or young forests. For many years, government agencies in the United States have routinely fought all wildfires, even those set naturally by lightning. Now the value of fire is being realized, though lumber companies and other special interests object strongly when fires are allowed to consume valuable lumber on large tracts.

Some densely settled forest areas cannot be allowed to burn because fire would endanger human lives or dwellings. To take the place of fire in the natural scheme of things, some wildlife authorities advocate clear-cutting. This has proved to be a valuable tool when done properly, but has resulted in the degradation of thousands of acres when not done in moderation or with proper concern for special conditions in the area.

Game departments throughout the world devote a large part of their resources to law enforcement. Without adequate enforcement, the best-laid set of wildlife regulations is next to worthless. Poaching is severe in many sections of the world, from the "civilized" states of the United States to the primitive bush in Africa. Certain game species face the threat of extermination from heavily poached areas. Rhinos of several types are threatened by poachers who kill for the horns, which are ground and sold as an aphrodisiac in Oriental countries. Elephant numbers have gone down drastically in recent years because poachers have killed the elephants only for their valuable ivory tusks.

The success of conservation depends in great measure on the attitudes and knowledge of the public. For this reason, conservationists on every continent are spending enormous sums on public education. In China, people are lectured on the value and importance of the giant panda. In Spain, attempts are made to persuade people that the brown bear, which lives in the remote mountains of the country and is essentially the same species that lives in North America, *Ursus arctos*, is worth saving. The developed countries publicize the dangers of pollution, clean-farming, and the rapidly skyrocketing human population, at the same time as they extol the values of wilderness preservation.

Of all the tools of the conservationist—whether he is a manager or a hunter—communication with the rest of mankind is probably the most important. If the world's wildlife is to survive the many threats directed toward it today, man must be convinced that the proper conservation of wildlife is essential to his very existence.

Less expensive methods of stopping game from wandering onto the roads include reflecting posts and markers. These reflect headlight beams and, hopefully, will scare off the animals, or at least make them wait until the vehicle has passed. One problem is that the reflecting surfaces have to be cleaned regularly.

Most road accidents involving moose occur during the summer months, as it is then that the previous year's calves leave the cows and begin to find their own way. Another bad period is in September and October, when the animals are in rut and are more or less unaware of any kind of impending danger. Dusk is the most dangerous time of the day, and it is then that most accidents occur.

Chapter 2

The Future of Game and Hunting

Richard F. LaRocco

One November day in 1976, two men—a 20-year-old automobile painter and a 71-year-old school custodian—experienced hunts that gave each an insight into the future of game and hunting. The younger man spent his day with his Brittany spaniel, hunting pheasants on his father's property along a muddy river. It was his last hunt there; the next spring, bulldozers would level the trees and brush, and fifty-three houses would be built. There would be no more room for the pheasants. The old man spent the day in a tree stand, a turkey permit stuffed in his pocket. He saw twenty turkeys and took a 13-lb (6 kg) gobbler. He was hunting on an abandoned farm in an area that had had no turkeys when he was a youngster. But farming there had become uneconomical during the years since his boyhood, and a hardwood forest now stretched over 350 acres (140 hectares) of once-cultivated farmland. Turkeys had been released there about five years earlier.

To the young man, hunting is an activity with no future. When he first started hunting at the age of twelve, pheasants had been common in the little valley where he lived. But soon, the valley became a suburb of a nearby city, and it was only on his father's farm that the last pheasants still persisted. Now, even it is gone.

To the old man, conservation has come a long way in the past fifty years. Not only are there turkeys on land that had none when he was a boy, but deer, grouse, and wood duck, all rare visitors once, have returned in number. Farming the steep, rocky ground is as unfeasible now as when the farm was abandoned, and the old hunter believes and hopes that the land will always provide food and shelter for game.

What *is* the future of hunting? Is there truly a place in tomorrow's world for wildlife? To answer these questions with any confidence, one would need a crystal ball; however, by studying past and current trends on the great hunting grounds of the world, one can get a fairly accurate idea of the direction things are taking.

What is inescapable will be the continuing effect of man's ecosystem on that of wildlife. The human population has grown fast over the past hundred years: from about 1 billion in 1850 to 2 billion in 1930, to 3 billion in 1960, to 4 billion in 1975. During this time, man's ecosystem has grown even faster, being enlarged by railways, motor vehicles, ocean, air, and space transportation, industrially constructed cities, and an industrially based agriculture. While only some parts of the world have had to absorb their combined direct impact in extreme forms, their indirect effects—their extractions and their refuse—has left, and will continue to leave, no part of the world untouched. And game and other animals thrive only when they do not trouble, or are not troubled by, any one of the parts of man's ecosystem.

Before about the middle of the nineteenth century, only a few parts of Europe and North America had been touched by the coming changes. In both these parts of the world there was—one can say with hindsight—perhaps the sense of a frontier. The limits of the untamed natural world had certainly been pushed back, and slow changes had been made to entire countrysides. For example, some 250 years of agricultural enclo-

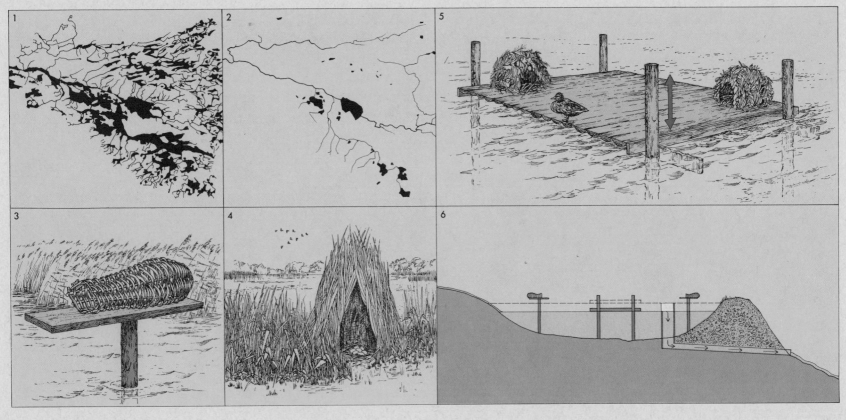

Excellent water-fowl breeding grounds like these are all too often subjected to draining, and this has a detrimental effect on the water-fowl population. *(1)* A water system with numerous connected expanses of water, interspersed with marshes and reedbeds. *(2)* If this is drained, the area changes character, and the breeding grounds that exist there will be destroyed. If a breeding population of birds is to return, it must have artificial nesting places *(3,4)*. Some nesting areas can float up and down as the water level changes *(5)*; in some places, a drain can be arranged *(6)*, so that flooding of the nests can be avoided.

The capture and release of wild turkeys. By this method, wild turkeys are transplanted from habitat with heavy populations of turkey to appropriate new areas that are unpopulated or only lightly populated. This increases the abundance and the distribution of the species, and in some cases, it saves whole turkey populations in areas where habitat will be reduced or disturbed by human activity. Several methods can be used for live trapping. The method shown here involves "cannon nets" *(1)*. A suitable clearing in a heavily populated habitat is baited with grain. At one edge of the clearing, a cannon with a large, light net is set up. When turkeys have gathered in the target area of the clearing, a concealed conservation officer fires the cannon, and the net shoots over the birds and traps them *(2)*. The turkeys are then transported in crates to the new area and released *(3)*.

sure in England had greatly changed the countryside's appearance and fauna. But even if some species were no longer to be seen in particular localities, and others—the dodo, the great auk, or the moa of New Zealand—had been made extinct, there must have been a sense that on the other side of the frontier, where man had certainly existed all the time, animals of all sorts still remained untouched in numbers that would have made our present fears incomprehensible.

It is largely with what still survives of those animals that hunters and conservationists are concerned today. But the demands of man's ecosystem are still increasing, and the role of the conservationist will be to moderate them if possible, and to make the best of them in any event.

What has the conservationist to contend with, then, and what means does he—or she—have available? The first part of the question is hardly difficult to answer: atmospheric, water-borne, chemical, heat, and noise pollution in all parts of the world; the increase in size and number of industrial activities, towns, and cities, and their domestic and industrial needs of land and water, in most parts of the world; mono-crop agriculture in North America, parts of Europe, Africa, and Asia; and the needs of rural populations in the poor countries for fuel and farming land. Within this worldwide context, conservationists have recourse to methods that are a mixture of the old and the new.

One of the persistent features of hunting for pleasure has been the protection of game in tracts of countryside reserved essentially for the use of the ruling classes, and the existence of laws providing fierce penalties for poaching. These conditions still obtain in many parts of the world, perhaps in their most developed form in Great Britain, where poaching laws have, however, been purged of their medieval barbarities. While England may be one of the most populated and industrialized countries in the world, and boasts royal game forests nearly 900 years old, it is unremarkable there that one person may own land, another may

farm it, a third may own the shooting rights, a fourth may lease the rights, while the local hunt may legally gallop across the land in the autumn, during the foxhunting season. All game animals, now including even deer, are owned by someone, even if it may sometimes be difficult to determine who that may be. Conservation is based firmly on the principle that shooting (and fishing) rights have a legal existence separate from that governing the land over which they are exercised, and can thus be bought, sold, and protected. Pollution, for example, or poaching thus infringes property rights.

Outside the reservations and the privately-owned hunting areas, conservationists must take account of the effects of agriculture on game animals and their food chains. That abandoned farm, where our 71-year-old hunted turkeys, had lost out, like tens of thousands of others, to industrial agriculture, a development of only the past three or four decades. Whole landscapes are now razed of hedges, fences, and ditches in the interests of highly sophisticated agricultural machinery that is used to process a single crop planted on an enormous scale. In Great Britain, some of the hedges that have been destroyed in this way dated back to the Middle Ages. In such a uniform environment, insect and plant pests endemic to the crop can spread explosively, so that they must be combated with chemicals on a large scale. Not only are birds and animals deprived of cover by the changes to the landscape, but their food is eliminated, while the residues of the chemicals inevitable affect water systems and harm the plant and animal life associated with them.

Industrial agriculture is perhaps more serious as a direct threat to wildlife, and a greater problem for conservationists, than industry itself, which is more concentrated spatially, and less direct in its effects. Agriculture and smaller game, at least, have always coexisted to some extent, for the damage done by such game was always to be balanced against the pleasure given by hunting it. There is little room for such

sentiments in industrial agriculture. Pesticide residues poison the fat of polar sea birds and animals, perhaps the most isolated of the world's creatures. Caribou and reindeer have high levels of radioactive strontium in their bones.

This is not to underestimate the effects of industrial pollution. Los Angeles, for example, has produced pollution that has killed or damaged an estimated 1.3 million ponderosa pine trees in the San Bernadino Mountains 75 miles (120 km) away. Animals depending on the trees for cover, food, or nesting have been reduced in number.

A vital part of intensive industrial agriculture is irrigation. It can cause streams and rivers almost to disappear, for rainfall is gathered up behind dams in reservoirs that themselves inundate valleys often richly stocked with game. When reservoir levels rise and fall in response to seasonal rainfall and take-offs, the shores cannot develop a stable waterside ecology, and it makes little difference from the hunter's point of view if the water is to be used for a hydroelectric plant, or for domestic or industrial use, or if it has been collected for flood control purposes. All of these instances, as well as large-scale drainage—something that has happened on a very large scale in Britain and mainland Europe—has caused riparian and other wetlands and their rich natural life to diminish. However, one cannot deny the positive side of man-made lakes. They can be stocked with fish and, gradually, an ecosystem that may be a novelty for the area is built up. Conservationists may feel themselves to be in a dilemma when this happens, for the introduction of exotic species is not always a good thing in the long run. Some extreme situations, however, require extreme solutions: power plants that pump out cooling water at a temperature of 80° to 90°F (27° to 32°C) have provided a new home for semi-tropical fish.

The introduction of exotic species is a process that has been going on at least since the Romans spread the pheasant over much of northwest Europe. Mistakes occur—taking rabbits to Australia is perhaps the best-known—but conservationists have seen brown trout and the ring-necked pheasant introduced successfully into North America, and many species there and elsewhere in the world have been preserved by planned re-introduction or establishment into areas where they once were, or could be made to feel, at home. Barbary sheep, for example, are now more numerous in the American Southwest than in their native North Africa, while Rocky Mountain goats have been successfully transplanted to the Wasatch Mountains of Utah. The "hot-holes" created by power-plant outflows have been stocked with such warm-water species as Florida-strain largemouth bass, tilapia, and hybrid striped bass, while birds that would otherwise migrate in winter remain all the year round and take advantage of waste grain in surrounding fields or of accessible aquatic plants.

Conservationists are directly concerned with such specific matters, and bring to bear an increasingly improved scientific knowledge of game and other animals in their ecosystems. They are concerned, too, with the implications for game of general industrial and agricultural pollution; nuclear power plants and their deliberate and accidental disposal of nuclear waste; the spread of suburbia in the industrial world, and that of farmlands and villages in the third world; the prospects of solar and wind-energy plants; and the overgrazing and exhaustion of farmlands, and the excessive clear-cutting of forests, with their attendant dangers of soil erosion.

Over-hunting has been a prime cause of the disappearance of many species and the near extinction of many more. Elk, whitetail deer, bison, and alligators are examples of species that have been saved at the last moment in the United States.

Improvements can flow from a better understanding of the role of predators in nature, to take one example, or from an appreciation that a

sentimental banning of the shooting or culling of does will lead to a rapid over-population that first severely damages the animals' environment and then leads to large numbers of deaths from starvation and disease. The effects of over-stocking of cattle—and therefore of over-grazing—are well known to conservationists. In the United States, the Bureau of Land Management, reporting on the rangelands of Nevada, stated that "uncontrolled, unregulated, unplanned livestock use is occurring on approximately eighty-five percent of the state and damage to wildlife habitat can be expressed only as extreme destruction." A similar situation surely exists in many other regions of the West and Midwest of America, while over-grazing in northern Africa is so severe that the Sahara Desert is moving southward. Over-grazing throughout the world has left depleted forage, damaged streams, and eroded soil. Too much stock has been competing for too long for too little food.

Knowledge has grown, too, of the importance of the controlled use of clearing and, even, of fire, in forest management. Wholesale felling has had, and continues to have, a major effect on animal life. This affected the eastern United States during the eighteenth and nineteenth centuries, affects India and Pakistan today, and has begun to affect parts of South America and Asia. Some species of deer thrive in the new growth that springs up after a fire, whereas a mature forest cannot provide this sort of grazing. Some game species, on the other hand—the turkey, for example—require mature forests. Too much felling, whether for game management purposes or to extract timber, can have far-reaching consequences if steep slopes are denuded of the vegetation that retains the soil. The dangers of such clear-cutting are both erosion and floods.

Today, game departments and conservation agencies are generally more cautious than they once were when introducing exotic animals. At one time, exotics were released into new habitats before their environmental needs had been evaluated and the possible effects of their new homes on their lives could be predicted. This resulted in a great number of failures or in "successes" in which the particular form of wildlife

introduced became pests. Bighorn sheep from the north of the United States, for example, had been unsuccessfully reintroduced into a number of southern states before researchers pointed out that animals were needed that had adjusted to the climatic conditions they would meet in the South.

Hunters and conservationists find that their interests to some extent clash directly with those of the native peoples of the affected areas. North American Indians and Eskimos have had their claims to certain hunting and fishing rights upheld, in some cases by the Supreme Court of the United States, in others by local officials of either the United States or Canada. These rights include that of taking certain migratory waterfowl and their eggs in the spring. In northern Canada, this is, in fact, subsistence hunting, but now officials are seeking to give this right to all Canadian Indians.

In Africa and Asia, population growth has not only resulted in deforestation in the interests of farming and fuel, but has put pressure on game reserves. Rhinoceros are poached not just for their horns but for meat (and poaching for meat increases in the industrialized countries, too, as the price of fresh meat rises). Elephants cannot be physically confined in game reserves, and so are shot when they intrude on the villages and farms that are spreading all the time in Africa.

In some countries, the government reimburses farmers and ranchers for damage caused by wildlife. As the value of food continues to rise, such payments may cease. Instead, the game will probably be shot for "trespass." An alarming trend is the inclination of governments to increase game-damage payments. Often, as in some of the western American states, the funds for such payments come from fees charged to hunters and fishermen. Thus, money that could have gone to the improvement of wildlife habitat is going instead to farmers and ranchers.

When game damage is particularly high in some areas, the government sometimes buys the land outright and allows wildlife to feed on it. An alternative is to buy land nearby and lure wildlife on to it by providing

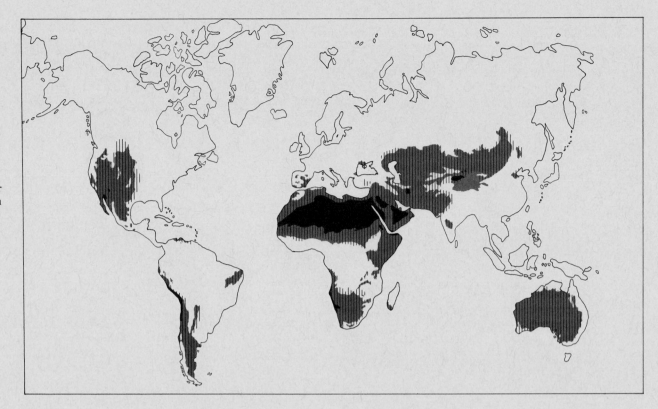

(Left) A herd of African cattle, still scrawny although the rains have begun, come home after a day's meager grazing. Too many cattle in proportion to the available growth progressively exhaust the grass, leading to soil erosion by winds and rain. (Right) Deserts, and the arid and semi-arid areas around them, are growing all over the world. Trees are cut for fuel for the cooking fire or are destroyed by elephants; areas of shade, which retain moisture, shrink. Irrigation can cause the ground-water level to rise: as ground water is rich in mineral salts, over-irrigated land can become infertile and end up as desert.

■ Extreme desert

■ Arid

▥ At risk

food for the animals. Certainly, the costs of these programs will increase dramatically, perhaps to impossibly high levels. Obviously, there would be no necessity for game feeding if the animals had sufficient undisturbed habitat.

Another factor that increases the demands made on rangelands today is the growing need for more food. Nowadays, at least in parts of the world, the needs of wildlife are considered before range managers set livestock quotas. The question of livestock will surely receive even more consideration as the demand for more food increases. The problem is that many ranges can produce food only indirectly—by supporting wild and domestic animals. Since domestic animals can be controlled more closely than wild animals and are not subject to wide population fluctuations, raising livestock will be seen as the most efficient way to produce meat on the ranges. Wildlife will be destroyed or its needs ignored, if the demand for food becomes too great.

Sometimes, however, domestic cattle and game animals can occupy the same environment. In the United States, for example, the pronghorn antelope population has risen from about 13,000 at the turn of the century to some 400,000 today, despite the fact that some 2 million have been shot since the 1920s. This antelope has food and water requirements that differ subtly from those of the cattle that have replaced the buffalo on the Plains. While cattle can be fenced in by relatively light barbed wire fences—which pronghorn will not jump if they are more than about 30 inches (91 cm) high—the antelope can still wriggle under a lower, unbarbed strand of wire, if it is at least 16 inches (41 cm) above the ground, thus maintaining the freedom of movement that they need for survival.

In comparison to loss of habitat, other threats to game and to hunting seem inconsequential. The anti-hunting movement seems unimportant when possible events of the future are analyzed. But in the short term, at least in parts of the world, anti-hunting sentiment *is* a real threat to hunters. Preservationist groups in the United States have filed suits to stop hunts several times. In 1974, four groups went to federal court to challenge the United States Fish and Wildlife Service's waterfowl hunting regulations because of their lack of environmental-impact statements. Eventually, this suit was dropped. Then the preservationists sued again, this time in an effort to stop federal taxes on sporting goods from going to programs designed to benefit fish and wildlife.

In Switzerland, the Canton of Geneva actually put the matter of hunting to a vote, and hunting was banned for good. This kind of voting could spread, and that could mean trouble for hunters, who are a minority almost everywhere. Some cities in the United States have banned hunting on wide-open lands lying within city limits. This has been done mainly for emotional reasons, although safety is the usual pretext given.

Because whitetail deer were overpopulating the Great Swamp National Wildlife Refuge in New Jersey, state and federal officials called for a hunt in 1970, hoping to cull the herd to a safe level. Several anti-hunting groups intervened in court and successfully blocked the hunt that year and for three more years. In the spring of 1974, biologists searched the refuge and determined that about 60 deer had died of starvation because there was too little forage. Incredibly, the anti-hunters tried to stop the hunt again, but it was allowed in December, 1974. Autopsies on 63 of the 127 deer shot showed evidence of what had happened to the herd. One buck carried tumors weighing 7 lb (3 kg) on his head and was virtually blind because of them. Tumors of this kind had not been seen before 1974 and were not seen again after the hunt was finally allowed. Six-month-old deer killed inside the refuge weighed an average of 10 lb (4.5 kg) less than deer of the same age outside its boundaries.

Increased knowledge about predators and their role in nature is a definite improvement. Just fifteen years ago, bears and mountain lions were classified as vermin to be shot on sight in several western United States. Now, they are either fully protected species or game animals, and populations have increased dramatically. Idaho's black-bear population

(Above) A growing problem in conservation today is the huge amounts of oil that are being spilled into the ocean. Countless sea birds die every year, and the effect on marine life in many areas is disastrous. Once a bird gets a lot of oil on its feathers, they lose their water-repellant properties, and this leads to the bird's death from exposure, if it has not already been poisoned by the oil.

(Below) Biocides and the effluent from industry are today a serious threat to wildlife. For instance, it has been shown that, in the past thirty years, the shells of the merlin's eggs have become thinner, resulting in a high rate of death among chicks in the shell. Many eggs, as this one, are infertile. In the long run, the whole species will become weakened, if nothing is done about pollution.

has risen to such a high level that elk herds are suffering from bear predation on their calves. As a result, the state has liberalized bear-hunting regulations in some game-management units. In designated areas, non-residents may shoot two bears with a minimum of licensing formalities.

Perhaps the most promising trend, as far as hunters are concerned, is the increased public awareness of the environment. Laws designed to protect and restore natural environments have multiplied like mice in the past decade. Such laws are aimed not only at reducing pollution and other visible environmental degradation, but also at protecting vital wildlife habitat. The beneficiaries include a great many wild creatures, from rare and endangered species to game animals. Nowadays, wildlife needs often are given priority over such interests as those of livestock growers, miners, and developers.

Intelligent land-use planning has increased considerably. Some planners set aside areas for nesting and breeding grounds, winter big-game ranges, and flood plains, and prohibit development of such important wildlife lands for other uses. In Britain, duck populations have greatly increased since World War II thanks to inland conservation stimulated partly by the Wildfowlers Association (a hunting organization), and partly by private landowners cultivating duck as a replacement for the partridge, which has been reduced in numbers by mechanized farming methods.

Tourism is on the upswing in many areas, not only because some countries are getting richer, but because people have more leisure than ever before. Tourism rarely damages wildlife resources and often can be credited with saving them. The only hope Africa's wildlife may have is the tourist who will pay to see it or hunt it.

Hunters today support the official departments that are responsible for wildlife conservation more consistently and vigorously than they commonly did twenty-five years ago. Despite occasional disagreements, the public generally understands the need for certain regulations. The harvesting of female deer furnishes an important example. Traditionally, sportsmen have killed only antlered male deer—trophies—unless there was an unusual need for meat. Gradually and subtly, the trophy tradition acquired absurd overtones of chivalry: A gentleman must protect all females, even if those females happen to be deer rather than humans. Thus, sportsmen were quick to advocate and support laws against doe shooting, even though most of them were willing to harvest any buck, whether or not its antlers qualified as a trophy.

In regions where deer were scarce and habitat was adequate, protection of does was a good conservation tool; it permitted great increases in the herds. But the problem in those regions is no longer underpopulation. It is just the opposite—deer overpopulation.

Years ago, when game departments first suggested the harvesting of does as a form of population control, sportsmen were appalled, and for a long time, they continued to oppose doe harvests. Now, these sportsmen support the doe-control regulation, and many of them apply for doe permits, having come to understand that shooting does as well is the only way to curtail a deer overpopulation that eventually causes severe habitat damage and a massive mortality rate. In the past few years, several governments have held successful doe hunts for the first time in many years, simply because hunters were finally convinced of the necessity.

Concurrently, sportsmen are also attaining a new level of awareness with regard to ethical behavior. This is reflected in the literature they read. Some sporting magazines today refuse to print anything having to do with hunting inedible creatures. They place emphasis on the joy of pursuit rather than killing. The sharpened ethical awareness is also seen in hunters' behavioral crusades, or movements, such as SPORT (Sportsmen Policing Our Ranks Together), HOW (Help Our Wildlife), and Operation Game Thief, in which hunters are encouraged to report poachers and game hogs. Perhaps we cannot entirely rid ourselves of hunters who violate game laws and ethical codes, but such people are no longer regarded with amusement. They are detested.

Will there be hunting a century from now? Probably. But it is likely that hunting opportunities will decrease, disappearing entirely in some regions. What kind of hunting will exist for our great-great-grandchildren depends on what courses of action we take today.

Another example of the effects of pollution is found among the seals of the Baltic. Sterility among the females is disastrously high—as few as twenty percent of them are fertile. This has been shown to be the result of PCB. The change in the ecosystem that will occur should the seal die out will eventually mean a change in the conditions under which we ourselves live. Some biologists warn that, for every species that dies out, mankind is taking a step nearer its own destruction.

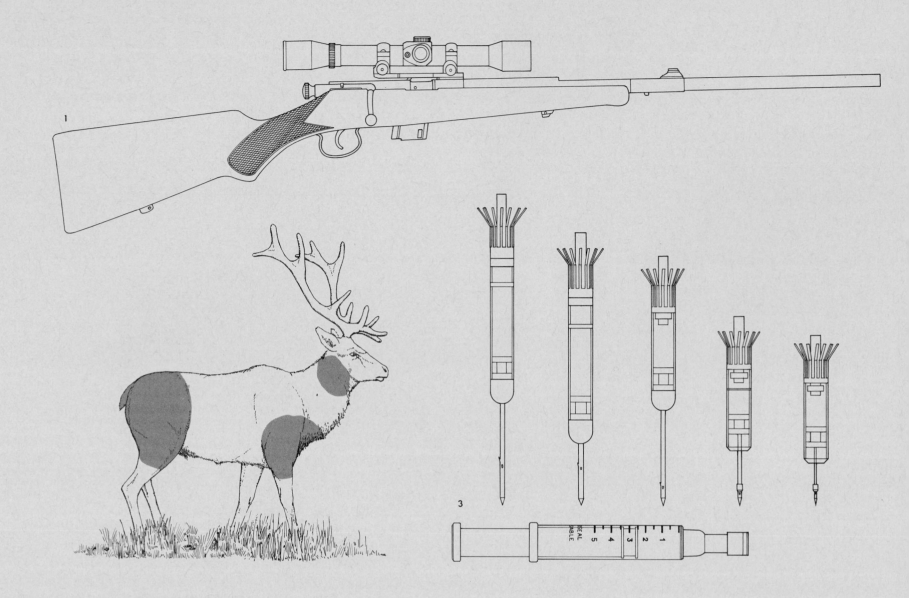

Tagging and radio-collaring various game species in order to monitor their activities and movements is an important part of game research. Often, it is important to be able to examine an animal (for instance, to take blood samples). For these purposes, some of the larger species are captured in baited pens; others are tranquilized or anaesthetized by means of a syringe projectile fired from a gun. Accurate marksmanship is a must when firing a syringe projectile at an animal. Drugs injected too close to the bone, in the joints between bones, or in tendons are more slowly absorbed than drugs injected in the muscle. The marksman should aim, therefore, at the animal's larger muscles in the rump, the foreleg, or the hind leg (here shown shaded on a deer). Great care must be taken when choosing the optimum dosage, for this can vary for the same animal, depending on such factors as the animal's condition, the time of

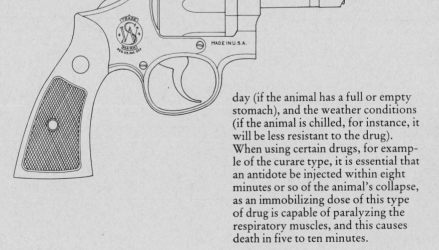

day (if the animal has a full or empty stomach), and the weather conditions (if the animal is chilled, for instance, it will be less resistant to the drug). When using certain drugs, for example of the curare type, it is essential that an antidote be injected within eight minutes or so of the animal's collapse, as an immobilizing dose of this type of drug is capable of paralyzing the respiratory muscles, and this causes death in five to ten minutes.

The guns and syringes shown here have been developed especially for the purpose by Paxarms, a New Zealand firm. (1) The Paxarms Mark 20 Syringe rifle. (2) The Paxarms Mark 10 Smith & Wesson Syringe pistol. (3) A selection of syringe projectiles and a filling syringe.

VIII The British Isles

Shooting Laws and Customs

Wilson Stephens

There has never been in Britain any conception of game as a communal resource. On the other hand, there is the right to hunt. This operates on two levels—the right to hunt at all, which is public; and the right to hunt in particular places, which is private. The effect is to place upon the active participants the responsibility for providing and safeguarding the game and the local environment which make their sport possible. The system grew over the years out of interaction between feudal pressures and the basic conviction of all Britons that Jack is as good as his master—a conviction, incidentally, which can exist only in a nation which has at least two social classes. Britain, of course, has many more than that.

The British sporting community extends from royalty to the nobility and the otherwise-wealthy, who own the land on which shooting takes place; thence to the farmers who rent the land, sometimes including the rights to the game upon it, and to those sufficiently well off to form the syndicates to lease the rights to game on land belonging to other people; thence to those insufficiently well off to do this but enabled by long-standing acquaintance, services rendered, personal charm, or sheer brass-neck to participate in what is being financed by others; thence to those who, being hardy men with a sense of adventure, base their sport on the wildfowl of the marshes and foreshore; thence to those who, rather than have no sport at all, are content to indulge in pigeon and rabbit shooting, and other forms of what the British regard as "vermin shooting" but enjoy none the less for that; not to mention those to whom the scatter-gun is anathema and who stalk with rifles the deer which, contrary to probability, have grown more abundant as the motorways spread across the rural landscape.

The community thus united by gun sport in Britain can be quantified. British law lays down that ownership of sporting weapons is dependent on permits issued at the discretion of the police, who have power of veto against which the applicant may appeal to the courts. These characteristi-cally convoluted British measures actually work. In addition, they reveal how many shooters there are. In 1980, the number of certificates issued for smooth-bore weapons stood at approximately 960,000. Add 172,638 rifle permits in England and Wales, where these are separately accounted for, and the figure emerges of 1,131,912 legitimate users of sporting weapons.

Of the near million holders of shotgun certificates, about thirty percent were estimated also to hold Game Licences. This additional formality (imposed by counties and hence not nationally aggregated) entitles the holder to shoot grouse, ptarmigan, pheasant, partridge, woodcock, and snipe, the species which rank as "game." All other species, both winged and furred, are fair quarry but not "game" in law. The major demarcation in the class distinctions of British shooting long rested upon the distinction between game and non-game. Game was for the privileged, non-game and vermin for everybody else. Before World War II, when this demarcation still existed, holders of the Game Licence totaled fewer than 30,000.

The marked increase in British game-shooters over a single generation reflects the greatly changed face of British shooting. The inter-war game-shooting community shot almost continuously, and those not wealthy enough to do so did not aspire to "game." Men and women financially able and occupationally free to make shooting virtually their only winter activity are now an extinct species. The typical modern British shooter follows his sport on an average of one day per week. The financial outlay for this frequency of sport brings it within the compass of income groups who could not have afforded the old style. Simultaneously, the virtual disappearance of domestic servants from the British way of life has rendered impossible the old system of high-society country-house par-ties, which were formerly the basis of game-shooting. Instead, the sport has become home-based for a greatly increased community, much aided by modern ease of travel.

These socio-economic changes have affected the character of gun sport in Britain. Shooting (the term by which it is known, in distinction from hunting, which in Britain means following on horseback or foot a quarry pursued by pack hounds) has been the fastest-growing component of the field sports trinity of shooting, hunting, and fishing. Although varying in regional emphasis, the pattern has been consistent.

The atmosphere of a British shoot, as of British life in general, is relaxed und unobtrusive. A shooting party is assumed to be a gathering of friends, acting in conformity with a recognized set of customs, and inclusive of all participants whatever their role. There are, of course, formalities, of which those most rigidly observed and penalized concern safety. He who fires a shot which endangers, or might endanger, another person or who behaves in a manner which might render such a shot possible, is not thereafter welcomed. Safety factors apart, the conven-tions of the sport reflect a traditional British ambivalence. It can be summed up by the generalization that all conform to custom while avoiding any possible indication that they are trying to do so.

In every kind of shooting, the British practice and value self-effacement, both actual and metaphorical. Shooting clothes are subdued in hue, to blend with the winter countryside, and so give camouflage. Britons are taciturn by nature, their utterances few and short at any time and, when out shooting, soft-spoken. The raised human voice, unless it be that of authority, has no place. There is no separation between the sporting side and the social side; shooting is a social occasion, and it remains precisely that, whether the birds are coming over or whether the drinks are passing round. Efficiency at either stage will be well regarded, but nobody refers to it.

These generalizations must be adjusted to the occasion, so those most likely to be encountered may be outlined. A formal pheasant shoot generally implies eight shooters, referred to as the Guns, but a total company of not fewer than forty people. They gather at some large house, or farm (perhaps the home of the owner of the land to be shot over, or of the leader of the party), or at an inn.

The Guns, in one way or another, bear the costs of the day, all other being paid for their efforts except on do-it-yourself shots, where neigh-boring country families band together in all-amateur enterprises. Apart from the gamekeeper, who is doing his normal job, the remaining participants are exercising jealously guarded rights not only to the payroll, but to their aspect of the sport. Here the widening spectrum of the class structure becomes apparent. Beaters are assumed to be local farmworkers enjoying a perquisite—because, for centuries, so they always were; but not now. Modern beating lines are certainly local, but not exclusively agricultural. Most include off-duty policemen and schoolmasters, soldiers on leave, the village postman, the filling station man, a shopkeeper, students, and anybody else aspiring to an invitation to shoot pigeons and rabbits when the game season ends.

The Guns may be peers of the realm, captains of industry, prosperous farmers, or such neighborhood-figures as doctors, lawyers, or parsons. For the purpose of the day they are co-equally Guns. The day is theirs, and everybody else's as well.

Regardless of the parts they play, there is recognition that all present are out to enjoy themselves. Except for the keeper, nobody is anybody's servant. The much-discussed British class structure dissolves into the wry courtesies of the British countryside. Christian names abound; Harry may be a belted earl or the game-cart driver. Not even tone of voice will give much clue to which, in the context of the moment, is the more important. Britons have a genius for forming closed communities which make all of them equal. This is one of them.

Through the day, this easy companionship persists, as it does throughout the whole gamut of British shooting. Such a formal shoot may be very definitely upper crust, or it may be one of the thousands which take place at a density of about one per village in rural Britain. The comradeship is identical with that of informal shoots, when two or three friends go out with dogs and guns, more in hope than expectation, or when wildfowling partners head for bleak wildernesses of swamp and coast. The act of sharing is a distinguishing element in British shooting. Another is the force of unwritten laws. Be it never more empty, no gun must ever point at or near any part of another human being; indeed at nothing except earth or sky, the weapon being carried either upright or down-pointing. Every gun is always unloaded on crossing any hedge, ditch, stile, gate, or bridge. Increasingly, though not yet invariably, it is the custom for guns to be carried open as proof of unloading, unless sleeved.

A Gun does not pick up (either in person or by his dog) game shot by another. On being told where to stand at a drive, he does not thereafter move, even a single stride. If his neighbor is not within sight, the Gun declares his own presence by voice until he receives a reply. It is his responsibility to know the orders of the day as to what species are to be shot, and what not. At the end of the day, he will not leave without thanking the keeper, and leaving a gift of money.

While unwritten laws govern the conduct of British shooting, written laws in the form of statutory enactments safeguard its existence. They give the sport an actual monetary value. This, responding to market factors of supply and demand, is at present extremely high. In consequence, the game populations and other facilities, which make the right to shoot a reality, are correspondingly well cared for, so that they remain profitable, both in terms of the pleasure they give and the income they produce.

The system rests on the principle of "separate enjoyment." This originated in a law of the Norman King William I (The Conqueror) whereby the right to hunt deer over a tract of forest in Hampshire was assigned to the Crown, the land itself remaining the property of its then possessors. Since then, the law has recognized that the ownership of land can be separated from its "enjoyments." This means that a landowner may let or sell the right to farm or to shoot on the land he owns. Alternatively, he may sell the land and retain the right to shoot, or exercise any other combination of the options.

Although the "separate enjoyment" principle thus establishes the right to sport as a negotiable asset, it does not confer the ownership of the game or other wild creatures living on the land in question. Non-domesticated species, whether deer and pheasants or rats and foxes, rank in British law as *ferae naturae* (creatures of the wild). As such, they are no man's property until they are legally "reduced into possession," which is generally interpreted as meaning "coming to hand." Thus, the owner of a shoot does not own the birds upon it, even though he may have spent much money in preserving them. Only when he, or somebody acting for him, has legally had a bird in his hand, does he become its owner.

It is not enough that he should shoot the bird while he is on his own ground and the bird within his boundaries. Even if he kills it, the bird may fall beyond the boundary on to a neighbor's land, whence its recovery would be an act of trespass by him or his dog (if the neighbor pressed the point, which most neighbors do not). From this, it follows that a poacher (one who takes game where the sporting rights belong to somebody else) does not commit theft, since things cannot be stolen which, at the time, had no possessor. What the poacher has done is to usurp another man's right and for that he may well go to prison. A simple trespasser, however, will not go to prison, unless he is exceptionally foolish and obdurate. His offence is in being on somebody else's land, and provided he leaves when asked to do so, the law holds him liable only for any damage he may have caused, it being up to the landowner to prove this.

Across the centuries, many laws for the protection of wild life have been passed in Britain, the last and perhaps the best being the 1954 Protection of Birds Act. This gives total permanent protection to all birds, but then schedules two sets of exceptions—those game and other birds which are fair quarry for the gun outside their close seasons, and those which, being agricultural pests, may be shot at any time.

Subject to observing these provisions, the owner of sporting rights may do as he likes, and may extend the privilege to others, on the land to which the rights apply. The consequence has been an integrating network of watch-and-word systems which, being motivated by the immediate interest of those who carry them out, are in practice efficient—certainly more efficient than any government effort could be. As a result, Britain is free of state-imposed limits on the amount of game which individuals may shoot, and the actual game populations permit the privately imposed allocations of sport by the holders of sporting rights to be set much higher than state-imposed limits elsewhere.

The force of unwritten law is never greater than in the conventions governing the weapons used in British sporting shooting. Nowhere in British law is there a single line of statutory stipulation affecting the proper usage of shotguns. Only in the last decade has Parliament belatedly (and then only weakly) declared the rifle to be the proper weapon for deer shooting. Sporting custom, however, is clear and definite—and doubtlessly the more binding on the British, who have no great taste for a proliferation of official laws.

For all forms of sporting shooting, a double-barreled breechloader is normal. Side lock and side-by-side is the preferred design, but the growing popularity of trap-shooting has led to increasing numbers of over-and-unders being used. Twelve-bore is the most popular size for men, many ladies preferring 16- or 20-bore for lightness, while 28-bore and .410 are the weapons with which most boys and girls learn. Wildfowlers, with geese in mind, use 8- or 10-bores. Single-barreled versions are mostly used for vermin control.

In the interests of giving a fair chance to the quarry, a basic principle of all sporting shooting in Britain is that the shooter should never be able to fire more than two shots before reloading. Hence, repeaters are not used.

Shotguns are regarded as proper weapons to use in shooting hares and rabbits, but not deer. That the three chief indigenous British species—red, fallow, and roe—should never be shot with anything but a rifle is now generally accepted by all with a legitimate reason to shoot them. In addition to the species named, many areas of Britain have now been colonized (through escapes from wild-life parks) by Japanese sika, muntjac, and Chinese water deer.

The long-term and appreciating value of shooting rights has affected the character of the British countryside, always to the benefit of wildlife in general. The small mixed woodlands (spinneys and coppices in local parlance) which dot lowland landscapes in apparently careless symmetry have been so positioned because they are tactically useful in holding pheasants, and because they route them over the valleys where Guns can be faced with the most testing shots. The shelter-belts which separate the wide fields of the corn counties were planted so that partridges could be driven over them, again to provide challenging marksmanship. That the pheasant coverts have preserved many species of woodland birds, as well as of foxes and deer, while the partridge belts have prevented wind-erosion of light soils, are both bonuses. Neither was the prime intention. Sport was.

Though it has left so positive a mark on the scenery, the trend goes back little more than a century. In British terms, this is a development so new that its impact is only now being appreciated. Like so much else, it stemmed from the introduction of the breechloading shotgun. The more rapid reload meant that high concentrations of game could be engaged, especially when each shooter had two guns, and a helper to do the re-loading. The result was the fashion for the battue, in which the sport was measured by the number of birds shot, and by nothing else. Happily, it is now long outmoded.

That brief and unattractive interlude ended with World War I. Differ-ent criteria now govern the sport. Chiefly, these are the nature of the surroundings and the quality of the shooting. But the aftermath of those days left both the sport and the landscape permanently changed for the better. Whereas previously the pheasant had been a bird of the open country, surviving against all odds in small groups based on hedges, shaws, and reedbeds, it is now a bird of the light woodlands. There, the environment can be controlled in the pheasant's favor, protection can be provided, and food made available when necessary. The guardianship of gamekeepers can thus be applied to immensely greater numbers of birds.

So the pheasant has become in Britain, as elsewhere, the common denominator of game shooting, having supplanted the partridge in this respect. Throughout the United Kingdom, from the English Channel to northern Scotland, the pheasant is found everywhere except in towns, block forestry, or at high altitude. Because pheasants need sunshine, they are birds of woodland edges; small plantations, with their greater ratio of edge to interior, meet their needs, but close planting cannot. Hardy as pheasants are, the British weather above the 1,000-foot (300 m) contour is not for them. On the other hand, they have adapted well to the intensive-farming methods on the drained marshes of East Anglia, where the prevailing crop, sugar beet, shelters large populations every year.

For a small island, Britain's contrasts in sporting background are wide. It is arguable that the best British pheasant country (if this could be defined) is in the mixed-farming counties of the South and Midlands, where the pattern of specially planting holding grounds is most developed; or on the lower slopes of steep mountainsides in Wales and Scotland, where the birds come over highest and the shooting is most difficult; or on the treeless flat landscapes of the Fens, where the mere quantity of birds is distracting to all but well-practiced locals.

Traditionally, the classic English manors, where a generation ago partridge shooting almost dictated the way of life, were in the open corn country of East Anglia, east Yorkshire, the plain of York itself, and on the high chalk downs of Wessex. There, the English gray partridge—fast, low-flying, swinging in the wind, and coming over in coveys of a dozen or so—demanded a very specialized form of gun handling. To take two in front and two behind with one gun in the few brief seconds between their coming and going was the feat of practiced perfectionists. To take five was a minor miracle, the secret being to reload after the first shot, take two more in front, reload as the birds passed overhead, and take the final two as they receded.

Some farming innovations since World War II proved adverse to gray partridge. Disappointing seasons followed while landowners, gamekeep-ers, and the Game Conservancy sought remedies. Meanwhile, confi-dence in the future of the English partridge waned, and gamekeeping

effort was diverted toward the more cost-effective and easily managed pheasant. Latterly, the situation has stabilized on a new basis.

The problems raised by attempts to aid the independent, wary gray partridge apply less to the red-legged (or French) partridge. This had long existed as a minority species in Britain. Now, it is in a majority. It responds better to artificial rearing, hence gamekeeping effort devoted to it is almost as productive as with pheasants. Cross-breeding with the Asiatic chukar and the rock partridge of the Mediterranean produced hardy hybrids resistant to the British weather. There is no firm evidence yet that they can self-regenerate in the wild, while there are plenty of indications that perhaps they cannot. However, this matters little on the growing number of shoots which now restock annually with hand-reared birds from game farms, in preference to producing their own.

What has been gained from this is the resurgence of partridge shooting under the wide skies of Britain's open country. What has been lost is much of its special character. The red-legged partridge and its derivatives seldom fly in coveys but, generally, in pairs or as singletons. The sport survives but lacks its acid test, except where gray partridge remain.

Although pheasant and partridge provide the bulk of British game-shooting, grouse provide its greatest distinction. The red grouse of the heather-clad moors is indigenous solely to the British Isles and has been established elsewhere only on a small scale (in Belgium and intermittently in Scandinavia).

Much myth and glamor surrounds grouse shooting in Britain. Some arises from its unfamiliarity to most people because of the bird's lonely habitat, some from the rumored social overtones, which are artificially fostered by the Press and readily absorbed abroad. The realities can be easily stated.

Despite its name, the British grouse is not red, but brown touched with white; it has small red patches above its eyes. Though often thought of, especially by indoor Britons, as a Scottish bird, it exists in higher densities in northern England, in smaller numbers as far south as Derbyshire, Staffordshire, Shropshire, and Herefordshire, and in a limited area of Somerset. It breeds in every county in Wales and Ireland (both Northern and Southern).

Grouse are more difficult to shoot than pheasant and less difficult than driven partridge. Grouse shooting is no more confined to the nobility than any other form of British shooting, although the nobility, like anybody else, shoot grouse when they get the chance. Foreign sharing of grouse shooting on a paying-guest basis is more marked than in pheasant and partridge shooting. Scottish grouse shooting, though excellent, is not necessarily better than any other. The cream of it is generally in York-shire, close to the sites of heavy industry. Its quality, of course, varies regionally and seasonally according to the weather at breeding time.

The grouse, therefore, is not a rare bird and is very widely distributed. Its exploitation for sport depends on conservation measures different from those applying to other game. Grouse do not thrive under hand-rearing. Nor do they thrive at elevations of less than 1,000 feet (300 m). They need entirely open country, being allergic to trees. They must, therefore, reproduce themselves in maximum numbers on ground which is unprotectable from severe, sometimes ferocious, weather, and where their only food source is heather. They can be helped only by making this stark environment as suitable for them as possible by burning off old heather to make way for younger and more nutritious growth, by better drainage, by supplies of grit to aid digestion, and by protection from disturbance in the nesting season.

For most of the year, a moor keeper's life is an act of faith. Around him, the birds live their lives unseen. The harsh sequence of gale, downpour, and blizzard takes its course. The chill, dun-colored land-scapes roll endlessly away, unvaried and seemingly lifeless through three of the four seasons. Then, late in summer, the moors burst into color—

the glowing, royal purple of flowering heather. Grouse shooters have every reason to feel on top of the world.

The great grouse family is represented in Britain by ptarmigan, black grouse, and capercaillie. The two last-named are also familiar on the European mainland and in Scandinavia, while the name ptarmigan is used in North America, but for yet another form of grouse. The British ptarmigan is a high-altitude version of the red grouse, having evolved a gray protective coloration as camouflage among the bare rocks and snowfields of the Scottish mountain tops. It is held in affection by moor men but is not highly regarded as quarry. Seldom seeing human beings, it has a confiding disposition and, having not learned fear, is too easy to be worth shooting by experienced sportsmen.

Capercaillie, a yard long from beak to tail and looking like grayish-black, flying turkeys, are the largest grouse of all. Black grouse (the female is known as gray hen, and, collectively, the species is called black game), handsome birds with lyre-shaped tails, though larger than red grouse, are less gigantic than capercaillie. Both frequent woodland. Capercaillie prefer old hardwoods where felling and wind-blow have created open patches where birds of their size can fly without colliding with branches. Black game favor young plantations where tree height does not exceed 10 feet (3 m), or edges of older forests where trees are well spread out. Both species are fair quarry at the discretion of shooting-rights owners, but neither is shot in numbers comparable to those in which the grouse is shot.

The list of game birds is completed by woodcock and snipe, wetland birds which are familiar in identical species or subspecies throughout the northern hemisphere of both the Old and New Worlds. Neither are normally chief quarry at formal shoots but are incidentals to days at grouse, pheasant, or partridge. However, when hard weather builds up their numbers in western Britain or Ireland (the warm Atlantic coasts being the last refuge from severe continental conditions), snipe drives out of bogs are organized, and special woodcock shoots are held over spaniels, the birds being flushed from laurels or rhododendrons.

More often, both these species are taken at rough-shoots—a term which has the British characteristic of defining the opposite of what it implies. There is nothing rough about it; much to the contrary. The distinction between "rough" and "formal" shoots is that, in the former, the Guns operate without human assistance, the range of quarry being identical. Instead of waiting at numbered pegs for beaters to put the game over them, rough-shooters keep moving, using their fieldcraft and knowledge of nature to locate their quarry in the most favorable circumstances for shooting it, aided by well-trained dogs. It is a sport for fit, active, experienced men, and its element of "hunt" has a special appeal to those of independent mind who prefer any success to be the result of their own unaided efforts. There are many connoisseurs who regard a rough-shoot with well-chosen companions as the cream of sport.

But not all. Half the shooters in Britain, if asked to name their personal high-spot, would think not of moor or manor, woodland or stubble, but of marsh and foreshore. What Britons know as wildfowling—where the quarry are ducks, geese, and wading birds which rank among the world's wariest creatures—is a world of its own, and its devotees are largely a community on their own.

Wildfowling country is not a magnet to the less privileged only. Undoubtedly, those with little money are in a majority there. But they are joined by many who enjoy game-shooting at its most luxurious and, yet, find it not enough. The reason is simple. Wildfowling, with its many hardships and a very fair share of dangers, is a sport that measures men by their manhood, not by their social position or income level. Rich men as well as poor feel this desire to go out and prove themselves to themselves, and afterwards enjoy the companionship of those of like

mind, whatever their level in life. Wildfowling is for individualists or for partnerships of two.

In British law, the rights of a landowner whose boundary is the sea extend to the (high) tideline, and there they stop. Between this and low tide may stretch a few yards of sand and gravel, or several miles of mud, rocks, and marine grass. Whatever its width, this zone constitutes the foreshore, which belongs to no one person but to all among the Queen's subjects. Therefore, the right to shoot there is free and unrestricted to all who possess their guns legally.

Great estuaries, such as those of the Thames, Humber, Mersey, Severn, Solway, Forth, and Tay, enclose enormous areas of mud and sandbanks, intersected by deep runnels, tideraces, and quicksands. In them gather the wintering flocks of Arctic-breeding geese (whitefront, pink foot, graylag, bean, and barnacle), native sea ducks, and roosting flocks of inland feeders (mallard, teal, shoveler, pintail, pochard, widgeon, gadwall, and tufted), and gray and golden plover, redshank, and curlew.

Inland from the foreshores, the saltings carry cattle and sheep in summer but are empty of all life except wintering birds in winter. The saltings include the Wash, Chichester and Poole Harbours, Morecambe Bay, and the mouths of Scottish sea lochs. Strangers need guides in all wildfowling zones. Every year claims lives, even from the locals, when men who lose their bearings are cut off by the tide or find themselves faced by quicksands instead of a safe route back while the sea builds up around them.

Wildfowling provides challenge, fascination, and thrills in plenty—but it is not for men who like things to be made easy for them; very definitely, it is not for softies. It is for anybody with the brains and hardihood, both mental and physical, to withstand its stresses—and the weather.

Those who regard it as their heritage have been conscientious in preserving both the well-being and the good name of wildfowling. The Wildfowlers Association of Great Britain and Ireland has as its motto "For Sport and Conservation." Its efforts in insisting on proper standards of behavior, the improvement of the environment, the welfare of all wild birds, but especially the migrant species, and respect for other people's interests, have greatly enhanced the resources on which coastal shooting depends. Simultaneously, another conservation development has expanded the scope of inland wildfowling.

When partridge populations fell and shoots found themselves dependent on pheasant alone, the immediate effect was the loss of September and October as shooting months. They had previously been devoted to partridge, since pheasant shooting, though legal in October, is not practical in many places until after the November frosts and leaf fall have opened up the woodlands. As a substitute for partridge, many inland shooters combined in organizing duck-rearing schemes. The result has been massive increases in non-coastal mallard populations, and a corresponding increase in the opportunities available to non-game shooters.

Game shooting and wildfowling have their open and close seasons, which are laid down by law. Other shooting continues throughout the year and probably gives pleasure to as many. This includes pigeon (analogous to dove in North America) and rabbit shooting, plus what Britons describe as "various," which means the birds and animals which are shot in defence of particular farming and forestry operations. In fact, all the quarry in this category are harmful to something, but this does not prevent two of them from also being major sporting quarry.

The woodpigeon, or ring dove, is the greatest avian pest of British farming. Shooting goes on throughout the close season for game and is at its most concentrated in early spring, when trees are bare and each neighborhood organizes its own concerted pigeon shoot. Every flighting place is manned, and every gun is in action half-a-dozen times in

February and March. Woodpigeon are dashing and elusive fliers, and perhaps the most demanding of all sporting birds.

Rabbits are a traditional countryman's perquisite, much prized for the pot, and he who excels at the difficult art of shooting them stands high in local esteem. Formerly, they constituted an even greater agricultural pest than the woodpigeon. Then the epidemic disease myxomatosis rendered them temporarily almost extinct. Now, their numbers, and the sport they provide, are recovering.

Hares—the brown hare of England, Wales, and the lowlands, and the blue hare of the Scottish highlands—can also be a cause of serious loss to farmers; three of them eat as much as one sheep, and a par figure for organized shoots in southern England is 300 per 1,000 acres (405 hectares). Such shoots take place in February and March, when cover and crops are at their minimum and visibility at its maximum in the winter-starved countryside. Except among the sophisticated, the hare is less popular than the rabbit. Many countryfolk retain a distrust of it, for which there is no rational explanation except superstition deriving from witchcraft. Hare shoots are not regarded as sporting occasions but specifically as vermin destruction.

This also applies to the gray squirrel, introduced from North America and destructive in British forestry, and most corvine birds. The latter are tolerated until their numbers reach levels which can cause severe damage, at which point shoots are organized to reduce them to acceptable levels. The birds chiefly concerned are rooks, for their damage to farming, and crows, jackdaws, magpies, and jays, for their destruction of the young of other species, including game.

All forms of wing shooting in Britain involve the use of dogs, some forms being wholly dependent on them. Britons have a long tradition in stockbreeding, British breeds of horses, cattle, and sheep being familiar in every continent. The development of gundogs in Britain has been equally wholehearted. To the British sportsman, the dog and the gun are complementary components of the sport.

In British shooting, pointers and setters work on grouse moors, and in stubble and root fields, where they quest for pheasant and partridge. Shooting over them is a specially skilled branch of the sport, with particular appeal to those who "read the dog," thereby anticipating where and when game will appear. Labradors and golden and flat-coated retrievers are used on formal shoots at the purpose for which they were intended, and in wildfowling. Spaniels find their ideal role in rough-shooting but, being the most versatile of all gundogs, they can play any other part equally well.

The one form of shooting in which dogs have no part is deerstalking, the growth of which has been one of the surprises on the British scene during the inter-war years. The sport divides itself into open-hill stalking in Scotland, and woodland stalking in England and Wales.

Once a sport becomes established, the natural species on which it depends is saved from threat of extinction. The red deer of the Scottish forests (still so called despite the absence of trees for the last 200 years) thrived under the protection of their sporting value. Meanwhile, the fallow and roe deer of the English woodlands survived tenuously in isolated areas until, against all apparent odds, their numbers rapidly increased after the end of World War II. What had happened was that returning soldiers had learned in Germany and Austria the excellent sport of woodland stalking. Previously, Britons had thought stalking with a rifle either impossible or not worth doing except on an open hill. Discovery to the contrary gave a sporting value to the deer of the lowlands, and with it the same revaluation and protection earlier accorded to the deer of the highlands. Lifted above vermin status, their numbers and range have both increased. So, two sports are now followed instead of one.

On the open, high ground of Scotland, traditional rituals are followed in a form of hunting demanding great skill where the natural odds are stacked heavily in favor of the deer. The shooter, known as the Rifle, is guided by a local professional stalker, and followed at a distance by a ghillie with a pony on which to bring home the kill. In that vast setting, devoid of cover, moving men can be seen miles away and can be winded from almost as far. Tactical approach to the chosen stag can take hours over the most daunting country. A man who is up to it, whatever his origin, earns high local respect. Again, the British social system, seemingly as enduring as the Norman conquest, proves itself resilient in the name of sport. Highland stalking is a princely pastime, but a stag is there for him who can get it — without bending the rules, of course.

In woodlands, the company of a local stalker is customary in places, but not mandatory. According to the lie of the countryside, the stalking method may be that of a tracker in careful pursuit, or of an ambush from a high seat. Roe deer are many times more numerous than fallow or sika (descended from escapes from private parks), and a good roe head is regarded as a more worthwhile trophy.

Sport having become supra-national, participation in distant countries is now a reality for a widening section of sporting communities everywhere. The British are well aware of this and have a practical understanding of the idea of interchange. In the days of Empire, only recently ended, Britons learned their sport in distant countries as often as at home. Travel, either in the armed forces or in the course of earning a living, taught them in the wider vistas overseas that most essential and basic of all sporting motivations, the simple fact of nature herself, unspoiled and offering adventure.

Britain still has unspoiled nature left and is energetically preserving it. Because of this pre-understanding, there is little of the aloofness which those of other nations seem to expect of Britons. There is, however, a natural preference for those ready to take to British sport in a British way, which is a little different. The participation of some sportsmen—welcomed because they do just that—from North and South America, Europe, the Near and Far East, and former Imperial territories, is nothing new. Their presence in increasing numbers is a fact of life.

Grouse shooting and deerstalking have appealed longest to shooters from other countries. Recently, appreciation of the British way with pheasants and partridges has spread among some of those who formerly thought their own version sufficient for their needs. Each shooting season now sees an increasing influx.

For the newcomer to the British scene—more particularly perhaps to the English scene, the Scots and Welsh being less surprised when visitors behave differently from themselves—the fundamental fact to remember is that, for practical purposes, all British shooting is private. The very small proportion of shooting country which is not legally private soon becomes somebody's territory by force of local custom and will be jealously guarded by those who have not the wish, even if they had the right, to be hospitable.

The way in, therefore, for the visiting sportsman is by invitation to the privacy of those who do wish to be hospitable and are ready to talk frankly of the terms on which this may be done. The basis of the paying-guest shooter has many modifications on such points as short-term or long, singly or in parties, experienced or not, and many more. The essential need is to make contact and discuss these points.

Reputable agencies exist to whom shoot owners indicate their readiness to be hosts to visiting sportsmen. Some leading land and property agents operate departments of their business for this purpose. With their aid, making an entry is less difficult than it may at first seem.

IX Reference

Hunter's Lexicon

Jerome Knap
Wilson Stephens

Action: The breech mechanism of a gun, by means of which it is loaded and which secures the cartridge in the chamber, preventing the cartridge from discharging to the rear. Also, a field-trial term describing the manner in which a dog moves in the field; the British term is "style."

Afon: A stream in Wales.

Aperture Sight: See **Sights.**

Autoloader: See **Semiautomatic.**

Automatic: Any firearm which continues to fire, to the extent of the capacity of its magazine, so long as the trigger is depressed. Sometimes erroneously applied to semiautomatic firearms.

Automatic Safety: See **Safety.**

Backing: An expression of a dog's pointing instinct, when a dog comes to point at sight of another dog's point, to "back" him, or "honor" his point.

Balance: In theory, the balance is that point between butt and muzzle where a gun balances when rested on a fulcrum. A gun balances properly when the point of balance is midway between the points where the hands naturally hold the gun in shooting. However, this is not the common understanding of the term. In most cases, balance is understood to mean the feel it gives the shooter in handling the gun—that is, whether correctly balanced or either muzzle-light or muzzle-heavy.

Ballistics: The theory of the motion of projectiles. The shooter loosely considers "ballistics" to mean data relative to the velocity, energy, trajectory, and penetration of a cartridge, and sometimes to related factors such as chamber pressure and a powder's burning characteristics.

Barrens: Flat wasteland with low, stunted vegetation. Also, a broad, flat marsh.

Bay: Second point of antlers, after the brow and before the tray; sometimes spelt "bey."

Bead: See **Sights.**

Beat (n): An area to be beaten or driven to flush out game.

Beat (v): To beat bushes etc., to drive out game.

Beater (n): One who beats, in order to send the game over the shooters at a covert shoot or grouse drive.

Beck: A stream in northern England.

Bed: Where big game—or even hares or rabbits—have been sleeping or resting. Another term for a rabbit or hare bed is "form."

Belted Cartridge: A cartridge, primarily of the heavy-caliber, high-velocity type, which is rimless but has a belt around the base.

Belton: A type of color formed in English setters when two colors blend so closely as to lose individual identity. Blue belton is a combination of black and white; orange belton a combination of orange and white.

Bench Rest: A wooden shooting bench, heavily constructed and firmly placed, with suitable "rest" for the muzzle or barrel, at which the shooter may sit to engage in accuracy tests of the firearm.

Bevy: A group of game birds, such as quail, generally a brood.

Big-bore: A rather loose adjective, normally applied in North America to rifles of calibers larger than .25, but applied in some countries only to much larger calibers. Also, large-bore.

Blind: A natural or man-made hiding place from which a hunter shoots ducks, turkeys, or other game. The British term is "hide."

Block: Colloquial word for a duck decoy.

Blowback: Automatic or semiautomatic action in which extraction, ejection, and reloading are accomplished by means of the force exerted rearward by the gas of the fired cartridge.

Blowdown: A thick tangle of fallen trees and brush, usually the result of severe winds.

Blown Primer: A cartridge case in which the primer was blown out during firing. Can cause serious injury, even blindness, to the shooter; one good argument for use of shooting glasses.

Bluebird Weather: Sunny, windless conditions which are the bane of the wildfowler's existence, as waterfowl normally do not move in such weather or else fly very high.

Boat-tail Bullet: A bullet with a tapered rear end designed to obtain greater efficiency at longer ranges.

Bore: The inside of the barrel of a shotgun, rifle, revolver, or pistol, the diameter of which is the caliber or gauge of the weapon. The term is also a synonym for "gauge" of a shotgun.

Brace: Standard term for two quail, partidge, pheasant, grouse, hares, or dogs.

Breech: The base (as opposed to the muzzle) of a gun barrel; the rear portion of the barrel, which, in a modern rifle, is chambered to hold the cartridge.

Breeding: The ancestry of a dog.

Brocket: A male red deer in his third year.

Broken: Term for a finished, completely trained bird dog.

Brood: All young together born or hatched by one female. See **Bevy** and **Covey.**

Brow: The first, or brow, point of antlers.

Browse: Branches of trees, small saplings, or low brush, which serve as food for members of the deer family and other ruminants.

Brush-cutter: A bullet, usually of large caliber and considerable weight, having enough velocity and weight to continue its original course without being deflected by light brush.

Brush Gun: A rifle or shotgun with a barrel shorter than average, designed for ease of movement through heavy brush.

Buck: American term for the male of various species, including antelope, goat, deer, and rabbit; in Britain, of non-native deer imported to Britain, and of the rabbit. Also, an accessory used in teaching retrieving, sometimes called a retrieving dummy.

Buckshot: Large lead or alloy shot used in shotgun shells, principally for big game such as deer.

Buffer: A biological term used to designate small forms of animal life upon which predators will feed, thus reducing the mortality of game. When enough "buffers" are present, predators eat fewer game animals.

Bugle: The sound a bull elk (wapiti) makes during the rutting (breeding) season to advertise his presence to the females and to issue challenges to the other bulls. The British term is "roaring" for stags of European red deer. In some regions, "bugling" is also used to describe the cries of hounds.

Bump: Slang for accidental flushing of game birds by a pointing dog.

Burn: An area which has been burned over by a forest fire; also, a stream in Scotland.

Burst: Generally, the first part of the run when hounds are close upon the fox; any fast part of a chase.

Butt (1): The rear part of a gun stock from the grip area rearward.

Butt (2): Camouflaged embrasure in which a shooter waits for the birds at a grouse drive. Also, the backing behind a target that stops the bullets.

Butt Plate: The metal, plastic, or hard-rubber plate covering the rear of a gunstock, usually checkered or corrugated to prevent slipping. See **Recoil Pad** or **Stock.**

Calf: Young, either sex, of the red deer until a year old.

Caliber: The diameter of the bore of a rifled arm in hundredths of an inch or in millimeters, usually measured from land to land (raised portion between grooves), which gives the true diameter of the bore prior to the cutting of grooves.

Caller: A hunter who does the calling when hunting ducks, geese, or turkeys, or other game.

Cape: The hide or pelage covering the head, neck, and foreshoulders of a game animal, often removed for mounting as a trophy. The British term is headskin.

Carbine: A short-barreled rifle, normally much lighter in weight than a standard rifle.

Carrier: The mechanism in a magazine or repeating firearm (other than a revolver) which carries the shell or cartridge from the magazine into a position to be pushed into the chamber by the closing of the breechbolt.

Carry the Line: When hounds are following the scent, they are "carrying the line."

Cast: The spreading out, or reaching out, of a pointing dog in search of game or of hounds in search of a scent. Also, in archery, the speed with which the bow will throw an arrow. Also, in falconry, a group or flight of hawks.

Centerfire: A cartridge of which the primer is contained in a pocket in the center of the cartridge base.

Chalk: White excreta of a woodcock, indicating the presence of birds in a covert.

Chamber: The enlarged portion of the gun barrel at the breech, in which the cartridge fits when in position for firing.

Charge: Load of powder and/or shot in a shotshell, or the load of powder in a muzzle-loading gun. Also, an old command, still occasionally used, to a hunting dog to lie down; it derives from the time when gun dogs were required to lie down while the guns were charged.

Cheeper: Game bird too young to be shot.

Chilled Shot: Shot containing a greater percentage of antimony than soft lead. All shot except buckshot and steel shot is dropped from a tower. Buckshot of the large sizes is cast, as are single balls.

Choke: The constriction in the muzzle of a shotgun bore by means of which control is exerted upon the shot charge in order to throw its pellets into a definite area of predetermined concentration. Degree of choke is measured by the approximate percentage of pellets in a shot charge, which hit within a 30-inch circle at 40 yards. The following table gives the accepted percentages obtained with various chokes:

Full Choke...65 % minimum
Improved Modified..60–70 %
Modified...50–65 %
Improved Cylinder...35–50 %
Cylinder..25–35 %

Choke Constriction: The amount of constriction at the muzzle of various gauges, which produces choke, is as follows:

Gauge	Full Choke		Modified Choke		Improved Cylinder		Cylinder	
	inch	mm	inch	mm	inch	mm	inch	mm
10	.035	.889	.017	.432	.007	.178	0	0
12	.030	.762	.015	.381	.006	.152	0	0
16	.024	.610	.012	.305	.005	.127	0	0
20	.021	.533	.010	.254	.004	.102	0	0
28	.017	.432	.008	.203	.003	.076	0	0

Clip: Detachable magazine of a rifle or a pistol. A metal container designed to contain a given number of cartridges for a repeating rifle.

Cock (n): Male bird.

Cock (v): Make ready a firearm for firing by pulling back the hammer or firing pin to full cock. A firearm with a visible hammer usually has half-cock and full-cock positions.

Cold Line: The faint scent of the quarry.

Comb: The upper and forward edge of a gunstock against which the shooter rests his cheek.

Conseil International De La Chasse: An organization comprising members from various European countries, which assumes responsibility for the classification and measurement system employed in recording trophies of European big game.

Coon: A colloquialism for raccoon.

Cope: Muzzle for a ferret.

Couple: Two woodcock, snipe, waterfowl, shorebirds, or rabbits. Also used to describe two hounds.

Course: In fox hunting, to run by sight and not by nose. Also, the territory to be covered in a field trial for bird dogs and spaniels.

Cover: Trees, undergrowth, grass, or reeds in which game may lie. A place to be hunted.

Covert: In fox hunting, a place where fox may be found. Also, woodland. Also, the name for a place where any game may be found. Same as cover.

Covert-shoot: Pheasant shooting in which the shooters wait in line outside woodland from which the birds are driven by beaters.

Coverts: The wing feathers which cover the base of the flight feathers.

Covey: A group of game birds such as quail; a bevy. Also, a British term for a family group of grouse or partidge, generally four to sixteen birds.

Crimp: That portion of a cartridge case or shotshell, which is turned inward to grip the bullet or to hold the end wad in place, respectively.

Cripple: A game bird that has been shot down but not killed. This term is normally employed in duck shooting. (In upland shooting, the term "winged" is more often used.)

Cross Hairs: The cross-hair reticule or aiming device in a telescopic sight on a rifle. Wire or nylon is now used instead of hair.

Cry: The voice of a hound. The cry varies during the chase. By its tone, the other hounds can tell how strong the scent is and how sure the line is.

Dancing Ground: An area where such birds as prairie chicken, sharptail grouse, sage grouse, and black grouse perform their courtship dances in the spring.

Doe: Female of fallow, roe, or imported deer, and of the hare or rabbit.

Dogging: The shooting of grouse or partidges over pointers or setters.

Double: Any shotgun with two barrels, whether the side-by-side type or the over-and-under. Also, when a fox, raccoon, or other game animal turns back on his course to elude hounds.

Drag: Scent left by a fox as he returns to his den; or an artificial trail made by dragging a scented bag for hounds to follow.

Dram: Unit of weight, which is the equivalent of 27.5 grains. There are 256 drams in one pound avoirdupois (454 g).

Dram Equivalent: In the early days of black-powder shotshells, the powder charge was measured in drams. Dram for dram, today's smokeless powder is more powerful. The term "3 dram equivalent" means that the amount of smokeless powder used produces the same shot velocity as would 3 drams of black powder.

Drift: Deviation of any projectile, bullet, or arrow from the plane of its departure, caused by wind. Also, the deviation of the projectile from the plane of departure due to rotation. In all sporting firearms, the drift from the plane of departure due to rotation is so slight as to be of no consequence.

Drive (v): To move game toward the shooters.

Drive (n): A self-contained operation during a day's shooting in which the shooters remain stationary while game is driven from a particular direction.

Driven Game: Birds which are moved toward the shooters by beaters.

Driving: Method of hunting in which the hunters are divided into two groups. One group moves to an area to take up stands or watches covering a wide terrain; the other group moves toward the first, making sufficient noise to drive the game toward the group on watches. The individuals on watch are termed "standers" and those driving the game "drivers," or in Britain, "beaters."

Drop: Distance below the line of sight of a rifle or shotgun from an extension of this line to the comb and to the heel of the stock. See **Drop at Comb** and **Drop at Heel.**

Drop at Comb: Vertical distance between the prolonged line of sight and the point of the comb. The drop and thickness of the comb are the most important dimensions in the stock of a shotgun or rifle. They are affected by the drop at heel. If the dimensions are correct, the eye is guided into and held steadily in the line of aim. For hunting purposes, the best standard drop at comb on both rifles and shotguns is $1\frac{1}{4}$ to $1\frac{5}{8}$ inches (3.8–4.1 cm). Drop differs for target shooting. Ideal stock dimensions for field or target shooting are attained only by custom fitting.

Drop at Heel: The vertical distance between the prolonged line of sight and the heel of the butt. The amount of drop varies, depending upon the ideas and build of the shooter. Most shotgun hunters require a drop of about $2\frac{1}{4}$ inches (6.4 cm).

Earth: The hole of some burrowing animal, such as a woodchuck, appropriated by a fox. Also, the den.

Eclipse Plumage: The plumage of a male bird before the time when he takes on his full breeding plumage.

Ejector: Mechanism which ejects an empty case or loaded cartridge from a gun after it has been withdrawn, or partly withdrawn, from the chamber by the extractor. In a double-barreled shotgun, ejector often means extractor; "selective ejection" means automatic ejection of the fired shell only and is otherwise called automatic ejection.

Ejector Hammers: In a double-barreled shotgun, the driving pistons which eject the fired shells.

Elevation: The angle which the rear sight must be raised or lowered to compensate for the trajectory of the bullet and ensure the desired point of impact at different ranges.

Exotic: Any game bird or animal which has been imported.

Extractor: The hooked device which draws the cartridge out of the chamber when the breech mechanism is opened.

Fault: A check or interruption in a run by hounds caused by loss of scent.

Fawn: Offspring of the year of any deer other than red deer.

Field Dressing: The minimum dressing-out of a game animal in the field, merely enough to ensure preservation of the meat and the trophy, means usually the removing of the entrails and visceral organs.

Firing Pin: The pointed nose of the hammer of a firearm or the separate pin or plunger which, actuated by the hammer or the mainspring, dents the primer, thus firing the cartridge.

Firelighting: See **Jacklighting.**

Flag: The tail of a whitetail deer. Also, the long hair on a setter's tail.

Flat Trajectory: A term used to describe the low trajectory of high-velocity bullets which travel for a long distance over a flatter arc than other bullets. Scientifically an incorrect term, for no trajectory is truly flat. See also **Trajectory.**

Flighting: Ambushing duck or pigeon at their roosts or feeding grounds.

Fling: A period of aimless running before an enthusiastic bird dog settles to hunting.

Flush (n): The act of a questing dog putting game birds into the air, or an animal on foot.

Flushing Wild: Rise of game birds which have not been obviously disturbed, or birds that have been flushed out of shotgun range.

Flyway: Migration route of birds between breeding and wintering grounds. Also, the route waterfowl use between feeding and roosting areas.

Forearm: Synonymous with fore-end, although some use "forearm" when the butt stock and foregrip are separate pieces. See **Fore-end.**

Fore-end: Portion of the wooden gunstock forward of the receiver and under the barrel.

Forest: Open mountains, devoid of trees, on which stags are stalked in Scotland.

Fresh Line: Opposite of "cold line"— a fresh, or "hot," scent of game pursued by hounds.

Fur: All four-legged quarry.

Gaggle: A flock of geese. An old British term.

Game: In British law, pheasants, all partridges, all grouse, woodcock and snipe; by custom, also deer and hares.

Gang: A flock of brant. Also, an old British term for a group of European elk (moose).

Gas-operated: Said of a semiautomatic firearm which utilizes the gases generated by the powder combustion, before the bullet emerges from the muzzle, to operate a piston which extracts, ejects, and reloads the arm to the extent of the number of rounds in the magazine.

Gauge: The bore size of a shotgun. The number of the gauge has no relation to the linear measurement of the bore. Gauge is determined by the number of equal spheres, each of which exactly fits the barrel of the gun, which may be obtained from 1 lb (454 g) of lead. For example, a 12-gauge gun has a bore diameter the same as one of the twelve identically-sized spheres which can be made from a pound of lead. See **Bore.**

Gauge Measurements: The bore diameters of various gauges are as follows:

10 gauge	.775 inches (19 · 69 mm)
12 gauge	.725 inches (18 · 42 mm)
16 gauge	.662 inches (16 · 81 mm)
20 gauge	.615 inches (15 · 62 mm)
28 gauge	.550 inches (13 · 97 mm)
.410 gauge	.410 inches (10 · 41 mm)

Ghillie: Attendant, usually in charge of the pony, who accompanies a stalking party in Scotland. Also, an attendant on a fisherman.

Glass (v): To scan terrain with binoculars or telescope to locate game.

Grain: Abbreviated gr. Weight measurement. One ounce equals 437.5 gr. There are 7,000 gr in 1 lb (454 grams). In reference to gunstocks, grain indicates the direction of the fibers on the surface of the stock.

Gralloch (v): To field dress big-game animals immediately after shooting by removing the viscera and entrails. See **Field Dressing.**

Gram: Abbreviated g. Weight measurement. The equivalent of 15.43 grains.

Graze: Grasses, weeds, and similar low growths upon which deer and other ruminants feed.

Grip: That part of the stock of a rifle or shotgun which is grasped by the trigger hand when firing the gun. The two most common types of grips are the "pistol grip" and the "straight grip" found on some double-barreled shotguns.

Group: A series of shots fired at a target with a constant sight setting and point of aim. The diameter of the group is measured from the centers of the outer holes.

Group Diameter: The distance between centers of the two shots most widely separated in a group.

Gun: Any smooth-bore weapon projecting a charge of pellets; see also **Rifle.** Also, a participant in a British shooting party, as distinct from a helper or spectator.

Hair Trigger: A trigger requiring extremely light pressure for the release of the hammer.

Hammer: That part of a firearm, actuated by the mainspring and controlled by the trigger, which strikes either the cartridge rim or primer, or strikes and drives forward the firing pin so that it indents the primer or rim of the cartridge, to discharge the cartridge.

Hammerless: Of firearms having the hammer concealed within the breech mechanism.

Handgun: A firearm that is normally fired with one hand. A pistol or revolver.

Handloads: Cartridges loaded by hand for precision shooting, as opposed to commercial or "factory loads."

Hang-fire: Delayed ignition of the powder in a cartridge after the hammer has fallen and the primer has been struck.

Hard-mouthed: Of a dog that chews or crushes birds when retrieving.

Hart: The male deer. Usually used to refer to male red deer in Britain. A stag.

Head (n): The antlers of a deer, of any species and either sex.

Head (v): For a shooter to take post in advance of others to intercept birds flushing out of range of the rest.

Headspace: The space between the head of the bolt or breechblock and the base of the cartridge. Excessive headspace is exceedingly dangerous and can result in the bursting of the receiver.

Headstamp: The letters or number, or both, on the base of a cartridge.

Heel (n): Upper part of the butt of a shotgun or rifle. Also, a command to a dog to walk quietly beside or at the heel of the person giving the order.

Hide: Camouflaged embrasure in which a shooter waits for duck or pigeon. See **Blind.** Also, the skin of an animal.

High-base Shell: A shotgun shell furnished with high inside base wad, approximately ¾ inch (19 mm) thick before forming.

High-brass Shell: High-velocity shotgun shell on which the brass base extends a considerable distance up the plastic tube.

High Intensity: A term associated with a rifle or cartridge having a velocity of more than 2,500 foot-seconds (762 m/seconds).

High Power: A term associated with a rifle or cartridge having a velocity of more than 2,000 foot-seconds (609 m/seconds).

Hind: The female of the red deer.

Hochstand (Ger.): The seat at tree-top height from which deer are shot in woodland.

Hull: Empty cartridge or shell.

Hummle: A mature red deer stag which has grown no antlers.

Hunting: In British usage, the pursuit by a pack of hounds of ground quarry (fox, deer, hare) with followers mounted or on foot; gun sport is "shooting" in British idiom.

Imperial Bull: A bull elk (wapiti) that has seven points on each antler; a relatively rare and highly desirable trophy. Also, imperial stag in the case of European red deer.

Iron Sight: See **Sights.**

Jack: The male of the hare.

Jacklighting: The illegal practice of shooting game at night with the help of artificial light, which is reflected by the eyes of the game. Synonymous with firelighting.

Jump-shooting: A method of duck hunting in which the hunter stealthily approaches ducks by boat, or by stalking toward water, until within range and then flushes them.

Juvenile: A bird which, though having attained full growth, has not attained full adult characteristics or plumage. See also **Cheeper.**

Kentucky Windage: A term used by American riflemen to describe the process of "holding off" to the left or right of a target to allow for the effect of the wind on the bullet, but making no adjustment in the sight setting.

Knobber: Male red deer in his second year.

Lead (n): Term used to designate the distance it is necessary to hold ahead of any bird or animal to compensate for its speed of movement and the time required for the bullet or hot charge to reach it. The British term is forward allowance.

Lead (v): To cause a dog to follow under restraint, by means of a cord or leather thong attached to the dog's collar.

Leash: A group of three quail, partridge, pheasant, grouse, or hares. Also, a cord to lead a dog, a dog lead.

Length of Stock: The distance in a straight line from the center of the trigger to a point midway between the heel and toe of the buttplate, on the surface of the plate. Required stock length depends upon the build of the shooter, men of short stature or short arms requiring short stocks. The standard length for hunting arms is 14 inches (35.6 cm) for shotguns and 13½ inches (34.3 cm) for rifles. Also called length of pull.

Line: The track or trail of an animal indicated by the scent the hounds are following. Also, the shooters deployed at a formal shoot, called "the line."

Line of Sight: The straight line between the eye of the shooter and the target. See **Trajectory.**

Line-running: Of a dog that casts in straight lines rather than hunts in places where birds are usually found.

Line Shooting: A form of scoter (sea duck) shooting along the North American Atlantic coast, in which several boats line up across a known scoter flyway to shoot at the birds as they fly past.

Live Weight: The computed or estimated weight of a game animal before it is dressed out.

Loader: Attendant who holds and re-loads the second weapon when a shooter uses two guns at a covert shoot where many birds are expected.

Loch: A lake in Scotland (also lough (Ireland) and llyn (Wales).

Lock: The combination of hammer, firing pin, sear, mainspring, and trigger which serves to discharge the cartridge when the trigger is pulled.

Lock Time: The time elapsed between the release of the hammer by the sear and the impact of the firing pin on the primer. Also called lock speed.

Lubrication of Bullets: Most lead bullets have to be lubricated with grease or wax on their surface or in their grooves to prevent leading the bore. Outside-lubricated cartridges have the lubricant placed on the surface of the bullet outside the case. Inside-lubricated bullets have the lubricant in grooves or cannelures on the bullet where it is covered by the neck of the case.

Lug: In a break-down, breech-loading shotgun or rifle, a lug on the barrel secures the barrel to the frame. Lugs on the front of a bolt or breechblock which rotate into slots to lock the action for firing are termed locking lugs.

Magazine: The tube or box which holds cartridges or shells in reserve for mechanical insertion into the chamber of a repeating firearm.

Magazine Plug: Plug or dowel placed inside or against the magazine spring of a slide-action or semiautomatic shotgun to limit the capacity of the magazine in order to comply with the law. (In the United States,

311

waterfowlers may have no more than three shells in their guns; some individual states limit magazine capacity for other game.)

Mark: A call used to warn another shooter of the flushing or approach of a game bird. The term is often accompanied by a direction: "mark right" or "mark left."

Mark Down: To use some terrain feature to mark the location of a fallen game bird in order to facilitate retrieving.

Market Gunner: One who hunted for the purpose of selling the game he killed, a practice now illegal in North America. A market hunter.

Mask: The head or pate of a fox, raccoon, wolf, or coyote.

Match Rifle: A rifle designed for competitive shooting, a target rifle.

Minute of Angle: This is the unit of adjustment on all telescopic, and most aperture, sights, being indicated by a series of fine lines. One minute of angle is equivalent to the following distances at the ranges indicated:

British and American	Metric
25 yards ......¼in	25 m .... .69 mm
50 yards ......½in	50 m ....1.39 mm
100 yards 1in	100 m ....2.78 mm

Moor: High, treeless land such as that inhabited by grouse.

Mounts: Metal bases used to secure a telescopic sight to the barrel or receiver of a firearm.

Muzzle Brake: A device on the muzzle of a shotgun or rifle which, by means of vents and baffles, deflects gases to the rear to reduce recoil.

Muzzle Energy: The energy of a bullet or projectile on emerging from the muzzle of the firearm that discharges it. Usually designated in foot-pounds or kilogram-meters.

Muzzle Velocity: The speed of a bullet or projectile at the moment of emerging from the muzzle. Usually expressed in feet or meters per second.

O'Clock: A means of indicating a location on the target or over a range or field, corresponding to similar locations on the face of a clock, 12 o'clock being at the top of the target, or at the target end of the rifle range. Thus, a shot striking the target immediately to the left of the bull's-eye is a hit at 9 o'clock, and a wind blowing from the right at a right angle to the line of fire is a 3 o'clock wind.

Offhand: Shooting in a standing position, without the use of a rest or sling.

Over-and-under: Double-barreled firearm with one barrel superimposed over the other.

Palmated: Of the shape of the antlers of moose, caribou, and fallow deer that is similar to the shape of the palm of a hand with fingers outspread.

Pass-shooting: A form of shooting in which the hunter places himself in position under a known flyway or travel route of ducks, geese, pigeons, or doves. The birds are shot as they pass, without the enticement of decoys.

Pattern: The distribution of a charge of shot fired from a shotgun.

Pattern Control: Control of the shot pattern by means of choke.

Peep Sight: See **Sights.**

Peg: The numbered stick indicating the position of a shooter at a covert shoot or partridge drive.

Pelage: The fur, hair, or wool covering of a mammal.

Pellet: Round shot, of any size, a given number of which make up the shot charge.

Picker-up: One who, helped by dogs, finds and gathers what is shot.

Piece: The mid-day meal carried by a shooter.

Piston: In an automatic or semiautomatic arm, a metal plunger which, when forced down a cylinder by powder gases, operates a mechanism to extract and eject the fired cartridge, and to reload and cock the arm.

Pitch: This can be observed by resting a gun upright beside a wall with the butt or butt plate flat on the floor. If the barrel is exactly parallel with the wall, the gun is said to have no pitch. If the breech touches the wall and the barrel inclines away from it, the distance between the muzzle and the wall is the "negative pitch." If the barrel inclines toward the wall, so that there is a distance between the breech and the wall, this distance is what is called, simply, the "pitch." A pitch of 2 to 3 inches (5 to 8 cm) is desirable on a repeating rifle because it causes the butt to remain in place at the shoulder when the rifle is fired rapidly.

Point: The motionless pose assumed by a dog which indicates the proximity of game birds.

Points: The horn features of an antlered head which determine its ranking as a trophy (e.g. "a twelve-pointer" is brow, bay, tray, and three on top of each antler).

Point of Aim: The bottom edge of the bull's-eye for a target shooter using iron sights; the center of the bull's-eye for one using a telescopic sight.

Pointing Out: A method of shotgun shooting in which the shooter selects a point ahead of the moving target at which to shoot so that the shot charge and target will meet. Opposite shooting style to "swinging past."

Post Sight: See **Sights.**

Pot-hunter: One who hunts primarily for meat rather than sport.

Powder: The finely divided chemical mixture that supplies the power used in shotgun and metallic ammunition, technically propellant powder. When the powder is ignited by the flash of the priming composition it burns with a rapidly increasing gas which develops a pressure of 6,000 to 55,000 lb per square inch (420 to 3,900 kg per square cm) in the chamber and bore of the gun. This gas furnishes the propelling force of the bullet or charge of shot. Originally, all propellant powder was black powder formed in grains of varying size, with the size of the grain determining the rate of burning and suitability for various cartridges. Modern powders are smokeless and their base is nitroglycerine or nitrocellulose or a combination of both, the product then being called double-base powder. The rate of burning is controlled by the composition, by the size and shape of the grains, and whether or not coated with some retarding substance called a deterrent. Those so coated are called progressive-burning.

Primaries: The outer and longest flight feathers of a bird; quill feathers.

Primer: The small cup, or cap, seated in the center of the base of a centerfire cartridge and containing the igniting composition. When the primer is indented by the firing pin, the priming composition is crushed and detonates, thus igniting the charge of powder. Rimfire cartridges contain the priming composition within the folded rim of the case, where it is crushed in the same manner. The British term is cap.

Pull: The distance between the face of the trigger and the center of the butt of the gunstock. Also, the amount of pressure, in pounds, which must be applied to the trigger to cause the sear to disengage and permit the hammer to fall. Also, the command given to release a skeet or trap target.

Pump Gun: Common name for the slide-action rifle or shotgun. See **Slide Action.**

Quartering: A hunting-dog term for the act of ranging back and forth across the course.

Quartering Bird: A bird which approaches the shooter at an angle, either right or left.

Rat-tailed: Lacking long hairs on the tail, as in the case of such dogs as the Irish water spaniel.

Receiver: The frame of a rifle or shotgun including the breech, locking, and loading mechanism of the arm.

Receiver Sight: See **Sights.**

Recoil: The backward movement, or "kick," of the firearm caused by the discharge of the cartridge.

Recoil-operated: Of a firearm which utilizes the recoil, or rearward force exerted by the combustion of the powder, to operate the action and extract, eject, and reload to the extent of the number of rounds in the magazine.

Recoil Pad: A soft rubber pad on the butt of a firearm to soften its recoil.

Reduced Load: A cartridge loaded with a lighter than standard powder charge, for use at a short range.

Reticule (or **Reticle**): The crossed wires, picket, post, or other divisional system installed in a telescopic sight to permit its use as a gunsight, or in a pair of binoculars to permit the use of a scale for estimating distances.

Retrieving: Dog's act of finding and bringing an object, generally dead or wounded game bird, to the handler.

Revolver: Any handgun embodying a cylindrical magazine, as opposed to a single-shot or semiautomatic handgun, either of which is usually called a "pistol."

Rib: The raised bar or vane, usually slightly concave on its upper surface and usually matted, which forms the sighting plane extending from breech to muzzle of a gun. It is used on all double-barreled shotguns.

Rifle: A firearm projecting a single rotating bullet. Also, as the Rifle, the member of a stalking party who will fire the shot (cf. the Gun).

Rifled Slug: A bullet-shaped projectile with hollow base and rifled sides used in a shotgun for hunting big game. Will not harm shotgun barrels and will not "ream out" any type of choke.

Rifling: Parallel grooves cut into the bore of a rifle or pistol, spiraling from the breech to the muzzle, causing the bullet to spin in its flight.

Rig: A setting of decoys in front of a boat or blind; also used to describe the entire hunting outfit.

Rimfire: A cartridge in which the priming compound is contained in a rim at the base.

Ring Hunt: A form of driving in which a large number of shooters and beaters form a ring and gradually close in, to drive the game toward its center. An ancient method, still used in Europe, primarily for hunting hares and foxes.

Rough-shooting: The pursuit and taking of game and other quarry by Guns who have no human assistants but are generally aided by spaniels. See also **Dogging.**

Royal: Fourth point, after the tray and before the fifth, of antlers.

Royal Bull: A bull elk (wapiti) that has six points on each antler. A very desirable trophy. Also, royal stag of the European red deer.

Run: In some regions, a game trail or path created by animals over a period of time.

Safety: The device which locks a firearm against the possibility of discharge; sometimes called a safety catch. In common practice, the term applies primarily to the button, pin, or toggle which, when set in the "safe" position, prevents the discharge of the arm by pulling the trigger. A safety which automatically resets itself in the "safe" position when the gun is opened during the reloading process is called an automatic safety. Such a safety is most common on double-barreled shotguns.

Scapulars: The feathers on each side of the back of a bird's shoulders.

Scope: Telescope or telescopic sight.

Sear: The device in the lock of a firearm which holds the hammer or firing pin in its cocked position. When the trigger is pulled to the rear, it depresses the sear, which in turn releases the hammer or firing pin.

Secondaries: The wing feathers inside the primaries.

Semiautomatic: Any firearm which will fire, extract, eject, and reload by means of pressure on the trigger, but requires repeated pressure on the trigger to fire each round.

Set: A "rig" or setting of decoys.

Set Trigger: A trigger, the sear of which is "set up" by a preliminary movement or by pressure on another trigger, permitting the sear to disengage the hammer at the slightest touch or pressure on the trigger.

Most set triggers are adjustable for the amount of pressure desired.

Sewelling: Cords carrying colored streamers which, when activated, cause birds to flush far enough back to ensure that they are flying high when over the Guns.

Shell: Empty case of any cartridge. Also, an American term for a loaded shotgun cartridge.

Shock Collar: A collar with an electronic device which can be set off by remote control to give a dog an electric shock to punish it when it does not obey or does something wrong. The shock collar is a dangerous instrument in the hands of a novice trainer because it can ruin a dog when used incorrectly.

Side-by-side: A double-barreled shotgun with the barrels positioned side by side, as opposed to the over-and-under configuration.

Sight Radius: The distance between the front and rear sights. The longer the distance the greater the accuracy of the firearm.

Sights: The aiming device on a firearm. On most rifles and handguns, the factory-installed sights consist of two elements called "front sight" and "rear sight," which together frequently are called "iron sights" because they are made of principally metal. The front sight, located on the barrel near the muzzle, is usually post-shaped or bead-shaped and hence sometimes called post or bead. The rear sight is usually located partway down the barrel, near the breech or on the receiver. If it consists of a V- or U-shaped notch in a flat piece of metal, it is called an "open" sight. An open sight with a deep U-shaped notch with protruding wings is called a "buckhorn sight." The rear sight can also consist of an aperture in a disk. It is then called an aperture, or peep, sight. When the aperture sight is attached to the receiver it is called a "receiver sight" and when it is attached to the tang it is called a "tang sight." When the aperture adjustments have micrometer settings, such a sight is sometimes called a "micrometer sight." A hunting shotgun usually has only one sight consisting of a bead near the muzzle, but most trap and skeet guns have a second bead halfway down the barrel. There are also telescopic sights for rifles and handguns.

Sign: Any indication of the presence of game. Sign may include tracks, droppings, marks on trees, or any other indication that the area has recently been visited by a game animal.

Silvertip: Colloquial name for the grizzly bear.

Singing Ground: An open area used by the male woodcock for its courtship display.

Six o'Clock, or Six-o'Clock Hold: A term for the aiming point indicating that a rifle or handgun has been sighted-in to place the bullet not at the point of aim on a bull's-eye but well above it, so that the shooter aims at the center of the bottom edge. If the bull's-eye is a clock face, the point of aim is at 6 o'clock, but the impact point is at the exact center, midway between 6 and 12 o'clock. Target shooters prefer to aim in this way, when using iron sights, as it permits them to "rest" the bull's-eye on the top of the front sight and center the bull's-eye in the rear-sight aperture. See **O'Clock.**

Slide Action: A repeating firearm action in which the breech is closed and opened and the action operated by means of a sliding fore-end that acts as a handle for sliding the breech into the opened or closed position. Also **Pump Gun.**

Small-bore: Specifically, of a .22-caliber rifle chambered for a rimfire cartridge. Sometimes applied to rifles chambered for centerfire cartridges up to .25 caliber and shotguns under 20 gauge.

Smoked Sights: Sights after they have been blackened by soot from a candle or blackening lamp, thus eliminating any shine or glare. Commercial spray blackeners are also available.

Smoothbore: A firearm without rifling.

Sneakbox: A term for the Barnegat Bay duck-boat.

Spike-collar: A dog-training accessory—a slip collar with small spikes on the inside, used to force obedience to commands.

Spook (v): To frighten game. A term used by a hunter to indicate that a bird or animal flushed or jumped from cover at his approach, or when it winded or heard him.

Spooky: Of any animal or bird that is extremely wary or constantly alert.

Spoor: Tracks or footprints of animals. Sometimes used to mean all game sign.

Spotting Scope: A telescope with sufficient magnification to permit a shooter to see bullet holes in a target at long range, and to permit hunters to see game and evaluate trophy animals at long range. The average sporting scope is 24 power.

Spread: The overall area of a shotgun pattern. Also, the inside distance between right and left antlers or horns at their widest separation or at the tips.

Spy: An interlude of halting, waiting, and watching in which a deer shooter observes his quarry and its movements before deciding the tactics of his approach.

Stag: The mature male of the red deer.

Stalker: The professional who guides and advises those seeking to shoot deer on open forests in Scotland; also, a shooter of deer in woodland who approaches the deer by stealth.

Stalking: A method of hunting in which the hunter locates game and then stealthily follows a predetermined route to arrive within shooting range of the quarry.

Stanch: Firm and decisive; describing a dog's style while pointing. The dog that establishes a point and holds it, without caution or admonition, until his handler flushes his birds, may be regarded as stanch. Also spelled "staunch."

Stand: The position at which the shooters are placed for each drive at a covert shoot (hence "first stand," "second stand," etc.).

Start: The moment when a hound first finds scent or a trail.

Steady: Of a dog's behavior after birds are flushed. The dog is "steady to wing and shot" when he retains his position after the birds are flushed and the shot is fired.

Still-hunt: A method of hunting in which a hunter moves very slowly and silently through cover in search of game, pausing frequently to scan the terrain. The word "still," in this context, means silent rather than motionless.

Stock (n): The wooden part of a shotgun or rifle, or the handle of a pistol or revolver. The butt section of a stock is called a buttstock.

Stock (v): In game management or preserve operation, to stock is to release game in suitable habitat.

Stop: An assistant tactically placed to prevent pheasants approaching the shooters too closely, or evading them, at a covert shoot.

Swinging Past: A method of shotgun shooting in which the target is overtaken and passed by the sight, and the swing with the target is continued as the trigger is pressed. See **Pointing Out.**

Switch: A mature male deer whose antlers have no points.

Take-down: Of a firearm in which the barrel and adjacent parts can be readily separated from the receiver or action, thus permitting the arm to be packed in a short container.

Tang Sight: See **Sights.**

Team: An old British term for a flock or group of ducks.

Telescopic Sight: A telescope with reticule, permitting an aim of greater accuracy and clearness than that of an ordinary sight.

Tertials: The wing feathers inside the secondaries that are closest to the body.

Throwing Off: Of a rifle that is performing erratically or failing to give reasonable accuracy. This often results from improper bedding of the barrel.

Timberline: The upper limit of forest growth at high altitude.

Toe: The lower part of the butt of a shotgun or rifle.

Tolling Dog: A dog once widely used in Europe, and used now only in Nova Scotia, to entice wildfowl to enter a trap or to lure them within range of the gun. The action of the dog in running back and forth on the shore stimulates the birds' curiosity. In Nova Scotia, these dogs are bred to resemble a red fox and are registered by the Canadian Kennel Club as the Nova Scotia tolling retriever.

Trade (v): Of game, to move back and forth over a given area: "The ducks were trading along the far shore."

Trailer: A dog which continually or frequently follows his bracemate.

Trailing: Act of following game. See **Tracking.**

Trajectory: The course described by a projectile in flight. It forms an arc due to the effect of gravity. Usually, measured in terms of height above the line of sight at midrange.

Tray: The third point of antlers of a deer, after the brow and bay (or bez). The word is sometimes spelt "trez."

Trigger Guard: A guard surrounding the trigger or triggers of a firearm.

Trigger Pull: The pressure required to bring about the release of the sear notch on the hammer, permitting the hammer to fall.

Tularemia: A virulent disease, known also as "rabbit fever." Rabbits are its major victims, and great care should be exercised when skinning rabbits. The disease can be communicated to humans if a cut or scratch on the hands or arms makes contact with an infected animal. The disease can be fatal. No harmful effects result from eating of an infected bird or animal, as thorough cooking destroys the virus.

Turkey Shoot: Originally, turkey shoots utilized a turkey as a target as well as a prize. The bird was placed behind a shield with only its head protruding. In early turkey shoots, contestants were permitted one shot in the standing position at 10 rods (55 yards/50 m); later, the ranges varied. At modern turkey shoots, a regulation target is used or clay targets are thrown from a trap, the turkey going to the shooter with the best score.

Turning to Whistle: A hunting-dog term for breaking the cast and turning the dog in response to the handler's whistle.

Twist: The angle or inclination of the rifling grooves off the axis of the bore. Twist is designated by measuring the number of turns or fractions of turns to the inch of barrel length. A "14-inch twist" means that the grooves make one complete turn inside the bore every 14 inches (35.6 cm).

Upland Game: A general term for all small game, including birds and mammals.

Various: In Britain, fair but unexpected quarry for which no category is provided in normal game records (e.g. jay, gray squirrel).

Varmint: A colloquial American term (stemming from "vermin") for a generally undesirable animal. Woodchucks and foxes are widely considered varmints. In some regions, the term is also used for predators such as bobcats. However, many predatory and non-predatory animals that were formerly classed as varmints are now protected or managed as game animals.

Varmint Cartridge: Cartridge designed to give exceptionally good accuracy, high retained velocity, and consequently flatter trajectory. Varmint cartridges are so called because they were originally developed for long-range shooting at woodchucks and prairie dogs.

Varminter: A rifle employed primarily for long-range varmint shooting. Many such rifles have long, heavy barrels for maximum velocity and accuracy.

Velocity: The speed of a bullet or shot charge, usually designated in feet per second or meters per second.

Velvet: Soft vascular tissue which covers the antlers of deer until they have attained their full growth and form, at which time membranous tissue dies and is removed when the animal rubs its antlers against brush and trees.

Ventilated Rib: A raised sighting plane affixed to a shotgun barrel by posts, allowing the passage of air to disperse the heat from the barrel which would otherwise distort the shooter's view of the target. Very useful on trap and skeet guns.

Vernier Sight: A rear sight, the aperture of which is raised or lowered by means of a threaded post with a knurled knob. A vernier scale on the frame indicates the elevation in hundredths of an inch.

Walk-up: A shooting method, chiefly for partridges and grouse, in which the shooters and their companions advance in line through a crop, stubble or heather, taking birds as they flush.

Wild Flush: The rise of game birds for no apparent reason, usually far from the gun.

Wing: All feathered quarry. See **Fur.**

Winged: A term indicating that a game bird has been hit but not killed. Used primarily by upland shooters. See **Cripple.**

Yard: An area, usually within a forest, in which a large number of deer, moose, elk, or similar mammals herd together, tramping down the snow and feeding on the browse supplied by the low branches. Used especially by whitetail deer when snow becomes deep enough to impede normal travel through browse areas.

Yaw: To vary from a straight course. A bullet which does not travel exactly "nose on" but wobbles slightly sideways is said to "yaw."

Yeld: A female deer without offspring; if a red hind, and barren, generally the leader of the herd.

Zero: The adjustment of the sights on a rifle to cause the bullet to strike a calculated impact point at a given range. A rifle with the sights zeroed for 100 yards will, under normal conditions, place the bullet in the center of the target at that range.

Bibliography

ACKLEY, P. O. **Home Gun Care & Repair.** Harrisburg, Pennsylvania, 1969.

ANDERSON, L. A. **How to Hunt Small American Game.** New York, 1969.

BAILLIE-GROHMAN, WILLIAM A. and BAILLIE-GROHMAN, F., eds. **Edward of Norwich: Oldest English Book on Hunting.** Repr. of ed. of 1909.

BARBER, JOEL D. **Wild Fowl Decoys.** New York, 1934.

BARNES, F. C. **Cartridges of the World.** Northfield, Illinois, 1972.

BERNSEN, PAUL S. **The North American Waterfowler.** Seattle, Washington, 1972.

BEST, G. A. and BLANC, F. E., eds. **Rowland Ward's Records of Big Game (Africa).** 15th ed. London, 1973.

BOUGHAN, ROLLA B. **Shotgun Ballistics for Hunters.** New York, 1965.

BOVILL, E. W. **The England of Nimrod and Surtees: 1815–1854.** London, 1959.

BRISTER, BOB. **Shotgunning: The Art and the Science.** Tulsa, Oklahoma, 1976.

BURK, BRUCE. **Game Bird Carving.** New York, 1972.

BUTLER, ALFRED J. **Sport in Classic Times.** Los Altos, California, 1975.

CAMP, RAYMOND R. **The Hunter's Encyclopedia.** Harrisburg, Pennsylvania, 1966.

CAPSTICK, PETER H. **Death in the Long Grass.** New York, 1978.

CARMICHEL, JIM. **The Modern Rifle.** Tulsa, Oklahoma, 1975.

CHURCHILL, ROBERT. **Churchill's Shotgun Book.** New York, 1955.

CONNETT, EUGENE V., III. **Duck Decoys.** Brattleboro, Vermont, 1953.

COYKENDALL, RALF. **Duck Decoys and How to Rig Them.** New York, 1955.

DALRYMPLE, BYRON. **Complete Guide to Hunting Across North America.** New York, 1970.

—**How to Call Wildlife.** New York, 1975.

DANIELSSON, BROR., ed. **William Twiti's the Art of Hunting.** Atlantic Highland, New Jersey.

DARTON, F. HARVEY. **From Surtees to Sassoon: Some English Contrasts 1838–1928.** Darby, Pennsylvania.

DA SILVA, S. NEWTON. **A Grande Fauna Selvagen de Angola.** Luanda, Angola, 1970.

DE HAAS, F. and AMBER, J. T., eds. **Bolt Action Rifles.** Northfield, Illinois, 1971.

DELACOUR, JEAN. **The Waterfowl of the World.** 4 vols. London, 1954–64.

DORST, JEAN. **Field Guide to the Larger Mammals of Africa.** London, 1970.

DUFFEY, D. M. **Bird Hunting Know-How.** Princeton, New Jersey, 1968.

—**Hunting Dog Know-How.** New York, 1972.

EDMAN, IRWIN., ed. **Socrates' Passages in Plato's "Dialogues."** New York, 1956.

ELLIOTT, CHARLES. **Care of Game Meat & Trophies.** New York, 1975.

ELMAN, ROBERT. **1001 Hunting Tips.** Tulsa, Oklahoma, 1978.

—**The Hunter's Field Guide.** New York, 1974.

ELMAN, ROBERT., ed. **All About Deer Hunting in America.** Tulsa, Oklahoma, 1976.

ELMAN, ROBERT and PEPER, GEORGE., eds. **Hunting America's Game Animals & Birds.** New York, 1975.

ERRINGTON, PAUL. **Of Men and Marshes.** Iowa City, Iowa, 1957.

FALK, JOHN R. **The Practical Hunter's Dog Book.** New York, 1971.

FITZ, GRANCEL. **How to Measure & Score Big-Game Trophies.** New York, 1977.

FORRESTER, REX and ILLINGWORTH, NEIL. **Hunting in New Zealand.** Wellington, New Zealand, 1967.

GATES, ELGIN T. **Trophy Hunter in Asia.** New York, 1971.

GREENER, W. W. **The Gun and Its Development.** London, 1881. Repr. 9th ed. New York, 1968.

GRESHAM, GRITS. **The Complete Wildfowler.** South Hackensack, New Jersey, 1973.

HALTENORTH T. and TRENSE W. **Das Grosswild der Erde und Seine Trophäen.** Munich, 1956.

HEILNER, VAN CAMPEN. **A Book of Duck Shooting.** New York, 1947.

HENDERSON, L. M. **Pocket Guide to Animal Tracks.** Harrisburg, Pennsylvania, 1968.

[HERBERT, W. H.] **Frank Forester's Field Sports of the United States.** New York, 1849.

HERNE, BRIAN. **Uganda Safaris.** Tulsa, Oklahoma, 1980.

HINMAN, BOB. **The Duck Hunter's Handbook.** Tulsa, Oklahoma, 1974.

HULL, DENISON B. **Hounds and Hunting in Ancient Greece.** Chicago, Illinois, 1964.

JOHNSGARD, PAUL A. **Waterfowl, Their Biology and Natural History.** Lincoln, Nebraska, 1968.

KNAP, JEROME. **Where to Fish & Hunt in North America: A Complete Sportsman's Guide.** Toronto, Canada.

KOLLER, L. **Shots at Whitetails.** New York, 1970.

KRIDER, JOHN. **Krider's Sporting Anecdotes.** Philadelphia, 1853.

MACKEY, WILLIAM J., Jr. **American Bird Decoys.** New York, 1965.

MARTIN, ALEXANDER C.; ZIM, HERBERT S.; and NELSON, ARNOLD L. **American Wildlife & Plants.** New York, 1951. MARTIN, ALEXANDER C., ed. Repr. ed. New York, 1961.

MELLON, JAMES et al. **African Hunter.** New York, 1975.

O'CONNOR, JACK. **The Art of Hunting Big Game in North America.** New York, 1977.

—**The Hunting Rifle.** Tulsa, Oklahoma, 1970.

—**Sheep and Sheep Hunting.** Tulsa, Oklahoma, 1974.

ORMOND, CLYDE. **Complete Book of Hunting.** New York, 1972.

ORTEGA Y GASSET, JOSÉ. **Meditations on Hunting.** New York, 1972.

OWEN, T. R. H. **Hunting Big Game with Gun and Camera.** London, 1960.

PETERSON, ROGER; MOUNTFORT, GUY; and HOLLOM, P. A. D. **A Field Guide to the Birds of Britain and Europe.** 3rd ed. London, 1974.

PETERSON, ROGER TORY. **A Field Guide to the Birds.** Boston, 1947.

—**A Field Guide to Western Birds.** Boston, 1969.

PETZAL, DAVID E., ed. **The Experts' Book of the Shooting Sports.** New York, 1972.

—**The Experts' Book of Upland Bird & Waterfowl Hunting.** New York, 1975.

REID, WILLIAM. **Arms Through the Ages.** New York, 1976.

REIGER, GEORGE. **Wings of Dawn.** New York, 1980.

RICE, F. P. and DAHL, J. I. **Game Bird Hunting.** New York, 1965.

ROURE, GEORGES. **Animaux Sauvages de Côte d'Ivoire.** Abidjan, Ivory Coast, 1962.

RUE, LEONARD L., III. **Sportsman's Guide to Game Animals.** New York, 1969.

SCOTT, PETER. **A Coloured Key to the Wildfowl of the World.** Slimbridge, England, 1957.

SPRUNT, A., IV and ZIM, H. S. **Pistols, A Modern Encyclopedia.** Harrisburg, Pennsylvania, 1961.

STEPHENS, WILSON. **The Guinness Guide to Field Sports.** London, 1978.

STEWART, J. and STEWART, D. R. M. "The Distribution of Some Large Mammals in Kenya." **Journal of the East African Natural History Society and Coryndon Museum** 24 (June 1963). Nairobi, Kenya.

SURTEES, R. S. **The Analysis of the Hunting Field.** New York, 1966.

TERRES, JOHN K. **Flashing Wings: The Drama of Bird Flight.** New York, 1968.

THOMAS, GOUGH. [GARWOOD, G. T.] **Gough Thomas's Gun Book.** New York

—**Gough Thomas's Second Gun Book.** New York 1972.

—**Shooting Facts & Fancies.** London, 1978.

TRENCH, CHARLES CHENEVIX. **The Desert's Dusty Face.** Edinburgh and London, 1964.

VILLENAVE, G. M. **La Chasse.** Paris, France.

WATERMAN, CHARLES F. **Hunting in America.** New York, 1973.

WELS, B. G. **Fell's Guide to Guns and How to Use Them.** New York, 1969.

WHITEHEAD, G. KENNETH. **Deer of the World.** New York, 1972.

WOLTERS, RICHARD A. **Water Dog.** New York, 1964.

WOOLNER, F. **Grouse and Grouse Hunting.** New York, 1970.

YOUNG, GORDON. **Tracks of an Intruder.** New York, 1970.

Index

Page numbers in italics indicate an illustration. The Latin names of the animals and birds follow in a separate index.

Latin Names